I0828976

THE MUTUAL LIFE INSURANCE CO.

OF

NEW-YORK.

FREDERICK S. WINSTON, PRESIDENT.

OFFICE, 144 and 146 BROADWAY.

Statement of the affairs of the Company for the year ending Oct. 31*st*, 1864:

Net Cash Assets, 1st November, 1863,		$9,542,047 16
RECEIPTS DURING THE YEAR:		
For Premiums, viz.:		
Originals,	$ 451,584 31	
Renewals,	1,254,325 66	
War Extras,	29,998 08	
	$ 1,735,908 05	
For Annuities,	4,192 52	
" Profit and Loss,	2,008 39	
" Interest,	777,355 74	
		2,519,464 70
		$ 12,061,511 86
DISBURSEMENTS DURING THE YEAR:		
Paid Claims by Death,	$ 515,250 00	
" Additions,	162,188 12	
" Surrender of Policies,	90,131 38	
" Annuities,	9,170 54	
" Commissions,	104,499 96	
" Expenses,	146,866 53	
		1,028,106 53
Net Cash Assets, November 1st, 1864,		$ 11,033,405 33
INVESTED AS FOLLOWS:		
Cash on hand and in Bank,	$ 705,879 06	
Bonds and Mortgages,	4,738,536 87	
United States Stocks, (cost,)	4,916,658 75	
Real Estate,	647,876 85	
W. J. Bunker, Loan Account,	418 50	
Balances due by Agents,	24,036 30	
		$ 11,033,405 33
Add Interest accrued, say		163,400 00
do. due and unpaid,		2,970 01
Premiums due, not yet received,		37,679 04
do. deferred, semi and quarterly, say		225,000 00
Gross Assets, 1st November, 1864,		$ 11,462,454 38

POLICY ACCOUNT.

In force November 1st, 1864,	17,369,	insuring	$ 51,569.076
" " " 1863,	14,376,	"	41,620,815
Net increase during year,	2,993,	insuring	$ 9,948,261
Issued during the year,	3,836,	"	12,300,245

SECRETARY, ISAAC ABBATT. ACTUARY, SHEPPARD HOMANS.
ASSISTANT SECRETARY, THEODORE W. MORRIS. CASHIER, FREDERICK M. WINSTON.

MEDICAL EXAMINER, MINTURN POST, M. D. ASS'T MEDICAL EXAMINER, ISAAC L. KIP, M. D.

COUNSEL, WILLIAM BETTS, LL.D., HON. LUCIUS ROBINSON.

ATTORNEY, RICHARD A. MCCURDY.

PURELY MUTUAL LIFE INSURANCE.

NEW-YORK LIFE INSURANCE CO.

ESTABLISHED 1845.

Home Office, 112 & 114 Broadway, N. Y.

ASSETS, $3,000,000—SECURELY INVESTED.

☞ There is "nothing in the Commercial world which approaches, even remotely, to the SECURITY of a well established and prudently managed Life Insurance Company.—*DeMorgan.*

☞ A Policy of Life Insurance is always an evidence of prudent forethought, and no man with a dependent family is free from reproach if his life is not insured.—*The late Lord Lyndhurst,* Chancellor of England.

This is one of the OLDEST, SAFEST, and most SUCCESSFUL Life Insurance Companies in the United States and offers advantages *not excelled,* and, in some respects, NOT EQUALLED, by any other. It has paid to widows and orphans of the assured over EIGHTEEN HUNDRED THOUSAND DOLLARS. Its Trustees in New-York City are of the very first and most reliable names.

It is STRICTLY MUTUAL, the policy holders receiving the entire profits.

☞ Special care in the selection of its risks,—strict economy,—and a safe and judicious investment of its funds,—emphatically characterize the management of this Company. ☜

Premiums received QUARTERLY, SEMI-ANNUALLY or ANNUALLY, at the option of the assured. Policies issued in all the various forms, of WHOLE LIFE, SHORT TERM, ENDOWMENT, ANNUITY, &c

DIVIDENDS DECLARED ANNUALLY.

The mortality among its members has been *proportionately less* than that of any other Life Insurance Company in America—a result consequent on a most careful and judicious selection of lives, and one of great importance to policy holders.

It offers to the assured *the most abundant security in a large accumulated fund, amounting now to*

THREE MILLION DOLLARS.

It accommodates its members in the settlement of their premiums, by receiving a note for a part of the amount when desired—thus furnishing Insurance for *nearly double the amount* for about the SAME CASH PAYMENT, as is required in an "all cash Company."

The **NEW FEATURE** in Life Assurance, recently introduced by this Company of issuing

LIFE POLICIES NOT SUBJECT TO FORFEITURE,

is regarded with universal favor, and annihilates the only argument of any weight which can possibly be brought against the system of Life Insurance.

The lively prosperity and success of this Company is shown in the FACT, that for the last three years it has taken the lead of ALL the Life Insurance Companies in this country; *the Official Returns of the Massachusetts Insurance Commissioners* showing that the amount of its NEW BUSINESS for the year 1862, nearly ***equalled the combined business of any other two Companies*** in the United States. (*See Statement, next page.*) OVER.

EXAMINE THIS TABLE CAREFULLY.

Table of Premiums for a Non-Forfeiture Policy, requiring only Ten Annual Premiums in Cash to secure $1000 at the Death of the Assured.

AGE.	Annual Prem. for Ten Years.	AGE.	Annual Prem. for Ten Years.	AGE.	Annual Prem. for Ten Years.
18	$39.63	31	$52.11	44	$68.33
19	40.38	32	53.09	45	69.61
20	41.15	33	54.16	46	71.00
21	41.98	34	55.31	47	72.46
22	42.87	35	56.54	48	74.05
23	43.81	36	57.82	49	75.90
24	44.80	37	59.15	50	78.41
25	45.84	38	60.52	51	81.27
26	46.91	39	61.95	52	84.24
27	48.05	40	63.35	53	87.33
28	49.19	41	64.64	54	90.54
29	50.24	42	65.88	55	93.90
30	51.17	43	67.08		

Dividends declared upon the ordinary Life Table Rate. If the premiums of a Non-Forfeiture Policy are paid all cash, the Dividends operate as an Annuity to the party during his whole life.

If the party insured on this plan desires to discontinue payments after the second payment, he will be entitled to a *PAID-UP POLICY* of as many tenths of the original amount insured as he has paid annual premiums.

Below will be found a summary of the business of this Company, as reported to the Insurance Commissioners of the State of Massachusetts, as required by the laws of that Commonwealth, on the first of November, 1863.

Number of New Policies issued during the year, 4,338.

Receipts for Premiums and Interest the same time, ...	$1,110,123.74
Losses and Expenses during the year, ...	495,294.72
Balance in favor of Policy Holders, who are the only Stockholders in this Co.,	614,829.02
Total Assets, November 1st, 1863	$2,566,923.03
Guarantee Capital, ...	None.

The following statement, taken from the OFFICIAL RETURNS of the Massachusetts Insurance Commissioners, showing the number of policies issued in the years 1861, 1862, and 1863, exhibits at a glance THE PRESENT COMPARATIVE SUCCESS of the principal Life Insurance Companies in this country:

NAME OF COMPANY.	When Organized.	Number of Policies issued in 1861.	Number of Policies issued in 1862.	Number of Policies issued in 1863.
New-York Life	**1845**	**1160**	**3302**	**4338**
Mutual Life	1843	1120	1833	2594
Connecticut Mutual	1846	1087	1775	4230
Mutual Benefit	1845	866	1741	2840
New England Mutual	1843	817	1498	1729
Manhattan	1850	688	1149	1464
Equitable	1859	536	1233	1271
Home	1860	869	788	1751
United States	1850	651	666	819
Massachusetts Mutual	1851	600	662	808
Knickerbocker	1853	242	551	739
Guardian	1859	230	688	885
Germania	1860	240	722	2018
Union Mutual, Me	1850	436	334	939
National, Vt	1850	111	170	218
Washington	1860	179	362	445
State Mutual	1846	198	129	137
Berkshire	1852	237	149	169
North America	1862		71	740
Charter Oak				695

From the above it will be seen that the number of policies issued in 1861, 1862, and 1863, by the "New York Life," exceeded that of any other Company in the United States. Much of this success is due to the NON-FORFEITING PLAN originated by this Company, and more fully described on the next page.

Banking Houses, Nos. 30 and 32 Wall Street, New York. 1864-1865.

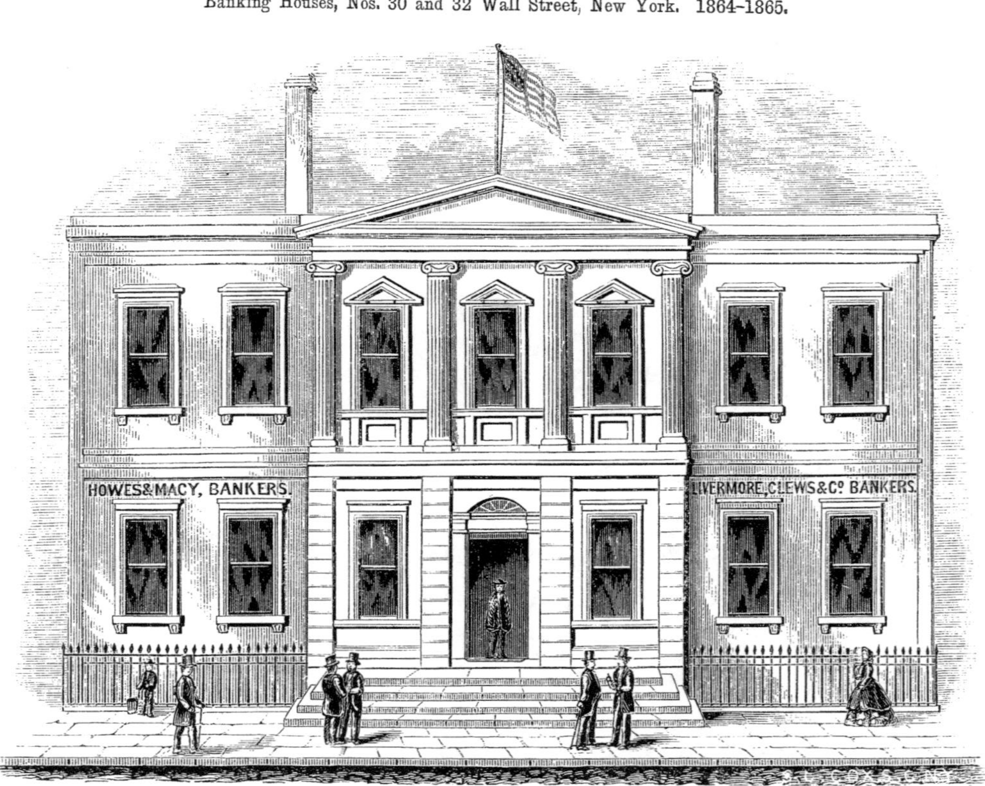

HOWES & MACY, BANKERS, No. 30 WALL ST. LIVERMORE, CLEWS, & CO., BANKERS, 32 WALL ST.

THE

Railroad and Insurance

ALMANAC

FOR

1865.

"Steam is estimated to be equal to the manual labor of four hundred millions of men."
SMILES.

"Mutual Insurance is economy in its most economical form."—*London Quar. Rev.*

NEW YORK:
Carleton, Publisher, 413 Broadway.
M DCCC LXV.

Price Two Dollars.

The "RAILROAD AND INSURANCE ALMANAC FOR 1866" will be published in December, 1865; with the latest information on the subjects of railroads and insurance, foreign and domestic. Communications and information for the volume may be addressed to CARLETON, PUBLISHER, 413 BROADWAY, NEW YORK.

The price of the "*Railroad and Insurance Almanac*" for 1865, has been fixed at Two Dollars. Copies of the work may be had in extra binding, with a RAILROAD MAP, showing the divisions of all the States and Territories (including WEST VIRGINIA and MONTANA); their area, population, etc., and the proposed lines of railroad from the Atlantic to the Pacific, viz.:—1. THE INTERNATIONAL PACIFIC RAILROAD; through Canada, British Columbia, etc. 2. THE NORTH PACIFIC RAILROAD; from St. Paul to Fort Walla-Walla, Washington Territory. 3. THE UNION PACIFIC RAILROAD; from Leavenworth to San Francisco. 4. THE SOUTH PACIFIC RAILWAY; from Fort Smith to Fort Yuma, San Diego, etc. Copies to be had of the publisher only.

Price Three Dollars.

R. CRAIGHEAD, PRINTER,
Caxton Building,
81, 83, *and* 85 *Centre Street, N. Y.*

CONTENTS

OF THE

RAILROAD AND INSURANCE ALMANAC

FOR 1865.

ENGRAVINGS.

Capital and Labor.—"Rightfully considered, no principle is more conservative than that which identifies the laborer with the capitalist."—*Edinburgh Review*, 1864.

Co-operation.—"The co-operative principle is that the workers are the capitalists. By this, if it is found practicable, the opposition between Capital and Labor is annihilated."—*Edinb. Rev.* 1864.

The New World.—"America and Australia are the two fields in which the intelligence and inventions of our own age find their widest application. The ordinary growth of centuries is here compressed into two or three generations; and the surface of the earth submitted to changes which have no parallel in the earlier history of nations."—*Edinburgh Review*, 1864.

Railroads.—"Look further at those admirable constructions, both in Europe and America, by which the railroad is carried across mountain chains, climbing tortuously their steep acclivities, or forced by tunnels through the rock. In the Copiapo Railway of Chili, the locomotive carries its train four thousand and seventy feet above the sea. In the several railroads which cross the Alleghany Mountains, the summit levels are from two to three thousand feet. The new Empire of Brazil boasts a work of similar kind, just completed. In the section, now open, of the St. Ander railroad in Spain, an elevation is reached of two thousand five hundred and twenty-four feet. The Sömmering Pass, between Vienna and Gratz, carries the traveller three thousand feet above the sea. Tunnels from two to three miles in length are familiar to us in England and elsewhere. That which is now in progress under Mount Cenis has for its object and ambition to win a passage into Italy without crossing the Alps. * * * The traveller gains a few hours of time upon his journey, and emerges into Italy through a hole in a rock!"—*Edinburgh Review*, 1864.

Human Progress.—"It is, in truth, a wonderful picture of human progress—of progress continuous, yet so marvellously quickened during the last fifty years, that the dullest observer of the world around him feels that he is living in a new age; and the most cautious philosopher scarcely ventures to set a limit to what may hereafter be attained. While the instincts and acts of other animals have remained stationary from the earliest recorded time, human intelligence, working with, and in part controlling, the great forces of nature, has covered the globe with monuments of its activity and power. The whole may be received as evidence of the high destiny which God has given to Man on earth; a destiny mingled at present with much that is obscure to reason and painful to feeling, but capable of, and intended, as we believe, for some higher and nobler development in the time yet to come."—*Edinburgh Review*, 1864.

Free Trade.—"We have, in great degree, confined ourselves to proving how unsound is the social philosophy embodied in the Free Trade policy. It would be even an easier task to prove its pernicious moral tendencies. It is in its very essence a mercenary, unsocial, demoralizing system; opposed to all generous actions, all kindly feelings. Based on selfishness—the most pervading as well as the most powerful of our vicious propensities—it directs that impulse into the lowest of all channels, the mere sordid pursuit of wealth. It teaches competition and isolation, instead of co-operation and brotherhood; it substitutes a vague and impracticable cosmopolitanism for a lofty and ennobling patriotism; it disregards the claims of humanity towards the poor, if opposed to the pecuniary interests of the rich; it takes no account of all that should exalt man in the scale of being, but elevates to exclusive importance his most degrading tendencies. Wealth is its end and aim, and Mammon its divinity. We cannot altogether regret with Burke that 'the age of chivalry is past,' and though we do with him regret that 'an age of sophists, of economists, and of calculators has succeeded,' we still trust that 'the glory of England is not yet extinguished for ever.'"—*London Quarterly Review*.

JANUARY.

MOON'S PHASES.

First Quarter, 4d. 10h. 46m. M.	Third Quarter, 19d. 9h. 40m. E.
Full Moon,... 11d. 6h. 4m. E.	New Moon,... 27d. 4h. 34m. M.

Day of Month.	Day of Week.	PREMIUM ON GOLD, IN JANUARY, AT NEW-YORK.						SUN.	
		1862.		1863.		1864.		Rises.	Sets.
		LOWEST.	HIGHEST.	LOWEST.	HIGHEST.	LOWEST.	HIGHEST.	H. M.	H. M.
1	**Sun**	..	..	*Holi*	*day.*	*Holi*	*day.*	7 25	4 43
2	Mon	..	..	*$33\frac{5}{8}$	35	$51\frac{7}{8}$	$52\frac{1}{8}$	7 25	4 44
3	Tues	..	..	$33\frac{5}{8}$	$34\frac{3}{4}$	**Sun**	..	7 25	4 45
4	Wed	..	..	**Sun**	..	*$51\frac{1}{2}$	$51\frac{7}{8}$	7 25	4 46
5	Thu	..	..	$34\frac{5}{8}$	35	$51\frac{5}{8}$	$51\frac{7}{8}$	7 25	4 46
6	Frid	..	..	34	$34\frac{1}{2}$	$51\frac{1}{2}$	$51\frac{7}{8}$	7 25	4 47
7	Sat	..	..	$34\frac{1}{4}$	35	$51\frac{7}{8}$	$52\frac{1}{4}$	7 25	4 48
8	**Sun**	..	..	$35\frac{5}{8}$	$36\frac{5}{8}$	$51\frac{3}{4}$	$52\frac{1}{8}$	7 25	4 49
9	Mon	..	..	$37\frac{3}{4}$	$38\frac{1}{4}$	$51\frac{7}{8}$	$52\frac{1}{8}$	7 25	4 50
10	Tues	..	..	$38\frac{1}{8}$	39	**Sun**	..	7 24	4 51
*11	Wed	..	..	**Sun**	..	$52\frac{3}{8}$	$52\frac{1}{2}$	7 24	4 52
12	Thu	..	..	$40\frac{3}{4}$	42	$53\frac{3}{4}$	$54\frac{1}{4}$	7 24	4 53
13	Frid	..	..	42	44	$53\frac{3}{4}$	$53\frac{7}{8}$	7 23	4 54
14	Sat	..	..	$46\frac{1}{2}$	$47\frac{1}{4}$	$54\frac{3}{8}$	$54\frac{7}{8}$	7 23	4 55
15	**Sun**	..	..	48	$48\frac{1}{4}$	$55\frac{1}{4}$	$55\frac{1}{2}$	7 22	4 57
16	Mon	..	..	$45\frac{1}{2}$	47	$55\frac{1}{2}$	$56\frac{1}{2}$	7 22	4 58
17	Tues	..	..	$46\frac{7}{8}$	$47\frac{1}{4}$	**Sun**	..	7 21	4 59
18	Wed	..	..	**Sun**	..	$59\frac{1}{8}$	$59\frac{1}{4}$	7 20	5 1
19	Thu	..	..	$47\frac{7}{8}$	$48\frac{1}{4}$	$59\frac{1}{4}$	*$59\frac{3}{8}$	7 20	5 2
20	Frid	..	..	$47\frac{1}{2}$	48	$58\frac{1}{4}$	$58\frac{7}{8}$	7 19	5 3
21	Sat	..	..	$47\frac{3}{4}$	$48\frac{1}{4}$	$56\frac{1}{4}$	57	7 18	5 4
22	**Sun**	..	..	$47\frac{1}{2}$	48	$56\frac{3}{4}$	$57\frac{5}{8}$	7 18	5 5
23	Mon	..	..	$47\frac{1}{2}$	48	56	$56\frac{5}{8}$	7 17	5 6
24	Tues	..	..	$48\frac{3}{4}$	$49\frac{3}{4}$	**Sun**	..	7 16	5 7
25	Wed	..	..	**Sun**	..	$57\frac{5}{8}$	$57\frac{7}{8}$	7 16	5 8
26	Thu	..	..	$48\frac{7}{8}$	$51\frac{1}{4}$	58	$58\frac{1}{8}$	7 15	5 9
27	Frid	..	..	53	$54\frac{1}{4}$	57	$58\frac{1}{8}$	7 14	5 11
28	Sat	..	..	53	$54\frac{1}{2}$	$57\frac{1}{8}$	$57\frac{1}{4}$	7 13	5 12
29	**Sun**	..	..	53	$54\frac{7}{8}$	$56\frac{3}{4}$	$57\frac{1}{2}$	7 13	5 13
30	Mon	..	..	56	$57\frac{1}{4}$	$56\frac{3}{4}$	$57\frac{1}{8}$	7 12	5 15
31	Tues	..	..	$59\frac{1}{2}$	*60	**Sun**	..	7 11	5 16

A Warning.—By a series of arbitrary acts on the part of government, and by connecting some splendid and illusory schemes with the bank, Law succeeded in putting in circulation about four hundred and twenty millions of dollars in bank notes, or more than twice the amount of the currency then wanted in France. This paper was made a legal tender, to the total exclusion of the precious metals. But the laws and all the power of the French government were unequal to the task of sustaining that excess of currency. The price of every species of merchandise naturally rose 100 per cent. Government, with a view probably to prevent a final catastrophe, reduced, by a decree, the notes to one-half their original value.—A. Gallatin.

EVENTS OF THE YEAR 1864.

JANUARY.

1. Meeting of the waters of the Nile with the Red Sea—celebrated with appropriate ceremonies. Proposals issued for a loan of $35,000,000 to the United States. Governor SEYMOUR deposes the old Police Commissioners, and appoints new ones.

3. Discovery of $6,000,000 in Confederate bonds, printed in New-York for the Confederate government. MAXIMILIAN'S acceptance of the Mexican throne announced. Death of Archbishop HUGHES, at New-York, aged 65 years. Surrender of 300 Union troops to the rebels, at Jonesville, Va.

6. Extreme stringency in the money market, at New-York. Death of Judge CALEB B. SMITH, at Indianapolis, aged 56 years, late Secretary of the Interior.

7. Discovery of great frauds at the New-York Custom-house—A. M. PALMER (private secretary of Collector BARNEY) arrested.

8. Birth of a son to the Prince of Wales.

9. About 400 rebels, under MOSBY, defeated in Loudon County, Va., by Union cavalry, under Major COLE. The steamer *Chesapeake*, seized by rebels, and run into Halifax, N. S., ordered by the Admiralty Court to be returned to her owners in New-York.

10. Discovery of frauds upon the government in the Brooklyn Navy Yard.

11. New-York banks receive $33,500,000 of five per cent. interest-bearing notes. Proclamation of Major-General BANKS for holding an election in Louisiana for State officers. Several extensive paper warehouses in Beekman-street, New-York, destroyed by fire—loss, $200,000. M. THIERS, in the French legislature, declared himself in favor of Universal Suffrage.

12. Gunboats and transports of SHERMAN'S and PORTER'S expedition, up the Yazoo river, attacked by 3,000 rebels.

15. GARIBALDI issues a proclamation to promote Italian union. A new Spanish ministry formed. Terrific gunpowder explosion in Liverpool, on board of a vessel—great destruction of glass, but no lives lost. MALCOLM CAMPBELL, LOUIS BENJAMIN and L. J. OLMSTEAD arrested on a charge of shipping goods for the use of the rebels.

16. Extensive fire at 144 Duane-street, N.Y. Losses estimated at $450,000.

17. Failure of several London and Coventry firms announced. The French government advertises for a loan of £12,000,000. A railway train from Philadelphia to Pittsburgh, Pa., precipitated into the Juniata river.

18. Denmark rejects the Austro-Prussian ultimatum. Bids opened at Paris for the French loan, £12,000,000 sterling, and found to amount to $160,000,000.

20. Union Gen. SEYMOUR, at Olustee, Florida, defeated by the rebels. Fight between Gen. STURGIS and the rebels under Generals HOOD and JOHNSON, at Danville, Tennessee.

22. Fight between the United States troops and the rebels in Arkansas.

23. Restrictions on trade in Missouri and Kentucky removed by order of the Treasury.

28. Blockade runner *Rosetta* captured by the United States steamer *Western Metropolis*. Defeat of rebels by Union troops under Gen. STURGIS near Fair Garden, Tenn. Explosion of detonating powder at No. 65 Maiden Lane, New-York—one person killed, and one seriously injured. New commercial treaty signed at Yeddo, between the United States and Japan.

29. Capture of Scottsville, Ky., by the rebels.

31. The Danes summoned to evacuate Schleswig forthwith, and the demand not being complied with, the Prussian army crossed the frontier, and shots were exchanged. A wagon train captured by the rebels near Williamsport—heavy loss on both sides. Union troops at Batchelor's Creek, N. C., defeated by the rebels.

FEBRUARY.

MOON'S PHASES.

FIRST QUARTER, 2d. 8h. 12m. E.	THIRD QUARTER, 18d. 4h. 42m. E.
FULL MOON,... 10d. 11h. 31m. M.	NEW MOON,... 25d. 3h. 7m. E.

Day of Month.	Day of Week.	PREMIUM ON GOLD, IN FEBRUARY, AT NEW-YORK.						SUN.			
		1862.		1863.		1864.		Rises.		Sets.	
		LOWEST.	HIGHEST.	LOWEST.	HIGHEST.	LOWEST.	HIGHEST.	H.	M.	H.	M.
1	Wed	..	..	**Sun**	..	$57\frac{3}{8}$	58	7	10	5	18
2	Thu	..	..	$56\frac{3}{4}$	$57\frac{1}{2}$	*$57\frac{1}{8}$	$57\frac{5}{8}$	7	9	5	19
3	Fri	..	..	$54\frac{1}{2}$	55	$57\frac{1}{2}$	$58\frac{1}{2}$	7	8	5	20
4	Sat	..	..	57	$57\frac{1}{2}$	$57\frac{5}{8}$	$58\frac{1}{8}$	7	7	5	21
5	**Sun**	..	..	$56\frac{3}{4}$	$57\frac{1}{8}$	$57\frac{3}{4}$	$58\frac{1}{4}$	7	6	5	22
6	Mon	..	..	$57\frac{1}{8}$	$57\frac{1}{2}$	$57\frac{7}{8}$	59	7	5	5	24
7	Tues	..	..	$56\frac{5}{8}$	$57\frac{1}{4}$	**Sun**	..	7	4	5	25
8	Wed	..	..	**Sun**	..	$57\frac{7}{8}$	$59\frac{1}{2}$	7	3	5	26
9	Thu	..	..	$55\frac{1}{4}$	$55\frac{3}{4}$	$59\frac{1}{2}$	$59\frac{7}{8}$	7	2	5	28
*10	Frid	..	..	*$52\frac{1}{4}$	$53\frac{3}{4}$	59	$59\frac{1}{2}$	7	0	5	29
11	Sat	..	..	$52\frac{1}{2}$	56	59	$59\frac{5}{8}$	6	59	5	30
12	**Sun**	..	..	$54\frac{1}{8}$	$54\frac{1}{2}$	$59\frac{1}{8}$	$59\frac{3}{8}$	6	58	5	32
13	Mon	..	..	$55\frac{1}{2}$	$55\frac{7}{8}$	$59\frac{3}{8}$	$59\frac{5}{8}$	6	56	5	33
14	Tues	..	..	$55\frac{1}{2}$	$55\frac{3}{4}$	**Sun**	..	6	55	5	34
15	Wed	..	..	**Sun**	..	$59\frac{7}{8}$	60	6	54	5	35
16	Thu	..	..	$55\frac{5}{8}$	$57\frac{5}{8}$	60	*61	6	53	5	36
17	Frid	..	..	$58\frac{1}{4}$	59	$59\frac{3}{4}$	$60\frac{1}{4}$	6	51	5	37
18	Sat	..	..	61	$61\frac{1}{2}$	$59\frac{7}{8}$	$60\frac{1}{8}$	6	50	5	38
19	**Sun**	..	..	$61\frac{1}{2}$	64	58	$59\frac{3}{8}$	6	49	5	39
20	Mon	..	..	$63\frac{1}{8}$	$63\frac{3}{4}$	$59\frac{1}{8}$	$59\frac{1}{2}$	6	47	5	41
21	Tues	..	..	$62\frac{1}{2}$	$62\frac{3}{4}$	**Sun**	..	6	46	5	42
22	Wed	..	..	**Sun**	..	$58\frac{1}{8}$	$59\frac{1}{4}$	6	44	5	43
23	Thu	..	..	$64\frac{3}{4}$	$64\frac{7}{8}$	$57\frac{1}{4}$	$58\frac{1}{8}$	6	43	5	45
24	Frid	..	..	68	$71\frac{1}{4}$	$57\frac{1}{4}$	$58\frac{1}{4}$	6	41	5	46
25	Sat	..	..	$71\frac{1}{2}$	*$72\frac{3}{8}$	$58\frac{1}{4}$	$58\frac{1}{2}$	6	39	5	47
26	**Sun**	..	..	$69\frac{1}{2}$	$71\frac{3}{4}$	$58\frac{1}{4}$	$58\frac{5}{8}$	6	38	5	48
27	Mon	..	..	$69\frac{5}{8}$	71	$57\frac{3}{4}$	$58\frac{3}{8}$	6	37	5	49
28	Tues	..	..	$71\frac{1}{2}$	72	**Sun**	..	6	36	5	49
29	..	..	..	..	..	$58\frac{3}{4}$	$59\frac{1}{4}$	..		..	

PUBLIC CREDIT.—Credit, public and private, is of the greatest consequence to every country; of this, it might be emphatically called the invigorating principle. No well informed man can cast a retrospective eye over the progress of the United States, from their infancy to the present period, without being convinced that they owe, in a great degree, to the fostering influence of credit, their present mature growth. This credit has been of a mixed nature, mercantile and public, foreign and domestic. Credit abroad was the trunk of our mercantile credit, from which issued ramifications that nourished all the parts of domestic labor and industry. The bills of credit emitted from time to time by the different local governments, which passed current as money, co-operated with that resource.—ALEXANDER HAMILTON.

FEBRUARY.

1. The Treasury Department issued a circular in favor of a revision and codification of the Customs and Navigation laws. England protests against the Federal occupation of Schleswig. President LINCOLN issues a proclamation for a draft for 500,000 men, to serve for three years.

2. Raid by rebels on the Baltimore and Ohio Rail-Road. Estimated damage to property, $1,000,000. Rebel attack on Newbern, N. C. repulsed. The gunboat *Underwriter* destroyed by the rebels. RODDY's rebel cavalry driven out of Tennessee.

3. The Danes evacuate Schleswig and the Dannerwerke. Restrictions on trade in West Virginia removed by the Treasury Department. Defeat on the Upper Potomac of the rebels under Colonel ROSSER, by General AVERILL. Blockade runner *Wild Dayrell* destroyed by the U. S. steamers *Sassacus* and *Florida.*

4. Union forces capture Jackson City and Yazoo City, Mississippi.

5. Destruction of COLT's patent fire-arms manufactory, at Hartford, Connecticut, by fire. Loss $500,000.

6. President LINCOLN issues a proclamation, removing restrictions on trade in the states of Kentucky and Missouri.

7. An expedition under General GILMORE ascends St. John's river, Florida, enters Jacksonville and captures 100 prisoners, 8 pieces of artillery and other property.

8. Accident on the Harlem Rail-Road at Brewster's Station. Three cars broken, but only one person injured. Fight with the rebels at Germania Ford, Va., without definite results. Loss considerable on both sides. Democratic State Convention of New-Hampshire. E. W. HARRINGTON nominated for Governor. Advance of Union troops from Jacksonville, Florida, into the interior, and capture of property valued at $150,000. Engagement between Russian troops and Polish insurgents.

9. Frightful accident on the Grand Trunk Rail-Road of Canada Two freight cars run off a bridge 125 feet high. Three persons crushed Severe cavalry fight with rebels at Strawberry Plains. Schleswig occupied by the Prussians.

10. General decline in the prices of stocks at New-York.

11. The infant prince, DON CARLOS, solemnly recognised as the successor to the crown of Portugal.

12. A Danish loan of £1,200,000 at 5 per cent., brought out in London. Accident on the Northern Central Rail-Road, of Maryland. One passenger killed, and six mortally wounded. A train on the Harlem Rail-Road thrown down an embankment. About fifteen persons seriously injured.

13. The premises 174 Washington-street, New-York, partially destroyed by fire.

15. The confederate steamer *Georgia* escaped from the port of Cherbourg.

16. Treaty of amity, commerce and navigation between Hayti and Liberia.

18. Fire at Gloucester, Massachusetts. Seventy-five buildings destroyed, involving a loss of over $400,000. Republican State Convention of Connecticut, held. Union forces under Generals SMITH, SHERMAN, and others, make a successful raid into Alabama. They destroy over 1,000,000 bushels of corn, and capture 1,500 mules and horses, and over 800 prisoners.

19. Stock market in New-York "rampant wild." The Enrollment Bill passed the Senate by vote of 36 to 16, and the House (on 12th) by 93 to 60.

20. Boiler explosion in the iron foundry of CORWIN & REED, Brooklyn.

22. Unconditional Union State Convention of Maryland, held at Baltimore. Steamship *Bohemian*, of the Montreal and Liverpool line, lost near Cape Elizabeth. Thirteen passengers lost.

23. Bombardment of Fort Powell, Mobile harbor, by Admiral FARRAGUT.

25. Tunnell Hill, Georgia, captured by Union troops under Gen. GRANT. Athens, Alabama, captured by the rebels under General RODDY.

26. The rebels beaten at Athens and Florence, Alabama, by Union troops. The Boston board of brokers appropriate $1,000 for the relief of the people of East Tennessee. The rank of Lieutenant-General conferred on ULYSSES S. GRANT.

28. Successful reconnoissance by General CUSTER, towards Gordonsville, Va.

29. Blockade runner *Scotia* (steamer) captured by the United States steamer *Connecticut.* Meeting of bank officers held at the American Exchange Bank.

MARCH.

MOON'S PHASES.

First Quarter, 4d. 7h. 23m. M.	Third Quarter, 20d. 7h. 40m. M.
Full Moon,... 12d. 5h. 46m. M.	New Moon,... 27d. 0h. 32m. M.

Day of Month.	Day of Week.	PREMIUM ON GOLD, IN MARCH, AT NEW-YORK.						SUN.			
		1862.		1863.		1864.		Rises.		Sets.	
		LOWEST.	HIGHEST.	LOWEST.	HIGHEST.	LOWEST.	HIGHEST.	H.	M.	H.	M.
1	Wed	$2\frac{3}{8}$	*$2\frac{3}{4}$	**Sun**	..	$59\frac{3}{4}$	60	6	35	5	50
2	Thu	**Sun**	..	71	$71\frac{1}{2}$	*$59\frac{1}{4}$	$60\frac{1}{8}$	6	33	5	51
3	Frid	2	$2\frac{3}{8}$	$71\frac{3}{8}$	*$71\frac{3}{4}$	60	$60\frac{7}{8}$	6	32	5	53
4	Sat	$1\frac{7}{8}$	2	65	68	$61\frac{1}{8}$	$61\frac{1}{2}$	6	30	5	54
5	**Sun**	2	2	57	58	$61\frac{7}{8}$	62	6	29	5	55
6	Mon	2	$2\frac{1}{8}$	50	54	**Sun**	..	6	27	5	56
7	Tues	2	$2\frac{1}{8}$	$54\frac{3}{4}$	$55\frac{1}{2}$	$61\frac{1}{2}$	$62\frac{1}{8}$	6	26	5	58
8	Wed	$1\frac{5}{8}$	2	**Sun**	..	$62\frac{1}{4}$	$64\frac{5}{8}$	6	24	5	59
9	Thu	**Sun**	..	$55\frac{3}{4}$	$57\frac{1}{4}$	65	69	6	23	6	0
10	Frid	2	2	60	63	$63\frac{3}{4}$	$64\frac{3}{4}$	6	21	6	1
11	Sat	$1\frac{5}{8}$	$1\frac{7}{8}$	$57\frac{7}{8}$	$58\frac{1}{2}$	63	$64\frac{3}{4}$	6	19	6	2
*12	**Sun**	$1\frac{5}{8}$	$1\frac{5}{8}$	$58\frac{1}{2}$	$60\frac{1}{2}$	$60\frac{7}{8}$	63	6	17	6	3
13	Mon	$1\frac{1}{2}$	$1\frac{1}{2}$	$59\frac{1}{8}$	62	**Sun**	..	6	15	6	4
14	Tues	$1\frac{1}{2}$	$1\frac{5}{8}$	$57\frac{3}{4}$	$58\frac{3}{4}$	$60\frac{1}{2}$	$61\frac{3}{4}$	6	14	6	5
15	Wed	$1\frac{3}{8}$	$1\frac{1}{2}$	**Sun**	..	$61\frac{3}{8}$	63	6	12	6	6
16	Thu	**Sun**	..	$54\frac{1}{2}$	55	$60\frac{3}{4}$	$63\frac{1}{4}$	6	10	6	7
17	Frid	$1\frac{1}{4}$	$1\frac{3}{4}$	$54\frac{5}{8}$	$55\frac{1}{4}$	$60\frac{1}{4}$	61	6	9	6	8
18	Sat	$1\frac{3}{8}$	$1\frac{5}{8}$	$53\frac{1}{2}$	55	62	63	6	7	6	9
19	**Sun**	$1\frac{1}{2}$	$1\frac{5}{8}$	$54\frac{7}{8}$	$55\frac{7}{8}$	$61\frac{5}{8}$	$62\frac{1}{2}$	6	5	6	10
20	Mon	$1\frac{1}{4}$	$1\frac{3}{8}$	$54\frac{1}{2}$	55	**Sun**	..	6	3	6	12
21	Tues	$1\frac{1}{4}$	$1\frac{1}{2}$	$53\frac{7}{8}$	$54\frac{7}{8}$	$61\frac{7}{8}$	$63\frac{1}{4}$	6	2	6	13
22	Wed	$1\frac{1}{8}$	$1\frac{3}{8}$	**Sun**	..	$63\frac{1}{4}$	$63\frac{7}{8}$	6	0	6	14
23	Thu	**Sun**	..	51	$53\frac{5}{8}$	$64\frac{1}{4}$	$65\frac{5}{8}$	5	59	6	15
24	Frid	$1\frac{1}{4}$	$1\frac{3}{8}$	$45\frac{1}{2}$	49	$65\frac{5}{8}$	$66\frac{1}{2}$	5	58	6	16
25	Sat	*$1\frac{1}{8}$	$1\frac{3}{8}$	$41\frac{1}{4}$	43	*Fast*	*day.*	5	56	6	17
26	**Sun**	$1\frac{1}{4}$	$1\frac{1}{4}$	*39	$40\frac{1}{4}$	$68\frac{1}{2}$	*70	5	55	6	18
27	Mon	$1\frac{1}{4}$	$1\frac{3}{8}$	40	$40\frac{7}{8}$	**Sun**	..	5	54	6	19
28	Tues	$1\frac{1}{4}$	$1\frac{3}{8}$	$42\frac{1}{4}$	$43\frac{1}{8}$	$64\frac{1}{2}$	$66\frac{1}{2}$	5	52	6	20
29	Wed	$1\frac{1}{2}$	$1\frac{1}{2}$	**Sun**	..	$64\frac{3}{4}$	66	5	51	6	21
30	Thu	**Sun**	..	$44\frac{1}{2}$	$47\frac{1}{4}$	$63\frac{1}{8}$	$65\frac{1}{4}$	5	49	6	22
31	Frid	$1\frac{3}{8}$	$1\frac{3}{4}$	$48\frac{1}{2}$	50	64	65	5	47	6	23

Directors.—Directors are, *virtute officii*, something more than irresponsible dummies. They are not, it is true, strictly trustees, in every sense of the word; they are not, for all purposes, like persons in whom property is vested upon specific trusts; but they fill what the law calls a fiduciary character. They are at all times, in the nature of trustees, partaking of their liabilities and participating in their immunities; and they are, as to the application of funds belonging to the company which come into their hands, or which are dealt with by their orders, in general, strictly trustees.

MARCH.

1. Annihilation of a colored regiment by guerillas at Tecumseh Landing, Miss.

2. Successful raid by Gen. KILPATRICK, near Richmond. Oil wells, at Oil Creek, Pa., take fire—upwards of 2,000 barrels of oil consumed.

5. The rebels attack Yazoo City, Miss. The Danes, in Jutland, defeated by German troops. The sovereign States of Apure, Aragua, Barcelona, Barquisimeto, Carabobo, Caraccas, Cojedes, Coro, Cumana, Guarico, Guiana, Maracaibo, Merida, Nueva Esperta, Portuguesa, Tachira, Trujillo, Yacacuy and Yamara, unite and form a free and independent nation, under the name of the United States of Venezuela.

6. Imperial manifesto of the Czar of Russia, emancipating the peasants in Poland.

7. Attempt to burn the Free Academy, New-York.

8. The Danes defeated near Vielle. Gen. SHERMAN returns to Vicksburgh from Alabama and Mississippi. Fire at Meriden, Conn.—loss, $80,000. State election in New-York, decided that soldiers may vote.

9. Major-General GRANT receives his commission as Lieut.-General from President LINCOLN. Council of war between the President, the Cabinet and General GRANT.

10. Death of the King of Bavaria. Panic in coal stocks—decline from 9 to 14 per cent. Expedition under General A. J. SMITH left Vicksburgh for the Red River. Constitutional Convention of West Virginia adopted a resolution to abolish slavery.

11. Two hundred and fifty lives lost in Sheffield, by the public reservoir.

13. Capture of Alexandria, La., by Union troops.

14. Blockade of Acapulco and Manzanilla, Mexico, by the French, announced. Fort De Russey, on Red river, Louisiana, captured by Union troops under Gen. A. J. SMITH. Major-General HALLECK retired from the position of Commander-in-Chief.

15. The rebels make a daring attempt to recapture Seabrook, near Hilton Head. Call by President LINCOLN for 200,000 men, for the army, navy and marine.

16. The gold bill passed by the House of Representatives. Explosion at LEET & Co.'s cartridge factory, Mass.—sixteen persons killed or badly wounded.

17. Lieut.-Gen. GRANT assumes command of all the armies of the United States. Fort De Russey blown up accidentally—four men killed and six wounded.

18. Speculation rampant in New-York—great rise in the price of gold, &c. The rebels appear on a new raiding expedition towards Washington.

20. Reconnoissance by Union troops, under General MOWER, up Red river, La.—200 rebels and four cannon captured. Fall of a block of twenty buildings in Memphis—forty negroes and six white soldiers buried in the ruins.

21. Act of Congress to admit Nevada and Colorado as States.

23. Several tenement houses and a print manufactory in Thirty-sixth-street, New-York, destroyed by fire—loss, $200,000.

23. Gen. FORREST commenced an invasion of Kentucky. President LINCOLN issued an order for the re-organization of the army.

24. Union City, Tenn., attacked by General FORREST; Col. HAWKINS, in charge, surrendered to the rebels. An extensive shell foundry at Mauch Chunk, Pa., destroyed by fire—loss, $30,000. Capture of Alexandria, La., by Union troops.

25. The rebels, under General FORREST, enter Paducah, Ky. Severe gale—several vessels driven ashore along the coast.

26. Republican State Convention of California, held at San Francisco. President LINCOLN issues a new amnesty proclamation.

27. Gold advances from 164 to 169. Union troops, under General MOWER, capture seventeen cannon from the rebels near Alexandria, La.

28. Gold declines from 169 to 166¼. Stock market rampant, and a general advance in prices. Election in Louisiana for delegates to a State Convention. Gen. FORREST, (rebel,) with 7,000 men, advances to the vicinity of Columbus, Ky.

29. Decline in the stock market, New-York. The protocol, putting an end to the English protectorate over the Ionian Islands, signed in London.

30. The chapel of the Presbyterian Church, in Fourth avenue, New-York, damaged by fire $1,000. An expedition, under Col. CLAYTON, to Mount Elba and Longview, Ark., captured 320 prisoners, 300 horses. The United States steamer *Maple Leaf* blown up in the St. John's river, Florida.

31. New Canadian ministry formed.

APRIL.

MOON'S PHASES.

First Quarter, 2d. 8h. 23m. E. | Third Quarter, 18d. 6h. 24m. E.
Full Moon, ... 10d. 11h. 31m. E. | New Moon,... 25d. 9h. 18m. M.

Day of Month.	Day of Week.	PREMIUM ON GOLD, IN APRIL, AT NEW-YORK.						SUN.			
		1862.		1863.		1864.		Rises.		Sets.	
		LOWEST.	HIGHEST.	LOWEST.	HIGHEST.	LOWEST.	HIGHEST.	H.	M.	H.	M.
1	Sat	1⅞	2	56⅜	57½	*66	68½	5	45	6	24
2	**Sun**	2	2⅛	53¼	57	66¼	66½	5	42	6	25
3	Mon	1¾	1⅞	53	53½	**Sun**	..	5	41	6	26
4	Tues	1¾	1⅞	54¾	55¼	66	67½	5	39	6	27
5	Wed	1⅞	2	**Sun**	..	67¾	68⅛	5	37	6	28
6	Thu	**Sun**	..	51	52⅞	68	70½	5	35	6	29
7	Frid	2⅛	2¼	50	52½	70⅝	71	5	33	6	30
8	Sat	2	2⅛	*45½	47	69¼	70	5	31	6	31
9	**Sun**	1¾	1⅞	46½	48	69⅝	71⅝	5	30	6	32
*10	Mon	1¾	1⅞	46½	49	**Sun**	..	5	28	6	33
11	Tues	1⅞	1⅞	50½	52⅛	71	72¼	5	26	6	34
12	Wed	1¾	2	**Sun**	..	73⅛	75	5	25	6	35
13	Thu	**Sun**	..	57	*57⅝	74½	79	5	24	6	36
14	Frid	1¾	1⅞	55	55¾	74¼	*89	5	22	6	37
15	Sat	1¾	1⅞	52	54	72	75	5	21	6	38
16	**Sun**	1⅝	1⅝	52	53¾	71	73¾	5	20	6	39
17	Mon	1½	1⅝	53¼	53¾	**Sun**	..	5	18	6	40
18	Tues	1½	1½	51¼	52⅝	70¾	71¼	5	16	6	41
19	Wed	1⅜	1½	**Sun**	..	69⅛	70	5	15	6	42
20	Thu	**Sun**	..	48¾	50¾	67½	68	5	13	6	44
21	Frid	1⅝	1⅝	46	47	67	69⅜	5	11	6	45
22	Sat	1⅝	1⅝	45¾	47¾	72½	74½	5	10	6	46
23	**Sun**	1⅝	1¾	48⅜	50	74⅛	79	5	9	6	47
24	Mon	1½	1⅝	51½	52	**Sun**	..	5	7	6	48
25	Tues	1½	1½	52	54	78¾	83½	5	6	6	49
26	Wed	1⅝	1⅝	**Sun**	..	79¾	85	5	5	6	50
27	Thu	**Sun**	..	50	53⅞	77	81½	5	3	6	51
28	Frid	1⅝	1¾	49⅝	50⅝	77¼	79⅜	5	2	6	52
29	Sat	1¾	1⅞	50	50⅝	78	81⅛	5	1	6	53
30	**Sun**	2	2	*Fast*	*day.*	70	80	5	0	6	54

Requisites of Bankers.—A banker should possess a sufficiency of legal knowledge to make him suspect what may be defects in proffered securities, so as to submit his doubts to authorized counsellors. He must in all things be eminently practical. Every man can tell an obviously sufficient security and an obviously abundant security, but neither of these constitute any large portion of the loans that are offered to a banker. Security practically sufficient for the occasion is all that a banker can obtain for the greater number of loans he must make. If he must err in his judgment of securities, he had better reject fifty good loans than make one bad debt; but he must endeavor not to err on the extreme of caution or the extreme of temerity; and his tact in these particulars will, more than any other, constitute the criterion of his merits as a banker.—A. B. Johnson.

APRIL.

1. Terrible explosion in a percussion cap manufactory at Waterbury, Connecticut. A band of rebels attack the United States government plantations on the Yazoo.
2. Business portion of Demarara destroyed by fire—loss $3,000,000.
3. GARIBALDI arrives in England. Union troops defeated at Shreveport, La.
4. WILLIAM A. BUCKINGHAM re-elected governor of Connecticut.
5. A distillery, &c., in Robinson-street, New-York, destroyed by fire—loss $70,000 Union powder mills at New-Durham, N. H., blown up—four men killed.
6. Advance of gold to 171—also a general advance in price of stocks. Explosion in MERRICK's foundry, Philadelphia—seven workmen killed, and thirty wounded.
7. A block and a half of buildings at Oil City, Pa., destroyed by fire—loss not ascertained. One hundred and forty-four buildings at Gonaives, Hayti, destroyed by fire, incurring a loss of $5,000,000. Foreign merchants nearly ruined.
8. Defeat of Union troops under STONEMAN, at Pleasant Hill, La.—loss, 2,000.
9. Fight at New Falls City, near Shreveport, La.; defeat of the rebels. Fight at Grand Ecore, La. Attempt to blow up the United States frigate *Minnesota.*
10. Several buildings in Cedar-street, N. Y., destroyed by fire—loss about $40,000.
11. Explosion of caisson at Huntsville, Ala.—six men blown to pieces.
12. The blockade steamer *Alliance* captured by the United States gunboat *South Carolina.* Capture of Fort Pillow by the rebels under General FORREST. Steamer *Golden Gate*, laden with U. S. government stores, captured by rebels. MAXIMILIAN solemnly invested with the new honors as Emperor of Mexico
13. The surrender of Fort Halleck, Columbus, Ky., demanded by Gen. BUFORD.
14. About 100 rebels, 200 horses, and 300 small arms, captured by Union troops at Half Mountain, Ky. The Chincha Islands, belonging to Peru, seized by Spain.
15. Explosion of a boiler on board the United States gunboat *Chenango*, in New-York harbor. The Knoxville Convention for State of East Tennessee adjourn.
16. A French armed transport is allowed to go up the James river, to Richmond, for tobacco. The issue of gold certificates by Sub-Treasury suspended.
17. Fire in buildings 77 and 79 Cliff-street, New-York—loss about $50,000. The rebels attempt to capture Plymouth, N. C., but are repulsed with great slaughter. A portion of Hickman, Ky., burned by the rebels. Convention or treaty between France and Mexico published. Female riot in Savannah, Ga.
18. A rebel ram at Plymouth, N. C., attacks and sinks the gunboats *Bombshell* and *Southfield.* Great panic in Wall-street, New-York; many heavy failures among the leading "bull" operators; decline in prices. Death of the Bishop of Peterborough, formerly tutor of Queen VICTORIA. Duppel surrendered by the Danes. Act of Congress to admit Nebraska as a State.
20. A general advance in gold and stocks. Fire at Lowell, Mass.—loss, $25,000. Surrender of Gen. WESSELS and 2,500 Union troops at Plymouth, N. C.; losses in killed 150, and 25 pieces of artillery. New Japanese Embassy visits Paris.
21. Rail-road bridge at Rock Island, Chicago and Dixon line, destroyed by fire.
22. Advance in gold from 170 to 175. Incendiary fire in Concord, N. H.—losses, $30,000. Fire in Ann-street, New-York—loss about $25,000. Fight between Union troops, under Gen. BANKS, at Cane river, near Alexandria, Va.—1,000 rebels and nine cannon captured.
23. The gunboat *Petrel* captured by rebels, under WIRT ADAMS, near Yazoo City.
24. The Architectural Iron Works, Fourteenth-street, New-York, destroyed by fire—loss, $100,000. Large advance in the price of stocks.
25. Boiler explosion in Philadelphia—three persons killed. The blockade-running schooner *Three Brothers* captured and the rebel schooner *Wild Pigeon* sunk. One hundred thousand troops, for 100 days, tendered for the Union army by the Governors of Indiana, Ohio, Michigan and Illinois. Advance in price of gold to 173. Gov. SEYMOUR signs the new Metropolitan Police bill.
25. A train of 250 wagons captured by rebels near Pine Bluff, Ark.
27. A large building in West-street, New-York, destroyed by fire. Decline in stocks. Advance in Confederate loan in London.
29. Fire in Thirty-fourth-street, New-York—loss, about $8,000. Madison Court House, Va., burned by Union troops.

MAY.

MOON'S PHASES.

First Quarter, 2d. 11h. 8m. M.	Third Quarter, 18d. 1h. 44m. M.
Full Moon,... 10d. 3h. 27m. E.	New Moon,.... 24d. 5h. 54m. E.

Day of Month.	Day of Week.	PREMIUM ON GOLD, IN MAY, AT NEW-YORK.						SUN.	
		1862.		1863.		1864.		Rises.	Sets.
		LOWEST.	HIGHEST.	LOWEST.	HIGHEST.	LOWEST.	HIGHEST.	H. M.	H. M.
1	Mon	*2⅛	2⅛	50¾	51½	**Sun**	..	4 59	6 55
2	Tues	2½	2⅝	49⅞	50⅛	77⅛	78¼	4 58	6 56
3	Wed	2½	2¾	**Sun**	..	77⅛	79¾	4 57	6 57
4	Thu	**Sun**	..	48¼	50	78⅝	80¼	4 56	6 58
5	Frid	3⅛	3½	48½	51½	77¼	78¼	4 55	6 59
6	Sat	2⅝	3⅜	52¼	54	74	76	4 54	7 0
7	**Sun**	2⅜	2¾	54¼	*55⅜	71	73	4 53	7 1
8	Mon	2¾	3	52⅝	54½	**Sun**	..	4 52	7 2
9	Tues	3⅛	3¼	49	50¼	68¾	71¾	4 51	7 3
*10	Wed	3⅜	3⅜	**Sun**	..	*68	69¾	4 50	7 4
11	Thu	**Sun**	..	48½	49	72⅜	76½	4 49	7 5
12	Frid	3⅜	3⅝	48⅛	49¼	73⅛	75	4 48	7 6
13	Sat	3¼	3⅜	49¾	49¾	70	73½	4 47	7 7
14	**Sun**	3¼	3¼	49¾	50⅛	71¼	72½	4 45	7 8
15	Mon	3¼	3⅜	49¾	50	**Sun**	..	4 44	7 9
16	Tues	3	3⅛	49¾	50	73	74½	4 43	7 10
17	Wed	3	3⅛	**Sun**	..	77¼	78½	4 42	7 11
18	Thu	**Sun**	..	49¾	50	82½	84	4 41	7 12
19	Frid	3¼	3¼	48⅛	49½	81½	83	4 40	7 13
20	Sat	3⅜	3⅜	48⅝	49	80½	81½	4 39	7 14
21	**Sun**	3½	3½	48¾	50	82	83¼	4 38	7 15
22	Mon	3½	3⅝	48½	49¾	**Sun**	..	4 37	7 16
23	Tues	3½	3⅝	48½	49½	81¾	82⅝	4 36	7 17
24	Wed	3½	3⅝	**Sun**	..	82½	86	4 35	7 18
25	Thu	**Sun**	..	44¾	46¼	84¾	85⅛	4 35	7 19
26	Frid	4	4	43½	45	83	84	4 34	7 20
27	Sat	4	*4⅛	43⅝	44⅝	86	87	4 33	7 21
28	**Sun**	3⅞	4	*43½	43⅞	85¾	88	4 33	7 22
29	Mon	3⅝	3⅞	44¼	45⅛	**Sun**	..	4 32	7 23
30	Tues	..	..	44⅞	45¼	88	*94⅜	4 31	7 24
31	Wed	3½	3⅝	**Sun**	..	90	90½	4 31	7 25

Power of Taxation.—Congress has the power to lay stamp duties on notes, on bank notes, and on any description of bank notes. That power has already been exercised, and the duties may be laid on to such an amount, and in such a manner, as may be necessary to effect the object intended. This object is not merely to provide generally for the general welfare, but to carry into effect, in conformity with the last paragraph of the eighth section of the first article, those several and express provisions of the Constitution, which vest in Congress exclusively the control over the monetary system of the United States, and more particularly those which imply the necessity of a uniform currency.—A. Gallatin.

MAY.

1. Gunboat *Eastport* and two transports blown up by Union forces, near Alexandria, La., to prevent their falling into possession of the rebels.
2. Fire at 210 Chatham-street, New-York—five persons burned to death.
3. Admiral WILKES suspended from duty three years. Gen. GRANT commences movements against Richmond. Fight between Gen. STURGIS and Gen. FORREST.
4. Union troops, under Gen. BUTLER, advance up the Peninsula. The army of the Potomac, under Gen. GRANT, cross the Rapidan without opposition.
5. Gen. BUTLER transports his army from Yorktown to City Point. Fire in Second Avenue, New-York—loss about $6,000. Two gunboats and three transports destroyed by the rebels near Alexandria, La. Act of Congress granting lands to Minnesota for a rail-road from St. Paul to Lake Superior. Act of Congress granting lands to Wisconsin for rail-roads.
6. A battle at Mine Run between Gen. LEE and Gen. GRANT; Brig.-Gen. JAS. S. WADSWORTH and Brig. ALEX. HAYS among the killed.
7. Gold declines to 171. Gen. THOMAS occupied Tunnel Hill, Ga.
8. Dalton, Ga., occupied by Union troops under Gen. THOMAS. Freight and passenger depot of the Northern Rail-Road, at New London, Conn., destroyed by fire—loss, $100,000. Major-Gen. JOHN SEDGWICK killed at battle of Spotsylvania C. H.
9. Gen. BANKS and Admiral PORTER at Alexandria. Fight between Gen. BUTLER and Gen. HILL, near Petersburg, Va. The Danish blockade of certain ports in the Baltic pronounced ineffectual. Battle near Spotsylvania Court House.
10. Gen. SHERMAN completes a successful raid in rear of LEE's rebel army in Virginia. Fight between Gen. BUTLER's troops and those of Gen. BEAUREGARD.
11. Arrest of Col. ARGUELLES, by the United States officials, in New-York. The rebel army in Georgia driven by Gen. SHERMAN to Buzzard's Roost mountain.
12. Major-Gen. HANCOCK captures 7,000 rebels and thirty guns in a battle near Spotsylvania, Va. Union troops evacuate Washington, N. C. The outer line of works of Fort Darling carried by Union troops under Generals GILMORE and SMITH. Gen. SHERIDAN captures the outer line of fortifications in front of Richmond. Dalton, Ga., evacuated. Act of Congress granting lands to Iowa for two rail-roads.
14. Bombardment of Charleston and Fort Sumter, S. C., renewed with vigor.
15. Blockade-running steamer *Tristam Shandy* captured. Resaca, Ga., captured by Gen. SHERMAN. Gen. SIGEL defeated at Rood's Hill, in the Shenandoah Valley.
16. President LINCOLN calls upon Governor PARKER, of New-Jersey, for all the militia he can raise for 100 days' service. Steamship *Greyhound* captured by the U. S. gunboat *Connecticut*. Defeat of the rebels by Gen. SHERMAN.
17. Republican Convention of Vermont. Postal money order system passed.
18. A bogus proclamation of President LINCOLN published. Battle between Union troops under Gen. A. J. SMITH, and a rebel division in Louisiana—300 rebels captured.
20. Defeat of Gen. SIGEL by Gen. BRECKENRIDGE, in the Shenandoah.
21. Post-office and Masonic Hall, in Ware, Mass., destroyed by fire—loss, $25,000. The rebels assault Gen. BUTLER's lines, near Fort Darling, and are repulsed.
23. Gen. GRANT makes a grand flank movement against Gen. LEE. JOSEPH HOWARD, Jr., and FRANCIS A. MALISON arrested and sent to Fort Lafayette, charged with forging the bogus proclamation of President LINCOLN. Gen. LEE's rebel army fall back to the South Anna river. Over 600 rebel soldiers captured by Union troops.
24. Advance in price of gold to 185.
25. Republican State Convention of New-York held, to elect delegates to the National Convention at Baltimore. The rebels, under Gen. FITZ HUGH LEE, attack the Union forces at Wilson's Wharf, on the James river, and are repulsed.
26. Gen. GRANT makes another flank movement on LEE's rebel army. Surgeon-General HAMMOND, U. S. A., convicted by court-martial. Act of Congress creating the Territory of Montana. Bank of England reduced its rate from 8 to 7 per cent.
28. Rapid advance in the price of gold to 188.
29. Fight between Gen. MCPHERSON's corps and the rebels, at Dallas, Ga. Fire at No. 75 Division-street, New-York; loss of property about $3,000.
31. Meeting of the Radical Republican National Convention at Cleveland. Gold advances to 194.

JUNE.

MOON'S PHASES.

FIRST QUARTER, 1d. 3h. 25m. M. | THIRD QUARTER, 16d. 6h. 57m. M.
FULL MOON, ... 9d. 4h. 45m. M. | NEW MOON, ... 23d. 3h. 2m. M.
FIRST QUARTER, 30d. 8h. 34m. E.

Day of Month.	Day of Week.	DAILY PREMIUM ON GOLD, IN JUNE, AT NEW-YORK.						SUN.	
		1862.		1863.		1864.		Rises.	Sets.
		LOWEST.	HIGHEST.	LOWEST.	HIGHEST.	LOWEST.	HIGHEST.	H. M.	H. M.
1	Thu	**Sun**	..	46	*47½	*87½	89¼	4 31	7 24
2	Frid	*3½	3⅝	46¾	47¼	89⅞	91	4 30	7 25
3	Sat	3½	..	46¾	46⅞	90¼	92½	4 30	7 25
4	**Sun**	3½	3⅝	46	46½	90¾	91	4 29	7 26
5	Mon	3¾	4	46	46¼	**Sun**	..	4 29	7 27
6	Tues	4	4¼	45⅛	45⅝	93½	94¼	4 28	7 27
7	Wed	4	4⅛	**Sun**	..	92	94	4 28	7 28
8	Thu	**Sun**	..	43	43½	93	94⅛	4 28	7 28
9	Fri*	4¼	4⅜	42⅛	42⅜	95	98¼	4 28	7 29
10	Sat	4¼	4⅜	*40½	40¾	97½	99	4 28	7 29
11	**Sun**	4⅜	4½	41¾	42	94½	98	4 28	7 30
12	Mon	4¾	5¼	41¼	41⅜	**Sun**	..	4 28	7 30
13	Tues	5¼	5½	42¼	42½	93⅝	96½	4 28	7 31
14	Wed	5⅝	5¾	**Sun**	..	96⅜	98	4 28	7 31
15	Thu	**Sun**	..	44½	46½	96¾	97¾	4 28	7 32
16	Frid	6½	6¾	47¾	48⅜	97	97¼	4 28	7 32
17	Sat	6	6½	45⅜	45¾	97	98	4 28	7 33
18	**Sun**	5¾	6½	43⅜	43¾	95	95¼	4 28	7 33
19	Mon	6½	6⅝	43	43⅜	**Sun**	..	4 29	7 34
20	Tues	6⅜	6⅞	43¼	43¾	98	98½	4 29	7 34
21	Wed	6⅜	6½	**Sun**	..	99½	108	4 29	7 34
22	Thu	**Sun**	..	43⅜	43¾	105	135	4 29	7 34
23	Frid	6¾	..	43⅜	43½	105	125	4 29	7 35
24	Sat	7¾	8¾	43½	44	110	117	4 30	7 35
25	**Sun**	8¼	8⅜	44¾	45¾	112	120	4 30	7 35
26	Mon	8⅞	9¼	44¾	45	**Sun**	..	4 30	7 35
27	Tues	9⅜	*9½	43⅞	45⅛	130	140	4 30	7 35
28	Wed	9	9⅛	**Sun**	..	130	140	4 31	7 35
29	Thu	**Sun**	..	46½	47¼	140	150	4 31	7 35
30	Frid	8⅞	9¼	46⅛	46¾	140	*151	4 31	7 35

LITERARY PURSUITS OF MERCHANTS.—Biography abounds in truth, with examples of the union of the pursuits of literature and science with those of every department of active life. The most elegant of the writers of ancient Rome was also the most renowned of her warriors. It was amid the hurry and toils of his campaigns that JULIUS CÆSAR is said to have written those commentaries, or memoirs of his military exploits, which have immortalized his name more than all his victories, and thus amply justified the anxiety he is recorded to have shown to preserve the work, when, being obliged to throw himself from his ship, in the bay of Alexandria, and swim for his life, he made his way to the shore, with his arms in one hand, holding his commentaries with his teeth.—*Lord Brougham.*

JUNE.

1. National Convention at Cleveland. A rebel iron-clad on the James river is repulsed. United States steamer *Pocahontas* sinks.

2. Count de Paris married in England to Princess ISABELLA, of Spain French fleet enter the harbor of Acapulco, Mexico. JOHN C. FREMONT resigns. A portion of Gen. SHERMAN's army occupy Altoona Pass, Ga. U. S. steamer *Water Witch* captured by rebels in Ossabaw Sound, Ga. Successful advance of Gen. GRANT's army to Cold Harbor, Va. Gen. FITZ HUGH LEE, and 500 rebel cavalry captured by Gen. BUTLER. Wharf boat burned at Mound City, Mo.—loss about $400,000. Rebel steamer *Rose* destroyed by U. S. steamer *Wamsutta*.

3. Gen GRANT attempts to drive the rebels across the Chickahominy, and is repulsed; Union loss in three days, 7.500. National bank act passed.

4. The rebels, under Gen. LEE, attack Union lines near Bottom's Bridge, on the Chickahominy, but are repulsed. Blockade-running steamer *Thistle* captured.

5. Buildings Nos. 58 and 60 Fulton-street, N. Y., destroyed by fire; loss, $75,000.

6. Blockade-running steamer *Daregan* captured by United States steamer. Gen. HUNTER defeats the rebels at Staunton, Va., capturing 1,500 prisoners. The rebel Gen. W. E. JONES killed. The rebels attack Gen. BURNSIDE, and are repulsed.

7. National Union Convention assembles at Baltimore. Gold advances to 194.

8. JOHN MORGAN's rebel forces enter Eastern Kentucky. The steamer *Berkshire* destroyed by fire. Explosion of a locomotive on the New-York Central Rail-Road; three persons killed.

9. JOHN MORGAN and his rebel band defeated at Mount Sterling, Ky. Blockade steamer *Perensey* run ashore by U. S. steamer *Newbern*, near Beaufort, S. C.; vessel and cargo valued at $1,000,000.

10. Gen. KAUTZ charges the rebel works in front of Petersburg, Va.

11. Fight between Gen. SHERIDAN and Gen. J. E. B. STEWART. United States gunboat *Lavendar* wrecked. Gen. HUNTER enters Lexington, Va. MAXIMILIAN enters the city of Mexico. JOHN MORGAN captures Cynthiana, Ky. Gen. BURBRIDGE defeats the rebels.

13. Gen. STURGIS defeated by Generals FORREST, LEE and RODDY—wagon and ammunition trains lost. Lexington, Va., captured by Generals CROOK and AVERILL.

14. Bids for $75,000,000 loan opened at the Treasury; $90.000,000 offered.

15. Gen. (BALDY) SMITH attacks Petersburg. The new line of steamships to Havre goes into operation. Terrific tornado at Penn Yan, N. Y.

16. C. L. VALLANDIGHAM returns from his exile, to Ohio.

17. Attempt to capture Petersburg, Va. Explosion at the Washington arsenal.

18. Repulse of Gen. HUNTER at Lynchburg. Surrender of Union troops by Lieut. DRISKEL at Bardstown, Ky. Gen. SHERMAN enters Marietta, Ga.

19. Fight off Cherbourg, between the *Alabama*, under Capt. SEMMES, and the *Kearsarge*, under Capt. WINSLOW. An invasion of Maryland and Pennsylvania.

20. The government of New-Grenada authorizes a loan of $8,000,000. Accident on the New-Haven and Hartford Rail-Road.

21. Repulse of the rebels at White House, Va Rebel cavalry attack Pine Bluff, Ark. Inter continental telegraph bill passed by Congress.

22. Desperate fight on the Weldon Rail-Road. ISAAC HENDERSON, Navy Agent, New-York, arrested.

23. Bill to repeal the Fugitive Slave Law passed by Congress.

24. Completion of the Atlantic and Great Western Rail-Road. The rebels capture the tin-clad gunboat *Queen City*. The Convention of Maryland adopt a clause in favor of prohibiting slavery in the State.

25. Accident on the Grand Trunk Rail-Road, near Montreal—87 bodies recovered.

26. Gen. HUNTER completes a successful raid into Dixie, capturing over $5,000,000 worth of property. Hostilities between Danish and Austro-Prussian armies resumed.

27. Blockade-running iron steamer *Jupiter* captured by steamer *Proteus*. Gen. SHERMAN makes an unsuccessful assault upon the rebel lines at Kenesaw mountain.

28. The Seneca flouring-mills at Minetta, N. Y., destroyed by fire—loss, $200,000. Buildings 138 and 140 Chatham-street, N. Y., destroyed by fire—loss, $50,000.

29. Another plot against the life of the Emperor NAPOLEON discovered.

30. Hon. SALMON P. CHASE resigns. New tariff bill passed. New internal revenue act passed. Act passed to raise 400 millions of dollars by six per cent. bonds.

JULY.

MOON'S PHASES.

Full Moon, ... 8d. 3h. 33m. E.	New Moon, ... 22d. 1h. 33m. E.
Third Quarter, 15d. 11h. 31m. M.	First Quarter, 30d. 2h. 13m. E.

Day of Month.	Day of Week.	DAILY PREMIUM ON GOLD, IN JULY, AT NEW-YORK.						SUN.	
		1862.		1863.		1864.		Rises.	Sets.
		LOWEST.	HIGHEST.	LOWEST.	HIGHEST.	LOWEST.	HIGHEST.	H. M.	H. M.
1	Sat	*8¾	9¼	44¾	*45	*125	185	4 31	7 35
2	**Sun**	9¼	9½	43⅞	44½	130	150	4 32	7 35
3	Mon	10⅛	10½	44	44¼	**Sun**	..	4 32	7 35
4	Tues	Holi	y.	Holi	day.	Holi	day.	4 33	7 34
5	Wed	9¾	10	**Sun**	..	140	149	4 33	7 34
6	Thu	**Sun**	..	38	39¼	148	161½	4 34	7 34
7	Frid	10	10¼	32½	38½	162	173	4 34	7 34
8	Sat*	10¾	11½	30⅝	31¾	169	176½	4 35	7 33
9	**Sun**	13½	16½	31¼	31⅝	160	175	4 36	7 33
10	Mon	15⅝	17½	32¼	33	**Sun**	..	4 37	7 33
11	Tues	14¾	16	32¼	32½	181	*185½	4 38	7 32
12	Wed	13⅞	14½	**Sun**	..	170	182	4 39	7 32
13	Thu	**Sun**	..	31¼	31⅝	168¾	173	4 39	7 31
14	Frid	15½	16½	31	31½	158	170	4 40	7 31
15	Sat	17	..	28⅛	29¼	142	157¼	4 41	7 30
16	**Sun**	16¾	17½	26	26⅛	148½	161¼	4 42	7 29
17	Mon	18	19	25¾	26	**Sun**	..	4 43	7 29
18	Tues	19	19¾	25	25¼	154½	162¼	4 43	7 28
19	Wed	18¼	19	**Sun**	..	160	168¾	4 44	7 27
20	Thu	**Sun**	..	*23½	25⅜	161	164	4 45	7 27
21	Frid	20	20¼	26	27⅜	156½	160	4 46	7 26
22	Sat	19¾	*20⅜	24½	25¾	150½	157¾	4 47	7 25
23	**Sun**	19	19½	25¾	26⅛	153½	155	4 48	7 24
24	Mon	17	17½	26⅛	26¼	**Sun**	..	4 49	7 23
25	Tues	14	17¼	25¾	25⅞	155⅜	159	4 49	7 22
26	Wed	17½	18	**Sun**	..	157¾	159	4 50	7 22
27	Thu	**Sun**	..	27¼	27½	154½	157¼	4 51	7 21
28	Frid	16⅝	17⅝	27½	27¾	148½	149	4 52	7 20
29	Sat	15¾	16½	27½	27¾	150⅞	153½	4 53	7 19
30	**Sun**	14¼	14½	27⅝	27¾	155	158	4 54	7 18
31	Mon	15	16	28½	29	**Sun**	..	4 55	7 17

Origin of Repudiation.—In proportion precisely as an individual is beyond the reach of compulsory process, should he be inclined to disregard the technicalities of mere law, and base himself upon the broader principles of natural justice. This is still more necessary when an independent sovereignty is concerned; because it is more difficult to procure redress for wrongs committed by a State. The relation between debtor and creditor, in all cases involving the repose of confidence, is pre-eminently a fiduciary relation when the debtor is a sovereign commonwealth. It should be distinguished by that *uberrima fides* which scorns the strict letter of the contract and regards its spirit and intention.—*Peleg W. Chandler.*

JULY.

1. Hon. Wm. P. Fessenden, of Maine, appointed Secretary of the Treasury. Destructive fire at Louisville, Ky.—loss, $1,000,000. Act "to facilitate trade on the Red river of the North." Act to incorporate the Metropolitan R. R., D. C.

2. Union cavalry, under Gen. Wilson, returns from a successful raid south of Petersburg. Destructive fire at the United States armory, Springfield, Mass. Act of Congress to repeal the gold bill of June 19. Act of Congress in favor of rail-road and telegraph from Lake Huron to Puget's Sound.

3. The rebels commence a new invasion of Maryland and Pennsylvania. General Sigel's forces driven from Martinsburg. Gen. Sherman flanks the rebels at Kenesaw. Collision of trains on the Erie Rail-Road—one man killed and two injured. Steamship *Locust Point* struck and sunk by the steamship *Matanzas*—19 persons lost.

4. Extensive water cure establishment at Saratoga destroyed by fire—loss, $60,000. Act of Congress to establish a branch mint at Dalles City, Oregon. One church and six dwellings destroyed by fire in Wooster-street, New-York—loss, $150,000.

5. Harper's Ferry and Hagerstown occupied by rebels; New-York and other States called upon to repel the invaders. The *habeas corpus* suspended, and martial law declared in Kentucky by proclamation of President Lincoln.

7. Advance in gold from 259 to 273. The rebels in Pennsylvania.

8. Artillery fight in front of Petersburg, Va. Blockade steamer *Little Ada* captured by United States steamer *Gettysburgh*. Frederick, Md., evacuated by Union troops under Gen. Wallace, and occupied by rebels, who levy $200,000 on the citizens.

9. Union troops, under Gen. Wallace, defeated by the rebels at Monocacy bridge. Mr. Briggs, bank clerk, London, murdered in a rail road car by Muller.

10. Steamship *Electric Spark*, of New-York, and four other vessels, destroyed by the *Florida*. Gunpowder bridge, on Baltimore and Philadelphia Rail-Road, destroyed by rebels; trains of cars also stopped. Steamer *John Potter*, and pier No. 1, N. R., New-York, destroyed by fire. President Lincoln issues a proclamation relative to a reconstruction of the Union. Rockville, Md., entered and robbed by rebels.

11. Governor Bradford's house robbed and burned by the rebels.

12. Frederick, Md., re-occupied by Union troops. Fires in the Bowery, also in Barclay and Baxter streets, New-York; total loss about $15,000.

13. The rebels retire across the Potomac.

14. Fight between Union and rebel troops at Tupelo, Miss.; defeat of the latter.

15. John Bellamy, tea merchant, 369 Broome-street, New-York, arrested on a charge of having set fire to his premises. Decline in gold from 260 to 250. Collision of trains on the Erie Rail-Road—over one hundred rebel prisoners killed and wounded. Destructive fire in Brooklyn; total loss about $1,000,000.

16. Gen. Sherman's army successfully crosses the Chatahooche river.

18. Rebels whipped at Snicker's Gap by Gen. Crook. Proclamation for 500,000 volunteers. Death of Nathaniel Marsh, President of Erie R. R. Company, aged 52.

20. The walls of the Female Lunatic Asylum, Philadelphia, fall and kill eighteen of the inmates, and injure twenty others. Severe fights between Gen. Sherman and Gen. Hood, in front of Atlanta; seven assaults of Hood successfully repulsed.

21. Steamboat *B. M. Runyon* sunk by a snag in the Mississippi river, by which about fifty lives were lost. Nixon paper-mills, at Manayunk, Pa., destroyed by fire—loss about $125,000. Peace conference at Niagara Falls.

22. Terrible battle in front of Atlanta; rebel loss estimated at 7,000, 18 stand of colors, and 5,000 stand of arms; Union loss, 3,200; Gen. McPherson (Union) killed.

24. Gen. Rousseau (Union) completes a successful raid in Alabama and Georgia, capturing about 800 mules and horses. Fire at Jamaica, L. I.—loss, $25,000.

25. Moses Taylor appointed Assistant Treasurer in New-York, (declined.) Sec Fessenden advertises for bids to the new $200,000,000 loan.

26. Union troops, under Gen. Averill, defeated by rebels at Martinsburg, Va.

27. The rebel troops on north side of James river surprised and defeated.

28. Severe fight in front of Atlanta between the rebel and Union armies; the rebels attack Gen. Sherman, and are repulsed with the loss of 1,000.

30. A mine exploded under rebel fortifications at Petersburg, Va..

31. A rebel force enters and burns nearly the whole of Chambersburg, Pa.

AUGUST.

MOON'S PHASES.

FULL MOON, ... 7d. 0h. 33m. M. | NEW MOON,... 21d. 2h. 21m. M.
THIRD QUARTER, 13d. 4h. 46m. E. | FIRST QUARTER, 29d. 6h. 50m. M.

Day of Month.	Day of Week.	PREMIUM ON GOLD, IN AUGUST, AT NEW-YORK.						SUN.	
		1862.		1863.		1864.		Rises.	Sets.
		LOWEST.	HIGHEST.	LOWEST.	HIGHEST.	LOWEST.	HIGHEST.	H. M.	H. M.
1	Tues	15⅛	15¾	29½	*29¾	151	158½	4 56	7 16
2	Wed	15	15¼	**Sun**	..	156	157½	4 57	7 15
3	Thu	**Sun**	..	27½	27¾	156½	158½	4 58	7 14
4	Frid	14⅝	15	28¼	28⅝	*Fast*	*Day.*	4 59	7 13
5	Sat	14½	14¾	27¾	27⅞	157¾	161¼	5 0	7 12
6	**Sun**	14⅝	14⅞	*Fast*	*Day*	159¼	*161¾	5 1	7 11
*7	Mon	14½	14⅞	27	27¾	**Sun**	..	5 2	7 10
8	Tues	12¾	13¼	26¼	..	156¾	159¼	5 3	7 9
9	Wed	*12½	12¾	**Sun**	..	153⅜	155	5 4	7 8
10	Thu	**Sun**	..	26⅛	26¾	154⅞	155¼	5 5	7 6
11	Frid	13⅛	14	26⅛	26¼	153⅞	156	5 6	7 5
12	Sat	13½	14	26¼	26⅜	156	157¼	5 7	7 3
13	**Sun**	14	14½	26⅝	27	154½	156	5 8	7 2
14	Mon	15	16	25½	26¼	**Sun**	..	5 9	7 0
15	Tues	14¾	15¼	25⅜	25½	155¾	156⅝	5 10	6 59
16	Wed	14⅜	15¼	**Sun**	..	155⅝	156¾	5 11	6 58
17	Thu	**Sun**	..	25⅝	25¾	155¾	156½	5 12	6 57
18	Frid	15	15¼	25⅝	26	157	157⅜	5 13	6 55
19	Sat	14⅞	15¼	25	25⅜	157	158	5 14	6 54
20	**Sun**	15	15½	24⅞	25	155	156	5 15	6 53
21	Mon	15½	16	25¼	25⅜	**Sun**	..	5 16	6 51
22	Tues	15	16¼	24¾	24⅞	156⅛	157⅛	5 17	6 50
23	Wed	15½	15¾	**Sun**	..	157⅛	158¼	5 18	6 49
24	Thu	**Sun**	..	24	24¼	154¼	157	5 19	6 47
25	Frid	15¼	15¾	22½	23⅛	154¼	155¾	5 20	6 45
26	Sat	15¼	15¾	*22½	23½	153⅝	156	5 21	6 43
27	**Sun**	15¼	15½	24½	24⅞	145	153	5 22	6 41
28	Mon	15½	15⅝	24½	24¾	**Sun**	..	5 23	6 40
29	Tues	16	*16½	24¾	24⅞	135½	145	5 24	6 38
30	Wed	15⅝	16	**Sun**	..	*131½	136	5 25	6 36
31	Thu	**Sun**	..	28	28¼	134	143	5 26	6 34

MR. JEFFERSON ON NATIONAL DEBTS.—"It is a wise rule, and should be fundamental in a government disposed to cherish its credit, and at the same time to restrain the use of it within the limits of its faculties, never to borrow a dollar without laying a tax in the same instant, for paying the interest annually and the principal within a given term; and to consider that tax as pledged to the creditors on the public faith. On such a pledge as this, sacredly observed, a government may always command on a reasonable interest all the lendable money of its citizens; whilst the necessity of an equivalent tax is a salutary warning to them and their constituents against oppression, bankruptcy, and its inevitable consequence, revolution."

AUGUST.

2. Special State election in Pennsylvania. A treaty of peace between Germany and Denmark agreed upon.
3. Rebels, under Gen. Early, occupy Martinsburg, Va., and Hagerstown, Md.
4. Fight between rebel and Union troops at New Creek, Md.
5. Admiral Farragut passes Forts Morgan, Gaines and Powell into Mobile harbor. The Union gunboat *Tecumseh* sunk.
6. Another rebel mine exploded in front of Gen. Grant's lines. Capture of Nankin, China, by the Imperialists, announced.
7. Gen. Sherman makes an important flank movement in front of Atlanta. The rebels make an attempt to re-capture Admiral Buchanan.
8. Fort Gaines (entrance of Mobile harbor) surrendered. Fort Powell abandoned by the rebels. Gen. Averill defeats the rebels under McCausland. Accident on Washington Branch Rail-Road.
9. Steamer *C. Vanderbilt* sunk on the Hudson river.
10. Explosion of army ordnance boat at City Point, Va. Brig *Billow*, of Salem, Mass., destroyed by the *Tallahassee*. Propeller *Racine* destroyed by fire on Lake Erie; about twenty persons lost their lives.
11. Pilot-boat *James Funk* and pilot-boat *No.* 22, of New-York, captured by the *Tallahassee*. Premises 409 Broadway, New-York, damaged by fire $12,000.
12. Riot in Londonderry, Ireland. Building No. 20 East-street, New-York, damaged by fire—loss, $6,500. Twenty-three buildings in Dover and Mott streets, New-York, partly destroyed by fire; damage, $50,000. Ship *Adriatic*, bark *Suliote*, pilot-boat *Wm. Bell*, and schooner *Carroll* captured by the rebel pirate *Tallahassee*.
13. Bark *Glenalvon* captured and destroyed by the *Tallahassee*.
14. Riot in Belfast, Ireland. Union troops, under Gen. Hancock, advance on the north side of James river.
15. Special State election in Connecticut. Three steamers captured by rebels near Shawneetown, Ill. Six vessels captured and destroyed by the *Tallahassee*. Freshet in front of Petersburg, Va. Gen. Wheeler (rebel) demands the surrender of Dalton.
16. Fire in Ninth-street, Brooklyn—loss, $1,500. Collision in the Erie Rail-Road tunnel, Jersey City, between two trains; two persons badly injured. Another advance of Union troops on the north side of James river.
17. Gen. Merritt's cavalry attacked in the Shenandoah Valley by Kershaw.
18. A peace convention assembles at Syracuse, attended by Vallandigham and F. Wood. Severe fight at Graysville, Ga., between Gen. Wheeler and Gen. Steadman. Accident on the Kennebec and Portland Rail-Road; about twenty-five persons badly injured. Lubricating oil works in Roxbury, Mass., blown up—loss, $23,000. The rebels attack Gen. Birney, and are repulsed with great slaughter.
19. Fire in East Twenty-fifth-street, New-York; damage, $3,000. Severe fight between the rebels and Gen. Warren. Martinsburg, Va., re-occupied by rebels.
20. Rail-road depot in Centre-street, N. Y., damaged by fire to amount of $8,000.
21. Battle on the Weldon and Petersburg Rail-Road; the rebels repulsed with fearful slaughter; Union loss about 3,000. Rebel Gen. Forrest attacks Memphis.
22. Fight between rebel and Union troops near Charlestown, Va. Gen. Kilpatrick returns from a successful raiding expedition.
23. Fort Morgan, Mobile harbor, Ala, surrendered to the United States forces.
24. A very large fire in Atlanta, caused by shells from Gen. Sherman's batteries.
25. The rebel privateer *Georgia* captured by the frigate *Niagara*. Fight between Gen. Early and a force of Gen. Sheridan's, near Leetown, Va. The rebels assault Gen. Warren, on line of Weldon Rail-Road. Muller, the murderer of Mr. Briggs, of London, arrested in New-York harbor.
26. Accident on the Indianapolis and Cincinnati R. R.; thirty persons injured.
28. The first broad gauge train of Atlantic and Great Western Rail-Road arrived at St. Louis, from New-York, without change of cars, in 44 hours running time. Great commercial crisis in Canada.

SEPTEMBER.

MOON'S PHASES.

Full Moon, . . . 5d. 8h. 56m. M.	New Moon, . . . 19d. 5h. 49m. E.
Third Quarter, 11d. 0h. 2m. M.	First Quarter, 27d. 9h. 50m. E.

Day of Month.	Day of Week.	Premium on Gold, in September, at New-York.						Sun.			
		1862.		1863.		1864.		Rises.		Sets.	
		Lowest.	Highest.	Lowest.	Highest.	Lowest.	Highest.	H.	M.	H.	M.
1	Frid	*16½	17⅛	*26⅞	27⅜	143	148	5	27	6	33
2	Sat	16½	17	27½	28	148½	154½*	5	28	6	32
3	**Sun**	17¾	19	29½	31¼	137¼	143½	5	29	6	30
4	Mon	17⅝	18¼	33¼	34½	**Sun**	..	5	30	6	29
*5	Tues	18¼	19⅛	31½	31¾	135	143½	5	31	6	27
6	Wed	18⅝	19	**Sun**	..	140⅝	142	5	32	6	26
7	Thu	**Sun**	..	33	33¼	140⅞	142¾	5	33	6	24
8	Fri	19	19¼	32	32⅛	135¾	141	5	34	6	23
9	Sat	18¾	19⅛	32⅜	32⅝	133¼	136	5	35	6	21
10	**Sun**	18⅝	18¾	31⅛	31⅜	118½	128½	5	36	6	19
11	Mon	18¾	19	29⅜	29¾	**Sun**	..	5	36	6	18
12	Tues	19	19⅜	28⅞	29	113½	126	5	37	6	16
13	Wed	18⅝	19	**Sun**	..	117½	128	5	38	6	14
14	Thu	**Sun**	..	30⅞	31⅝	123½	128	5	39	6	12
15	Frid	17½	17⅞	31	32⅛	127	129¼	5	40	6	10
16	Sat	16½	17¾	31⅜	32¼	123½	128	5	41	6	8
17	**Sun**	16⅞	17¾	32¼	32½	120⅞	123	5	42	6	7
18	Mon	16¾	17¼	33	33¾	**Sun**	..	5	43	6	7
19	Tues	16⅛	17¾	33¾	34	123⅞	126¾	5	44	6	4
20	Wed	16¾	17½	**Sun**	..	123	126¾	5	45	6	2
21	Thu	**Sun**	..	39¼	40	120	122⅛	5	46	6	1
22	Frid	16¾	17¼	37¼	38½	116	121¼	5	47	5	59
23	Sat	17⅜	18	37½	38¼	111	117	5	48	5	57
24	**Sun**	18⅝	19	36¾	37	110	112	5	49	5	55
25	Mon	20	20¾	38	38⅛	**Sun**	..	5	50	5	53
26	Tues	20⅛	20½	39	39¼	*85	98½	5	51	5	52
27	Wed	21⅜	21½	**Sun**	..	92½	95	5	52	5	50
28	Thu	**Sun**	..	42½	43⅛	95	105	5	53	5	49
29	Frid	21¾	23½	42½	*43¼	94¼	101	5	54	5	47
30	Sat	21½	*24	41¼	42	91	94	5	55	5	45

Specie and Paper.—The essential difference between banking and other commercial business is, that merchants rely, for the fulfilment of their engagements, on their resources, and not on the forbearance of their creditors; whilst the banks always rely not only on their resources but also on the probability that their creditors will not require payment of their demands. We have already seen that this probability is always increased or lessened in proportion as the issues of the banks are moderate or excessive. One of the most efficient modes to reduce the amount of bank notes, as compared to the total amount of the currency of the country, consists in the increase of the metallic currency which circulates amongst the people, independent of that which is kept in reserve in the vaults of the banks.—Albert Gallatin.

SEPTEMBER.

1. SIMEON DRAPER appointed Collector of the Port of New-York.

2. Atlanta, Ga., captured by Major-Gen. SHERMAN; 27 guns and 1,000 rebel prisoners taken. Fight in the Shenandoah Valley, near Berryville, Va.; defeat of the rebels. Rail-road accident near Berrymansville; five persons killed and seventeen injured.

3. Successful attack on Japanese fortifications by ships of war representing England, France, Holland and the United States. Prince and Princess of Wales embark at Dundee for Denmark, on a visit.

4. Fight with rebels at Greenville, Tenn.; JOHN MORGAN, the notorious guerilla chief, killed, and his force dispersed.

5. President LINCOLN issues a proclamation of thanks to Admiral FARRAGUT, and Generals CANBY, GRANGER, SHERMAN and SHERIDAN, for their signal victories over the rebels. A number of failures in England and Germany announced.

6. Vermont State election—success of the Republican party. Gen. CORTINAS, of Mexico, drives the rebels out of Brownsville, Texas, and holds the place.

7. The Republican State Convention of New-York held at Syracuse.

8. Gen. McCLELLAN accepts his nomination for the Presidency. Bids for United States bonds opened at Washington; bids received for $62,000,000.

9 Successful night attack by Union troops at Petersburg, Va.

11. State election in Maine—success of the Republican tickets.

13. Danish peace conference held at Vienna—a prolongation of the armistice.

15. Democratic Convention of New-York, at Albany; Gov. SEYMOUR re-nominated.

16. Daring raid by the rebels near Petersburg, Va.; loss of 3,000 head of cattle.

18. AVERILL's corps, at Martinsburg, Va., attacked by the Confederate General GORDON; the latter repulsed.

19. Desperate fight with the rebels at Opequan Creek, Shenandoah Valley; the Union troops, under Gen. SHERIDAN, capture 3,000 prisoners. The rebels capture the steamers *Parsons* and *Island Queen*, and convert them into privateers.

20. The British government order that no vessel belonging to the Confederates or United States shall enter British ports for the purpose of being dismantled or sold. Collision on the Pennsylvania Rail-Road; about fifty persons lost their lives.

21. Two steamers seized by the rebels on Lake Erie, re-captured, and the pirates arrested. Gen. J. C. FREMONT and Gen. JOHN COCHRANE withdraw.

22. Gen. SHERIDAN gains a great victory over the rebels at Fisher's Hill, Shenandoah Valley; captures twenty guns, besides caissons, horses, and 1,100 prisoners; Union Gen. RUSSELL killed. Serious riot at Turin, in consequence of the proposed transfer of the capital of Italy from that city to Florence; twenty of the rioters shot. New Italian ministry formed. Defeat of Gen. ORTEGO, in Mexico, by the French troops; every Mexican army said to be dispersed and the war closed. The Confederate loan declined 9 per cent. within a week.

23. War declared by Brazil against Uruguay. Cash payments suspended by the Bank of Brazil. Postmaster-General BLAIR resigns; ex-Governor DENISON, of Ohio, appointed. Financial panic in England; the Bank of Leeds stops payment.

24. Great depression in commercial circles in England. Fall in the price of cotton. Failure of several large houses in London, Liverpool and Leeds announced.

26. Gold panic in Wall-street, (New-York,)—great fall in prices.

27. Potosi, Mo., captured by the rebels. Decline of 6½ per cent. in the Confederate loan. Failure of several large firms in London announced.

28. Decline in prices of dry goods, articles of food, &c. Serious fracas in Cincinnati, O., between political gatherings.

29 Rebel fortifications at Chapin's farm, near Richmond, Va., stormed and taken by Union troops; fifteen guns and two hundred prisoners captured. Commercial panic in Chicago; fall in prices of gold, articles of provisions, clothing, &c.

30. Invasion of Missouri by the rebels; rail-road property at Franklin destroyed. Democratic State Convention held at Baltimore. The rebels make three unsuccessful attempts to drive the Union troops from Chapin's farm, in front of Richmond; advance of Union troops, and defeat of the rebels at Poplar Grove, near Petersburg, Va. Battle between French troops and Arab insurgents; 800 of the Arabs killed.

OCTOBER.

MOON'S PHASES.

Full Moon,... 4d. 5h. 35m. E. | New Moon,... 19d. 11h. 31m. M.
Third Quarter, 11d. 10h. 26m. M. | First Quarter, 27d. 10h. 54m. M.

Day of Month.	Day of Week.	PREMIUM ON GOLD, IN OCTOBER, AT NEW-YORK.						SUN.			
		1862.		1863.		1864.		Rises.		Sets.	
		LOWEST.	HIGHEST.	LOWEST.	HIGHEST.	LOWEST.	HIGHEST.	H.	M.	H.	M.
1	**Sun**	*22	22¾	*40⅛	40⅜	89	94	5	56	5	43
2	Mon	22⅜	23	43	43¼	**Sun**	..	5	57	5	42
3	Tues	22⅜	22⅝	43	43⅛	89	92½	5	58	5	41
*4	Wed	22½	23	**Sun**	..	90⅛	92¼	5	59	5	39
5	Thu	**Sun**	..	44	44¾	*88	91	6	0	5	37
6	Frid	23	23⅛	46	47¼	92¼	97	6	1	5	36
7	Sat	23½	24	46¼	46½	98	106	6	2	5	34
8	**Sun**	24½	25	46	46⅞	96¾	103¼	6	3	5	33
9	Mon	26	26⅝	46¾	47	**Sun**	..	6	4	5	31
10	Tues	27	29	48⅜	48½	96	99	6	5	5	29
11	Wed	28	28⅞	**Sun**	..	98¾	105	6	6	5	28
12	Thu	**Sun**	..	49½	50¼	102	104¾	6	7	5	26
13	Frid	29	30⅛	53¾	54¾	103¾	109¾	6	8	5	25
14	Sat	32	33½	52½	53¾	108	117¼	6	9	5	23
15	**Sun**	34	*37⅝	56	*56⅞	113¼	120	6	10	5	22
16	Mon	32½	35	54⅛	55½	**Sun**	..	6	11	5	20
17	Tues	32	33	49½	50	106½	123	6	12	5	19
18	Wed	29	30	**Sun**	..	106¼	117½	6	13	5	17
19	Thu	**Sun**	..	51¼	51½	107½	111½	6	14	5	16
20	Frid	27	29	49⅝	49¾	106¾	111¼	6	15	5	15
21	Sat	28¼	32	43¾	46	107⅜	109½	6	16	5	13
22	**Sun**	33	34	42¾	44¼	109½	113½	6	18	5	12
23	Mon	32½	33	45¾	46½	**Sun**	..	6	19	5	10
24	Tues	30¼	32½	46¾	47	112½	117⅞	6	20	5	8
25	Wed	30	31¼	**Sun**	..	115	118¾	6	21	5	7
26	Thu	**Sun**	..	49½	49¾	112½	117⅛	6	22	5	5
27	Frid	30	31¼	46	47¼	114¾	116½	6	24	5	4
28	Sat	31⅝	32¼	45¾	46½	115⅜	117¾	6	25	5	3
29	**Sun**	31¼	31¾	47	48	118⅛	120¾	6	26	5	2
30	Mon	30¼	30¾	46	46⅜	**Sun**	..	6	27	5	0
31	Tues	29½	30	45⅜	46¼	121½	*129¼	6	28	5	59

Rail-Roads and Steam.—Among the innumerable benefits derived from advancing knowledge, there are few more important than those improved facilities of communication, which, by increasing the frequency with which nations and individuals are brought into contact, have, to an extraordinary extent, corrected their prejudices, raised the opinion which each forms of the other, diminished their mutual hostility, and thus diffusing a more favorable view of our common nature, have stimulated us to develop those boundless resources of the human understanding, the very existence of which it was once considered almost a heresy to assert.—Buckle.

OCTOBER.

1. Secretary of the Treasury, FESSENDEN, advertises for a loan of $40,000,000. Pilot Knob, Mo., attacked by the rebels without important results. Heavy decline in gold, railway stocks, &c. GEORGE PEABODY, the distinguished banker, London, retired from business. Financial panic in England; more failures announced.

3. Great panic in the Stock market in New-York.

4. Severe fight between Gen. SHERMAN's forces and the rebels at Altoona, Tenn. Great excitement in Missouri, in consequence of the invasion of that State by the rebels, under Gen. PRICE. Capture of Athens, Ala., by the rebels. Betrothal of the Crown Prince of Russia to the Princess DAGMAR, of Denmark, officially announced. Failure of W. T. BROWN & Co., of Liverpool, and JULIUS MANDELL & Co., of London.

5. Terrible cyclone at Calcutta, causing the loss of a large number of vessels. Failure of A. SOLOMONS, of Manchester, Eng., announced. Run upon the banks of Chicago. Several banking houses of Chicago fail.

6. Advance in price of gold on account of unfavorable news from Richmond.

7. The rebel cruiser *Florida*, with twelve officers and fifty-eight of her crew, captured in the Bay of Bahia, Brazil, by the United States steamer *Wachusett*. Arrest of several persons in Indianapolis, Indiana, charged with treasonable organization.

8. Desperate fight with the rebels near Richmond; severe loss of life. Rome, Ga., captured by the rebels; some officers and 3,000 negroes taken prisoners.

9. Fight near Strasburg, Va.; about 350 rebels and eleven guns captured.

11. A Spanish steamer seized by the United States frigate *Niagara*, on suspicion of being a blockade runner. State elections held in Pennsylvania, Ohio and Indiana; the Republicans triumphant in each State.

12. Election in Maryland, to decide upon the adoption of a new constitution abolishing slavery; the new constitution adopted. Death of Chief Justice TANEY.

13. The bank of France shows a decrease of 17,000,000 francs within the week; rate of discount from 7 to 8 per cent. Accident on the Hudson River Rail-Road—two persons injured.

14. Failure of several large firms in London and Liverpool announced. Bids for the $40,000,000 loan at the Treasury Department; $30,000,000 offered in excess of the amount asked for. Failure of three New-York firms announced.

15. Gen. CORTINAS, of Mexico, gives in his adhesion to the Empire.

16. Convention at Quebec, to form a union or confederation of the British provinces. Accident on the New-Haven Rail-Road—thirty persons injured.

17. Steamship *Roanoke*, of New-York, captured and destroyed by the rebels. Capture of Ship Gap, Tenn., by Gen. SHERMAN. Lexington and Warrensburg, Mo., occupied by the rebels.

18. A party of twenty-five armed rebels enter St. Albans, Vt., and rob three banks of $150,000, and shoot five citizens; then flee to Canada, where they are arrested by the Canadian authorities.

19. Great battle in the Shenandoah Valley between the Union forces, under Gen. SHERIDAN, and the rebels, under Gen. EARLY; defeat of the latter, and capture of forty-three guns. Destruction of Brooklyn City Flour Mills by fire.

21. Failure of several extensive firms in London announced.

22. Cash in the Bank of France increased 3,500,000 francs. Gen. BLUNT defeated by the rebels under Gen. PRICE, at Lexington, Mo.

23. Fire in Eastport, Maine—loss estimated at $500,000.

24. Improvement in commercial and financial matters in England.

25. Suspension of diplomatic relations between Spain and Peru announced.

26. The King of Greece warns the national assembly to close their labors at an early day, or take the responsibility of the consequences.

28. The rebel ram *Albemarle* blown up in Roanoke river by a United States torpedo boat, under command of Lieut. CUSHING. Fight between Gen. PLEASANTON's Union army and Gen. PRICE's rebel army, at Newtown, Mo.; defeat of the latter; 2,000 rebels and 700 stand of arms captured. Decline in the price of gold.

29. Interview of the Emperor NAPOLEON, of France, with the CZAR at Nice.

30. The State of Nevada admitted to the Union, officially announced.

21. Capture of Plymouth, N. C., by Union troops.

NOVEMBER.

MOON'S PHASES.

FULL MOON, ...	3d.	3h.	7m.	M.
THIRD QUARTER,	10d.	0h.	49m.	M.
NEW MOON, ...	18d.	6h.	4m.	M.
FIRST QUARTER,	25d.	10h.	3m.	E.

Day of Month.	Day of Week.	PREMIUM ON GOLD, IN NOVEMBER, AT NEW-YORK.						SUN.			
		1862.		1863.		1864.		Rises.		Sets.	
		LOWEST.	HIGHEST.	LOWEST.	HIGHEST.	LOWEST.	HIGHEST.	H.	M.	H.	M.
1	Wed	29⅝	31¼	**Sun**	..	130	141½	6	29	4	59
2	Thu	**Sun**	..	45⅞	46½	129⅞	146	6	30	4	58
*3	Frid	30½	31½	46⅛	46¼	126¾	136¼	6	31	4	57
4	Sat	29½	31½	46	46⅛	131⅝	139	6	32	4	56
5	**Sun**	31½	32¼	46¼	47¼	135¼	145½	6	33	4	55
6	Mon	31½	32	48	48¾	**Sun**	..	6	35	4	53
7	Tues	31½	32	46¼	47⅜	138½	150¼	6	36	4	52
8	Wed	32	32¼	**Sun**	..	145½	149½	6	38	4	50
9	Thu	**Sun**	..	46¼	46⅝	146	*160	6	39	4	49
10	Frid	32¼	*33¼	45	45¾	138	153	6	40	4	48
11	Sat	31	32¾	45⅜	45¾	138⅞	145	6	41	4	47
12	**Sun**	31½	32	46⅝	47	142	145	6	43	4	46
13	Mon	31½	32	47	47⅜	**Sun**	..	6	44	4	45
14	Tues	32	33	46⅝	47	143	146½	6	45	4	44
15	Wed	31¾	32	**Sun**	..	137	144⅝	6	47	4	43
16	Thu	**Sun**	..	47	47	123½	140	6	48	4	42
17	Frid	32	32¼	47⅞	48½	118⅛	129	6	49	4	41
18	Sat	31⅜	32	49½	50	109¾	118½	6	50	4	40
19	**Sun**	30	31	51	52¾	116⅝	124¼	6	51	4	40
20	Mon	30¼	30½	52½	53¼	**Sun**	..	6	52	4	39
21	Tues	30¼	30⅝	53⅛	*54	117½	122	6	54	4	38
22	Wed	30½	30¾	**Sun**	..	122½	128¼	6	55	4	38
23	Thu	**Sun**	..	53	54	120½	124⅝	6	56	4	37
24	Frid	30⅛	30¾	50½	52	*Holi*	*day.*	6	57	4	36
25	Sat	29⅞	30	48¾	49	*116½	121	6	58	4	36
26	**Sun**	29¼	29½	*Holi*	*day.*	118	127⅝	6	59	4	35
27	Mon	*Thanks*	*giving.*	*43	45½	**Sun**	..	7	0	4	34
28	Tues	29¼	29½	44½	44⅝	126½	133¾	7	1	4	34
29	Wed	*28¾	29¼	**Sun**	..	132	136	7	2	4	33
30	Thu	**Sun**	..	48⅜	49	128	132½	7	4	4	33

THE STANDARD.—There is not, however, in nature, any perfect or altogether permanent standard of value. There is not a single commodity, the relative value of which, as compared to that of all other commodities, is not subject to great and permanent changes, as well as to temporary fluctuations. But it will be found that the nature of the demand for precious metals, the comparative regularity of the supply, and especially their much greater durability and intrinsic value than those of any other substance otherwise fitted for a circulating medium, restrain the fluctuations to which the relative value is liable, within far narrower limits, than is the case with any other commodity, which might have been selected for a currency. —A. GALLATIN.

NOVEMBER.

1. Great excitement in the Stock market, rise in the price of railway shares, &c. The Post-office money order system goes into operation in the United States. Articles of the Danish treaty of peace published.

3. Fight between Gen. SHERMAN and Gen. HOOD; defeat of the latter. Armed bands of rebels appear on the Lakes, and occasion great alarm along the northern frontier. Robbery of the Mercantile Bank of New-York of $340,000, by the paying teller, CHARLES WINDSOR, announced. Rebel troops, under Gen. PRICE, attack Fayetteville, Ark., and are repulsed.

4. Destruction of six United States vessels by two new rebel cruisers, the *Chickamauga* and *Olustee*, announced.

6. Disaster on the Erie Rail-Road—four persons killed and thirty wounded.

7. Night attack by rebels on Union troops in front of Petersburg, Va., repulsed.

8. ABRAHAM LINCOLN carries every State except Delaware, Kentucky and New-Jersey. State election in New-York—the Union ticket elected by about 7,000 majority.

9. Advance of 12½ per cent. in the price of gold. Gen. SHERMAN starts on a march through Georgia to the coast.

10. Bank of England reduced the rate of discount from 9 to 8 per cent.

11. Explosion on board the steamer *Tulip*, of the Potomac flotilla; fifty-five lives supposed to be lost. Rebels rush into Atlanta, and are handsomely whipped; 900 taken prisoners.

14. Gen. BRECKENRIDGE attacks Gen. GILLEM at Bull Gap, and captures 400 Union troops.

15. Fall of 6 per cent. in the price of gold.

16. Fall of 10 per cent. in the price of gold.

17. The rebels repulsed in a night attack on the Union lines at Bermuda Hundred.

18. Severe fight between rebel and Union troops at Strawberry Plains, Tenn. Forty-five Union scouts captured by the rebel Gen. MOSBY, at Charlestown, Va.

19. Norfolk, Va., Fernandina and Pensacola, Florida, opened for trade, the blockade being partially raised by proclamation of President LINCOLN. Fire at Newbern, N. C.; fifteen large buildings destroyed; in blowing up some buildings to arrest the flames, several soldiers were torn to pieces.

20. Building No. 1360 Broadway, New-York, and contents, damaged by fire to the amount of $9,500. Decline in gold to 216.

22. Battle between rebel and Union troops at Rood's Hill, Va., without important results. Explosion of a powder-mill near Newburgh, N. Y.

23. A tobacco warehouse in St. Louis destroyed by fire—loss, $25,000. Decline in gold to 221.

24. Fire in Frankfort, Ky.; damage, $50,000. Waynesboro', Tenn., occupied by rebel troops under Gen. HOOD.

25. An agent from England, with a numerously signed peace petition to be presented to President LINCOLN, arrives at New-York. Bancroft House, New-York, damaged by fire—loss on building and furniture, $28,000. Several hotels of New-York city set on fire by Southern incendiaries.

26. Gen. HOOD makes an assault on Union lines at Columbia, south of Duck river, Tenn.

27. Gen. BUTLER's dispatch steamer, *Greyhound*, destroyed by fire. Fire at Cincinnati—loss, $60,000.

28. Rebels, under Gen. PAINE, occupy New-Creek and Piedmont, and destroy considerable property; they are finally driven from the last named place. Breach in the Erie Canal, attended with loss of life; damage to canal, $50,000. Astounding frauds in the Philadelphia Navy-Yard made public.

29. President LINCOLN issues a proclamation that the treaty between the United States and the King of the Belgians, for the extinction of the Scheldt dues, has been ratified. ROGER A. PRYOR, of Virginia, captured by Union pickets in front of Petersburg, Va.

DECEMBER.

MOON'S PHASES.

Full Moon, ... 2d. 1h. 48m. E. | New Moon,... 17d. 11h. 49m. E.
Third Quarter, 9d. 7h. 17m. E. | First Quarter, 25d. 7h. 35m. M.

Day of Month.	Day of Week.	PREMIUM ON GOLD, IN DECEMBER, AT NEW-YORK.						SUN.	
		1862.		1863.		1864.		Rises.	Sets.
		LOWEST.	HIGHEST.	LOWEST.	HIGHEST.	LOWEST.	HIGHEST.	H. M.	H. M.
1	Frid	28½	31½	*47¾	48⅜	..	..	7 5	4 34
*2	Sat	31	31½	48½	48⅝	..	..	7 6	4 34
3	**Sun**	31	32	51½	52½	..	..	7 7	4 34
4	Mon	33	*34	52¼	*52¾	..	..	7 8	4 33
5	Tues	31½	32½	52¾	52	..	..	7 9	4 33
6	Wed	*30½	32	**Sun**	..	..	..	7 10	4 33
7	Thu	**Sun**	..	51	52⅛	..	..	7 11	4 33
8	Frid	31⅜	31½	48¾	49½	..	..	7 12	4 33
9	Sat	32⅜	33¼	48½	48⅝	..	..	7 13	4 33
10	**Sun**	32¼	32½	48¾	49⅝	..	..	7 14	4 33
11	Mon	32⅛	32¼	51	51½	..	..	7 15	4 33
12	Tues	31½	31¾	50	50⅜	..	..	7 15	4 33
13	Wed	31⅛	32	**Sun**	..	..	..	7 16	4 33
14	Thu	**Sun**	..	49¾	50⅜	..	..	7 17	4 34
15	Frid	31⅞	32¼	50¾	..	..	..	7 17	4 34
16	Sat	32	32⅞	49¼	49¾	..	..	7 18	4 34
17	**Sun**	32¾	33	50¼	50½	..	..	7 18	4 34
18	Mon	32⅓	32¾	51⅝	52⅛	..	..	7 19	4 35
19	Tues	32½	32¾	51½	52	..	..	7 19	4 35
20	Wed	32	32⅞	**Sun**	..	..	..	7 20	4 36
21	Thu	**Sun**	..	52⅛	52½	..	..	7 20	4 36
22	Frid	32¼	32⅝	52⅛	52¼	..	..	7 21	4 37
23	Sat	32⅛	32¼	52	52⅛	..	..	7 21	4 37
24	**Sun**	32	32⅛	51⅝	51¾	..	..	7 22	4 38
25	Mon	*Holi*	*day.*	*Holi*	*day.*	..	..	7 22	4 38
26	Tues	31⅞	32	51½	51¾	..	..	7 23	4 39
27	Wed	31⅞	32⅝	**Sun**	..	..	..	7 23	4 39
28	Thu	**Sun**	..	51¾	52⅝	..	..	7 24	4 40
29	Frid	31⅞	32¾	52⅝	52¾	..	..	7 24	4 40
30	Sat	32⅝	33	51¾	52½	..	..	7 25	4 41
31	**Sun**	33¼	33⅝	51⅞	52½	..	..	7 25	4 42

Statistics.—To those who have a steady conception of the regularity of events, and have firmly seized the great truth that the actions of men, being guided by their antecedents, are in reality never inconsistent; but, however capricious they may appear, only form part of one vast scheme of universal order, of which we, in the present state of knowledge, can barely see the outline—to those who understand this, which is at once the key and the basis of history, the facts just adduced, so far from being strange, will be precisely what would have been expected, and ought long since to have been known. * * * Statistics have already thrown more light on the study of human nature than all the sciences put together.—Buckle.

THE RAILWAYS OF GREAT BRITAIN.

Total Length, Capital, Passengers Conveyed, Receipts, and Working Expenses of Railways in England and Wales, Scotland, and Ireland.

I.—England and Wales.

Years.	Length of Lines open at the End of each Year.	Total Capital Paid up. (Shares, Loans, &c.)	Total Number of Passengers Conveyed (including Season-Ticket Holders).	Total of Traffic Receipts.	Total of Working Expenses.	Net Receipts
	Miles.	£	No.	£	£	£
1854	6,114	240,235,025	92,346,149	17,342,925	7,870,407	9,472,438
1855	6,210	249,805,306	99,175,923	18,363,369	8,845,924	9,517,445
1856	6,447	257,489,431	108,368,901	19,728,309	9,359,414	10,368,895
1857	6,773	263,198,206	115,858,806	20,527,748	9,707,498	10,820,250
1858	7,001	270,871,643	115,956,957	20,244,095	10,105,384	10,138,711
1859	7,309	277,665,518	124,881,202	21,723,926	(Not ascertained.)	
1860	7,583	288,691,611	136,989,404	23,472,946	11,258,104	12,214,842
1861	7,820	299,446,182	145,831,425	24,021,928	11,802,349	12,219,579
1862	8,176	....	152,402,287	24,529,062	....	....

II.—Scotland.

Years.	Miles	£	No.	£	£	£
1854	1,043	31,482,647	11,949,388	1,998,322	948,119	1,050,203
1855	1,083	32,571,108	12,206,926	2,144,398	1,045,719	1,098,679
1856	1,203	34,139,963	13,097,238	2,319,217	1,071,502	1,247,715
1857	1,250	35,078,482	14,733,503	2,501,478	1,093,970	1,407,508
1858	1,353	36,681,000	14,788,968	2,536,934	1,101,597	1.435,337
1859	1,428	37,564,105	15,480,713	2,723,512	(Not ascertained.)	
1860	1,486	38,838,741	16,503,050	2,925,229	1,306,128	1,619,101
1861	1,626	40,986,534	17,255,058	3,095,434	1,398,849	1,696,585
1862	1,777½	....	17,597,548	3,153,404	....	....

III.—Ireland

Years.	Miles	£	No.	£	£	£
1854	897	14,351,122	6,911,170	874,477	387,599	486,878
1855	987	15,208,295	7,212,286	999,832	408,066	591,766
1856	1,057	15,965,692	7,881,453	1,117,965	406,540	711,425
1857	1,071	16,880,570	8,416,579	1,145,384	438,771	706,613
1858	1,188	17,822,864	8,447,774	1,175,720	461,244	714,476
1859	1,265	19,133,305	9,445,233	1,296,064	(Not ascertained.)	
1860	1,364	20,599,775	9,991,118	1,368,447	623,136	745,311
1861	1,423	21,894,622	10,686,735	1,447,993	642,139	805,854
1862	1,568	....	10,420,210	1,446,092	....	....

United Kingdom (*see* p. 30.)

Total Length, Capital, Passengers Conveyed, Receipts, and Working Expenses of Railways in England and Wales, Scotland, and Ireland.—Continued.

UNITED KINGDOM.

YEARS.	Length at the End of each Year.	Capital paid up. (Shares, Loans, &c.)	Passengers Conveyed.	Traffic Receipts.	Working Expenses.	Net Receipts.
	Miles.	£	No.	£	£	£
1848	5,127	200,173,059	57,965,070	9,933,552	Cannot be given previous to 1854.	
1849	6,031	229,747,778	63,841,539	11,806,498		
1850	6,621	240,270,745	72,854,422	13,204,668		
1851	6,890	248,240,896	85,391,095	14,997,459		
1852	7,336	264,165,672	89,135,729	15,710,554		
1853	7,686	273,324,514	102,286,660	18,035,879		
1854	8,054	286,068,794	111,206,707	20,215,724	9,206,205	11,009,519
1855	8,280	297,584,709	118,595,135	21,507,599	10,299,709	11,207,890
1856	8,707	307,595,086	129,347,592	23,165,491	10,837,456	12,328,035
1857	9,094	315,157,258	139,008,888	24,174,610	11,240,239	12,934,371
1858	9,542	325,375,507	139,193,699	23,956,749	11,668,225	12,288,524
1859	10,002	334,362,928	149,807,148	25,743,502	(Not ascertained.)	
1860	10,433	348,130,127	163,483,572	27,766,622	13,187,368	14,579,254
1861	10,869	362,327,338	173,773,218	28,565,355	13,843,337	14,722,018
1862	11,551	385,218,438	180,420,065	29,089,100	14,268,409	14,810,691

Note.—The details for each division of the United Kingdom cannot be readily ascertained for the years previous to 1854.

"Great Britain is indebted to its Mines for its colonization in the mists of time—for much of its present importance—and, according to BOCHART and others, even for its name. Its whole history, indeed, is associated with these subterranean treasures. The most ancient nations of the East resorted to it for tin and copper. Julius Cæsar, like the Spanish conquerors of the West, was attracted to its shores chiefly by rumors of its mineral wealth: and Pliny, and even the severer Tacitus invested Britain with the splendors of an El Dorado. These golden visions, to be sure, were not realized. But the Romans worked extensively its mines of lead, and extracted silver from the produce. It was reserved for much later times to discover that the stratification of Britain was of almost unequalled variety, and that it contained, to an extent never dreamed of, the most abundant supplies of coal and iron. The manufacturing industry of the north originated in and was long satisfied with, the power derived from the uncertain streams issuing from its mountains. But the steam-engine at last opened out visions of national wealth more gorgeous than the mines of Peru. It not only enabled the deeper metallic and other mines to be worked, and thus added new realms of happy conquest to the nation, but it formed in itself a matchless power for all the industrial arts of life. All that this many-handed and munificent giant demanded for its unceasing labors, was a sufficient supply of its peculiar food; and fortunately for Britain, this food was found within her shores in a profusion and of an excellence unparalleled in Europe."

RAILROADS OF THE UNITED STATES.

I.—STATE OF MAINE.

Corporate Titles of Companies.	Mileage.			Cost of Property.		
	1850	1860	1865	1850	1860	1865
1. Androscoggin	....	37.0	68.0		$707,000	$1,253,000
2. Atlantic and St. Lawrence	48.0	149.0	149.0	$1,642,000	7,559,000	7,656,000
3. Bangor, Oldtown and Milford	11.0	12.5	12.5	135,000	245,000	247,000
4. Calais and Baring	....	6.0	6.0	....	226,000	226,000
5. Great Falls and S. Berwick	....	6.0	6.0	....	169,000	172,000
6. Kennebec and Portland (and Branch)	59.5	72.5	72 5	1,742,000	2,871,000	2,871,000
7. Lewy's Island	....	16.5	16.5	....	315,000	315,000
8. Machiasport	7.5	7.5	7.5	110,000	110,000	110,000
9. { Maine, Central	....	....	109.8	....	....	4,212,000
9. { Androscoggin and Kennebec	55.0	55.0	....	1,817,000	2,218,000	....
9. { Penobscot and Kennebec	....	54.8	....	....	1,880,000	....
10. Portland and Oxford Central	13.0	18.5	18.5	260,000	370,000	370,000
11. Portland, Saco and Portsmouth	51.3	51.3	53.5	1,294,000	1,500,000	1,500,000
12. Somerset and Kennebec	....	37.0	37.0	...	836,000	785,000
13. York and Cumberland	....	18.5	18.5	....	560,000	560,000
	245.3	542.1	575.3	$7,000,000	$19,616,000	$20,277,000
Deduct						
Atlantic and St. Lawrence, in Maine and Vermont		70.2	70.2		3,561,000	3,608,000
Total in Maine	245.3	471.9	505.1	$7,000,000	$16,055,000	$16,669,000

II.—STATE OF NEW HAMPSHIRE.

Corporate Titles of Companies.	Mileage.			Cost of Property.		
	1850	1860	1865	1850	1860	1865
1. Ashuelot	23.8	23.8	23.8	$506,000	$506,000	$506,000
2. Boston, Concord and Montreal	51.3	93.5	93.5	1,283,000	2,863,000	2,850,000
3. Cheshire	53.6	53.6	53.6	2,739,000	3,076,000	3,839,000
4. Cochecho	17.5	28 1	28.1	422,000	847,000	847,000
5. Concord	34.5	34.5	34.5	1,387,000	1,500,000	1,500,000
6. Concord and Portsmouth	18.2	47.8	49.9	478,000	1,109,000	385,000
7. Contoocook River	14.2	14.6	14.6	209,000	257,000	200,000
8. Eastern	16.6	16.6	16.6	525,000	525,000	525,000
9. Great Falls and Conway	6.6	20.1	20.1	134,000	433.000	433,000
10. Manchester and Lawrence	26.5	26.5	26.9	733,000	1,000,000	1,065,000
11. Manchester and N. Weare }	43.3	52.7	19.4	822,000	1,283,000	200,000
12. Merrimac and Conn. Rivers }			29·3			698,000
13. Northern (and Branch)	82.6	82.6	82.6	2,796,000	3,343,000	3,068,000
14. Peterboro and Shirley	....	9.4	9.4	....	246,000	94,000
15. Sullivan	24.7	25.3	25 3	930,000	1,250,000	1,481,000
16. White Mountains	....	20.8	20.8	....	871,000	200,000
17. Wilton	11.8	15.4	15.4	159,000	227,000	227,000
	425.2	564.5	563.8	$13,123,000	$18,836,000	$18,118,000
Deduct						
Cheshire, in Mass	10.5	10.5	10.5	548,000	615,000	768,000
	414.7	554.0	553.8	$12,575,000	$18,221,000	$17,350,000
Add						
Atlantic and St. Lawrence, from Me.	....	54.0	54.0	....	2,638,000	2,659,000
Boston and Maine, from Mass	40.2	40.2	40.2	1,651,000	1,794,000	2,042,000
Nashua and Lowell, from Mass	6.2	6.2	6.2	258,000	261,000	269,000
Worcester and Nashua, from Mass	6.6	6.6	6.6	176,000	172,000	169,000
Total in New Hampshire	467.7	661.0	660.3	$14,660,000	$23,086,000	$22,489,000

III.—STATE OF VERMONT.

Corporate Titles of Companies.	Mileage.			Cost of Property.		
	1850	1860	1865	1850	1860	1865
1. Connecticut and Passumpsic	40.0	90.7	110.3	$1,323,000	$2,531,000	$2,879,000
2. Rutland and Burlington	119.5	119.5	119.5	4,343,000	4,607,000	4,546,000
3. Rutland and Washington........	....	44.7	44.7	....	1,771,000	1,871,000
4. Rutl'd & Whitehall (and Branch).	....	8.4	8.4	....	256,000	256,000
5. Southern Vermont......	....	8.0	8.0	....	200,000	200,000
6. Vermont and Canada...........	....	47.0	55.5	....	1,350,000	1,678,000
7. Vermont Central.....	120.0	120.0	120.0	5,134,000	8,402,000	8,522,000
8. Vermont Valley.............	....	23.7	23.7	....	1,302,000	1,302,000
9. Western Vermont (and Branch)..	....	59.5	64.5	....	1,083,000	1,083,000
	279.5	521.5	554.6	$10,800,000	$21,502,000	$21,837,000
Deduct						
Rutland and Washington, in N. Y....	....	11.2	11.2	....	443,000	343,000
	279.5	510.3	543.4	$10,800,000	$21,059,000	$21,494,000
Add						
Atlantic and St. Lawrence, from Me.	....	16.2	16.2	....	923,000	949,000
Grand Trunk, from Canada.........	....	17.0	17.0	....	908,000	936,000
Vermont and Mass., from Mass......	10.5	10.5	10.5	466,000	466,000	473,000
Total in Vermont..........	290.0	554.0	587.1	$11,266,000	$23,356,000	$23,852,000

IV.—STATE OF MASSACHUSETTS.

Corporate Titles of Companies.	Mileage.			Cost of Property.		
	1850	1860	1865	1850	1860	1865
1. Agricultural Branch............	....	15.0	15.0	....	$360,000	$352,900
2. Amherst, Belchertown and Palmer		19.5	19.5	....	295,000	85,000
3. Berkshire	21.1	21.1	21.1	$600,000	600,000	600,000
4. Boston and Lowell (and Branch).	27.6	28.6	28.6	1,945,000	2,428,000	2,428,000
5. Boston and Maine (and Branches)	83.0	83.0	91.6	4,022,000	4,303,000	4,863,000
6. Boston & Providence (& Branches)	47.5	47.5	47.5	3,416,000	3,161,000	3,160,000
7. Boston & Worcester (& Branches)	68.4	68.4	68.4	4,883,000	4,738,000	4,508,000
8. Cape Cod...........	28.8	47.1	47.1	626,000	1,032,000	1,032,000
9. Connecticut River (and Branch)..	52.4	52.4	52.4	1,799,000	1,802,000	1,802,000
10. Danvers	....	9.2	9.2	....	233,000	244,000
11. Dorchester and Milton..........	3.3	3.3	3.3	132,000	137,000	137,000
12. Eastern (and Branches).........	58.5	72.5	74.6	3,095,000	4,169,000	4,322,000
13. Easton Branch................	....	3.8	3.8	....	56,000	56,000
14. Essex (and Branch)............	21.2	21.2	21.2	538,000	747,000	747,000
15. Fairhaven Branch).............	....	15.1	15.1	....	400,000	244,000
16. Fall River, Warren & Providence	....	....	5.7	....	....	120,000
17. Fitchburg (and Branches).......	65.8	67.8	85.8	3,552,000	3,540,000	3,540,000
18. Fitchburg and Worcester........	14.0	14.0	14.0	259,000	334,000	334,000
19. Grand Junction................	6.2	9.0	....	764,000	1,947,000	(*incl. in* 12)
20. Hampshire and Hampden.......	....	25.0	....	....	597,000	(*incl. in* 9 *Conn.*)
21. Horse Pond Branch.............	....	0.7	0.7	....	13,000	15,000
22. Lexington and West Cambridge..	6.6	6.6	6.6	242,000	251,000	251,000
23. Lowell and Lawrence...........	12.4	12.4	12.4	333,000	363,000	363,000
24. Mailboro Branch...............	....	3.9	....	....	157,000	(*incl. in* 17)
25. Medway Branch................	....	3.6	3.6	38,000	38,000	38,000
26. Middleboro and Taunton........	....	8.5	8.5	....	156,000	152,000
27. Midland (Norfolk Co., etc.)......	26.0	61.3	61.3	1,061,000	3,692,000	4,930,000
28. Nashua and Lowell............	14.6	14.6	14.6	651,000	655,000	655,000
29. New Bedford & Taunton (& Br'ch)	21.1	21.6	21.6	499,000	553,000	533,000
30. Newburyport..................	8.6	27.0	27.0	107,000	597,000	597,000
31. New York and Boston......... .	....	21.5	33.0	....	744,000	1,129,000
32. Old Colony and Newport........	87.3	87.3	87.3	3,362,000	3,434,000	3,434,000
33. Peterboro and Shirley...........	14.1	14.1	....	273,000	265,000	(*incl. in* 17)
34. Pittsfield and North Adams......	18.7	18.7	18.7	444,000	444,000	444,000
35. Providence and Worcester.......	43.4	43.4	43.4	1,825,000	1,762,000	1,622,000

MASSACHUSETTS.—Continued.

Corporate Titles of Companies.	Mileage.			Cost of Property.		
	1850	1860	1865	1850	1860	1865
36. Rockport..	....	4.0	4.0	....	$84,000	$91,000
37. Salem and Lowell	16.9	16.9	16.9	$317,000	464,000	464,000
38. South Reading Branch	8.2	8.2	8.4	293 000	300,000	300,000
39. South Shore	11.5	11.5	11.5	421,000	502,000	502,000
40. Stockbridge and Pittsfield	21.9	21.9	21 9	449,000	449,000	449,000
41. Stoneham Branch	....	....	1.6	....	....	31,000
42. Stony Brook	13.2	13.2	13.2	266,000	268,000	268,000
43. Stoughton Branch	4.0	4.0	4.0	93,000	93,000	101,000
44. Taunton Branch	11.7	11.7	11.8	307,000	313,000	313,000
45. Troy and Greenfield	....	7.0	7.0	....	1,040,000	1,946,000
46. Vermont and Massachusetts	69.0	77.0	77.0	3,406,244	3,269,000	3,043,000
47. Western	117.8	117.8	117.8	8,034,000	8,444,000	8,678,000
48. West Stockbridge	2 8	2.8	2.8	42,000	40.000	40,000
49. Worcester and Nashua	45.7	45.7	45.7	1,410,000	1,379,000	1,233,000
	1073.3	1310.4	1306.2	$49,504,000	$60,648,000	$60,596,000
Deduct						
Boston and Maine, in N. Hamp	40.2	40.2	40 2	1,651,000	1,794,000	2,042,000
Boston and Providence, in R. I	5.0	5.0	5.0	316,000	302,000	302,000
Midland, in Conn	....	8.0	8.0	....	200,000	200,000
Nashua and Lowell, in N. H.	6.2	6.2	6.2	258,000	261,000	269,000
Providence and Worcester, in R. I	18.0	18 0	18.0	756,000	808,000	626,000
Vermont and Mass, in Vt	10.5	10 5	10 5	466.000	466,000	473,000
Worcester and Nashua, in N. H	6.6	6.6	6 6	176,000	172,000	169,000
	986.8	1215.9	1211.7	$45,881,000	$56,645,000	$56,515,000
Add						
Cheshire, from N. Hamp	10.5	10.5	10.5	548,000	615,000	768,000
Hartford and New Haven, from Conn.	5.9	5.9	5 9	219,000	288,000	293,000
N. Haven & Northampton. from Conn.	....	....	25.0	....	....	525,000
Norwich and Worcester, from Conn.	21.0	21.0	21.0	829,000	831.000	831,000
New London, Northern	10.9	10.9	10.9	242,000	263,000	119,000
Total in Massachusetts	1035.1	1264.2	1285.0	$47,719,000	$58,642,000	$39,051,000

V.—STATE OF RHODE ISLAND.

Corporate Titles of Companies.	Mileage.			Cost of Property.		
	1850	1860	1865	1850	1860	1865
1. New York, Providence and Boston	50.0	50.0	50.0	$2,046,000	$2,158,000	$2,158,000
2. Newport and Fall River	....	...	17.3	....	....	365,000
3. Providence, Warren and Bristol.	....	13.6	13 6	....	449,000	449,000
	50.0	63.6	80.9	$2,046,000	$2,607,000	$2,972,000
Deduct						
New York, Providence and Boston, in Conn	5.0	5.0	5.0	205,000	216,000	216,000
	45.0	58.6	75.9	$1,841,000	$2,391,000	$2,756,000
Add						
Boston and Providence, from Mass	5.0	5.0	5.0	316,000	302,000	302,000
Providence & Worcester, from Mass.	18.0	18.0	18.0	756,000	808,000	626,000
Hartford, Providence and Fishkill, from Conn	....	26.3	26.3	....	904,000	904,000
Total in Rhode Island	68·0	107.9	125.2	$2,913,000	$4,405,000	$4,588,000

VI.—STATE OF CONNECTICUT.

Corporate Titles of Companies.	Mileage.			Cost of Property.		
	1850	1860	1865	1850	1860	1865
1. Danbury and Norwalk..........	....	33.8	28 8	....	$402,000	$411,000
2. Fairhaven and Westville........	....	....	6.0	....	....	150,000
3. Hartford and New Haven (and Branch)......................	72.4	72.4	72.4	$2,632,000	3,461,000	3,515,000
4. Hartford, Providence and Fishkill	50.8	122.4	122.4	2,077,000	4,205,000	4,205,000
5. Hartford and Weathersfield.....	....	....	9.0	....	....	200,000
6. Housatonic	74.0	74.0	74.0	2,400,000	2,440,000	2,440,000
7. Naugatuck......................	57.0	57.0	57.0	1,335,000	1,578,000	1,461,000
8. New Haven, New London and Stonington.......	....	62.0	62.0	....	1,852,000	1,852,000
9. New Haven and Northampton (and Branch).................	....	59.8	93.8	....	1,400,000	2,334,000
10. New London Northern..........	66.0	66.0	66.0	1,451,000	1,579,000	1,579,000
11. New York and New Haven......	62 3	62.3	62.3	3,006,000	5,316,000	5,487,000
12. Norwich and Worcester.........	66.4	66.4	66.4	1,598,000	2,614,000	2,614,000
13. Rockville Branch...............	....	....	4.8	....	....	200,000
	448.9	666.1	719.9	$15,499,000	$24,847,000	$26,448,000
Deduct						
Hartford and New Haven, in Mass...	5.9	5.9	5.9	219,000	288,000	293,000
Hartford, Providence and Fishkill, in Rhode Island....................	....	26.3	26.3	....	904,000	904,000
New Haven and Northampton, in Mass	....	....	25.0	....	....	525,000
New London, Northern, in Mass.....	10.9	10.9	10.9	242,000	263,000	119,000
New York and New Haven, in N. Y.	14.2	14.2	14.2	679,000	1,129,000	1,178,000
Norwich and Worcester, in Mass....	21.0	21.0	21.0	829,000	831,000	831,000
	396 9	587.8	616.6	$13,530,000	$21,482,000	$22,598,000
Add						
Midland, from Mass	....	8.0	8.0	....	200,000	200,000
New York, Providence and Boston, from Rhode Island...............	5.0	5.0	5.0	205,000	216,000	216,000
Total in Connecticut.......	401.0	600.8	629.6	$13,735,000	$21,848,000	$23,014,000

VII.—STATE OF NEW YORK.

Corporate Titles of Companies.	Mileage.			Cost of Property.		
	1850	1860	1865	1850	1860	1865
1. Albany and Boston...........	....	83.0 (1 and 2)	21.4	....	$2,020,000 (1 and 2)	$1,200,000
2. Albany and Vermont.	....		11.6	....		600,000
3. Albany and Susquehanna.....	....	....	35.0	....	....	1,257,000
4. Albany and West Stockbridge	38.3	38.3	38.3	$1,930,000	2,393,000	2,388,000
5. Atlantic and Great Western..	....	....	18.9	....	....	2,615,000
6. Avon, Geneseo and Mt. Morris	....	15.5	15.5	....	329,000	210,000
7. Blossburg and Corning.......	14.8	14.8	14.8	250,000	497,000	548,000
8. Brooklyn Central and Jamaica	11.0	11.0	14.5	370,000	370,000	805,000
9. Buffalo, New York and Erie...	....	142.0	142.0	....	3,151,000	3,369,000
10. Buffalo and State Line.......	....	68.3	68.3	....	2,788,000	2,788,000
11. Cayuga and Susquehanna....	34.6	34.6	34.6	380,000	1,096,000	636,000
12. Chemung	17 4	17.4	17.4	400,000	400,000	400,000
13. Coney Island and Brooklyn...	....	....	10.5	....	....	544,000
14. Elmira, Jefferson and Canandaigua	....	46.8	46.8	....	1,275,000	500,000
15 { Erie (and Branches).........	337.0	465.0	528.0 (15)	20,066,000	35,321,000	39,328,000 (15)
15 { Buffalo and New York City...	....	60.0		....	2,902,000	
16. Hicksville and Cold Spring....	....	4.0	4.0	....	45,000	45,000
17. Hudson and Boston..........	31.5	17.4	17.4	821,000	175,000	175,000
18. Hudson River................	74.7	143.7	143.7	6,667,000	11,388,000	12,616,000
19. Long Island (and Branch)....	86.5	86.5	96.5	2,192,000	2,566,000	2,928,000
20. New York Central (& Branches)	447.0	555.9	555.9	20,024,000	30,841,000	32,740,000

NEW YORK.—Continued.

Corporate Titles of Companies.	Mileage.			Cost of Property.		
	1850	1860	1865	1850	1860	1865
21. New York and Flushing.......	....	8.0	8.0	....	$245,000	$261,000
22. New York and Harlem (and Branch).................	80.2	132.9	132.9	4,666,000	8,023,000	10,202,000
23. Niagara Bridge and Canandaigua...................	....	100.4	100.4	....	3,211,000	1,000,000
24. Niagara Falls and Lake Ontario.....................	....	13.2	13 2	....	394,000	394,000
25. Northern (Ogdensburg)......	58.0	121.8	121.8	2,980,000	4,810,000	4,588,000
26. Oswego and Syracuse........	35.9	35.9	35.9	548,000	791,000	823,000
27. Plattsburg and Montreal.....	....	23.2	23.2	....	349,000	349,000
28. Rensselaer and Saratoga.....	25.3	25.3	25.3	687,000	912,000	939,000
29. Rochester and Genesee Valley.	....	18.5	18.5		654,000	656,000
30. Rome, Watertown & Ogdensburg	....	....	....	....	....	....
Potsdam and Watertown.....	....	75.4	189.6	....	1,600,000	3,460,000
Watertown and Rome.......	24.0	96.8	....	604,000	2,276,000	....
31. Sackett's Harbor, Rome & N. Y.	....	18.5	18.5	....	389,000	77,000
32. Saratoga and Schenectady...	21.5	21.5	21.5	396,000	481,000	481,000
33. Saratoga and Whitehall......	45.4	47.5	47.5	1,313,000	902,000	902,000
34. Staten Island................	....	13.2	13.2	....	288,000	315,000
35. Syracuse, Binghampton & N. Y.	....	80.9	80.9	....	2,854,000	2,903,000
36. Troy and Bennington........	....	5.4	5 4	....	236,000	236,000
37. Troy and Boston.............	....	34.9	34.9	....	1,535,000	1,829,000
38. Troy and Greenbush.........	6.0	6.0	6 0	283,000	295,000	295,000
39. Troy and Rutland...........	....	18.5	18.5	....	350,000	363,000
40. Troy Union and Depôt........	....	2.1	2.1	....	758,000	758,000
41. Utica and Black River.......	....	37.5	37.5	....	1,237,000	876.000
42. Warwick Valley.............	....	....	10.3	....		170,000
	1389.1	2691.6	2830.2	$64,779,000	$130,142,000	$137,564,000
Deduct						
Erie, in Pennsylvania...........	42.5	42.5	42.5	2,479,000	3,204,000	3,298,000
	1346.6	2649.1	2787.7	$62,298,000	$126,938,000	$134,266,000
Add						
Elmira and Williamsport, from Penn.........................	....	7.8	7.8	....	405,000	100,000
New York and New Haven, from Conn....	14.2	14.2	14.2	679,000	1,129,000	1,178,000
Rutland and Washington, from Vt.	....	11.2	11.2	....	443,000	343,000
Total in New York......	1360.8	2682.3	2820.9	$62,977,000	$128,915,000	$135,887,000

VIII.—STATE OF NEW JERSEY.

Corporate Titles of Companies.	Mileage.			Cost of Property.		
	1850	1860	1865	1850	1860	1865
1. Belvidere Delaware.............	...	64.2	64.2	....	$3,135,000	$3,170,000
2. Burlington and Mount Holly...	7.1	7.1	7.1	$100,000	120,000	120,000
3. Camden and Amboy (& Branches)	92.4	92.4	104 5	4,000,000	5,919,000	6,070,000
4. Camden and Atlantic...........	....	60.2	60.2	....	1,834,000	1,837,000
5. Central	9.5	63.8	73.8	236,000	5,835,000	7,209,000
6. Flemington......................	....	12.0	12.0	....	287,000	292,000
7. Freehold and Jamesburg........	....	11.5	11.5	....	231,000	231,000
8. Hackensack and New York......	....	....	4.9	....	....	136,000
Lodi Branch (private)........	....	....	0.8	....	....	20,000
9. Jersey City and Bergen Point....	...	....	10.0	....	....	200,000
10. Long Dock and Tunnel..........	....	....	2.9	....	....	2,480,000
11. Millstone and New Brunswick....	....	6.6	6.6	....	111,000	111,000
12. Millville and Cape May.........	....		39.0	....	....	400,000
13. Millville and Glasboro'..........	....	22.3	22.3	....	190,000	192,000

NEW JERSEY.—Continued.

Corporate Titles of Companies.	Mileage.			Cost of Property.		
	1850	1860	1865	1850	1860	1865
14. Morris and Essex	34.0	52.5	58.5	$1,232,000	$1,758,000	$2,400,000
15. Newark and Bloomfield	....	6.0	6.0	....	110,000	112,000
16. New Jersey	33.8	33.8	33.8	2,801,000	4,933,000	5,551,000
17. Northern New Jersey	....	21.3	21.3	....	412,000	422,000
18. Paterson and Hudson	14.5	14.5	14.5	630,000	630,000	630,000
19. Paterson and Ramapo	15.1	15.1	15.1	350,000	350,000	350,000
20. Perth Amboy and Woodbridge	....	....	8.0	....	....	160,000
21. Raritan and Delaware Bay	....	22.0	148.0	....	300,000	2,463,000
22. South Branch	....	....	16.0	....	....	320,000
23. Sussex	....	12.0	12.0	....	417,000	426,000
24. Vincentown Branch	....	....	4.5	....	....	60,000
25. Warren	....	21.0	21.0	....	1,877,000	1,908,000
26. West Jersey	....	22.0	86.0	....	517,000	1,622,000
Total in New Jersey	206.4	560.3	864.5	$9,349,000	$28,966,000	$38,892,000

IX.—STATE OF PENNSYLVANIA.

Corporate Titles of Companies.	Mileage.			Cost of Property.		
	1850	1860	1865	1850	1860	1865
1. Alleghany Valley	....	45.0	45.0	....	$1,765,000	$1,829,000
2. Atlantic and Great Western	....	....	165.0	....	....	5,634,000
3. Bald Eagle Valley	....	7.0	34.0	....	411,000	768,000
4. Barclay Coal	....	16.5	16.5	...	262,000	401,000
5. Beaver Meadow (& Branches)	20.5	52.3	52.3	$418,000	1,227,000	1,465,000
6. Bedford	....	....	12.3	....	....	193,000
7. Bellefonte and Snowshoe	....	18.3	22.0	....	367,000	382,000
8. Buffalo, Bradford and Pittsburg	....	....	12.0	....	....	380,000
9. Catasauqua	....	13.0	13.0	....	150,000	332,000
10. Catawissa	....	64.0	64.0	....	4,060,000	3,634,000
11. Chartiers Valley	....	....	....	....	....	342,000
12. Chester Valley	....	21.5	21.5	....	1,372,000	1,372,000
13. Chestnut Hill	....	4.2	4.2	....	122,000	122,020
14. Cumberland Valley	52.0	52.0	52.0	1,188,000	1,192,000	1,131,000
15. Delaware and Hudson	26.5	27.5	36.0	742,000	1,793,000	1,916,000
16. Delaware, Lackawanna and Western	....	113.5	113.5	....	9,146,000	9,179,000
17. East Brandywine	....	17.5	17.5	....	350,000	356,000
18. East Mahoney	....	....	8.0	....	....	381,000
19. East Pennsylvania	....	36.9	36.9	....	1,099,000	1,266,000
20. Ebensburg and Cresson	....	....	8.0	....	....	200,000
21. Elmira and Williamsport	....	78.0	78.0	....	4,050,000	1,000,000
22. Erie and North East	....	18.5	18.5	....	700,000	700,000
23. Erie and Pittsburg	....	40.3	80.5	....	800,000	2,000,000
24. Fayette County	....	12.7	12.7	....	154,000	107,000
25. Franklin	22.5	22.5	22.5	225,000	525,000	200,000
26. Gettysburg	....	17.1	17.1	....	275,000	274,000
27. Hanover Branch	....	12.2	12.2	....	202,000	229,000
28. Harrisburg and Lancaster	36.0	54.0	54.0	1,250,000	1,883,000	1,883,000
29. Hazleton	....	14.5	18.0	....	290,000	360,000
30. Hempfield	....	32.0	32.0	....	1,809,000	1,902,000
31. Huntingdon and Broad Top	....	42.5	50.5	....	1,355,000	1,927,000
32. Ironton	....	....	9.7	....	....	242,000
33. Jamestown and Franklin	....	....	40.0	....	....	1,000,000
34. Junction (Phila.)	....	....	4.6	....	....	225,000
35. Lackawanna (Grassy Island)	....	9.0	9.1	....	180,000	181,000
36. Lackawanna and Bloomsburg	....	80.0	82.0	....	2,400,000	2,803,000
37. Lehigh Luzerne	....	10.5	11.5	....	253,000	316,000
38. Lehigh and Susquehanna	19.7	19.7	19.7	1,000,000	1,380,000	1,390,000
39. Lehigh Valley	....	45.5	45.5	....	3,788,000	4,491,000
40. Lehigh and Mahoney	....	....	22.0	....	....	499,000

PENNSYLVANIA.—Continued.

Corporate Titles of Companies.	Mileage.			Cost of Property.		
	1850	1860	1865	1850	1860	1865
41. Little Saw Mill Run..........	....	....	30.0	....	....	$88,000
42. Little Schuylkill............	....	33.8	33.8	....	$3,299,000	3,372,000
43. Littlestown..................	....	7.3	7.3	....	76,000	76,000
44. Locust Gap...................	....	....	0.9	....	....	25,000
45. Lorberry Creek...............	5.1	5.1	5.5	$51,000	60,000	82,000
46. Lykens Valley................	15.5	19.7	19.7	300,000	429,000	415,000
47. McCauley Mountain............	....	6.0	6.0	....	200,000	200,000
48. Mahoney and Broad Mountain	....	6.0	6.0	....	200,000	200,000
49. Mauch Chunk and Summit Hill	13.0	26.3	28.3	600,000	1,300,000	1,454,000
50. Mill Creek and Mine Hill.....	8.3	12.5	16.8	233,000	311,000	324,000
51. Mine Hill and Schuylkill Haven	39.1	72.3	130.0	800,000	2,861,000	3,312,000
52. Mount Carbon (and Branches)	6.3	6.3	7.8	179,000	205,000	205,000
53. Mount Carbon and Port Carbon	2.5	2.5	6.3	231,000	282,000	282,000
54. Nanticoke....................	....	....	5.0	....	....	79,000
55. Nesquehoning Valley.........	....	....	13.1	....	....	236,000
56. Newcastle and Beaver Valley.	....	....	14.9	....	....	300,000
57. North Lebanon..............	....	8.2	8.2	....	309,000	307,000
58. North Pennsylvania..........	....	67.2	67.2	....	5,868,000	5,890,000
59. Oil Creek..................	....	....	54.0	....	....	1,879,000
60. Panther Creek..............	....	....	6.5	....	....	130,000
61. Penn Haven and White Haven	....	....	16.0	....	....	283,000
62 { Pennsylvania (and Branches)	218.1	278.0	278.0	} 10,112,000	25,646,000	26,058,000
{ Columbia Division	81.2	81.2	81.2			
63. Pennsylvania Coal...........	47.0	47.0	54.0	1,605,000	1,999,000	2,000,000
64. Phila. and Baltimore Central.	....	36.5	36.5	....	875,000	930,000
65. Philadelphia and Erie........	....	148.0	288.7	....	9,576,000	16,500,000
66. Philadelphia, Morristown and Germantown....	20.2	20.2	20.2	955,000	1,674,000	1,366,000
67. Philadelphia & Reading (& Br.)	95.0	154.0	154.0	16,325,000	24,126,000	24,735,000
68. Philadelphia and Trenton....	28.2	28.2	28.2	564,000	608,000	608,000
69. Phila., Wilmington & Baltim'e	98.0	98.0	98.0	6,052,000	7,789,000	8,575,000
70. Pittsburg and Connellsville...	....	59.5	59.5	....	2,920,000	2,198,000
71. Pittsburg, Ft. Wayne, Chicago.	....	467.5	467.5	....	17,480,000	18,191,000
72. Pittsburg and Steubenville. ..	....	....	23.0	....	....	1,384,000
73. Reading and Columbia.......	....	....	39.0	....	....	886,000
74. Schuylkill and Susquehanna..	....	54.0	55.0	....	1,259,000	1,311,000
75. Schuylkill Valley............	18.5	24.5	24.5	438,000	574,000	576,000
76. Shamokin Valley and Pottsville	28.0	29.2	29.2	560,000	1,696,000	1,492,000
77. Strasburg....................	4.3	4.3	4.3	42,500	42,500	67,000
78. Swatara......................	6.0	6.0	6.0	100,000	100,000	100,000
79. Tioga	25.8	29.6	29.6	427,000	574,000	837,000
80. Treverton....................	....	14.5	14.5	....	762,000	792,000
81. Tyrone and Clearfield........	....	22.0	22.0	....	440,000	500,000
82. Union Canal Railroad........	....	5.8	5.8	....	57,000	69,000
83. Westchester.................	10.3	10.3	10.3	100,000	107,000	113,000
84. Westchester and Philadelphia	....	26.4	26.4		1,485,000	1,390,000
85. Wrightsville, York and Gettysburg..................	13.0	13.0	13.0	426,000	401,000	393,000
	1260.6	2929.1	3698.5	$44,923,000	$158,950,000	$183,217,000
Deduct						
Elmira and Williamsport, in N. Y.	....	7.8	7.8	....	405,000	100,000
Franklin, in Maryland...........	6.0	6.0	6.0	60,000	131,000	40,000
Hempfield, in West Virginia......	....	8.0	8.0	....	452,000	317,000
Philadelphia, Wilmington and Baltimore, in Delaware and Md....	79.0	79.0	79.0	4,879,000	6,279,000	6,778,000
Pittsburg, Fort Wayne and Chicago, in Ohio, Ind. and Ill......	....	416.0	416.0	....	15,554,000	16,022,000
Pittsburg & Steubenville, in W. Va	....	....	8.0	....	....	464,000
	1175.6	2412.3	3173.7	$39,984,000	$136,129,000	$159,496,000
Add						
Cleveland, Painesville and Ashtabula, from Ohio...............	....	26.7	26.7	....	1,101,000	1,101,000
Cleveland & Pittsburg, from Ohio.	....	14.9	14.9	....	687,000	474,000
Erie, from New York............	42.5	42.5	42.5	2,479,000	3,204,000	3,298,000
Northern Central................	22.0	102.0	102.0	2,080,000	5,623,000	5,711,000
Total in Pennsylvania..	1240.1	2598.4	3359.8	$44,543,000	$146,744,000	$170,080,000

X.—STATE OF DELAWARE.

Corporate Titles of Companies.	Mileage.			Cost of Property.		
	1850	1860	1865	1850	1860	1865
1. Delaware	....	84.3	84.3	....	$1,552,000	$1,552,000
2. Junction and Breakwater	....	8.5	8.5	....	77,000	77,000
3. Newcastle and Frenchtown	16.2	6.0	6.0	$861,000	745,000	745,000
4. Newcastle and Wilmington	....	5.0	5.0	....	150,000	150,000
	16.2	103.8	103.8	$861,000	$2,524,000	$2,524,000
Add						
Philadelphia, Wilmington and Baltimore, from Penn.	23.0	23.0	23.0	1,421,000	1,828,000	1.976,000
Total in Delaware	39.2	126.8	126.8	$2,282,000	$4,352,000	$4,500,000

XI.—STATE OF MARYLAND.

Corporate Titles of Companies.	Mileage.			Cost of Property.		
	1850	1860	1865	1850	1860	1865
1. Annapolis and Elkbridge	21.5	21.5	21.5	$442,000	$442.000	$442,000
2. { Baltimore and Ohio	178.0	386.8	386.8	8.799,000	24.919,000	24,919,000
{ Washington Line	30.0	30.0	30.0	1,650,000	1,650,000	1,650,000
3. Cumberland	10.4	14.0	14.0	300,000	560,000	560,000
4. Cumberland and Pennsylvania	9.0	27.5	27.5	300,000	1,255,000	1,255,000
5. Eastern Shore	....	6.5	6.5	....	125 000	125,000
6. George's Creek	....	21.0	21.0	....	600,000	600,000
7. Northern Central	67.5	142.0	142.0	3,507,000	8,229,000	8,691,000
8. Western Maryland	....	18.0	40.0	....	300,000	884,000
	316.4	667.3	689.3	$14,998,000	$38,080,000	$39,126,000
Deduct						
Baltimore and Ohio, in W. Va	97.0	241.0	241.0	4,795,000	15,520.000	15,520,000
Northern Central, in Penn	22.0	102.0	102.0	2,080,000	5,623,000	5,711,000
	197.4	324.3	346.3	$8,123,000	$16,937,000	$17,895.000
Add						
Franklin, from Penn	6.0	6.0	6.0	60,000	131,000	40,000
Philadelphia, Wilmington and Baltimore, from Penn	56.0	56.0	56.0	3,458,000	4,451,000	4,802,000
Total in Maryland	259.0	386.3	408.3	$12,241,000	$21,519,000	$22,737,000

XII.—STATE OF WEST VIRGINIA.

Corporate Titles of Companies.	Mileage.			Cost of Property.		
	1850	1860	1865	1850	1860	1865
1. North-Western Virginia	....	203.5	103.5	....	$5,684,000	$5,684,000
Add						
Baltimore and Ohio, from Maryland	97.0	241.0	241.0	$4,795,000	15,520,000	15,520,000
Hempfield, from Penn	....	8.0	8.0	....	452,000	317,000
Pittsburg and Steubenville	....	....	8.0	....	....	464,000
Total in West Virginia	97.0	352.5	360.5	$4,795,000	$21,656,000	$21,985,000

XIII.—STATE OF KENTUCKY.

Corporate Titles of Companies.	Mileage.			Cost of Property.		
	1861	1860	1865	1850	1860	1865
1. Bardstown and Louisville.......	....	....	18.0	....	....	$360,000
2. Breckenridge Coal	....	8.5	8.5	...	$312,000	320,000
3. Covington and Lexington.......	....	80.2	80.2	....	4,019,000	4,529,000
4. Henderson and Nashville.......	....	....	12.0	....	....	300,000
5. Lexington and Big Sandy.......	....	17.9	21.0	....	694,000	694,000
6. Lexington & Southern Kentucky.	....	13.2	13.2	....	824,000	766,000
7. Lexington and Frankfort........	29.2	29.2	29.2	$551,000	646,000	674,000
8. Louisville and Frankfort.........	49.0	65.1	65.1	1,279,000	1,568,000	1,568,000
9. Louisville and Nashville (and Branch)	....	253.2	253.2	....	8,531,000	9,730,000
10. Maysville and Lexington.......	....	18.8	18.8	....	601,000	601,000
11. New Orleans and Ohio..........	....	59.6	59.6	....	1,172,000	1,224,000
12. Portland and Louisville..........	....	5.0	5.0	....	100,000	100,000
	78.2	550.7	583.8	$1,830,000	$18,467,000	$20,866,000
Deduct Louisville and Nashville, in Tenn....	....	45.0	45.0	....	1,421,000	1,621,000
	78.2	505.7	538.8	$1,830,000	$17,046,000	$19,245,000
Add Mobile and Ohio, from Alabama.....	....	20.5	20.5	....	800,000	1,592,000
Nashville and North-Western, from Tenn	....	7.5	7.5	....	200,000	225,000
Total in Kentucky.........	78.2	533.7	566.8	$1,830,000	$18,046,000	$21,062,000

XIV.—STATE OF OHIO.

Corporate Titles of Companies.	Mileage.			Cost of Property.		
	1850	1860	1865	1850	1860	1865
1 { Atlantic and Great Western..	....	....	246.0	....	....	$6,000,000
Cleveland Branch...........	....	....	50.0	....	....	1,000,000
2. Bellefontaine and Indiana....	....	118.2	118.2	....	$3,088,000	3,031,000
3. Carrollton..................	....	11.5	11.5	....	225,000	225,000
4. Central Ohio................	....	137.1	137.1	....	6,502,000	6,513,000
5. Cincinnati, Hamilton and Dayton......................	....	60.3	60.3	....	3,153,000	3,451,000
6. Cincinnati and Indiana.......	....	....	20.0	....	....	600,000
7. Cincinnati and Indianapolis Junction.................	....	42.0	42.0	....	1,050,000	1,287,000
8. Cincinnati and Zanesville.....	....	132.8	132.8	....	6,251,000	6,251,000
9. Cleveland and Mahoning (and Branch)..................	....	67.0	72.0	....	2,768,000	2,850,000
10 { Cleveland, Columbus and Cincinnati..................	135.4	141.2	} 191.0	{ $3,009,000	4,772,000	} 6,225,000
Springfield, Mount Vernon and Pittsburg..........	....	49.8		....	2,205,000	
11. Cleveland, Painesville and Ashtabula...	....	96.6	96.6	....	3,987,000	4,305,000
12. Cleveland and Pittsburg (and Branches)................	....	203.5	203.5	....	9,320,000	7,836,000
13. Cleveland and Toledo........	....	188.6	174.0	....	7,187,000	7,411,000
14. Cleveland, Zanesville and Cincinnati	....	61.4	61.4	....	1,575,000	1,575,000
15. Columbus and Indianapolis (and Branch)............	....	103.0	123.0	....	3,091,000	3,055,000
16. Columbus and Xenia.........	54.6	54.6	54.6	722,000	1,782,000	1,686,000
17. Dayton and Michigan........	....	144.0	144.0	....	5,200,000	5,967,000
18. Dayton and Western.........	....	36.3	38.3	....	1,104,000	1,104,000
19. Dayton, Xenia and Belpré....	....	16.2	16.2	....	860,000	860,000
20. Eaton and Hamilton.........	....	45.1	45.1	....	1,102,000	1,218,000

OHIO.—Continued.

Corporate Titles of Companies.	Mileage.			Cost of Property.		
	1850	1860	1865	1850	1860	1865
21. Frémont, Lima and Union....	....	36.0	40.0	....	1,311,000	1,500,000
22. Greenville and Miami........	....	32.0	32.0	....	888,000	888,000
23. Iron	....	13.0	13.0	....	219,000	251,000
24. Little Miami.................	83.4	83.4	83.4	1,419,000	4,291,000	4,600,000
25 { Marietta and Cincinnati......	....	204.4	} 272.0	{	10,684,000	} 10,722,000
25 { Scioto and Hocking Valley...	....	55.6		....	1,104,000	
26. Pittsburg, Columbus and Cincinnati..................	....	125.8	125.8	....	4,773,000	4,773,000
27. Sandusky, Dayton and Cincinnati......................	173.9	173.9	205.9	3,662,000	4,594,000	4,579,000
28. Sandusky, Mansfield & Newark	116.0	126.0	116.0	1,693,000	2,309,000	2,385,000
29. Springfield and Columbus.....	....	19.5	19.5	....	347,000	352,000
30. Toledo and Wabash..........	....	243.0	243.0	....	8,020,000	9,996,000
	563.3	2826.8	3188.2	$10,505,000	$103,762,000	$112,476,000
Deduct						
Cleveland, Painesville and Ashtabula, in Penn.................	....	26.7	26.7	....	1,101,000	1,101,000
Cleveland and Pittsburg, in Penn.	....	14.9	14.9	....	687,000	474,000
Cincinnati and Indianapolis Junction, in Ind..................	....	20.3	20.3	....	506,000	614,000
Toledo and Wabash, in Indiana...	....	166.0	166.0	....	5,676,000	6,591,000
	563.3	2595.9	2960.3	$10,505,000	$95,792,000	$103,696,000
Add						
Michigan Southern and Northern Indiana, from Mich........	12.0	82.6	82.6	280,000	2,657,000	2,657,000
Ohio and Mississippi, from Indiana	....	19.0	19.0	....	1,841,000	1,841,000
Pittsburg, Fort Wayne and Chicago, from Penn..............	....	249.0	249.0	....	9,311,000	9,389,000
Total in Ohio...........	575.3	2945.5	3310.9	$10,785,000	$109,601,000	$117,583,000

XV.—STATE OF MICHIGAN.

Corporate Titles of Companies.	Mileage.			Cost of Property.		
	1850	1860	1865	1850	1860	1865
1. Amboy, Lansing and Traverse Bay	....	....	30.0	....	....	$1,250,000
2. Bay de Noquet and Marquette...	....	20.5	22.5	....	$410,000	456,000
3. Chicago, Detroit and Canada Grand Junction...............	....	59.0	59.0	....	1,710,000	1,962,000
4. Detroit and Milwaukee..........	25.0	188.9	188.9	$408,000	9,118,000	8,918,000
5. Detroit, Monroe and Toledo.....	....	51.0	51.0	....	1,523,000	1,701,000
6. Flint and Père Marquette.......	....	35.0	35.0	....	1,000,000	1,272,000
7. Marquette and Ontonagon.......	....	....	10.0	....	....	400,000
8. Michigan Central............	226.0	284.8	284.8	6,340,000	13,159,000	13,805,000
9. Michigan Southern and Northern Indiana........	103.0	484.6	484.6	2,378,000	15,591,000	15,263,000
10. Peninsula	....	....	77.0	....	...	2,000,000
	354.0	1123.8	1242.8	$9,126,000	$42,511,000	$47,027,000
Deduct						
Michigan Central, in Indiana and Illinois	....	65.0	65.0	....	3,003,000	3,162,000
Michigan Southern, in Ohio, Indiana and Illinois......................	12.0	279.6	279.6	280,000	8,995,000	8,874,000
Total in Michigan.........	342.0	779.2	898.2	$8,846,000	$30,523,000	$35,091,000

XVI.—STATE OF INDIANA.

Corporate Titles of Companies.	Mileage.			Cost of Property.		
	1850	1860	1865	1850	1860	1865
1. Chicago and Great Eastern......	....	61.0	109.5	....	$1,250,000	$2,500,000
2. Cincinnati and Chicago.........	....	108.0	108.0	....	2,081,000	2,188,000
3. Cincinnati, Peru and Chicago....	....	29.1	29.1	....	1,161.000	1,184,000
4. Evansville and Crawfordsville....	....	132.0	132.0	....	2,466,000	2,472,000
5. Indiana Central................	....	72.4	72.4	....	2,233,000	1,941,000
6. Indianapolis and Cincinnati.....	....	89.8	89.8	....	3,038,000	3,038,000
7. Indianapolis and Madison (and Branch)	86.0	135.0	135.0	$1,812,000	2,668,000	1,464,000
8. Indianapolis, Pittsburg and Cleveland	28.0	82.8	82.8	813,000	1,902,000	1,848,000
9. Jeffersonville (and Extension)...	16.0	78.0	82.5	320,000	2,182,000	1,849,000
10. Knightstown and Shelbyville ..	27.0	27.0	27.0	270,000	366.000	400,000
11. Lafayette and Indianapolis......	....	64.0	64.0	....	1,856,000	1,856,000
12. Louisville, New Albany and Chicago........................	35.0	288.0	288.0	418,000	7,029,000	7,029,000
13. Ohio and Mississippi............	....	192.3	192.3	....	18,636,000	17,594,000
14. Peru and Indianapolis..........	....	74.0	74.0	....	2,371,000	2,871,000
15. Rushville and Shelbyville........	20.0	20.0	20.0	250,000	320,000	320,000
16. Shelbyville Lateral............	16.0	16.0	16.0	160,000	160,000	160,000
17. Terre-Haute and Richmond.....	....	73.0	73.0	....	1,611,000	1,611,000
18. Toledo, Logansport and Burlington	....	49.0	49.0	....	1.200,000	1,200,000
19. Union Track and Depôt..... ...	....	3.5	3.5	....	265,000	280,000
	228.0	1594.9	1647.9	$4,043,000	$52,795,000	$51,305,000
Deduct						
Chicago and Great Eastern, in Ill....	...	....	21.0	....	....	500,000
Ohio and Mississippi, in Ohio........	....	19.0	19.0	....	1,841,000	1,841,000
	228.0	1575.9	1607.9	$4,043,000	$50,954,000	$49,964,000
Add						
Cincinnati and Indianapolis Junction, from Ohio	....	20.8	20 8	....	506,000	614,000
Joliet and Northern Indiana, from Ill.	....	15.0	15.0	....	391,000	433,000
Michigan Central, from Mich........	....	52.0	52.0	....	2,463,000	2,571,000
Michigan Southern and Northern Indiana, from Mich.	....	185.0	185.0	....	5,952,000	5,817,000
Pittsburg, Fort Wayne and Chicago, from Penn.........	....	149.0	149.0	....	5.195,000	5,306,000
Toledo and Wabash, from Ohio......	....	166.0	166.0	....	5,576,000	6,591,000
Total in Indiana...........	228.0	2163.2	2195.2	$4,043,000	$71,087,000	$71,296,000

XVII.—STATE OF ILLINOIS.

Corporate Titles of Companies.	Mileage.			Cost of Property.		
	1850	1860	1865	1850	1860	1865
1. Chicago and Alton...........	...	220.0	220.0	....	$8,117,000	$8,281,000
2. { Chicago, Burlington & Quincy	18.0	138.0		$195,000	7.469,000	
Peoria and Oquawka........	....	96.0	400.0	....	3,770,000	13,927,000
Quincy and Chicago..... ...	....	100.0		....	1,979,000	
3. { Chicago and Milwaukee......	....	45.0	85.0	....	1,884,000	3,714,000
Milwaukee and Chicago......	....	40 0		....	1,830,000	
4. { Chicago and North-Western..	....	213.0		....	10·685,000	
Galena and Chicago Union...	42.5	261.3	535.5	696,000	9,352,000	28,000,000
Elgin and State Line.........	....	32 2		....	581,000	
5. Chicago and Rock Island.....	....	181 5	181.8	....	6,914.000	7,430,000
6. Great Western of 1859.......	55.0	182.0	182.0	1,550,000	5,083.000	4,039,000
7. Illinois Central..............	....	708.0	708.0	....	27,195,000	28,610,000
8. Illinois Coal................	....	4.0	4.0	....	100,000	100,000
9. Illinois and Southern Iowa...	....	....	26.0	....	....	400,000
10. Jacksonville, Peoria & Chicago	....	....	81.5	....	....	3,500,000
11. Joliet and Northern Indiana.	....	45.0	45.0	....	1,173,000	1.250,000
12. Joliet and Chicago...........	....	35.8	35.8	....	1,000,000	1,000,000

ILLINOIS.—Continued.

Corporate Titles of Companies.	Mileage.			Cost of Property.		
	1850	1860	1865	1850	1860	1865
13. Mound City	....	3.5	3.5	....	$60,000	$60,000
14. Northern Illinois	....	....	38.5	....	....	1,200,000
15. Ohio and Mississippi	....	148.0	148.0	....	4,871,000	4,871,000
16. Peoria and Bureau Valley	....	46.6	46.6	....	2,106,000	2,106,000
17. Quincy and Toledo	....	34.0	34.0	....	750,000	1,000,000
18. Rock Island and Peoria	....	11.0	11.0	....	220,000	220,000
19. Rock Island Bridge	....	1.0	1.0	....	250,000	250,000
20. Rockford	....	28.0	45.7	....	560,000	860,000
21. St. Louis, Alton and Terre-Haute	....	208.3	208.3	....	8,865,000	10,600,000
22. St. Louis, Jacksonville and Chicago	....	....	54.0	....	....	1,250,000
23. Sterling and Rock Island	....	....	52.0	....	...	1,250,000
24. Syracuse and Cortlandt	....	5.0	5.0	....	75,000	75,000
25. Toledo, Peoria and Warsaw	....	123.0	123.0	....	4,000,000	4,200,000
26. Warsaw and Peoria	....	13.0	13.0	....	300,000	300,000
	110.5	2923.2	3288.2	$2,441,000	$108,889,000	$128,493,000
Deduct						
Chicago and Milwaukee, in Wisc.	....	40.0	40.0	....	1,830,000	1,741,000
Chicago & North-Western, in Wisc.	....	147.0	176.0	....	7,374,000	10,000,000
Joliet & Northern Indiana, in Ind.	....	15.0	15.0	....	391,000	433,000
	110.5	2721.2	3059.2	$2,441,000	$99,294,000	$116,319,000
Add						
Chicago & Great Eastern, from Ind.	....	....	21.0	....	....	500,000
Michigan Central, from Mich.	....	13.0	13.0	....	540,000	591,000
Michigan Southern and Northern Indiana, from Mich.	....	12.0	12.0	....	386,000	400,000
Pittsburg, Fort Wayne and Chicago, from Penn.	....	18.0	18.0	....	1,048,000	1,327,000
Racine and Mississippi, from Wisc.	....	35.0	35.0	....	1,280,000	1,280,000
Total in Illinois	110.5	2799.2	3156.2	$2,441,000	$102,548,000	$120,417,000

XVIII.—STATE OF WISCONSIN.

Corporate Titles of Companies.	Mileage.			Cost of Property.		
	1850	1860	1865	1850	1860	1865
1. Beloit and Madison	....	17.3	47.0	....	$350,000	$1,000,000
2. Kenosha and Rockford	....	28.3	28.3	....	1,069,000	1,101,000
3. La Crosse and Milwaukee	....	95.0	95.0	....	3,500,000	3,500,000
4. Manitouwoc and Mississippi	....	7.5	7.5	....	200,000	200,000
5. Milwaukee and Prairie du Chien	20.0	234.4	234.4	$612,000	7,500,000	7,500,000
6. { Milwaukee and St. Paul	....	104.9	} 261.0	....	4,000,000	} 8,144,000
Milwaukee and Horicon	....	42.0		....	1,138,000	
Milwaukee and Western	....	57.2		....	1,499,000	
7. Mineral Point	....	32.0	32.0	....	1,814,000	1,000,000
8. Racine and Mississippi	....	104.0	104.0	....	3,802,000	3,802,000
9. Sheboygan and Fond du Lac	....	20.0	20.0	....	412,000	457,000
10. Wisconsin Central	....	10.0	....	....	250,000	....
	20.0	752.6	829.2	$612,000	$25,534,000	$26,704,000
Deduct						
Racine and Mississippi, in Illinois	....	35.0	35.0	....	1,280,000	1,280,000
	20.0	717.6	794.2	$612,000	$24,254,000	$25,424,000
Add						
Chicago and Milwaukee, from Ill.	....	40.0	40.0	....	1,830,000	1,741,000
Chicago and North-Western, from Ill.	....	147.0	176.0	....	7,374,000	10,000,000
Total in Wisconsin	20.0	904.6	1010.2	$612,000	$33,458,000	$37,165,000

XIX.—STATE OF MINNESOTA.

Corporate Titles of Companies.	Mileage.			Cost of Property.		
	1850	1860	1865	1850	1860	1865
1. Minnesota Central..............	....	....	35.0	....	....	$1,000,000
2. Minnesota Southern.............	....	....	10.0	....	...	250,000
3. St. Paul and Pacific.............	....	....	62.0	....	....	1,600.000
4. Winona and St. Peter...........	....	....	50.0	....	....	1,000.000
Total in Minnesota.........	....	....	157.0	....	....	$3,850,000

XX.—STATE OF IOWA.

Corporate Titles of Companies.	Mileage.			Cost of Property.		
	1850	1860	1865	1850	1860	1865
1. Burlington and Missouri.........	....	75.5	75.5	....	$1,498,000	$1,514,000
2. Cedar Rapids and Missouri......	....	25.4	81.0	....	612,000	2,430,000
3. Chicago, Iowa and Nebraska....	....	82.1	82.1	....	1,860,000	2,500,000
4. Dubuque and Pacific............	....	101.0	101.0	....	2,836,000	3,152,000
5. Dubuque, Marion and Western..	....	54.0	54.0	....	1,352,000	1,620,000
6. Keokuk, Fort Desmoines and Minnesota	....	92.0	92.0	....	2,879,000	3,000,000
7. Keokuk, Mt. Pleasant and Muscatine	....	25.2	25.2	....	1,022,000	1,200,000
8. Mahaska County...............	....	12 0	12.0	....	250,000	250,000
9. McGregor Western.............	....	...	61.0	....	....	1,830,000
10. Mississippi and Missouri.........	....	187.6	221.0	....	6,319,000	8,000,000
Total in Iowa.............	....	654.8	804.8	....	$18,623,000	$25,496,000

XXI.—STATE OF KANSAS.

Corporate Titles of Companies.	Mileage.			Cost of Property.		
	1850	1860	1865	1850	1860	1865
1. Union Pacific, E. D..............	....	....	40.0	....	....	$1,400,000

XXII.—STATE OF MISSOURI.

Corporate Titles of Companies.	Mileage.			Cost of Property.		
	1850	1860	1865	1850	1860	1865
1. Cairo and Fulton........	....	37.0	37.0	....	$1,213,000	$1,339,000
2. Hannibal and St. Joseph........	....	206.8	206.8	....	12,364,000	12,984,000
3. North Missouri	....	168.8	168.8	....	6,966,000	6.904,000
4. { Pacific........................	....	189.7	282.0	....	11,219,000	16,000,000
{ South-Western Branch..........	....	77.5	77 5	....	3,873,000	4,893,000
5. Platte County..................	....	37.0	52.0	....	925,000	2 000,000
6. Quincy and Palmyra............	...	10.5	10.5	....	250,000	250,000
7. St. Louis and Iron Mountain.....	....	90.2	90.2	....	5,582,000	5,676,000
Total in Missouri..........	....	817.5	924.8	....	$42,342,000	$50,046,000

XXIII.—STATE OF ARKANSAS.

Corporate Titles of Companies.	Mileage.			Cost of Property.		
	1850	1860	1865	1850	1860	1865
1. Memphis and Little Rock.........	....	38.5	38.5	....	$1,155,000	$1,155,000

XXIV.—STATE OF TENNESSEE.

Corporate Titles of Companies.	Mileage.			Cost of Property.		
	1850	1860	1865	1850	1860	1865
1. Central Southern...............	....	47.6	47.6	....	$1,079,000	$1,179,000
2. Cleveland and Chattanooga.....	....	30.6	30 6	....	867,000	867,000
3. East Tennessee and Georgia.....	....	110.8	110.8	....	3,638,000	3,638,000
4. East Tennessee and Virginia.....	....	130.3	130 3	....	2,866,000	2,866,000
5. Edgefield and Kentucky.........	....	46.7	46.7	....	1,290,000	1,290,000
6. Memphis and Charleston (and Branches)...................	....	290.9	290.9	....	6,745,000	6,745,000
7. Memphis and Ohio..............	....	130.6	130.6	....	2,612,000	2,612,000
8. Memphis, Clarksville and Louisville.........................	....	56.8	56.8	....	1,593,000	2,100,000
9. McMinnville and Manchester....	....	34.2	34.2	....	591,000	591,000
10. Nashville and Chattanooga......	....	158.7	158.7	....	3,633,000	3,633.000
11. Nashville and North-Western....	....	98.4	139.0	....	2,460,000	3,506,000
12. Rogersville and Jefferson........	....	....	14.0	....	...	280,000
13. Tennessee and Alabama.........	....	45.8	45.8	....	1,185,000	1,659,000
14. Winchester and Alabama........	....	38.1	38.1	....	630,000	639,000
	....	1219.5	1274.1	....	$29,189,000	$31,605,000
Deduct						
Memphis and Charleston, in Miss. and Ala..........................	....	188.0	192.0	....	4,357,000	4,413,000
Nashville and North-Western........	....	....	7.5	....	200,000	225,000
	....	1081.5	1074.6	....	$24,632,000	$26,967,000
Add						
Louisville and Nashville, from Ky...	....	45.0	45 0	....	1,421,000	1,621,000
Mississippi Central and Tennessee, from Miss.......................	....	49.0	49.0	....	1,188,000	1,188,000
Mississippi and Tennessee, from Miss.	...	9.8	9.8	....	238,000	238,000
Mobile and Ohio, from Ala	....	117.3	117.3	....	3,519,000	3,519,000
Total in Tennessee.........	....	1252.6	1295.7	....	$30,998,000	$33,533,000

XXV.—STATE OF VIRGINIA.

Corporate Titles of Companies.	Mileage.			Cost of Property.		
	1850	1860	1865	1850	1860	1865
1. Alexandria, Loudoun and Hampshire	....	41.5	41.5	....	$1,533,000	$1,533,000
2. Alexandria and Washington.....	....	6.1	6.1	....	122,000	122,000
3. Blue Ridge (State road).........	....	16.8	16.8	...	1,605,000	1,605,000
4. Clover Hill.....................	18.5	18.5	18 5	$185,000	185,000	185,000
5. Manassas Gap (and Branches). .	....	86.7	86.7	....	3,153,000	3,153,000
6. Norfolk and Petersburg...	....	80.0	80.0	....	2,129,000	2,129,000
7. Orange and Alexandria (and Branches)....................	....	156 7	156.7	....	6,422,000	6,422,000
8. Petersburg (and Branch)........	80 0	80.0	80.0	1,124,000	1,260,000	1,260,000
9. Richmond and Danville (and Branches)..................	27.7	143.2	143.2	1,406,000	3,726,000	3,726,000

VIRGINIA.—Continued.

Corporate Titles of Companies.	Mileage.			Cost of Property.		
	1850	1860	1865	1850	1860	1865
10. Richmond, Frederick and Potomac (and Branch)............	75.0	78.5	78.5	$1,510,000	$1,986,000	$1,986,000
11. Richmond and Petersburg (and Branch)......................	24.9	24.9	24.9	943,000	1,223,000	1,223,000
12. Richmond and York River.......	....	23.7	23.7	....	725,000	725,000
13. Seaboard and Roanoke..........	80.0	80.0	80.0	1,000,000	1,469,000	1,469,000
14. South Side......................	10.0	132 0	132.0	120,000	4,239,000	4,239,000
15. Virginia Central	70.1	189.2	189.2	944,000	5,494,000	5,494,000
16. Virginia and Tennessee (and Br'h)	....	214.9	214.9	....	7,431,000	7,431,000
17. Winchester and Potomac........	32.0	32 0	32.0	559,000	576,000	576,000
	418.2	1404.7	1404.7	$7,791,000	$43,278,000	$43,278,000
Deduct						
Seaboard and Roanoke, in N. Carolina..............................	16.8	16.8	16 8	200,000	294,000	294,000
Petersburg, in North Carolina.......	17.2	17.2	17.2	225,000	252,000	252,000
	384.2	1370.7	1370.7	$7,366,000	$42,732,000	$42,732,000
Add						
Roanoke Valley, from North Carolina	....	8.0	8.0	....	173,000	173,000
Total in Virginia.....	384,2	1378.7	1378.7	$7,366,000	$42,905,000	$42,905,000

XXVI.—STATE OF NORTH CAROLINA.

Corporate Titles of Companies.	Mileage.			Cost of Property.		
	1850	1860	1865	1850	1860	1865
1. Atlantic and North Carolina.....	....	94.9	94.9	....	$2,158,000	$2,158,000
2. North Carolina.................	....	223.0	223.0	...	4,235.000	4,235,000
3. Raleigh and Gaston.............	87.0	97.0	97.0	$870,000	1,240,000	1,240,000
4. Roanoke Valley..................	....	22.0	22.0	....	477,000	477,000
5. Piedmont (Greensboro to Danville)....	....	....	32.0	....	....	1,000,000
6. Western (Coal).................	....	41.5	41.5	....	830,000	830,000
7. Western North Carolina.........	....	84.0	96.0	....	1,740,000	2,000,000
8. Wilmington, Charlotte and Rutherfordton	....	110.0	112.5	....	2,200,000	2,500,000
9. Wilmington and Manchester. ...	....	161.5	161.5	....	2,869,000	2,869,000
10. Wilmington and Weldon (and Branch)......................	161.5	176.5	176.5	2,412,000	3,197,000	3,197,000
	248.5	1010.4	1056.9	$3,282,000	$18,946,000	$20,506,000
Deduct						
Roanoke Valley, in Virginia........	....	8.0	8.0	....	173.000	173,000
Wilmington and Manchester, in S. Carolina..................... ...	....	99.0	99.0	....	1,759,000	1,759,000
	248.5	903.4	949.9	$3,282,000	$17,014,000	$18,574,000
Add						
Petersburg, from Virginia...........	17.2	17.2	17.2	225,000	252,000	252,000
Seaboard and Roanoke, from Virginia	16.8	16.8	16.8	200,000	294,000	294,000
Total in North Carolina....	282.5	937.4	983.9	$3,707,000	$17,560,000	$19,120,000

XXVII.—STATE OF SOUTH CAROLINA.

Corporate Titles of Companies.	Mileage.			Cost of Property.		
	1850	1860	1865	1850	1860	1865
1. Blue Ridge (and Branch)........	....	33.0	33.0	....	$2,989,000	$2,989,000
2. Charleston and Savannah.......	....	103.3	103.3	....	2,320,000	2,320,000
3. Charlotte aud South Carolina (and Branches)..........	....	109.6	109.6	....	1,719,000	1,719,000
4. Cheraw and Darlington.........	....	40.3	40.3	....	612,000	612,000
5. Greenville and Columbia (and Branches)....................	47.0	164.3	164.3	$877,000	2,763,000	2,763,000
6. King's Mountain................	....	22.5	22.5	....	225,000	225,000
7. Laurens........................	....	32.0	32.0	....	543.000	543,000
8. North Eastern..................	....	102.0	102.0	....	2,054,000	2,054,000
9. South Carolina (and Branches)...	242.0	242.0	242.0	6,649,000	6,503,000	6,503,000
10. Spartanburg and Union.........	....	40.0	40.0	....	897,000	897,000
	289.0	889.0	889.0	$7,526,000	$20,625,000	$20,624,000
Deduct Charleston and Savannah, in Geo....	....	15.0	15.0	....	331,000	331,000
	289.0	874.0	874.0	$7,526,000	$20,294,000	$20,294,000
Add Wilmington and Manchester, from N. Carolina........................	....	99.0	99.0	....	1,759,000	1,759,000
Total in South Carolina....	289.0	973.0	973.0	$7,526,000	$22,053,000	$22,053,000

XXVIII.—STATE OF GEORGIA.

Corporate Titles of Companies.	Mileage.			Cost of Property.		
	1850	1860	1865	1850	1860	1865
1. Atlanta and West Point.........	...	86.7	86.7	....	$1,192,000	$1,192,000
2. Augusta and Savannah.........	....	53.0	53.0	....	1,032,600	1,032,000
3. Barnesville and Thomaston......	....	16.0	16.0	....	240,000	240,000
4. Brunswick and Florida..........	....	43.5	43.5	....	756,000	756,000
5. Central	190.7	190.7	190.7	$2,996,000	3,700,000	3,700,000
6. Etowah	....	8.9	8.9	.. .	113,000	113,000
7. Georgia (and Branches).........	213.0	232.0	232.0	4,000,000	4,156,000	4,156,000
8. Macon and Brunswick...........	..	37.5	37.5	....	927,000	1,000,000
9. Macon and Western....	102.0	102.0	102.0	1,276,000	1,502,000	1,502,000
10. Main Trunk (Atlantic and Gulf)..	....	109.7	109.7	....	2,194,000	2,194,000
11. Milledgeville and Eatonton......	....	22.0	22.0	....	276,000	276,000
12. Milledgeville and Gordon.......	....	17.0	17.0	....	214,000	214,000
13. Muscogee	....	50.0	50.0	....	1,000,000	1,000,000
14. Rome and Kingston............	....	20.0	20.0	....	250,000	250,000
15. Savannah, Albany and Gulf.....	....	68.1	68.1	....	1,387,000	1,387,000
16. South-Western (and Branches)..	....	209.7	209.7	....	4,218,000	4,218,000
17. Western and Atlantic...........	138.0	138.0	138.0	5,000,000	5,901,000	5,901,000
	643.0	1404.8	1404.8	$13,272,000	$29,058,000	$29,058,000
Add Charleston and Savannah, from S. Carolina	....	15.0	15.0	....	331,000	331,000
Total in Georgia..........	643.0	1419.8	1419.8	$13,272,000	$29,389,000	$29,389,000

XXIX.—STATE OF FLORIDA.

Corporate Titles of Companies.	Mileage.			Cost of Property.		
	1850	1860	1865	1850	1860	1865
1. Florida	....	154.2	154.2	....	$3,084,000	$3,084,000
2. Florida and Alabama	....	45.1	45.1	....	1,133,000	1,133,000
3. Florida, Atlantic and Gulf	....	59.3	59.3	....	1,212,000	1,212,000
4. Pensacola and Georgia	....	115.9	115.9	....	2,719,000	2,719,000
5. Perdido and Junction	....	6.0	6.0	....	60,000	60,000
6. Tallahassee	21.0	21.0	21.0	$210,000	420,000	420,000
Total in Florida	21.0	401.5	401.5	$210,000	$8,628,000	$8,628,000

XXX.—STATE OF ALABAMA.

Corporate Titles of Companies.	Mileage.			Cost of Property.		
	1850	1860	1865	1850	1860	1865
1. Alabama and Florida	....	115.6	115.6	....	$2,982,000	$2,982,000
2. Alabama and Mississippi River	....	30.8	88.3	....	618,000	2,000,000
3. Alabama and Tennessee River	....	109.8	109.8	....	2,447,000	2,447,000
4. Marion and Cahawba	....	14.0	14.0	....	280,000	280,000
5. Mobile and Gerard	....	57.8	57.8	....	1,506,000	1,506,000
6. Mobile and Great Northern	....	49.2	49.2	....	1,095,000	1,095,000
7. Mobile and Ohio	....	482.8	482.8	....	14,484,000	14,484,000
8. Montgomery and West Point (and Branch)	88.5	116.9	116.9	$1,286,000	2,266,000	2,266,000
9. Tennessee and Alabama Central	....	26.1	26.1	....	782,000	782,000
10. Tuscumbia and Decatur	44.0	....	...	660,000	....	....
	132.5	1002.0	1060.0	$1,946,000	$26,460,000	$27,842,000
Deduct Mobile and Ohio, in Miss., Tenn. & Ky.	....	420.3	420.3	....	12,594,000	12,594,000
	132.5	581.7	639.7	$1,946,000	$13,866,000	$14,248,000
Add Memphis and Charleston, from Tenn.	....	161.0	165.0	....	3,732,000	3,913,000
Total in Alabama	132.5	742.7	804.7	$1,946,000	$17,598,000	$18,161,000

XXXI.—STATE OF MISSISSIPPI.

Corporate Titles of Companies.	Mileage.			Cost of Property.		
	1850	1860	1865	1850	1860	1865
1. Grand Gulf and Port Gibson	8.0	8.0	8.0	$120,000	$120,000	$120,000
2. Mississippi Central	....	236.0	236.0	....	6,319,000	6,319,000
3. Mississippi and Tennessee	....	99.2	99.2	....	2,149,000	2,373,000
4. Raymond	7.0	7.0	7.0	100,000	100,000	100,000
5. Southern Mississippi	60.0	143.6	143.6	1,800,000	4,308,000	4,308,000
	75.0	493.8	493.8	$2,020,000	$12,996,000	$13,220,000
Deduct						
Mississippi Central, in Tenn.	....	49.0	49.0	....	1,188,000	1,188,000
Mississippi and Tennessee, in Tenn.	....	9.8	9.8	....	238,000	238,000
	75.0	435.0	435.0	$2,020,000	$11,570,000	$11,794,000
Add						
Memphis and Charleston, from Tenn.	....	27.0	27.0	....	626,000	626,000
Mobile and Ohio, from Alabama	....	282.5	282.5	...	8,475,000	8,475,000
New Orleans, Jackson and Great Northern, from La.	....	118.0	118.0	....	3,787,000	3,787,000
Total in Mississippi	75.0	862.5	862.5	$2,020,000	$24,458,000	$24,682,000

XXXII.—STATE OF LOUISIANA.

Corporate Titles of Companies.	Mileage.			Cost of Property.		
	1850	1860	1865	1850	1860	1865
1. Baton Rouge, Grosse-Tête and Opelousas	....	17.0	17.0	....	$327,000	$327,000
2. Clinton and Port Hudson	14.0	22.0	22.0	$400,000	751,000	751,000
3. Mexican Gulf	27.0	27.0	27.0	500,000	663,000	663,000
4. Milnburg and Lake Pontchartrain	4.5	6.0	6.0	120,000	213,000	213,000
5. New Orleans and Carrollton	8.0	15.0	15.0	300,000	500,000	500,000
6. N. O., Jackson and G't N'th'n	....	206.0	206.0	....	6,611,000	6,611,000
7. N. O,, Opelousas and G't West'n.	....	80.0	80.0	....	4,460,000	4,460,000
8. Vicksburg, Shreveport and Texas	....	53 8	53.8	....	1,663,000	1,663,000
9. West Feliciana	26.0	26.0	26.0	520,000	620,000	620,000
	79.5	452.8	452.8	$1,840,000	$15,808,000	$15,808,000
Deduct N. O., Jackson and G't N'th'n in Miss.	....	118.0	118.0	....	3,787,000	3,787,000
Total in Louisiana	79.5	334.8	334.8	$1,840,000	$12,021,000	$12,021,000

XXXIII.—STATE OF TEXAS.

Corporate Titles of Companies.	Mileage.			Cost of Property.		
	1850	1860	1865	1850	1860	1865
1. Buffalo Bayou, Brazos and Colorado	....	32.0	32.0	....	$1,000,000	$1,000,000
2. Eastern Texas	....	....	21.0	....	....	630,000
3. Galveston, Houston and Henderson	....	72.0	72.0	....	2,500,000	2,880,000
4. Houston and New Orleans	....	....	96.0	....	....	3,000,000
5. Houston Tap and Brazoria	....	60.0	80.0	....	1,800,000	2,400,000
6. Houston and Texas Central	....	90.0	98.0	....	4,232,000	4,829,000
7. San Antonio and Mexican Gulf	....	25.0	25.0	....	500,000	500,000
8. Southern Pacific	....	27.5	27.5	....	1,000,000	1,000,000
Total in Texas	....	306.5	451.5	....	$11,032,000	$16,239,000

XXXIV.—STATE OF CALIFORNIA.

Corporate Titles of Companies.	Mileage.			Cost of Property.		
	1850	1860	1865	1850	1860	1865
1. California Central	....	....	43.8	....	....	$2,500,000
2. Central Pacific	....	....	31.0	....	....	1,600,000
3. Sacramento Valley	....	22.5	22.5	....	$1,600,000	1,800,000
4. San Francisco and San José	....	....	50.0	....	....	2,000,000
Total in California	....	22.5	147.3	....	$1,600,000	$7,900,000

XXXV.—STATE OF OREGON.

Corporate Titles of Companies.	Mileage.			Cost of Property.		
	1850	1860	1865	1850	1860	1865
1. Cascades Transit	....	....	6.0	....	....	$200,000
2. Dallas and Deschuttes	....	....	13.5	....	....	500,000
Total in Oregon	....	....	19.5	....	....	$700,000

RECAPITULATION OF RAILROADS IN THE U. S., NUMBER OF COMPANIES IN EACH STATE, WITH THEIR MILEAGE AND COST, IN THE YEARS 1850, 1860, AND 1864.

From the Latest Official Reports.

STATES.	NUMBER OF COMPANIES.	MILEAGE.			COST OF PROPERTY.		
		1850	1860	1864	1850	1860	1864
Maine	18	245.3	471.9	505.1	$7,000,000	$16,055.000	$12,669,000
New Hampshire	17	467.7	661.0	660 3	14.660,000	23 086,000	22.489.000
Vermont	9	290.0	554.0	587.1	11,266,000	23.356.000	23,852.000
Massachusetts	49	1035.1	1264 2	1285.0	47,719,000	58 642,000	59,051,000
Rhode Island	8	68.0	107 9	125.2	2.913,000	4,405.000	4,588,000
Connecticut	13	401.9	600.8	629.6	13,735.000	21,848,000	23,014,000
N. E. States	104	2508.0	3359.8	3792.3	$97,293,000	$147,392,000	$149,663,000
New York	42	1360.8	2682.3	2820.9	$62,977,000	$128.915.000	$135.887.000
New Jersey	26	206.4	560.3	864.5	9,349.000	28.966.000	38.892.000
Pennsylvania	85	1240.1	2598 4	3359.8	44.543,000	146.744,000	170,080,000
Delaware	4	39.2	126.8	126.8	2 282,000	4 352,000	4.500,000
Maryland & D. of Col'bia.	8	259.0	386 3	408.3	12,241,000	21,519,000	2 ,737,000
Middle Atlantic States.	165	3105.5	6354.1	7580.3	$131,392,000	$330,496,000	$372,096,000
West Virginia	1	97.0	352.5	360.5	$4.795,000	$21.656,000	$21,985.000
Kentucky	12	78.2	533.7	566.8	1,830,000	18.046,000	21.062,000
Ohio	30	575 3	2945.5	3310.9	10,785,000	109.601.000	117 583,000
Michigan	10	342.0	779.2	898.2	8,846.000	30.523.000	35.091,000
Indiana	19	228.0	2163.2	2195.2	4,043,000	71.037,000	71.296,000
Illinois	26	110.5	2799.2	3156.2	2,441,000	102.548.000	120.417.000
Wisconsin	9	20.0	904.6	1010.2	612,000	33,458,000	37,165,000
Minnesota	4	....	....	157.0	....	....	3,850,000
Iowa	10	....	654.8	804.8	....	18,623,000	25.496,000
Kansas	1	....	....	40.0	....	....	1.400,000
Missouri	7	....	817.5	924 8	....	42,342,000	50,046.000
Arkansas	1	....	38.5	38 5	....	1.155,000	1.155,000
Tennessee	14	....	1252.6	1295.7	....	30,998,000	33,583,000
Interior States	144	1451.0	13,241 3	14,758.8	$33,352,000	$479,947,000	$540,079,000
Virginia	17	384.2	1378.7	1378.7	$7.366,000	$42,905,000	$42,905.000
North Carolina	10	282 5	937.4	983 9	3.707.000	17,560,000	19.120,000
South Carolina	10	289.0	973.0	973.0	7,526.000	22,053,000	22,053.000
Georgia	17	643.0	1419.8	1419.8	13.272.000	29.389,000	29,389.000
Florida	6	21 0	401 5	401.5	210,000	8,623,000	8.628,000
Alabama	10	182.5	742.7	804.7	1,946,000	17,598,000	18,161.000
Mississippi	5	75.0	862.5	862 5	2,020,000	24,458,000	24,682,000
Louisiana	9	79.5	334.8	334.8	1,840,000	12.021.000	12,621,000
Texas	8	....	306.5	451 5	....	11,032,000	16,239,000
Southern States	92	1956.7	7356.9	7610.4	$37,887,000	$185,644,000	$193,198,000
California	4	....	22.5	147.3	....	$1,600,000	$7,900,000
Oregon	2	....	....	19 5	....	....	700,000
Pacific States	5	....	22.5	166,8	....	$1,600,000	$8,600,000
North-Eastern States	104	2508.0	3659.8	3792.3	$97,293,000	$147.392,000	$149,663,000
Middle Atlantic States	165	3105 0	6354 1	7580 3	131,392,000	330.496,000	372,096,000
Interior States	144	1451 0	13 241.3	14,758.8	33,352.000	479.947.000	540,079,000
Southern States	92	1956.7	7356.9	7610.4	37,887,000	185.644,000	193,198,000
Pacific States	5	....	22 5	135.8	....	1,600,000	8,600,000
TOTAL United States.	510	9020.7	30,634.6	33,908.6	$299,924,000	$1,145,079,000	$1264, 336,000

PROGRESS OF RAILROADS

A Tabular Statement of the Mileage in each State and cluster of

States, etc.	1835	1836	1837	1838	1839	1840	1841	1842	1843	1844	1845	1846	1847	1848	1849	1850
1. Maine	....	....	11	11	11	11	11	62	62	62	62	62	62	90	168	245
2. N. Hamp	....	....	....	6	6	53	53	88	92	92	92	92	175	223	386	467
3. Vermont	....	....	....	....	....	....	....	....	....	....	....	....	....	103	214	290
4. Mass	113	139	139	169	219	301	373	435	485	485	567	626	718	790	948	1035
5. R. Island	....	....	50	50	50	50	50	50	50	50	50	50	68	68	68	68
6. Conn	....	....	....	18	36	102	102	176	176	176	202	202	202	202	289	402
N. E. States	113	139	190	254	322	527	589	811	865	865	973	1032	1225	1276	2073	2508
7. New York	104	191	269	314	374	374	538	636	648	715	721	727	764	869	1180	1361
8. New Jersey	99	133	183	133	174	186	186	186	186	186	186	186	185	206	206	206
9. Pennsyl	318	339	466	608	691	754	754	789	789	798	798	840	1006	1048	1120	1240
10. Delaware	16	16	24	39	39	39	39	39	39	39	39	39	39	39	39	39
11. Md. & D. C.	117	117	138	138	185	213	259	259	259	259	259	259	259	259	259	259
Mid. A. States	654	796	930	1232	1463	1566	1776	1909	1921	1997	2003	2051	2254	2421	2804	3105
12. W. Virginia	....	....	....	....	....	....	61	97	97	97	97	97	97	97	97	97
13. Kentucky	15	22	22	22	25	28	28	28	28	28	28	28	28	28	55	78
14. Ohio	....	....	....	....	....	....	36	84	84	84	84	129	274	301	319	575
15. Michigan	....	....	....	....	44	89	138	138	174	206	238	238	270	270	270	342
16. Indiana	....	....	....	....	....	....	....	....	....	....	30	30	42	86	86	228
17. Illinois	....	....	....	....	....	....	22	22	22	22	22	22	22	22	52	111
18. Wisconsin	....	....	....	....	....	....	....	....	....	....	....	....	....	....	....	20
19. Minnesota	....	....	....	....	....	....	....	....	....	....	....	....	....	....	....	....
20. Iowa	....	....	....	....	....	....	....	....	....	....	....	....	....	....	....	....
21. Kansas	....	....	....	....	....	....	....	....	....	....	....	....	....	....	....	....
22. Missouri	....	....	....	....	....	....	....	....	....	....	....	....	....	....	....	....
23. Arkansas*	....	....	....	....	....	....	....	....	....	....	....	....	....	....	....	....
24. Tennessee*	....	....	....	....	....	....	....	....	....	....	....	....	....	....	....	....
Int'r States	15	22	22	22	69	117	285	369	405	437	499	544	733	804	879	1451
25. Virginia*	93	93	125	125	125	147	223	223	223	223	223	270	303	303	303	384
26. North Car.*	....	....	....	....	....	53	87	87	87	87	87	87	87	87	154	283
27. South Car.*	137	137	137	137	137	137	204	204	204	204	204	204	204	241	263	289
28. Georgia*	....	....	7	57	100	185	271	323	368	452	516	576	609	609	609	643
29. Florida*	....	....	....	....	....	....	....	....	....	....	....	38	38	38	21	21
30. Alabama*	46	46	46	46	46	46	46	46	46	46	46	46	46	91	133	183
31. Mississippi*	....	....	....	....	....	....	14	14	26	26	42	42	60	60	60	75
32. Louisiana*	40	40	40	40	40	40	40	40	40	40	40	40	40	66	66	80
33. Texas*	....	....	....	....	....	....	....	....	....	....	....	....	....	....	....	....
South'n States	316	316	355	405	448	608	885	937	994	1078	1158	1303	1387	1495	1609	1957
34. California	....	....	....	....	....	....	....	....	....	....	....	....	....	....	....	....
35. Oregon	....	....	....	....	....	....	....	....	....	....	....	....	....	....	....	....
Pacific States	....	....	....	....	....	....	....	....	....	....	....	....	....	....	....	....

Recapitulation.

States, etc.	1835	1836	1837	1838	1839	1840	1841	1842	1843	1844	1845	1846	1847	1848	1849	1850
N. E. States	113	139	190	254	322	527	589	811	865	865	973	1032	1225	1276	2073	2508
Mid. A. States	654	796	930	1232	1463	1566	1776	1909	1921	1997	2003	2051	2254	2421	2804	3105
Interior States	15	22	22	22	69	117	285	369	405	437	499	544	733	804	879	1451
South'rn States	316	316	355	405	448	608	885	937	994	1078	1158	1303	1387	1495	1609	1957
Pacific States	....	....	....	....	....	....	....	....	....	....	....	....	....	....	....	....
Grand Total	1098	1273	1497	1913	2302	2818	3535	4026	4185	4377	4633	4930	5599	5996	7365	9021

* We have no reliable data from these States since the year

IN THE UNITED STATES.

States at the end of each Year, from 1835 to 1864, both inclusive.

	1851	1852	1853	1854	1855	1856	1857	1858	1859	1860	1861	1862	1863	1·64
1	293	323	334	360	415	429	451	468	472	472	472	505	505	505
2	537	568	644	644	657	657	657	657	661	661	661	661	661	661
3	413	471	506	512	529	529	529	529	546	554	562	562	587	587
4	1038	1047	1105	1144	1264	1264	1264	1264	1264	1264	1264	1285	12·5	1285
5	68	68	68	94	108	108	108	108	108	108	108	108	125	125
6	451	496	496	496	496	590	590	590	601	601	630	630	630	630
	2800	2973	3153	3250	3469	3577	3599	3616	3652	3660	3697	3751	3798	3798
7	1623	2031	2387	2534	2583	2629	2661	2661	2679	2682	2700	2728	2792	2821
8	303	318	347	375	466	485	507	516	546	560	587	633	756	864
9	1297	1372	1404	1537	1800	1925	2081	2340	2442	2598	2802	2066	3371	3360
10	39	39	39	44	56	79	115	127	127	127	127	127	127	127
11	274	327	327	327	327	327	352	352	277	386	386	408	408	408
	3636	4087	4504	4817	5232	5445	5716	5996	6961	6354	6602	6902	7254	7580
12	159	241	241	241	241	241	352	352	352	352	361	361	361	361
13	94	94	167	242	242	263	305	453	534	534	549	567	567	567
14	588	756	1200	1317	1456	1807	1895	2651	2812	2946	2946	3101	3311	3311
15	379	431	431	444	474	591	602	642	737	779	810	853	898	898
16	558	756	1209	1317	1406	1807	1895	1995	2014	2168	2175	2175	2175	2195
17	271	412	759	788	887	2235	2502	2734	2781	2799	2917	2998	3156	3156
18	50	71	71	97	187	276	630	647	826	905	933	961	990	1010
19	......	......	......	......	......	......	......	......	......	......	......	......	31	157
20	......	......	......	....	68	254	344	379	533	655	701	731	792	805
21	......	......	......	......	......	......	......	......	......	......	......	......	......	40
22	......	......	38	38	139	144	318	547	724	817	838	838	868	925
23	......	......	......	......	......	......	......	......	......	38	38	38	38	38
24	112	185	291	329	466	541	770	888	963	1253	1253	1253	1253	1296
	2211	2946	4416	4813	5516	8074	9613	11,293	12,276	13,241	13,521	13,876	14,440	14,759
25	520	632	752	839	912	951	1137	1168	1301	1379	1379	1379	1379	1379
26	283	351	420	572	582	691	733	849	937	937	937	937	984	984
27	378	598	652	669	759	848	879	9 5	973	973	973	973	973	973
28	795	910	962	9 3	1020	1165	1242	1297	1371	1420	1420	1420	1420	1420
29	21	21	21	21	21	56	128	198	290	402	402	402	402	402
30	183	214	304	304	334	454	532	582	628	743	743	805	805	805
31	75	96	96	222	278	413	483	604	698	862	862	862	862	862
32	80	80	89	198	203	249	261	251	295	335	335	335	335	335
33	......	......	......	32	40	71	157	205	284	307	392	451	451	451
	2335	2902	3296	3840	4149	4898	5552	6040	6777	7357	7443	7564	7610	7610
34	......	......	......	......	8	23	23	23	23	23	23	23	53	147
35	......	......	......	......	......	......	......	......	......	......	......	4	19	19
	......	......	......	......	8	23	23	23	23	23	23	27	72	166

Recapitulation.

1851	1852	1853	1854	1855	1856	1857	1858	1859	1860	1861	1862	1863	1864
2800	2973	3153	3250	3469	3577	3599	3616	3652	3660	3697	3751	3798	3798
3636	4087	4504	4817	5232	5445	5716	5996	6061	6354	6602	6902	7254	7580
2211	2946	4416	4813	5516	8074	9613	11 293	12,276	13,241	13,521	13,876	14,440	14,759
2335	2902	3296	3840	4149	4898	5552	6040	6777	7357	7443	7564	7610	7610
......	......	......	......	8	23	23	23	23	23	23	27	72	166
10,982	12,908	15,369	16,720	18,374	22,017	24,503	26,968	28,789	30,685	31,286	32,120	33,169	33,908

1861; we therefore give the figures mainly of that year.

RAILROADS OF THE UNITED STATES.

Statement exhibiting the Mileage of Railroads in its relation to Area, Population, and Wealth, for each State and cluster of States, deduced from the official returns for the year 1860; also, the Average Dividends on Stock in 1860.

STATES.	Area in square miles.	Population: Census 1860.	Wealth: Census 1860.	Mileage of Railr'ds.	One mile of Railroad to			Average Dividends.
					Sq. miles	Population.	Wealth.	
Maine	31,765	628,279	$190,211,600	471.9	67.3	1331	$403,076	2.7
New Hampshire	9,280	326,073	156,310,860	661.0	14.0	493	236,476	2.8
Vermont	10,212	315,098	122,477,170	554.0	18.4	569	221,078	0.5
Massachusetts	7,800	1,231.066	815,237,433	1264.2	6.1	974	644,864	5.1
Rhode Island	1,306	174,620	135,337,588	107.9	12.1	1619	1,254.287	3.4
Connecticut	4,674	460,147	444,274,114	600.8	7.7	766	739,471	2.8
New Eng. States	65,038	3,135,283	$1,863,848,765	3659.8	17.9	857	$509,276	....
New York	47,000	3,880,735	1,843,338,517	2682.3	17.5	1447	687,223	4.1
New Jersey	8,320	672,035	467,918,324	560.3	14.9	1199	835,121	6.7
Pennsylvania	46,000	2,906,215	1,416,501,818	2598.4	17.7	1118	545,144	3.9
Delaware	2,120	112,216	46,242,181	126.8	16.7	885	864.686	5.1
Maryland & D. C.	11,184	762,129	417,204,889	386.3	29.0	1973	1,080,000	2.4
Mid. Atl'tic States	114,624	8,333,330	$4,191,205,729	6354.1	18.0	1311	659,606	....
West Virginia*	20,541	399,679	198,312,420	352.5	58.3	1132	562,588	2.0
Kentucky	37,680	1,155,684	666,043,112	533.7	70.8	2165	1,247,973	0.4
Ohio	39,964	2,339,511	1,193,898,422	2945 5	13.6	709	405 329	2.9
Michigan	56,243	749,113	257,163,983	779.2	72.2	961	330,036	
Indiana	33,809	1,350,428	528,835,371	2163.2	15.6	624	244,469	0.8
Illinois	55,405	1,711,951	871,860,282	2799.2	19.8	612	311,468	2.7
Wisconsin	53,924	775,881	273,671,668	904 6	59.6	857	302,583	....
Minnesota	83,531	172,023	52,294,413	....	..	...	....	....
Iowa	55,045	674,913	247,338,265	654.8	84.1	1031	377,731	....
Kansas	78,418	107,206	81,327,895	...	....	....	....	....
Missouri	67,380	1,182,012	501,214,398	817.5	82.4	1445	613,106	....
Arkansas	52,198	435,450	219,256,473	38.5	1355.7	11,310	5,694,973	....
Tennessee	45,000	1,109,801	493,903,892	1252.6	35.9	886	394.303	1.2
Interior States	679,138	12,163,052	$5,535,120,594	13,241.3	51.3	919	$418,034	....
Virginia	40,816	1,197,239	594,937,261	1378.7	29.6	868	431,521	1.3
North Carolina	50,704	992,622	358,739,399	937.4	54.1	1059	382,698	2.8
South Carolina	29 385	703,708	548,138,754	973.0	30.2	723	563,349	2.3
Georgia	52 009	1,057,286	645,895,237	1419.8	36.6	731	454,920	3.7
Florida	59,268	140,424	73,101,500	401.5	147.6	349	182,079	....
Alabama	50,722	964,201	495,237,078	742.7	68.3	1298	666,806	1.4
Mississippi	47,156	791,305	607,324,911	862 5	54.6	917	704,029	....
Louisiana	46,431	708,002	602,118,568	334.8	138 7	2115	1,798,442	0.9
Texas	237,504	604,215	365.200.614	306.5	774 8	1971	1,191,519	....
Southern States	613,995	7,159,002	$4,290,693,322	7356.9	83.4	973	$583,220	....
California	188,982	379 994	207,874,613	22.5	8390.3	16,888	9,238,871	....
Oregon	95,274	52,465	28,930,637	....	....	....	....	....
Pacific States	284,256	432,459	$236,805,250	22.5	12,633.8	19,220	$10,524,677	....
No'th-East'n States	65,038	3,135,283	1,863,848,765	3659.8	17.9	857	509,276	....
Mid. Atl'tic States.	114,624	8,333,330	4,191.205,729	6354.1	18.0	1311	659,606	....
Interior States	679,138	12,163,052	5,535,120,594	13,241.3	51.3	919	418,034	....
Southern States	613,995	7,159,002	4,290,693.322	7356.9	83.4	973	583,220	....
Pacific States	284,256	432,459	236,805,250	22.5	12.633 8	19,220	10,524.677	....
GRAND TOTAL	1,757,051	31,223,126	$16,117,673,660	30,634.6	57.3	1019	$526,126	....

* Embraces one-third the area, and one-fourth the population and wealth of Virginia as it was in 1860.

THE MONTHLY PRICE OF **Bar Iron** (ENGLISH) PER TON; FROM JANUARY, 1825, TO DECEMBER, 1864.

Year.	January.	February.	March.	April.	May.	June.	July.	August.	September.	October.	November.	December.
	$ $	$ $	$ $	$ $	$ $	$ $	$ $	$ $	$ $	$ $	$ $	$ $
1825	85 00*a* 90 00	85 00*a* 90 00	95 00*a*	105 00*a*110 00	115 00*a*120 00	115 00*a*120 00	115 00*a*120 00	115 00*a*	110 00*a*	105 00*a*110 00	105 00*a*110 00	100 00*a*105 00
1826	95 00*a*100 00	95 00*a*100 00	95 00*a*100 00	95 00*a*100 00	95 00*a*100 00	95 00*a*100 00	90 00*a*100 00	85 00*a* 95 00	85 00*a* 95 00	85 00*a* 90 00	90 00*a* 95 00	90 00*a* 95 00
1827	90 00*a* 95 00	85 00*a* 95 00	85 00*a* 95 00	85 00*a* 95 00	85 00*a* 95 00	85 00*a*	.... *a* 80 00	80 00*a* 82 50	77 00*a* 80 00	80 00*a* 82 50	.... *a*	80 00*a* 82 50
1828	.... *a* 82 50	.... *a* 82 50	.... *a* 82 50	80 00*a* 82 50	77 50*a* 80 00	77 50*a* 80 00	77 50*a* 80 00	77 50*a* 80 00	77 50*a* 80 00	77 50*a* 80 00	.... *a* 80 00	80 00*a* ....
1829	80 00*a*	80 00*a*	80 00*a* 82 50	80 00*a* 82 50	80 00*a* 82 50	80 00*a* 82 50	78 00*a* 80 00	78 00*a* 80 00	78 00*a* 80 00	78 00*a* 80 00	78 00*a* 80 00	72 50*a* 75 00
1830	72 50*a* 75 00	72 50*a* 75 00	72 00*a* 75 00	72 00*a* 75 00	... *a* 75 00	.... *a* 75 00	.... *a* 75 00	75 00*a* 77 50	75 00*a* 77 50	75 00*a* 77 50	75 00*a* 77 50	72 50*a* 75 00
1831	72 50*a* 80 00	72 50*a* 75 00	72 50*a* 75 00	70 00*a* 72 50	70 00*a* 72 50	72 50*a* 74 00	72 00*a* 74 00	72 00*a* 74 00	70 00*a* 72 00	70 00*a* 72 00	.... *a* 72 00	.... *a* 72 00
1832	.... *a* 72 00	.... *a* 72 00	72 00*a*	72 00*a* 75 00	72 00*a* 75 00	72 00*a* 75 00	71 00*a* 72 00	72 00*a* 73 00	72 00*a* 73 00	72 00*a* 73 00	70 00*a* 72 00	75 00*a* ....
1833	75 00*a* ...	75 00*a*	75 00*a*	.... *a* 75 00	.... *a* 75 00	.... *a* 75 00	.... *a* 75 00	.... *a* 75 00	73 00*a* 75 00	71 00*a* 75 00	72 50*a* 75 00	.... *a* 75 00
1834	.... *a* 75 00	.... *a* 75 00	.... *a* 75 00	.... *a* 75 00	72 50*a* 75 00	72 50*a* 73 00	70 00*a* 72 50	67 00*a* 69 00	67 00*a* 70 00	67 50*a* 70 00	67 50*a* 70 00	67 50*a* 70 00
1835	67 50*a* 70 00	.... *a* 70 00	.... *a* 70 00	67 50*a* 70 00	67 50*a* 70 00	67 50*a* 70 00	67 50*a* 70 00	67 50*a* 70 00	67 50*a* 70 00	67 50*a* 70 00	67 50*a* 70 00	72 50*a* 75 00
1836	.... *a* 75 00	75 00*a* 77 00	80 00*a* 85 00	.... *a*100 00	100 00*a*105 00	100 00*a*105 00	100 00*a*105 00	100 00*a*	97 50*a*100 00	92 50*a* 95 00	95 00*a* 97 50	97 50*a*100 00
*1837	97 50*a*100 00	97 50*a*100 00	.... *a*105 00	.... *a*105 00	.... *a*105 00	.... *a*105 00	92 50*a* 95 00	.... *a* 90 00	.... *a* 85 00	85 00*a* 90 00	85 00*a* 90 00	85 00*a* 90 00
*1838	85 00*a* 90 00	87 50*a* 92 50	87 50*a* 92 50	87 50*a* 97 50	87 50*a* 92 50	87 50*a* 90 00	87 50*a* 90 00	85 00*a* 87 50	85 00*a* 87 50	85 00*a* 87 50	85 00*a* 87 50	85 00*a* 87 50
1839	87 50*a* 90 00	... *a* 92 50	95 00*a*	95 00*a*	.... *a* 90 00	87 50*a* 90 00	87 50*a* 90 00	87 50*a* 90 00	82 50*a* 85 00	82 50*a* 85 00	82 50*a* 85 00	82 50*a* ....
1840	82 50*a*	80 00*a* 82 50	.... *a* 80 00	75 00*a* 77 50	72 50*a* 75 00	72 50*a* 75 00	72 50*a* 75 00	70 00*a* 72 50	70 00*a* 72 50	70 00*a* 72 50	72 50*a* 75 00	72 50*a* 75 00
1841	72 50*a* 75 00	72 50*a* 75 00	72 50*a* 75 00	72 50*a* 75 00	72 50*a* 75 00	68 50*a* 70 00	62 50*a* 65 00	62 50*a* 65 00	65 00*a*	65 00*a*	62 00*a* 65 00	60 00*a* 62 50
1842	60 00*a* 62 50	60 00*a* 62 50	57 50*a* 60 00	57 50*a* 60 00	.... *a* 55 00	.... *a* 55 00	52 50*a* 55 00	50 00*a* 52 50	52 50*a* 55 00	57 50*a* 60 00	57 50*a* 60 00	57 50*a* 60 00
1843	57 50*a* 60 00	57 50*a* 60 00	57 50*a* 60 00	57 50*a* 60 00	55 00*a* 57 50	.... *a* 55 00	.... *a* 55 00	.... *a* 55 00	.... *a* 55 00	... *a* 57 50	.... *a* 57 50	.... *a* 57 50
1844	.... *a* 57 50	.... *a* 57 50	57 50*a* 60 00	.... *a* 57 50	57 50*a* 60 00	62 50*a* 65 00	62 50*a* 65 00	62 50*a* 65 00	62 00*a* 65 00	62 50*a* 65 00	62 50*a* 65 00	62 50*a* 65 00
1845	62 50*a* 65 00	62 50*a* 65 00	70 00*a*	77 50*a* 80 00	80 00*a* 85 00	77 50*a* 80 00	77 50*a* 80 00	75 00*a*	72 50*a* 75 00	72 50*a* 75 00	.... *a* 77 50	77 50*a* 80 00
1846	77 50*a* 80 00	77 50*a* 80 00	77 50*a* 80 00	77 50*a* 80 00	77 50*a* 80 00	77 50*a*	77 50*a*	77 50*a*	77 50*a*	75 00*a* 77 50	75 00*a* 77 50	75 00*a* 77 50
1847	75 00*a* 77 50	75 00*a* 77 50	70 00*a* 72 50	70 00*a* 72 50	70 00*a* 72 50	72 50*a* 75 00	72 50*a* 75 00	72 50*a* 75 00	70 00*a*	70 00*a*	70 00*a*	70 00*a* ....
1848	70 00*a*	70 00*a*	65 00*a* 67 50	65 00*a* 67 50	60 00*a*	57 50*a*	57 50*a*	52 50*a* 55 00	52 50*a*	52 50*a*	52 50*a*	50 00*a* ....
1849	50 00*a*	50 00*a*	50 00*a*	55 00*a*	55 00*a*	48 50*a* 50 00	40 00*a* 42 50	.... *a* 42 50	.... *a* 42 50	.... *a* 42 50	42 50*a* 45 00	42 50*a* 45 00
1850	42 50*a* 45 00	42 50*a* 45 00	42 50*a* 45 00	42 50*a* 45 00	42 50*a* 45 00	40 00*a* 42 50	40 00*a* 42 50	40 00*a* 42 50	40 00*a* ...	40 00*a*	40 00*a*	40 00*a* ....
1851	40 00*a* 41 00	40 00*a* 41 00	40 00*a* 41 00	40 00*a* 41 00	36 00*a* 37 00	36 00*a* 37 00	34 00*a* 35 00	34 00*a* 35 00	32 50*a* 33 50	33 00*a* 33 50	33 00*a* 33 50	34 00*a* 35 00
1852	34 00*a* 35 00	34 50*a* 35 00	34 00*a* 35 00	34 00*a* 35 00	34 00*a* 35 00	34 00*a* 35 00	37 50*a* 38 00	38 00*a* 40 00	40 00*a* 42 58	44 00*a* 45 00	53 00*a* 55 00	53 00*a* 55 00
1853	65 00*a* 70 00	65 00*a* 73 00	73 00*a* 75 00	65 00*a* 67 50	65 00*a* 70 00	60 00*a* 63 00	55 00*a* 57 50	55 00*a* 60 00	65 00*a* 67 50	65 00*a* 67 50	65 00*a* 67 50	62 50*a* 65 00
1854	65 00*a* 70 00	67 50*a* 70 00	.... *a* 72 50	.... *a* 75 00	75 00*a* 77 50	70 00*a* 72 00	70 00*a* 73 50	70 00*a* 73 50	70 00*a* 73 50	70 00*a* 73 50	70 00*a* 73 50	62 50*a* 65 00
1855	57 50*a* 60 00	57 50*a* 60 00	57 50*a* 60 00	55 00*a* 57 50	55 00*a* 60 00	50 00*a* 55 00	55 00*a* 57 50	57 50*a* 60 00	60 00*a* 62 50	62 50*a* 65 00	62 50*a* 65 00	55 00*a* 57 50
1856	60 00*a* 61 00	60 00*a* 61 00	60 00*a* 62 50	62 50*a* 65 00	62 50*a* 65 00	62 00*a* 62 50	60 00*a* 62 50	50 00*a* 60 00	55 00*a* 57 00	55 00*a* 57 00	57 50*a* 60 00	53 00*a* 55 00
*1857	55 00*a* 57 50	56 00*a* 58 00	60 00*a* 62 00	61 00*a* 62 50	61 00*a* 62 50	55 00*a* 56 00	52 00*a*	.... *a* 55 00	52 00*a* 54 00	53 50*a*	.... *a* 53 50	.... *a* 53 50
1858	52 50*a* 55 00	52 50*a* 55 00	52 50*a* 55 00	47 50*a* 50 00	45 00*a* 47 50	45 00*a* 49 50	45 00*a* 46 50	45 00*a* 46 50	45 00*a* 46 00	44 00*a* 45 00	45 00*a* 46 00	46 00*a* 47 00
1859	46 00*a* 47 00	48 00*a* 50 00	47 50*a* 48 00	47 50*a* 48 00	47 00*a* 47 50	44 00*a* 45 00	44 00*a* 45 00	43 00*a* 45 00	43 00*a* 45 00	43 00*a* 45 00	43 00*a* 44 00	42 50*a* 43 00
1860	42 00*a* 42 50	43 50*a* 44 00	42 00*a* 43 00	43 00*a* 43 50	41 00*a* 42 50	41 00*a* 42 50	41 00*a* 42 50	41 00*a* 42 50	42 50*a* 43 00	42 50*a* 43 00	42 00*a* 43 00	42 00*a* 43 00
1861	40 00*a* 42 50	38 00*a* 40 00	38 00*a* 40 00	46 00*a* 47 50	44 00*a* 45 00	44 00*a* 45 00	43 00*a* 44 00	43 00*a* 44 00	43 00*a* 44 00	45 00*a* 47 50	45 00*a* 47 50	47 50*a* 50 00
*1862	.... *a*	.... *a*	50 00*a*	52 50*a* 55 00	52 50*a* 55 00	52 50*a* 57 50	52 50*a* 57 50	... *a* 65 00	.... *a* 65 00	57 50*a* 60 00	65 00*a*	67 50*a* 70 00
*1863	75 00*a* 67 50	75 00*a*	.... *a*	.... *a*	... *a*	76 00*a*	76 00*a*	73 00*a* 75 00	73 00*a* 75 00	72 50*a* 75 00	.... *a*	.... *a* ....
*1864	105 00*a*	120 00*a*	115 00*a*116 00	105 00*a*	.... *a*	.... *a*	.... *a*190 00	205 00*a*220 00	205 00*a*220 00	185 00*a*200 00	175 00*a*190 00	175 00*a*190 00

* Years of bank suspension.

THE MONTHLY PRICES OF **Pig Copper** PER POUND, AT NEW YORK; FROM JANUARY, 1825, TO DECEMBER, 1864.

Year.	January.	February.	March.	April.	May.	June.	July.	August.	September.	October.	November.	December.
	cts. cts.	cts. cts.	cts. cts.	cts. cts.	cts. cts.	cts. cts.	cts. cts.	cts. cts.	cts. cts.	cts. cts.	cts. cts.	cts. cts.
1825	17 a 18	17 a 18	17 a 18	17 a 18	18 a 19	18 a 19	22 a 23	22 a 23	22 a 23	21 a 22	21 a 22	21 a 22
1826	20 a 21	20 a 21	20 a 21	20 a 21	17 a 18	17 a 18	17 a 18	17 a 18	17 a 18	17 a 18	17 a 18	17 a 18
1827	17 a ...	17 a	17 a	17 a	17 a	17 a	19 a 20	18 a 19	18 a 19	18 a 19	18 a 19	19 a 20
1828	19 a 20	19 a 20	19 a 20	18 a 19	18 a 19	17 a 18	17 a 28	17 a 18	17 a 18	17 a 18	17 a 18	17 a 18
1829	17 a 18	17 a 18	17 a 18	18 a 19	18 a 19	18 a 19	18 a 19	18 a 19	18 a 19	18 a 19	18 a 19	18 a 19
1830	18 a 19	18 a 19	18 a 19	18 a 19	18 a 19	18 a 19	17 a 18	16 a 17	16 a 17	16 a 17	17 a 18	17 a 18
1831	17 a 18	17 a 18	17 a 18	17 a 18	17 a 18	17 a 18	17 a 18	18 a 19	18 a 19	18 a 19	18 a 19	18 a 19
1832	18 a 19	18 a 19	18 a 19	18 a 19	18 a 9	18 a 19	16 a 17	16 a 17	16 a 17	17 a 18	17 a 18	16 a 17
1833	16 a 17	16 a 17	16 a 17	16 a 17	16 a 17	16 a 17	16 a 17	16 a 17	16 a 17	16 a 17	16 a 17	17 a 18
1834	16 a 17	16 a 17	16 a 17	16 a 17	16 a 17	16 a 17	16 a 17	16 a 17	16 a 17	15 a 16	15 a 16	15 a 16
1835	15 a 16	15 a 16	15 a 16	16 a 17	16 a 17	16 a 17	16 a 17	16 a 17	16 a 17	16 a 17	17 a 18	17 a 18
1836	18 a 19	18 a 19	18 a 19	20 a 21	21 a 22	21 a 22	21 a 22	21 a 22	21 a 22	21 a 22	21 a 22	21 a 22
1837	21 a 22	21 a 22	21 a 22	21 a 22	20 a 21	16 a 17	16 a 17	16 a 17	16 a 17	17 a 18	17 a 18	17 a 18
1838	17 a 18	17 a 18	17 a 18	17 a 18	16 a 17	16 a 17	16 a 17	16 a 17	16 a 17	16 a 17	17 a 18	17 a 18
1839	17 a 18	17 a 18	17 a 18	16 a 17	16 a 17	16 a 17	16 a 17	17 a 18	17 a 18	17 a 18	17 a 18	17 a 18
1840	17 a 18	17 a 18	17 a 18	18 a 19	18 a 19	18 a 19	18 a 19	18 a 19	18 a 19	18 a 19	19 a 20	18 a 19
1841	17 a 18	18 a 19	18 a 19	18 a 19	18 a 19	18 a 19	17 a 18	17 a 18	17 a 18	17 a 18	17 a 18	17 a 18
1842	17 a 18	17 a 18	17 a 18	17 a 18	17 a 18	17 a 18	17 a ...	17 a	16 a 17	16 a 17	17 a 18	16 a 17
1843	16 a 17	17 a 18	17 a 18	17 a 18	17 a 18	17 a 18	16 a 17	16 a 17	16 a 17	16 a 17	16 a 17	16 a 17
1844	17 a 18	17 a 18	17 a 18	17 a 18	17 a 18	17 a 18	17 a 18	16 a 17	17 a 18	17 a 18	17 a 18	17 a 18
1845	17 a 18	17 a 18	17 a 18	17 a 18	17 a 18	17 a 18	17 a 18	17 a 18	17 a 17	17 a 18	16 a 17	16 a 17
1846	16 a 17	16 a 17	16 a 17	16 a 17	18 a 19	18 a 19	18 a 19	18 a 19	18 a 19	18 a 19	18 a 19	18 a 19
1847	18 a 19	18 a 19	18 a 19	18 a 19	18 a 19	18 a 19	18 a 19	18 a 19	17 a 18	17 a 18	17 a 18	17 a 18
1848	17 a 18	17 a 18	17 a 18	18 a 19	18 a 19	18 a 19	18 a 19	18 a 19	18 a 19	18 a 19	17 a 18	17 a 18
1849	17 a 18	17 a 18	17 a 18	17 a 18	17 a 18	17 a 18	17 a 18	17 a 18	16 a 17	16 a 17	16 a 17	16 a 17
1850	16 a 17	16 a 17	16 a 17	17 a 18	17 a 18	17 a 18	17 a 18	17 a 18	17 a 18	17 a 18	17 a 18	17 a 18
1851	17 a 18	17 a 18	17 a 18	17 a 18	17 a 18	17 a 18	17 a 18	17 a 18	17 a 18	17 a 18	17 a 18	17 a 18
1852	17 a 18	18 a 19	18 a 19	18 a 19	18 a 19	18 a 19	19 a 20	19 a 20	20 a 21	21 a 22	21 a 22	21 a 22
1853	23 a	23 a	... a	.... a	.... a	.... a	.... a	25 a	.... a	.... a	.... a	.... a ....
1854	.... a	30 a 31	30 a 31	30 a	29 a ..	29 a	29 a	29 a	29 a	29 a ...	28 a 29	.... a ....
1855	24 a 25	24 a 25	24 a 25	24 a 25	24 a 25	24 a	23 a	23 a ...	.... a 25	.... a 25	.... a 25	.. a 25
1856	24 a 25	24 a 25	26 a 28	26 a 28	26 a 28	26 a 18	26 a	25 a 26	23 a 24	23 a 24	23 a 24	23 a 24
1857	.... a	.... a 28	... a 27	.... a 27	26 a	26 a	24 a ...	24 a	23 a 24	.... a 22	23 a	23 a ....
1858	23 a 24	23 a 24	23 a 24	24 a 25	22 a 28	22 a ...	.... a	.... a	.... a	.... a	.... a	.... a ....
1859	.... a	.... a	.... a	.... a	... a	.... a	.... a	.... a	.... a	.... a	.... a	.... a ....
1860	.... a	.... a ...	.... a	.... a	.... a	.... a	.... a	.... a	.... a	.... a	.... a	.. a ....
1861	.... a	.... a	.... a	... a	.... a	.... a	.. a	.... a ..	.... a	.... a	.... a	.... a ....
1862	.... a	.... a ...	.... a	.... a	.... a	.... a ...	.... a	.... a	.... a ...	.... a	.... a	.... a ...
1863	.... a	.... a	.... a ...	.... a	.... a	.... a	.... a ..	.... a	.... a	.... a	.... a	.... a ....
1864	37¾ a 39	40¼ a 42	40¾ a 42	40½ a 42½	43 a 44	43 a 44	46½ a 50	50¾ a 53	50½ a 53	47 a 47½	47½ a 48	48½ a 50

THE MONTHLY PRICES OF **Sheet Iron** AT NEW YORK; FROM JANUARY, 1825, TO DECEMBER, 1864.

Year.	January.	February.	March.	April.	May.	June.	July.	August.	September.	October.	November.	December.
	$ $	$ $	$ $	$ $	$ $	$ $	$ $	$ $	$ $	$ $	$ $	$ $
1825	6 50 *a* 8 00	6 50 *a* 8 00	6 50 *a* 8 00	7 50 *a* 9 00	7 50 *a* 9 00	7 50 *a* 9 00	7 50 *a* 9 00	7 50 *a* 9 00	7 50 *a* 9 00	7 50 *a* 9 00	7 50 *a* 9 00	7 50 *a* 8 75
1826	7 50 *a* 8 75	7 50 *a* 8 75	7 50 *a* 8 75	7 50 *a* 8 75	7 50 *a* 8 75	7 50 *a* 8 75	7 50 *a* 8 75	7 50 *a* 8 75	7 50 *a* 8 75	7 50 *a* 8 75	8 75 *a*10 00	8 75 *a*10 00
1827	8 75 *a*10 00	7 75 *a* 9 00	7 00 *a* 8 00	8 00 *a* 9 00	8 00 *a* 9 00	6 50 *a* 7 50	6 50 *a* 7 50	6 50 *a* 7 50	6 50 *a* 7 50	6 50 *a* 7 00	6 50 *a* 7 00	6 50 *a* 7 00
1828	6 50 *a* 7 00	6 50 *a* 7 00	6 50 *a* 7 00	6 50 *a* 7 00	6 50 *a* 7 00	6 50 *a* 7 00	6 70 *a* 8 00	6 75 *a* 8 00	6 75 *a* 8 00	6 75 *a* 8 00	6 75 *a* 8 00	6 75 *a* 8 00
1829	6 75 *a* 8 00	6 75 *a* 8 00	6 75 *a* 8 00	6 75 *a* 8 00	6 75 *a* 8 00	6 75 *a* 8 00	6 75 *a* 8 00	6 75 *a* 8 00	6 75 *a* 8 00	6 75 *a* 8 00	6 75 *a* 8 00	6 75 *a* 8 00
1830	6 75 *a* 8 00	6 75 *a* 8 00	6 75 *a* 8 00	6 75 *a* 8 00	6 75 *a* 8 00	6 75 *a* 8 00	6 75 *a* 8 00	6 75 *a* 8 00	6 75 *a* 8 00	6 75 *a* 8 00	6 75 *a* 8 00	6 75 *a* 8 00
1831	6 75 *a* 8 00	6 75 *a* 8 00	6 75 *a* 8 00	6 75 *a* 8 00	6 75 *a* 8 00	6 75 *a* 8 00	6 75 *a* 8 00	6 75 *a* 8 00	6 75 *a* 8 00	6 75 *a* 8 00	6 75 *a* 8 00	6 75 *a* 8 00
1832	6 75 *a* 8 00	6 75 *a* 8 00	6 75 *a* 8 00	6 75 *a* 8 00	6 75 *a* 8 00	6 75 *a* 8 00	6 75 *a* 8 00	6 75 *a* 8 00	6 75 *a* 8 00	6 75 *a* 8 00	6 75 *a* 8 00	6 75 *a* 8 00
1833	6 75 *a* 8 00	6 75 *a* 8 00	6 75 *a* 8 00	6 75 *a* 7 50	6 75 *a* 7 50	6 75 *a* 7 50	6 75 *a* 7 50	6 75 *a* 7 50	6 75 *a* 7 50	6 75 *a* 7 50	6 25 *a* 6 75	6 25 *a* 6 75
*1834	03¼ *a* 03¾	03¼ *a* 03¾	03¼ *a* 03¾	03¼ *a* 03¾	03¼ *a* 03¾	03¼ *a* 03¾	03¼ *a* 03¾	03¼ *a* 03¾	03¼ *a* 03¾	03¼ *a* 03¾	03¼ *a* 03¾	03¼ *a* 03¾
1835	.... *a*	.... *a*	.... *a*	.... *a*	.... *a*	.... *a*	.... *a*	.... *a*	.... *a*	.... *a*	.... *a*	.... *a* ....
1836	06 *a*	06 *a*	06 *a*	06 *a*	07 *a* 08	07 *a* 08	07 *a* 08	07 *a* 08	07 *a* 08	07 *a* 08	07 *a* 08	07 *a* 08
1837	07 *a* 08	07 *a* 08	07 *a* 08	07 *a* 08	07 *a* 08	07 *a* 08	07 *a*	07 *a*	07 *a*	07 *a*	07 *a*	07 *a* ....
1838	07 *a* 08	07 *a* 08	06 *a* 07	06 *a* 07	06 *a* 07	06 *a* 07	06 *a* 07	06 *a* 07	06 *a* 07	06 *a* 07	06 *a* 07	06 *a* 07
1839	06 *a* 07	06 *a* 07	06 *a* 07	06 *a* 07	06 *a* 07	06 *a* 07	06 *a* 07	06 *a* 07	06 *a* 07	06 *a* 07	06 *a* 07	06 *a* 07
1840	06 *a* 07	06 *a* 07	06 *a* 07	06 *a* 07	06 *a* 07	06 *a* 07	06 *a* 07	06 *a* 07	06 *a* 07	06 *a* 07	06 *a* 07	06 *a* 07
1841	06 *a* 07	06 *a* 07	06 *a* 07	06 *a* 07	06 *a* 07	06 *a* 07	06 *a* 07	06 *a* 07	06 *a* 07	06 *a* 07	06 *a* 07	06 *a* 07
1842	13 *a* 14	13 *a* 14	13 *a* 14	13 *a* 14	13 *a* 14	13 *a* 14	13 *a* 14	13 *a* 14	13 *a* 14	13 *a* 14	13 *a* 14	13 *a* 14
1843	11 *a* 12	11 *a* 12	11 *a* 12	11 *a* 12	11 *a* 12	11 *a* 12	12 *a* 13	13 *a*	13 *a* 14	13 *a* 14	.... *a* 13	12 *a* 13
1844	05 *a* 06	05 *a* 06	05 *a* 06	05 *a* 06	05 *a* 06	05 *a* 06	05 *a* 06	05 *a* 06	05 *a* 06	05 *a* 06	05 *a* 06	05 *a* 06
1845	11 *a* 12	11 *a* 12	11 *a* 12	11 *a* 12	11 *a* 12	11 *a* 12	11 *a* 12	12 *a* 13	12 *a* 13	11 *a* 12	11 *a* 12	11 *a* 12
1846	12 *a* 12	11 *a* 12	11 *a* 12	11 *a* 12	11 *a* 12	11 *a* 12	11 *a* 12	11 *a* 12	11 *a* 12	11 *a* 12	11 *a* 12	11 *a* 12
1847	11 *a* 12	11 *a* 12	11 *a* 12	12 *a*	11 *a* 12	11 *a* 12	11 *a* 12	11 *a* 12	11 *a* 12	11 *a* 12	11 *a* 12	11 *a* 12
1848	11 *a* 12	11 *a* 12	11 *a* 12	11 *a* 12	11 *a* 12	11 *a* 12	11 *a* 12	11 *a* 12	11 *a* 12	12 *a* 13	12 *a* 13	12 *a* 13
1849	12 *a* 13	12 *a* 13	12 *a* 13	12 *a* 13	12 *a* 13	12 *a* 13	12 *a* 13	12 *a* 13	13 *a* 14	13 *a* 14	13 *a* 14	13 *a* 14
1850	13 *a* 14	13 *a* 14	13 *a* 14	13 *a* 14	13 *a* 14	13 *a* 14	13 *a* 14	13 *a* 14	13 *a* 14	13 *a* 14	13 *a* 14	13 *a* 14
1851	13 *a* 14	13 *a* 14	13 *a* 14	13 *a* 14	13 *a* 14	13 *a* 14	13 *a* 14	13 *a* 14	13 *a* 14	13 *a* 14	13 *a* 14	10 *a* 11
1852	10 *a* 11	10 *a* 11	10 *a* 11	10 *a* 11	10 *a* 11	10 *a* 11	10 *a* 11	10 *a* 11	11 *a* 12	11 *a* 12	11 *a* 12	11 *a* 12
1853	11 *a*	11 *a* ...	11 *a*	11 *a*	11 *a*	11 *a*	11 *a*	11 *a* 12	11 *a* 12	11 *a* 12	11 *a* 12	11 *a* 12
1854	11 *a*	11 *a*	11 *a*	11 *a*	13 *a*	13 *a* ...	13 *a*	13 *a*	14 *a* 15	14 *a* 15	13 *a* 14	13 *a* ...
1855	13 *a*	13 *a*	13 *a* 14	15 *a* 16	14 *a* 15	15 *a* 17	15 *a* 17	15 *a* 17	15 *a* 17	15 *a* 22	15 *a* 22	15 *a* 22
1856	15 *a* 22	15 *a* 22	15 *a* 22	18 *a*	18 *a*	17 *a* ...	13 *a* 14	13 *a* 14	11 *a*	12 *a*	13 *a*	13 *a* ....
1857	13 *a*	13 *a*	13 *a*	13 *a*	13 *a*	13 *a*	12 *a*	11 *a*	11 *a*	11 *a*	11 *a*	11 *a* ....
1858	11 *a*	11 *a*	11 *a*	11 *a*	... *a*	.... *a*	11 *a* 12	12 *a* 14	12 *a* 14	13 *a*	11 *a*	11 *a* ....
1859	11 *a*	11 *a*	10 *a* 11	10 *a* 11	10 *a* 11	10 *a* 11	10 *a* 11	11 *a*	11 *a* 12	11 *a*	11 *a*	11 *a* ....
1860	11 *a*	11 *a*	11 *a*	12 *a*	12 *a* 13	13 *a*	14 *a*	14 *a* 15	14 *a*	14 *a* 15	15 *a* 16	15 *a* 16
1861	16 *a* 17	16 *a* 17	16 *a* 17	16 *a*	16 *a*	16 *a*	16 *a*	16 *a*	16 *a*	16 *a*	16 *a*	15 *a* ....
1862	13 *a*	16 *a* 17	15 *a* 16	15 *a* 16	15 *a* 16	15 *a* 16	15 *a* 16	16 *a* 17	16 *a* 17	14 *a* 15	16 *a* 17	16 *a* 17
1863	16 *a* 17	16 *a* 17	.... *a*	.... *a* ...	.... *a*	... *a*	.... *a*	17 *a* 18	17 *a* 18	17 *a* 18	17 *a* 18	17 *a* 18
1864	.... *a* 21½	.... *a*	.... *a* ...	24 *a* 28	25 *a* 39	25 *a* 30	... *a*	33 *a* 40	32 *a* 34	29 *a* 32	28 *a* 31	30 *a* 33

* From this date per pound.

THE MONTHLY PRICE OF **Anthracite Coal** AT NEW YORK, PER TON; FROM JANUARY, 1825, TO DECEMBER, 1864.

Year.	January.	February.	March.	April.	May.	June.	July.	August.	September.	October.	November.	December.
	$ $	$ $	$ $	$ $	$ $	$ $	$ $	$ $	$ $	$ $	$ $	$ $
1825	9 00 *a* 11 00	9 00 *a* 10 00	9 00 *a* 10 00	8 00 *a* 10 00	8 00 *a* 10 00	8 00 *a* 10 00	8 00 *a* 10 00	8 00 *a* 10 00	8 00 *a* 10 00	8 00 *a* 10 00	8 00 *a* 10 00	8 00 *a* 10 00
1826	12 00 *a*	.... *a*	.... *a*	.... *a*	.... *a*	11 00 *a*	11 00 *a*	11 00 *a*	11 00 *a*	11 00 *a*	11 00 *a* ...	12 00 *a* ...
1827	12 00 *a*	12 00 *a* 12 50	12 00 *a* 12 50	12 00 *a*	11 00 *a*	11 00 *a*	11 00 *a*	11 00 *a*	11 00 *a*	10 50 *a* 11 00	10 50 *a* 11 00	.... *a* 11 00
1828	11 00 *a* 12 00	11 00 *a* 12 00	11 00 *a*	11 00 *a*	11 00 *a*	11 00 *a*	11 00 *a*	11 00 *a*	10 50 *a*	10 00 *a*	10 00 *a*	11 00 *a* 12 00
1829	11 00 *a* 12 00	.... *a* 12 00	.... *a* 12 00	.... *a*	.... *a* 11 00	10 00 *a*	10 00 *a*	10 00 *a*	10 00 *a*	10 00 *a* 11 00	10 00 *a* 11 00	10 00 *a* 11 00
1830	.... *a* 12 00	11 00 *a* 12 00	10 00 *a* 11 00	8 75 *a* 9 00	8 75 *a* 9 00	8 75 *a* 9 00	8 00 *a* 9 00	8 00 *a* 9 00	8 00 *a* 9 00	7 00 *a* 8 00	7 00 *a* 8 00	7 00 *a* 8 00
1831	7 00 *a* 8 00	7 00 *a* 9 00	7 00 *a* 9 00	7 00 *a* 9 00	6 00 *a* 7 00	6 00 *a* 7 00	6 00 *a* 7 00	6 00 *a* 7 00	6 00 *a* 7 00	6 00 *a* 7 00	6 00 *a* 7 00	7 50 *a* 8 50
1832	10 00 *a* 15 00	10 00 *a* 14 00	13 00 *a* 16 00	10 00 *a* 11 00	10 00 *a* 11 00	8 50 *a* 10 00	7 50 *a* 9 00	7 50 *a* 9 00	7 50 *a* 10 00	8 50 *a* 10 00	9 00 *a* 10.00	8 50 *a* 10 00
1833	8 50 *a* 10 00	8 00 *a* 9 00	6 50 *a* 9 00	6 50 *a* 9 00	6 00 *a* 7 00	6 00 *a* 7 00	6 00 *a* 7 00	5 50 *a* 6 25	5 50 *a* 6 25	5 50 *a* 6 25	5 50 *a* 6 00	5 50 *a* 6 00
1834	5 50 *a* 6 50	5 50 *a* 6 50	5 50 *a* 6 50	5 50 *a* 6 50	5 50 *a* 6 50	5 50 *a* 6 50	5 50 *a* 6 50	5 50 *a* 6 50	5 50 *a* 6 50	5 50 *a* 6 50	5 50 *a* 6 50	5 50 *a* 6 50
1835	5 50 *a* 6 50	6 00 *a* 7 00	6 00 *a* 7 00	6 00 *a* 7 00	6 00 *a* 7 00	6 00 *a* 7 50	6 00 *a* 7 50	6 00 *a* 7 50	6 00 *a* 7 50	6 00 *a* 7 50	6 00 *a* 7 50	7 00 *a* 9 00
1836	7 00 *a* 9 00	7 00 *a* 9 00	8 00 *a* 10 00	8 00 *a* 10 00	.... *a*	7 00 *a* 8 00	7 00 *a* 8 00	7 00 *a* 8 00	8 00 *a* 9 00	8 00 *a* 9 00	9 00 *a* 10 00	10 00 *a* 11 00
1837	10 00 *a* 11 00	10 00 *a* 11 00	10 00 *a* 11 00	10 00 *a* 11 00	10 00 *a* 11 00	.... *a*	8 50 *a* 9 50	8 50 *a* 9 50	8 50 *a* 9 50	8 50 *a* 9 50	8 50 *a* 9 50	8 50 *a* 9 50
1838	8 50 *a* 9 50	7 00 *a* 8 50	7 00 *a* 8 50	7 00 *a* 8 50	7 00 *a* 8 50	7 00 *a* 8 50	7 00 *a* 8 50	7 00 *a* 8 50	7 00 *a* 8 50	7 00 *a* 8 50	7 00 *a* 8 50	7 50 *a* 9 00
1839	7 50 *a* 9 00	7 50 *a* 9 00	7 50 *a* 9 00	7 50 *a* 9 00	7 50 *a* 9 00	7 50 *a* 9 00	7 50 *a* 9 00	7 50 *a* 9 00	7 50 *a* 9 00	7 50 *a* 8 50	6 50 *a* 8 50	6 50 *a* 8 50
1840	6 50 *a* 8 50	6 50 *a* 8 50	6 50 *a* 8 50	6 50 *a* 8 50	6 50 *a* 8 00	6 50 *a* 7 50	6 00 *a* 6 50	6 00 *a* 6 50	6 00 *a* 7 50	6 50 *a* 7 50	6 50 *a* 8 00	7 00 *a* 9 00
1841	7 00 *a* 9 00	8 00 *a* 9 00	6 50 *a* 8 00	6 50 *a* 8 00	6 50 *a* 8 00	6 00 *a* 7 50	5 00 *a* 7 00	6 50 *a* 8 00	7 00 *a* 8 50	7 00 *a* 8 50	8 00 *a* 9 00	8 00 *a* 9 00
1842	8 00 *a* 9 00	6 50 *a* 8 50	6 25 *a* 8 00	6 00 *a* 7 50	5 25 *a* 7 00	5 50 *a* 7 00	5 50 *a* 7 00	5 00 *a* 5 50	5 00 *a* 5 50	5 50 *a* 6 50	5 00 *a* 6 00	5 00 *a* 6 50
1843	5 00 *a* 6 50	4 50 *a* 6 00	4 50 *a* 5 50	4 50 *a* 6 00	4 50 *a* 6 00	4 50 *a* 5 25	4 50 *a* 5 00	4 50 *a* 5 00	4 75 *a* 5 50	4 50 *a* 5 25	4 50 *a* 5 50	5 00 *a* 6 00
1844	5 00 *a* 5 50	5 00 *a* 5 50	5 00 *a* 5 50	4 75 *a* 5 50	4 50 *a* 5 50	4 25 *a* 5 25	4 25 *a* 5 25	4 25 *a* 5 25	4 50 *a* 5 50	4 50 *a* 5 50	4 50 *a* 5 75	5 00 *a* 6 00
1845	5 00 *a* 6 00	5 00 *a* 6 00	5 00 *a* 6 00	5 00 *a* 6 00	5 00 *a* 6 00	4 50 *a* 5 50	4 50 *a* 5 50	4 50 *a* 5 50	4 50 *a* 5 50	5 00 *a* 6 00	5 00 *a* 6 00	5 00 *a* 6 00
1846	5 00 *a* 6 00	5 50 *a* 6 50	5 50 *a* 6 00	5 00 *a* 6 00	5 00 *a* 6 00	5 00 *a* 6 00	5 00 *a* 6 00	5 50 *a* 6 00	5 00 *a* 6 00	5 00 *a* 6 00	6 00 *a* 6 50	6 00 *a* 7 00
1847	6 00 *a* 7 00	6 00 *a* 7 00	6 00 *a* 6 50	5 50 *a* 6 00	5 00 *a* 6 00	5 00 *a* 6 00	5 00 *a* 5 50	5 00 *a* 5 50	5 00 *a* 5 50	5 00 *a* 5 50	5 50 *a* 6 00	5 50 *a* 6 00
1848	5 50 *a* 6 00	5 50 *a* 6 00	5 50 *a* 6 00	5 50 *a* 6 00	5 50 *a* 6 00	5 50 *a* 6 00	5 50 *a* 6 00	4 50 *a* 5 25	4 50 *a* 5 00	4 75 *a* 5 25	4 50 *a* 5 25	4 75 *a* 5 25
1849	5 00 *a* 5 50	5 00 *a* 6 00	5 00 *a* 6 00	5 00 *a* 6 00	5 00 *a* 6 00	5 00 *a* 6 00	5 00 *a* 6 00	5 50 *a* 6 00	5 50 *a* 6 00	5 50 *a* 6 00	5 62 *a* 6 00	5 50 *a* 6 00
1850	5 50 *a* 6 00	5 50 *a* 6 00	5 50 *a* 6 00	5 50 *a*	5 50 *a*	5 50 *a*	5 00 *a* 5 50	5 00 *a* 5 50	5 00 *a* 5 50	6 00 *a* 6 50	6 00 *a* 6 50	6 50 *a* 7 00
1851	6 50 *a* 7 00	6 50 *a* 7 00	6 00 *a* 6 50	5 00 *a* 5 50	4 50 *a* 5 25	4 25 *a* 5 00	4 25 *a* 5 00	4 25 *a* 5 00	4 25 *a* 5 00	4 25 *a* 5 00	4 50 *a* 5 00	4 50 *a* 5 25
1852	5 00 *a* 5 50	6 00 *a* 7 00	5 75 *a* 6 00	5 50 *a* 6 00	5 50 *a* 6 00	4 75 *a* 5 50	4 75 *a* 5 50	4 75 *a* 5 50	4 75 *a* 5 50	5 00 *a* 5 50	5 00 *a* 5 50	5 00 *a* 5 50
1853	5 00 *a* 5 50	5 50 *a* 6 00	5 50 *a* 6 00	5 25 *a* 5 50	5 00 *a* 5 50	5 00 *a* 5 50	5 00 *a* 5 50	5 00 *a* 5 50	5 50 *a* 6 00	6 00 *a* 6 50	6 50 *a* 7 00	6 50 *a* 7 00
1854	6 50 *a* 7 00	.... *a* 7 00	.... *a* 7 00	6 00 *a* 6 50	6 00 *a* 6 50	6 50 *a* 7 00	6 50 *a* 7 00	7 00 *a* 7 50	7 00 *a* 7 50	7 00 *a* 7 50	7 00 *a* 7 50	7 00 *a* 7 50
1855	7 00 *a* 7 50	7 00 *a* 7 50	7 00 *a* 7 50	6 50 *a* 7 00	6 00 *a* 6 50	5 50 *a* 6 50	5 50 *a* 6 50	5 50 *a* 6 50	5 50 *a* 6 50	5 50 *a* 6 00	5 50 *a* 6 00	5 50 *a* 6 00
1856	5 90 *a* 6 00	5 90 *a* 6 00	6 00 *a* 6 50	6 25 *a* 6 50	5 50 *a* 6 00	5 50 *a* 6 00	5 50 *a* 6 00	5 50 *a* 6 00	5 50 *a* 6 00	5 50 *a* 6 00	5 50 *a* 6 00	5 50 *a* 6 00
1857	6 50 *a*	7 00 *a*	.... *a* 6 50	.... *a* 6 00	.... *a* 6 00	.... *a* 6 00	.... *a* 6 00	.... *a* 6 00	... *a* 6 00	.... *a* 6 00	.... *a* 6 00	.... *a* 6 00
1858	5 00 *a* 6 00	5 00 *a* 6 00	5 00 *a* 6 00	5 00 *a* 5 50	5 00 *a* 5 25	5 00 *a* 5 25	5 00 *a* 5 25	5 00 *a* 5 25	5 00 *a* 5 25	5 00 *a* 5 25	5 00 *a* 5 25	5 00 *a* 5 25
1859	.... *a* 5 25	.... *a* 5 50	.... *a* 5 50	.... *a* 5 50	.... *a* 5 25	.... *a* 5 25	.... *a* 5 25	.... *a* 5 25	.... *a* 5 25	.... *a* 5 25	.... *a* 5 25	.... *a* 5 25
1860	.... *a* 5 50	.... *a* 5 50	.... *a* 5 50	.... *a* 5 50	.... *a* 5 50	.... *a* 5 50	.... *a* 5 50	... *a* 5 50	.... *a* 5 50	.... *a* 5 50	.... *a* 5 50	5 50 *a* 6 00
1861	5 50 *a* 6 00	5 50 *a* 6 00	5 50 *a* 6 00	5 50 *a* 6 00	5 50 *a* 6 00	5 50 *a* 6 00	4 50 *a* 5 50	4 50 *a* 5 00	4 50 *a* 5 00	4 50 *a* 5 00	4 20 *a* 5 00	4 20 *a* 5 00
1862	4 25 *a* 5 00	4 50 *a* 5 00	4 50 *a* 5 00	4 50 *a* 5 00	4 50 *a* 5 00	4 50 *a* 5 00	5 00 *a* 6 00	5 00 *a* 6 00	5 50 *a* 6 00	7 00 *a* ...	8 00 *a* ...	8 00 *a* 8 50
1863	.... *a* 8 50	.... *a* 8 50	7 50 *a* 8 00	7 00 *a* 7 50	7 00 *a* 7 50	7 00 *a* 8 00	9 00 *a* 10 00	8 00 *a* 8 50	8 00 *a* 8 50	.... *a* 9 50	.... *a* 11 00	10 50 *a* 11 00
1864	9 50 *a* 10 00	9 50 *a* 10 50	9 00 *a* 10 00	9 00 *a* 9 50	9 00 *a* 10 50	9 00 *a* 10 50	11 00 *a* 11 50	14 00 *a* 15 00	12 00 *a* 14 00	9 50 *a* 12 00	9 50 *a* 11 00	9 00 *a* 10 50

THE MONTHLY PRICE OF **Pig Iron** AT NEW YORK, PER TON (ENGLISH), FROM JANUARY, 1825, TO DECEMBER, 1864.

Year.	January.	February.	March.	April.	May.	June.	July.	August.	September.	October.	November	December.
	$ $	$ $	$ $	$ $	$ $	$ $	$ $	$ $	$ $	$ $	$ $	$ $
1825	35 00 a 50 00	35 00 a 50 00	35 00 a 50 00	40 00 a 50 00	40 00 a 50 00	75 00 a	75 00 a	75 00 a	70 00 a 72 50	70 00 a	70 00 a	60 00 a 70 00
1826	60 00 a 70 00	60 00 a 70 00	60 00 a 70 00	60 00 a 70 00	60 00 a 70 70	60 00 a 70 00	60 00 a 70 00	50 00 a 65 00	50 00 a 65 00	50 00 a 65 00	50 00 a 60 00	50 00 a ....
1827	50 00 a	50 00 a	50 00 a 55 00	50 00 a 55 00	50 00 a 55 00	50 00 a 55 00	50 00 a 55 00	50 00 a 55 00	50 00 a 52 00	50 00 a 52 00	50 00 a 52 00	50 00 a 52 00
1828	50 00 a 52 00	50 00 a 52 00	50 00 a 52 00	52 00 a 55 00	50 00 a 55 00	50 00 a 55 00	50 00 a 55 00	50 00 a 55 00	50 00 a 55 00	50 00 a 55 00	50 00 a 55 00	50 00 a 55 00
1829	50 00 a 55 00	50 00 a 55 00	50 00 a 55 00	50 00 a 55 00	50 00 a 55 00	50 00 a 55 00	50 00 a 55 00	40 00 a 50 00	40 00 a 50 00	40 00 a 50 00	40 00 a 50 00	40 00 a 50 00
1830	40 60 a 50 00	40 00 a 50 00	40 00 a 50 00	40 00 a 50 00	40 00 a 50 00	40 00 a 50 00	40 00 a 50 00	40 00 a 45 00	40 00 a 45 00	40 00 a 45 00	40 00 a 45 00	40 00 a 45 00
1831	40 00 a 45 00	40 00 a 45 00	40 00 a 45 00	40 00 a 45 00	40 00 a 47 50	40 00 a 47 50	40 00 a 47 50	40 00 a 47 50	40 00 a 47 50	40 00 a 47 50	40 00 a 47 50	40 00 a 47 50
1832	40 00 a 47 50	40 00 a 47 50	40 00 a 47 50	40 00 a 47 50	40 00 a 47 50	40 00 a 47 50	40 00 a 47 50	40 00 a 45 00	40 00 a 45 00	40 00 a 45 00	40 00 a 45 00	40 00 a 45 00
1833	40 00 a 45 00	40 00 a 45 00	40 00 a 45 00	37 50 a 45 00	37 50 a 45 00	37 50 a 45 00	37 50 a 45 00	37 50 a 45 00	37 50 a 45 00	37 50 a 45 00	37 50 a 45 00	38 00 a 47 50
1834	33 00 a 47 50	38 00 a 45 00	38 00 a 45 00	38 00 a 45 00	38 00 a 45 00	38 00 a 45 00	33 00 a 45 00	38 00 a 45 00	38 00 a 45 00	38 00 a 45 00	38 00 a 42 50	38 00 a 42 50
1835	38 00 a 42 50	33 00 a 42 50	38 00 a 42 50	33 00 a 42 50	38 00 a 42 50	38 00 a 42 50	38 00 a 42 50	38 00 a 42 50	38 00 a 42 50	33 00 a 42 50	38 00 a 42 50	38 00 a 42 50
1836	38 00 a 42 50	40 00 a 44 00	40 00 a 45 00	55 00 a 60 00	55 00 a 60 00	55 00 a 60 00	52 50 a 60 00	52 50 a 55 00	52 50 a 55 00	52 50 a 55 00	55 00 a 60 00	57 50 a 62 50
1837	60 00 a 70 00	65 00 a 70 00	62 50 a 65 00	57 50 a 60 00	50 00 a 52 50	40 00 a 45 00	40 00 a 45 00	40 00 a 45 00	40 00 a 42 50	42 50 a 45 00	50 00 a 55 00	50 00 a 55 00
1838	50 00 a 55 00	50 00 a 52 50	47 50 a 50 00	45 00 a 47 50	45 00 a 47 50	40 00 a 45 00	40 00 a 45 00	37 50 a 42 50	35 00 a 37 50	37 50 a 40 00	37 50 a 40 00	37 50 a 40 00
1839	37 50 a 40 00	40 00 a 42 50	40 00 a 40 45	40 00 a 45 00	40 00 a 43 00	37 50 a 40 00	37 50 a 40 00	37 50 a 40 00	37 50 a 40 00	37 50 a 40 00	37 50 a 40 00	37 50 a 40 00
1840	37 50 a 40 00	37 50 a 40 00	35 00 a 40 00	34 00 a 33 00	32 50 a 35 00	32 50 a 35 00	32 50 a 35 00	32 50 a 35 00	32 50 a 35 00	32 50 a 35 00	32 50 a 35 00	32 50 a 37 50
1841	35 00 a 37 50	35 00 a 37 50	35 00 a 37 50	35 00 a 37 50	35 00 a 37 50	33 00 a 35 00	32 00 a 35 00	32 00 a 33 00	32 00 a 33 00	32 50 a 34 00	36 00 a 37 50	34 00 a 35 00
1842	34 00 a 35 00	34 00 a 35 00	31 00 a 32 50	30 00 a 31 50	25 00 a 29 00	25 00 a 28 00	25 00 a 27 00	23 50 a 24 50	26 00 a 27 50	27 00 a 27 50	26 00 a 27 50	26 00 a 27 50
1843	27 00 a 27 50	27 00 a 27 50	27 00 a 27 50	25 00 a 27 00	25 00 a 27 00	25 00 a 26 00	22 50 a 24 00	22 50 a 24 00	22 50 a 24 00	25 00 a 26 00	27 00 a 29 00	30 00 a 32 00
1844	31 00 a 33 00	32 00 a 34 00	.... a 32 50	30 00 a 32 00	30 00 a 31 50	35 00 a	35 00 a	34 00 a 35 00	33 00 a 34 00	32 00 a 33 00	30 00 a 31 00	30 00 a 31 00
1845	30 00 a 31 00	30 00 a 31 00	32 50 a 35 00	42 50 a 45 00	50 00 a 52 50	40 00 a 42 50	35 00 a	35 00 a 36 00	32 50 a 35 00	.... a 37 50	40 00 a 42 50	41 00 a 42 50
1846	38 00 a 40 00	38 00 a 40 00	38 00 a 40 00	40 00 a 42 50	40 00 a 42 50	38 00 a 40 00	38 00 a 40 00	38 00 a 40 00	35 00 a 37 50	35 00 a 36 00	35 00 a 36 00	35 00 a 36 00
1847	33 00 a 34 00	33 00 a 34 00	.... a 35 00	.... a 35 00	.... a 35 00	.... a 30 00	.... a 30 00	30 00 a	32 50 a 35 00	34 00 a 36 00	40 00 a 42 50	40 00 a 42 50
1848	35 00 a 37 50	35 00 a 37 50	32 50 a	32 50 a	27 50 a 30 00	26 50 a 27 50	26 50 a 27 50	26 50 a 27 50	25 00 a 26 00	25 00 a 26 00	25 00 a 26 00	25 00 a 26 00
1849	25 00 a 26 00	24 00 a 25 00	26 00 a 27 50	26 00 a 27 50	26 00 a 27 50	22 50 a 23 00	22 50 a 23 00	22 50 a 23 00	23 00 a 24 00	23 00 a 24 00	23 00 a 24 00	23 00 a 24 00
1850	23 00 a 24 00	23 00 a 24 00	23 00 a 24 00	23 00 a 24 00	23 00 a 24 00	22 00 a 23 50	22 00 a 23 50	22 00 a 23 50	21 00 a 22 00	22 00 a 22 50	22 00 a 22 50	22 00 a 22 50
1851	22 00 a 22 50	22 50 a 25 00	22 50 a 25 00	22 50 a 25 00	21 00 a 21 50	20 00 a 21 00	19 00 a 19 50	19 50 a 20 00	19 50 a 20 00	19 75 a 20 25	21 00 a 21 50	20 00 a 21 00
1852	19 50 a 20 75	20 50 a 21 00	20 50 a 21 00	20 00 a 21 00	20 00 a 21 00	19 25 a 20 00	19 00 a 19 75	20 25 a 20 75	22 00 a 23 00	26 50 a 27 50	30 00 a 31 00	30 00 a 31 00
1853	30 00 a 32 00	37 00 a 37 50	38 00 a 40 00	37 50 a 39 00	33 00 a 34 00	28 50 a 30 00	28 50 a 30 00	34 00 a 35 00	35 00 a 36 00	36 00 a 37 50	36 00 a 37 00	37 00 a 38 00
1854	37 50 a 38 50	39 00 a 40 00	38 00 a 39 50	41 00 a 42 50	39 00 a 40 00	38 00 a 40 00	40 00 a 41 50	40 00 a 41 00	39 00 a 40 00	37 00 a 38 00	32 00 a 34 00	33 00 a 35 00
1855	27 50 a 30 00	29 00 a 31 00	31 00 a 32 00	29 00 a 31 00	27 00 a 29 00	26 50 a 27 00	29 50 a 30 50	31 00 a 31 50	.... a 35 00	36 00 a 37 00	35 00 a 36 00	30 00 a 31 00
1856	32 00 a 33 00	33 00 a 34 00	36 00 a 37 00	36 00 a 37 00	32 00 a 33 00	30 00 a 32 00	30 50 a 32 00	31 50 a 32 50	31 50 a 32 50	31 00 a 31 50	30 00 a 31 00	29 00 a 30 00
1857	30 00 a 31 00	30 50 a 32 00	30 00 a 32 00	36 00 a 37 50	35 00 a 37 50	31 00 a 32 00	30 00 a 32 00	30 00 a 31 00	29 00 a	28 00 a 28 50	28 00 a 29 00	28 00 a 29 00
1858	26 00 a 27 00	24 00 a 27 00	26 00 a 27 00	24 00 a 26 00	25 50 a 26 50	24 00 a 24 50	22 00 a 24 00	23 00 a 23 50	23 00 a 23 50	22 00 a 23 00	22 50 a 23 50	25 00 a 26 00
1859	25 00 a 28 00	23 00 a 30 00	30 00 a 31 50	25 00 a 28 00	24 00 a 24 50	24 00 a 25 00	23 00 a 24 00	24 00 a 25 00	23 00 a 23 50	22 00 a 23 00	24 00 a 25 00	23 00 a 24 00
1860	24 00 a 25 00	25 00 a 25 50	25 50 a 27 00	24 00 a 25 00	24 00 a 24 50	22 50 a 23 00	22 50 a 23 00	22 50 a 23 50	22 60 a 23 00	22 75 a 23 00	22 00 a 22 50	20 50 a 21 50
1861	20 00 a 21 00	20 00 a 21 00	20 00 a 21 50	21 00 a 22 00	20 00 a 22 00	21 00 a 23 00	21 00 a 23 00	21 00 a 23 00	22 50 a 24 50	23 00 a 25 00	24 00 a 25 00	24 00 a 24 50
1862	21 00 a 23 00	22 00 a 24 00	23 00 a 25 00	22 00 a 23 50	22 00 a 24 00	24 00 a 25 00	24 00 a 25 00	27 00 a 28 00	28 00 a 29 00	27 00 a 28 00	31 00 a 32 00	33 00 a 33 50
1863	33 00 a	36 00 a 37 00	38 00 a 40 00	37 00 a 39 00	36 00 a	32 50 a 34 00	34 00 a 35 00	34 00 a 35 00	33 00 a 34 50	40 00 a 42 50	42 00 a 43 00	42 50 a 45 00
1864	43 00 a 45 00	47 50 a 50 00	49 00 a 50 00	49 50 a 51 00	60 00 a 62 00	58 00 a 60 00	70 00 a 72 50	77 00 a 80 00	72 00 a 75 00	60 00 a 63 00	60 00 a 63 00	60 00 a 62 00

PIG IRON AND BAR IRON

Manufactured in the United States in the year 1860, *according to the Census Report.*

STATES.	PIG IRON.		BAR IRON.	
	Tons.	Value.	Tons.	Value.
Maine			5,300	$332,000
N. Hampshire	3,224	$92,910	70	7,000
Vermont			1,100	63,250
Massachusetts	13,700	403,000	20,285	1,291,200
Connecticut	11,000	379,500	2,060	175,500
Total, N. England	27,924	$875,410	28,815	$1,868,950
New York	63,145	$1,385,208	38,275	$2,215,250
Pennsylvania	553,530	11,427,379	259,709	12,643,500
New Jersey	29,048	574,820	25,006	1,370,725
Total, Middle States	645,723	$13,387,407	322,990	$16,229,475
Ohio	94,647	$2,327,261	10,439	692,000
Indiana	375	9,375	2,000	105,000
Michigan	10,400	291,400		
Wisconsin	2,000	40,000		
Total, Western States	107,422	$2,668,036	12,439	$797,000
Maryland	30,500	$730,600	7,000	$556,000
Virginia	9,096	251,173	17,870	1,147,425
North Carolina			1,007	92,948
Tennessee	18,417	457,000	5,024	483,248
Kentucky	23,362	534,164	6,200	514,000
Missouri	22,000	575,000	4,678	535,000
South Carolina			275	24,750
Total, Southern States	103,375	$2,547,937	42,054	$3,353,371
" Western "	107,422	2,668,036	12,439	797,000
" Middle "	645,723	13,387,407	322,990	16,229,475
" N. England "	27,924	875,410	28,815	1,868,950
Total	884,444	$19,478,790	406,298	$22,248,796

Bar Iron, value	$22,248,796
Pig Metal, value	19,478,790
Total Pig and Bar Iron	$41,727,586
Of which Pennsylvania made	24,070,885
	$17,656,701

Census Report on Pig Iron and Machinery.

The quantity of Pig Iron returned by the census of 1860 was 884,444 tons, valued at $19,487,790, an increase of 44.4 per cent.

upon the value returned in 1850. Bar and other ROLLED IRON amounted to 406,298 tons, of the value of $22,248,796, an increase of 39.5 per cent. over the united products of the rolling mills and forges, which in 1850 were of the value of $15,938,786. This large production of over one and a quarter million of tons of iron, equivalent to 92 pounds for each inhabitant, speaks volumes for the progress of the nation in all its industrial and material interests. The manufacture holds relations of the most beneficial character to a wide circle of important interests intimately affecting the entire population; the proprietors and miners of ore, coal, and limestone lands; the owners and improvers of woodlands, of railroads, canals, steamboats, ships, and of every other form of transportation; the producers of food, clothing, and other supplies, in addition to thousands of workmen, merchants, and capitalists and their families, who have directly participated in the benefits resulting from this great industry. It has supplied the material for an immense number of foundries, and for thousands of blacksmiths, machinists, millwrights, and manufacturers of nails, hardware, cutlery, edged tools, and other workers in metals, whose products are of immense aggregate value and of the first necessity. The production of so large a quantity of iron, and particularly of bar iron, and the demand for additional quantities from abroad, tell of the progress of the country in civil and naval architecture and all the engineering arts; of the construction of railroads and telegraphs, which have spread like a net over the whole country; of steam-engines and locomotives; of spinning, weaving, wood, and metal working, milling, mining, and other machinery; and of all the multiform instruments of science, agriculture, and the arts, both of peace and of war; of the manufacture of every conceivable article of convenience or luxury of the household, the field, or the factory. The aggregate statistics of iron exhibit the extent to which the general condition of the people has been improved by this great agent of civilization during the ten years embraced in this retrospect.

The materials for the manufacture of iron—ore, coal, and other fuel, water power, etc.—are so diffused, abundant, and cheap, that entire independence of foreign supplies appears to be alike desirable and attainable at no distant period.

Probably no class of statistics possesses more general interest, as illustrating the recent progress of the country in all the operative branches and in mechanical engineering, than those relating to MACHINERY. Nearly every section of the country, particularly the Atlantic slope, possesses a great affluence of water power, which has been extensively appropriated for various manufacturing purposes. The construction of hydraulic machinery, of stationary and locomotive steam-engines, and all the machinery used in mines, mills, furnaces, forges, and factories; in the building of roads, bridges, canals, railways, etc.; and for all other purposes of the engineer and manufacturer, has become a pursuit of great magnitude.

RAILWAY ACCIDENTS.

BY LORD BROUGHAM.

From the Transactions of the National Association for the Promotion of Social Science.

THE time appears to be come, if, indeed, it has not long since arrived, when some effectual precaution should be taken for the security of life and limb in railway travel; and there are some propositions on this subject so manifest upon the least attention which can be given to it, that we may venture to begin by stating them, with hardly any demonstration.

1. It is undeniable that the vast extent of railway traffic renders it not only justifiable, but necessary, for the public authority to interpose, and endeavor to prevent needless risks being run by the community.

2. It is not a valid objection to such interposition, that the conduct of their business should be left to the Company themselves, and that the State has no right to interfere with private concerns. The concerns are not private. No railway can be established without an Act of Parliament, and every such Act gives powers, not only of an extraordinary but of a transcendental kind, to the undertakers. They are authorized to travel through men's lands without their consent: they can force the sale of those lands at a price assessed, not by the vender, but by a jury. They have many other privileges, by special laws made in their favor, and against the law of the land. But enough has been said on this head when we state that all rights of property, all settlements by will or by marriage contract, all bargains previously made by the landowners, are utterly disregarded, and the whole is thrown under the power and at the mercy of the Companies.

3. It is equally undeniable, that when the safety and welfare of the public is concerned we have no right to regard the interest or the caprices of one class any more than the interest or the good pleasure of the railway companies. Suppose it were admitted that certain arrangements are required to satisfy one, even a considerable body of persons; if those arrangements are plainly prejudicial to the rest of the travellers, not merely displeasing to them but perilous to them, the question is decided that such arrangements should not be permitted; and the only matter for consideration is how they shall be prevented.

4. It may be alleged that persons unconnected with railway administration are not sufficiently qualified to form a sound opinion upon the different matters involved in the inquiry, whence arise the accidents so much complained of, and how they are to be prevented. But this being admitted as a general proposition, it may very likely be also quite true that there are some things so palpably evident, that any one is as capable of understanding them as if he had spent all his life at a railway board, and that no proof needs be given of them because they are next to self-evident.

Now, to apply these general principles there wants but little consideration of the subject. In the *first* place, without the least railway experience, every one must be aware that the whole plant, and all the carriages and tackle of a railway, is inevitably and constantly undergoing a great wear and tear, very much greater than in any other travelling establishment, because the great velocity of the movement unavoidably increases the friction exceedingly, and causes more jolts and other concussions, which directly affect the rails, and the carriages, and the tackle. *Secondly*, the disposition of the companies will always be to grudge the necessary outlay for repairing damage and preventing its recurrence, because the amount of the dividend is the primary object, in order to maintain the market value of the shares; and their manner of grudging it will be underrating the necessity. *Thirdly*, the damage occasioned by wear and tear has an unavoidable tendency to increase, in geometrical progression, each injury, if not remedied, becoming the foundation of other injuries. *Fourthly*, if there can be pointed out a cause either certain or very likely to produce injuries, either by increasing unnecessarily the wear and tear, or by augmenting the number of concussions, or by rendering them greater when they do happen, or even only by increasing the risk of their happening, that cause ought to be removed at once, instead of trusting to the efficacy of vigilant superintendence, or inquiring into the existence of injuries as actually sustained, because such superintendence and inquiry may or may not prove effectual, whereas the removal of the cause must altogether prevent the evil or greatly lessen its amount; and we are here speaking only of the wear and tear. *Fifthly*, such wear and tear must, if not either prevented or remedied, occasion so great a risk of accidents as almost to become a certainty. *Sixthly*, the length of time that most of the great railways have been established makes it manifest that they have very much greater chance of accidents now than they ever had before. *Seventhly*, the prevention of accidents, otherwise than by the effects of wear and tear, is most likely also to be secured by whatever lessens that wear and tear; *e.g.*, accidents caused by concussions and by collisions. Now, all these considerations point to one thing—the great speed of the movements; and it is too clear to require a word of proof, that whatever lessens the speed diminishes both the wear and tear, the injuries to the carriages, the risks of their running off the line, and if they do of their being damaged, and the risks of collision, either with other carriages or with fixed obstacles. It is enough to name the rates, in order to be satisfied that they expose to serious risks of collision, and produce the certainty of great wear and tear. Hardly any rate is known in this country under an average of forty miles an hour, while some have fifty, and some as much as sixty, or a mile a minute; and even where such is not the average, excessive speed is occasionally given to make up for lost time; so that an average of forty implies occasionally one of sixty, and an average of sixty, one of seventy, eighty, or it may be more.

Now it is quite manifest that the risks are very great arising from such rapid movement, both by the damage done to the rails, carriages, and tackle, and by the accidents thence arising, and also where no mischief arises from the disrepair, by the collisions and other consequences of rapid movement; and the prevention of such movement removes the risk and renders the travelling reasonably safe, even if a very considerable speed should still be permitted. Suppose the maximum of twenty-five or thirty miles an hour were fixed, and a prohibition of exceeding this in order to make up lost time; in a word, suppose the inconvenience to be inflicted upon travellers of arriving somewhat later at their journey's end, and of occasionally waiting at the station on account of some accidental delay not allowed to be prevented by increase of speed, can this be put in the balance and weighed against the absolute, or nearly absolute, security against bad accidents which would thus be given? That is the only question; and it does not seem to admit of much doubt.

Let it be observed that no reference has been made to the clear opinion given by the most experienced engineers, such as Mr. G. Stephenson, upon the too great speed being the cause of accidents, because it is better to rely upon the nature of the thing itself; and no testimony, nor any authority is wanted, to prove that such rapid motion *must* produce the consequences ascribed to it. Then it remains to consider the justification of the proposed prohibition. The advantages of such travelling, as saving time, and thus giving valuable facilities to the transaction of business, as well as accommodation to persons bent upon change of residence for other pursuits, cannot be denied. Nor can it be doubted that there are many who, if asked whether they would for the sake of the speed incur the risk, would answer in the affirmative. But it is equally undeniable, that a very great majority of those who travel would prefer the security, and declare themselves satisfied with a moderate speed —with going from London to York or Liverpool in eight hours, and to Edinburgh in sixteen. Why are they to be sacrificed because some others insist on moving with double that speed? It is a common remark of those who reflect little upon the subject, that if accidents happen it is the fault of the public which calls for fifty or sixty miles an hour; and they add, '*Volenti non fit injuria.*' But the *volentes* are only few, comparatively, and the body of the travellers, that is, the public, make no such demand.

The anxious vigilance with which our law, like that of all civilized communities, watches over life, is not to be lost sight of. Severe punishment is inflicted on any carelessness from which fatal consequences result, only less severe than what is inflicted when deliberate intention of mischief is proved. Nay, the act of self-destruction is regarded as a great offence, and whoever is so grossly negligent of his own personal safety as to occasion his death without intending it, may be said to commit an offence which assumes the same relation to suicide that manslaughter does to murder. But suppose a person at the request of another, puts him to death, the law treats this as murder, and the assent, nay, the instance and request of the deceased, is not any kind of defence, and does not make the act manslaughter. These remarks apply, first, to the class who hazard their own lives in the desire to save time: they are incurring the moral guilt of an offence akin to suicide; but next, the remarks apply to the same class, as risking the lives of others, and thus committing a most grievous offence. It is manifest that the risk which they run themselves is no defence against the charge of involving others in the same hazard, any more than a duellist stands acquitted of risking the taking away his neighbor's life by the fact that he also risks his own. But we have here to deal not with the minority, or their conduct in requiring the dangerous rate of travelling; our concern is with the supreme power in the State, the legislature, which is bound to watch over the safety of the whole community, and to prohibit such conduct as exposes its safety to unnecessary hazards—hazards, too, of the gravest description. If it should be said that the fixing of a maximum speed, with the prohibition of exceeding it to make up for loss of time accidentally incurred, would diminish the security of the public, by making the companies more careless, the answer is, that this never could be the result as long as the present liabilities continued, because no one contends that by fixing the maximum the law should declare the parties absolved from all other duty except that of not exceeding the prescribed rate. Every other neglect would be either punishable as an offence, or entail the reparation, by way of damages, according to the nature of the negligence; and it would be no kind of defence, nor even any matter of extenuation, so as to mitigate the sentence in the case of a criminal proceeding, or reduce the damages in a civil action, if the party proved that the requisitions of the law respecting speed had been scrupulously complied with. There can be no doubt that in France, Germany, and Belgium, where the rate does not exceed twenty-five miles an hour, accidents are very much more rare than in this country. It can be as little denied, that by better regulations time might be saved at the stations, both here and in those countries. It may probably be found expedient, for the benefit both of the shareholders and of the public, to introduce a better system of management, by paying the functionaries more liberally, and casting more entire responsibility upon them, so as to suffer no interference of the unpaid directors. But this is a large subject, and connects itself with the whole railway administration, as well as the branch immediately under consideration—the prevention of accidents.

British Railroads.—There are now in the British Islands three hundred and seventy-five district railway companies, who own eleven thousand five hundred miles of road. They carry above eighty million passengers yearly, and above thirty million tons of merchandise and minerals. They give employment to probably not less than two hundred thousand persons.

STEEL FOR SHIPBUILDING.

Messrs. Jones, Queggan, & Co., of Liverpool, have built two large ships of steel—one a sailing ship, named the *Formby*, of 1271 tons tonnage, built for the East India trade; the other a paddlewheel steamer named the *Hope*, of 1492 tons. At a *déjeûner* which took place after the launch, Mr. Jones made some remarks on these vessels. He said that steel is much stronger than iron, weight for weight, and consequently in shipbuilding that equal strength can be given with less weight of steel than of iron. The strain resisted by iron-built ships had been found to be from 19 to 20 tons per square inch, while the resistance of steel is found to range from 42 to 48, giving a mean of 45 tons for steel, or considerably more than double that of iron. Keeping these results in view, the *Formby*, a vessel built of steel, required 500 tons of material in her hull, while a similar ship made of iron would have required 800 tons. The difference in weight of hull would cause a difference of nearly two feet in displacement in favor of the steel vessel, requiring also less propelling power. In the case of steamers the advantages were still more obviously in favor of steel. If the *Persia*, a steamer of 3600 tons and 900 horse power, had been built of steel instead of iron her displacement would have been diminished about one-sixth, and she would have been enabled to carry double her present cargo. Mr. Reed, the Chief Constructor in the Royal Navy, who was present, said he should watch with great interest the career of the two ships which had just been launched. He remarked that merchant ships can be built to test a principle when war ships cannot, as the former can be examined and repaired annually, while the latter are sent abroad for periods of three or four years. He perfectly agreed with what had been said of the importance of steel for the construction of small ships, and stated that the government took great interest in the question of employing steel as a material for shipbuilding.—*Times*.

CHARING-CROSS RAILWAY BRIDGE.

This novel railway construction has been described to the Institution of Civil Engineers by Mr. Harrison Hayter.

It was stated that the bridge consisted of nine spans—six of 154 ft. and three of 100 ft.—the centre opening of the Hungerford Suspension-bridge having been divided into four spans each of 154 ft., that on the Surrey side into two spans also of 154 ft. each, and the opening on the Middlesex side into three spans each of 100 ft., the superstructure over the latter being fan-shaped. The width of the river, at the side of the bridge, was 1350 ft. The greatest depth of water between the two brick piers of the original bridge was 13 ft. below low-water spring tides, and the average depth was about

9 ft.; the rise of spring tides being 17½ ft. The level of the rails was 31 ft. above Trinity high-water mark, and there was a clear minimum headway under the bridge of 25 ft. above the same datum.

The superstructure was carried by cylinders sunk into the bed of the river, and by the piers and abutments of the suspension-bridge, the abutments having been considerably lengthened. The cylinders, excepting at the fan end, were 14 ft. diameter below the surface of the ground, and 10 ft. diameter above, the junction between the two sizes being effected by a conical length. There were four piers formed of these cylinders, each consisting of two cylinders, 49 ft. 4 in. apart from centre to centre. They were of cast iron, 1⅛ in. in thickness throughout, and the circumference was divided into segments, with interior flanges round all the edges, through which the segments were bolted together; and a horizontal interior rib was also cast in the middle of each segment. There were thus continuous vertical lines of ribs, securing a strong columnar arrangement.

The strata through which the cylinders were sunk consisted of mud and gravel, of varying thicknesses, overlying the London clay. The sinking was effected by excavating the material from the inside—at first by divers, but after the London clay was reached and the water was pumped out, in the ordinary way—and by weighting the cylinders, to an average load of 150 tons each. These cylinders were sunk to depths of 52 ft., 62 ft., and in one case to 72 ft., below Trinity high-water mark. They were filled with Portland cement concrete up to where the conical length commenced, and above with brickwork, set in Portland cement mortar, to the underside of the granite bearing blocks, which were 2 ft. 6 in. in thickness, and projected 1 in. above the top of the cylinders, in order that the weight might not come on the upper edge of the ironwork. With a view of testing the strength of the foundations, the two cylinders in the pier nearest to the Surrey side, after being completed up to the level of high water, and filled with concrete and brickwork, were each weighted with 700 tons, being about equal to the greatest load they could possibly have to sustain, supposing the four lines of rails on the bridge to be loaded with locomotive engines. This caused the cylinders to sink permanently 4 inches. To bring the other cylinders to a bearing, so as to prevent any settlement after the completion of the bridge, from the weight of the permanent and moving loads, they were each weighted with 450 tons, when it was found that they permanently sank, on an average, 3 in. each. Each pair of cylinders forming a pier was connected together transversely by a wrought-iron box girder, 4 ft. deep, which also served as a cross-girder for supporting the roadway. Assuming the four lines of way on the bridge to be loaded with locomotive engines, the pressure on the base of the cylinders would amount to eight tons per square foot, and on the brickwork at the top of the cone to about nine tons per square foot.

The superstructure of each of the 154-feet openings consisted of two main girders, to the under side of which were suspended cross-girders for carrying the roadway platform. These cross-girders extended beyond the main girders, and formed a series of cantilevers on the outer sides, for supporting two footpaths, each 7 feet wide in the clear. The main girders were of wrought-iron, and were not continuous, but extended only over one opening. Each girder had to support, inclusive of its own weight, a maximum distributed load of 750 tons. The extreme depth of these girders was 14 feet, and the depth between the centres of gravity of the top and bottom members was 12 feet 9 inches. The sides of the girders between the bearings were divided into fourteen equal parts by a pair of vertical bars, connected to the top and bottom by pins of puddled steel, 7 inches diameter at the ends of the girder, decreasing to 5 inches diameter at the centre; and each division contained a double set of two diagonals crossing each other. The top and the bottom of these girders were of boiler plate, and consisted of horizontal tables 4 feet and 3 feet wide respectively, and of four vertical ribs, the two outer rows being 24 inches deep, and the two inner rows 21 inches deep. The aggregate thickness of the plates in the horizontal table of the top in the centre of the girder was $3\frac{1}{8}$ in., and in the bottom $3\frac{13}{16}$ in., without the angle-irons, and of $4\frac{1}{8}$ in. and $4\frac{13}{16}$ in. respectively with the angle-irons, but exclusive of the angle-iron covers. It was arranged that, with the greatest load, the maximum strains should not exceed 4 tons per square inch in compression, and 5 tons per square inch in extension. All the rivet-holes were drilled by machines capable of drilling several holes at one time. This plan was, under the circumstances, less costly than punching, besides which a great saving was effected in putting the work together. The diagonals acting as ties were of Howard's rolled suspension links, each separate tie being composed of two or three links, as required, riveted together. The diagonals acting as struts were each in one solid forging, and were united together in pairs by zigzag bracing of wrought iron. In the centre of the girder, where the diagonals acted as both struts and ties, the pairs were united together in the two central spaces by the zigzag work. The dimensions of the struts varied from 12 in. by 3 in. at the ends to 6 in. by $2\frac{1}{2}$ in. in the middle, and of the ties from 12 in. by $2\frac{1}{2}$ in. at the ends to 6 in. by 2 in. in the middle. The ends of the girders over the piers were boxed in with plates $\frac{3}{8}$ in. thick, stiffened by angle and T irons. Over the cylinders the girders rested on sheet lead, laid upon the granite blocks. On the brick piers and the Surrey abutment they rested upon roller bed-plates. The girders were put together in place on a staging, the upper and lower platforms of which were accurately adjusted to the proper camber. The whole of the plates were drilled, and the struts and ties were completed before being sent to the works. The weight of each main girder was 190 tons. One of the main girders was tested when in its place with a distributed load of 400 tons, when the greatest deflection observed was $1\frac{5}{16}$ in., and the permanent deflection after the load was removed was $\frac{1}{2}$ inch.

The cross girders of the 154 ft. openings were of wrought iron, and were generally similar in character to the main girders, from which they were suspended at intervals of 11 ft. apart, from centre to centre. They were 4 ft. deep in the middle, and 2 ft. 1⅛ in. deep where the cantilevers were united to them outside the main girders. The top and bottom consisted of two plates, 18 in. wide by ⅝ in. thick, the sides being of lattice bars united to the top and bottom by angle-irons. The cantilevers decreased from 2 ft. 1⅛ in. at their junction with the cross girders to 1 ft. 2 in. deep at their extremities. Each cross girder, including the two cantilevers, weighed 9 tons. When two of these cross girders, without the cantilevers, were tested with a load of 140 tons, equivalent to 70 tons on each girder, the maximum deflection in the centre was 1 in., and the permanent deflection when the load was removed was ¼ inch.

The superstructure of the three 100 ft. openings of the fan end was supported by the brick pier and abutment on the Middlesex side of the suspension bridge, and intermediate to these by two rows of seven and of nine cast iron cylinders respectively. These cylinders were 10 ft. diameter below the ground level, the outer ones being 8 ft. diameter, and the inner ones 6 ft. diameter above that level. They were sunk to depths averaging 40 ft. below Trinity high-water mark, and were filled with Portland cement concrete to about 5 ft. above that level; but it was not considered necessary to fill in the remaining portion of these cylinders. On account of the great width of the fan end, which increased from 49 ft. 4 in. at the brick pier to 168 ft. at the abutment, the plan of supporting the roadway on cross girders, suspended from outside main girders, was inadmissible; and as it was not desirable to introduce intermediate main girders, projecting above the line of rails, the roadway was carried by interior plate girders, laid at right angles to the piers and abutment, and by the outside main girders, which were laid at the angle of inclination of the fan. The outside main girders were of the same depth, and were generally of the same character, although lighter in all the parts, and were fixed at the same level as the girders of the 154 ft. openings. The interior plate girders were of the ordinary construction, 5 ft. deep, or one-twentieth of the span, and weighed 26 tons each. The triangular spaces between the outside main girders and the outer interior plate girders were filled in with cross girders, terminated by cantilevers; projecting beyond the face girders, and similar to those outside the main girders of the 154 ft. openings.

The roadway platform over the 150 ft. openings consisted of planking 4 in. thick, spiked to longitudinal timbers, 15 in. by 15 in., placed underneath the rails, and bolted to the cross girders. Over the fan end, the platform consisted of planking 6 in. thick, secured to the girders. The footpath platforms were of planking 6 in. thick.

The first cylinder of the Charing-cross bridge was pitched on the 6th June, 1860, and its construction extended over a period of about three years. The weight of wrought iron in the bridge, including the steel pins, was 4950 tons and of cast iron 1950 tons. The total cost, including the abutments, would be 180,000*l.*, or 1*l.* 15s. per square foot, and 131*l.* per lineal foot. The cylinders of the 154 ft. openings cost complete 20*l.* per lineal foot; the outer cylinders of the piers of the fan end cost about 12*l.* and the inner ones about 10*l.* per lineal foot. The bridge was designed by Mr. Hawkshaw (President Inst. C. E.), the engineer to the Charing-cross Railway Company, and was carried out under his immediate supervision, Mr. John H. Stanton being the resident engineer. Mr. George Wythes was the contractor for the construction of the railway, but this bridge was sublet to Messrs. Cochrane & Co., whose representative on the works was Mr. Joseph Phillips.

But it is as an engineering work chiefly that the bridge is best worth notice, and presents some very curious features, one of these being the enormous strength concentrated both in the cylinder piers and in the girders in the smallest compass. The cylinders obtained for the column of brickwork built inside them afterwards, a foundation as solid as rock itself, and one not likely to be disturbed by any changes which may occur in the bed of the river by the scour which may be expected from the formation of the Thames Embankment, the scour being a source of evil which has hitherto proved fatal to the foundation of nearly all our metropolitan bridges. Again, with the superstructure, although the span is moderate, 154 ft., yet the quantity of metal required in each of these girders amounts to 200 tons, and the skilful way it has been massed together to afford the requisite strength, and yet give little indication of it in its light and almost elegant appearance, is certainly unsurpassed.

This account of the Charing-cross Extension would be incomplete, if we did not add that it is intended to connect the Charing-cross station by a double line of rails with the North-Western, Great Northern, and Midland lines. Fortunately, the level of the Charing-cross station, with regard to those termini, is such that an underground line in an open cutting, passing by tunnel under all the streets and under the Strand, can yet make its junction at a level into the Hungerford-bridge. With such an important link connecting the southern lines with the great systems north of the Thames, passengers can book through from Southampton, Dover, or Brighton, to any part of England or Scotland without changing carriages. The importance of such a saving of inconvenience and time will be understood by all travellers who know that to traverse London from the north to catch a southern train is, in point of loss of time, equal to 100 miles of rail added to their journey. In point of trouble and annoyance it is infinitely worse than 200.—*Proceedings of the Institution of Civil Engineers.*

An iron railway bridge is also in course of construction from the Southwark bank, opposite Cory's wharf, to Steelyard wharf, on the City side of the river. This bridge will be constructed of iron girders, supported on cast iron cylinders. Its total length will be about 645 ft., and the width of the roadway, to carry 5 lines of rails, will be about 60 ft. It will not be provided with a footway for passengers; the roadway will be carried over the river on cylinders 12 ft. in diameter, filled with solid brickwork. Between these there will be five openings or waterways, each about 130 ft. wide, while the distance between high-water mark and the girders of the central span will be 25 ft. The Engineer is Mr. Hawkshaw, and the contractors are Messrs. Cochrane, of Dudley Woodside. The estimated cost of this City bridge, which will be about half the length of that at Charing-cross, is about 120,000*l.*

INSTITUTION OF CIVIL ENGINEERS.

THE Council of the Institution of Civil Engineers have awarded the following Premiums for papers read at the meetings during the session 1862–63:—

1.—A Telford medal, and a Telford premium, in books, to John Brunton, M. Inst. C.E., for his "Description of the Line and Works of the Scinde Railway."

2.—A Telford medal, and a Telford premium, in books, to James Robert Mosse, M. Inst. C. E., for his Paper on "American Timber Bridges."

3.—A Telford medal, and a Telford premium, in books, to Zerah Colburn, for his Paper on "American Iron Bridges."

4.—A Telford medal, and a Telford premium, in books, to Harrison Hayter, M. Inst. C.E., for his Paper on "The Charing-Cross Bridge."

5.—A Telford premium, in books, to William Michael Peniston, M. Inst. C.E., for his Paper on "Public Works in Pernambuco, in the Empire of Brazil."

6.—A Telford premium, in books, to William Henry Preece, Assoc. Inst. C.E., for his Paper "On Railway Telegraphs, and the Application of Electricity to the Signalling and Working of Trains."

7.—A Telford premium, in books, to Alexander Woodlands Makinson, M. Inst. C.E., for his Paper "On some of the Internal Disturbing Forces of Locomotive Engines."

8.—A Telford premium, in books, to Daniel Miller, for his Paper on "Structures in the Sea, without Cofferdams—with a Description of the Works of the New Albert Harbor at Greenock."

9.—A Telford premium, in books, to Robert Crawford, Assoc. Inst. C.E., for his Paper on "The Railway System of Germany."

10.—A Telford premium, in books, to William Cudworth, M. Inst. C.E., for his Paper on "The Hownes Gill Viaduct, on the Stockton and Darlington Railway."

11.—A Telford premium, in books, to James Grant Fraser, M. Inst. C.E., for his Paper, "Description of the Lydgate and of the Buckhorn Weston Railway Tunnels."

NEW METHOD OF WORKING RAILWAYS BY STATIONARY ENGINES.

A PAPER by Messrs. Hawthorn, describing their new method of Working Railways by Stationary Engines, has been read to the British Association. Messrs. Hawthorn, after referring to other systems of working railways by fixed engines and ropes, in all of which the rope was attached to the carriage, proceeded to describe their method, as follows:—They propose with the ordinary construction and gauge of railway to place in the intermediate space between a double line of rails a series of double-grooved sheaves, fixed in spindles or axles, which pass across under the rails, extending a little over the centre of each line; a plain wheel or roller is fixed upon each end of these axles by which the motion is communicated to the train from a stationary engine or engines placed at a convenient point of the line, by the means of an endless wire or other rope, passing alternately over and under the grooved sheaves to the extremity of a section of the line, where it is taken round a large loop-sheave and returned to the engine, now passing over each sheave which it before passed under, and *vice versâ*—the double groove providing for the rope crossing itself without contact.

From this arrangement of the rope on the sheaves, it will be seen that every alternate sheave runs in the same direction, and every intermediate sheave in the contrary direction; and this motion is communicated to the traction wheels or rollers before mentioned. It is proposed to construct the carriages for passenger lines on the principle of those used in America and on the Canadian railways, of a length of from 60 to 75 ft., and supported on bogies, and capable of seating from 120 to 150 passengers, each carriage to be fitted with traction bars—these bars extending over two or more alternate traction rollers—and to be furnished with the ordinary flanged wheels for running on the rails. The traction bars, of which there are two, are placed side by side, at such a distance from each other as may be necessary to meet the requirements of the line; and these traction bars are worked either in connexion with or independent of each other by a suitable arrangement of levers or other gearing, by which either of the bars can be raised or depressed, thereby bringing a portion of the weight of the carriages upon the traction wheels or rollers, thus giving motion to the train of carriages in either direction; or both these bars can be raised out of contact with the traction wheels or rollers, and the train left free from all tractive force. The traction bars will be nearly the full length of the carriage, and the traction rollers will be placed about 18 ft. apart, or at the rate of 293 per mile. The carriage made in this way is adapted for running with either end first, being provided at each end with a platform, on which the driver stands to work the traction bars; and it is considered that for ordinary traffic one carriage will be sufficient to form a train, but two or more may be attached to each other, or the number of trains of a single carriage increased to meet the requirements of the traffic. The motion of the train can be quickly and certainly retarded or stopped by raising one bar and depressing the other, in the manner of a brake, thereby reversing the direction of the driving motion. A separate or independent traction carriage may be used, fitted with the traction bars and gear; but it is considered that such an arrangement would, in most cases, only be adding a useless and unnecessary weight to the useful portion of the train.

The present line of underground railway through London, from Paddington to Farringdon street, is favorable to the use of the locomotive engine, where so much of the surface of the ground under which it passes is unoccupied by buildings, and readily admits of a good deal of open cutting and ventilation at the stations, which cannot be the case where the railway passes under the densely populated parts of a city, as those projected in London must do. In such cases it will be necessary to provide for working in a continuous tunnel of perhaps three or four miles in length, in which the steam and smoke of locomotive engines would prove obnoxious to a much greater extent than is experienced on the present line, which is only partially an underground railway. As there does not appear to be any means of remedying these evils, except at a very extravagant cost, it is believed that the new system may be introduced with advantage in such cases as are above referred to, viz. railways passing under large towns, or in situations where opportunities do not occur of having openings to the surface. The maintenance of the engines will be considerably less than with locomotives, to balance the expense of keeping in working order the sheaves, ropes, &c., which will cost more than an ordinary line. Both calculation and experiment on the adhesion required to propel a train remove any reasonable doubt of being able, by the new system, to obtain sufficient tractive force by the traction bars and rollers, and it is evidently quite feasible to increase this tractive force if required.

INDIAN RAILWAY PROGRESS—THE BHORE GHAUT INCLINE.

This highly important railway communication has been opened in the Bombay Presidency; bringing the high lands of the Deccan —2000 feet above the sea level—into close connexion with the low lands of the Presidency, and with the town of Bombay itself; and thus converting the Deccan into a kind of suburban district for the citizens. The Bhore Ghaut Incline of the Great Indian Peninsula Railway has occupied more than seven years in construction; and during the greater part of that time there have been 45,000 workmen daily employed upon it. The incline is a series of tunnels through mountains of rock, and viaducts stretching across valleys, alternating with each other; each part a triumph of modern science and skill.

The incline reaches at one long lift the height of 1832 feet, the highest elevation yet attained by any railway incline. It is 15½ miles long, and its average gradient consequently 1 in 46.39. The highest gradient is 1 in 37, and the sharpest curve 15 chains radius. The tunnels are twenty-five in number, the greatest length of any of them being 341⅓ yards. There are eight viaducts, one consisting of eight arches of 50 feet, and being 129 feet high, and another of a like number of arches with a maximum height of 143 feet. The quantity of cutting amounts to 2,067,738 cubic yards, and of embankments to 2,452,308 cubic yards. There are twenty-two bridges of various spans, and seventy-four culverts. The total cost of the works has been 1,100,000*l.* or 68,750*l.* a mile.

The construction of the incline was let by contract to Mr. Faviell, during the autumn of 1855. In March, 1859, Mr. Faviell relinquished his contract, and the Company carried on the works under the management of their resident engineers, Messrs. Adamson and Clowser, until the following November, when Mr. Solomon Tredwell, to whom the contract had been re-let in England (in the previous August), commenced operations. On Mr. Tredwell's decease, shortly thereafter, Mrs. Tredwell conducted the business of the contract, until, in March, 1860, Messrs. Adamson and Clowser were permitted to resign the Company's service and accept the office of contractor's managers; Messrs. West and Tate being appointed resident engineers on the part of the Railway Company.

NEW STUPENDOUS RAILWAY BRIDGE.

Among the extensive railway works projected is the construction of a Railway Bridge across the Forth, to facilitate the communication between the Eastern Lowlands of Scotland and the North; the traffic at present passing either by the route of the Western Lowlands to the North, *i.e.*, *viâ* the Scottish Central Railway, to Stirling and Perth, or by a railway ferry at Burnt Island, which is found expensive, cumbrous, and liable to detention. The point proposed to construct a bridge at first was Queensferry, but the Admiralty object to any structure which would prevent their ships passing to the anchorage above; while the depth of the water is also another reason why the only bridge permissible there should be a railway bridge. But the span of such a bridge would exceed anything hitherto known. Consequently, a point farther up the river had to be selected. The point which the Parliamentary notices state to have been fixed upon is a point about four miles above Queensferry, and is stated to be the point at which the Edinburgh and Glasgow Railway on the south side, and the Dunfermline Railways on the north side of the Frith, run nearest to the respective shores.

This new bridge is proposed to be constructed by an independent company; who will afford running powers and facilities to all the railway companies choosing to make use of it. It is obvious that it must be used by the several lines running to the east coast from Edinburgh, and also, we should apprehend, by the Caledonian. These lines will all be able to reach the bridge by very short extensions.

This bridge, which will be built on about fifty piers, will necessarily be of great length—nearly as long, it is said, as the Victoria Bridge across the St. Lawrence. It will not, however, involve by any means the same cost of construction. The cost of the Frith of Forth Bridge is not estimated to exceed half a million; whilst the Victoria Bridge, which had to be exported, as it were, to Canada, cost nearly a million and a half.

VIBRATION OF RAILWAY TRAINS.

The vibrations occasioned by railway trains passing through a tunnel, formed the subject of experiments by Sir James South, made by him in 1847 over the Watford tunnel, in Cassiobury Park, the property of the Earl of Essex, in consequence of the attempt, in 1846, to run a line of railway through Greenwich Park, in what seemed a dangerous proximity to the Royal Observatory. Suitable first class apparatus was set up in an observatory erected for the purpose, so that night or day, if clear, an observer could have the reflected image of the star in the mercurial vessels ready to testify against the tremors caused by any train. In *The Proceedings of the Royal Society* Sir James has recently printed the result of his observations, thinking that, although all danger to the Observatory is past at present, yet that no observatory can now be considered secure from railway injury. He says that, "with the ordinary disturbance to which an observatory is liable (as wind, carriages, or persons moving near it), the reflected image of a star breaks up into a line of stars perpendicular to the longest side of the mercury vessel. With increased agitation another line of stars perpendicular to the first appears, making a cross. With still more the cross becomes a series of parallel lines of stars; still more makes the images oscillate, and at last all becomes a confused mass of nebulous light. The first of these (the line) is not injurious to one class of observations; but the others are, and therefore the second (the cross) was taken as a measure of the beginning and end of injurious disturbance. Signal-shots were fired when a train passed the southern entrance of the tunnel, and a shaft 1162 yards from it. Hence the train's velocity was obtained, and thence its position at any given time." These observations led Lord Auckland, then First Lord of the Admiralty (1847), to say that "they would be quite conclusive if the question of carrying a tunnel through Greenwich Park were again agitated."

IMPROVED RAILWAY SIGNALS.

MR. W. PATERSON has described to the Scottish Society of Arts an improved Signal, and method of working single lines of railway without accident. The method suggested by Mr. Paterson was, carrying out the suggestion of Captain Tyler, in his report on the Winchburgh Railway accident, that main signals, as well as distant signals, ought to be placed at both ends of single lines; that distant signals, with the necessary gearing, be placed from 500 to 600 yards distant from each connexion; that main signals be placed at the point where two lines begin to converge to the point of junction, whether at crossing places or single lines, or where the double line is closed in one line. These last-mentioned signals it is proposed to improve by making them lock signals. The pointsman at either end would have full control of the respective distant signals, but not so of the main signals. In working, should an engine or train approach one end of the signal line, and the pointsman, finding that it could not be let on (he not being in possession of the handle for opening the main signal) then in that case he would turn the distant signal to caution, and thereby permit the engine or train to draw in between the distant and main signals, the former being turned to danger so soon as the engine had passed within it—in that way protecting the standing engine or train—and then so soon as the pointsman received the handle of the main signal (which could be carried along the single line either by the engine-driver or by the guard of a train, or by a pilot-engine) he would open it and permit the train or engine to proceed.

Travellers on the Midland Railway, passing Kegworth, may have observed at that place a new signal, which is likely to cause a revolution in this class of work. It consists of a clock, with a face 4 ft. in diameter, placed on the top of a column 15 ft. high. Only a quarter of the clock is shown, which is formed of ground glass, with red figures 0.5.10.15., and has only one hand. Attached to the clock is a rod connected with a treadle about 16 ft. long, which lies along the inside of one of the rails. On the train passing over the treadle it is depressed slightly by the wheel flange, and the clock hand is set at liberty and is so adjusted by a counterpoise that it turns to the figure 0. Immediately the train has passed over the hand begins again to mark the time up to 15 minutes, when it is stopped, thus indicating to the next train exactly how long up to 15 minutes the preceeding train has passed the signal. The same clock works two faces, one for the up and one for the down line. The signal is illuminated at night. The simplicity of this signal is such, that it is almost an impossibility for it to get out of order, and it is so arranged that a passing train takes off all pressure from the clock, so that the great difficulty hitherto experienced in self-working signals is successfully overcome. The Midland Railway Company, who have erected the one above described, have every reason to be satisfied with the result of the experiment.

It is calculated that when adopted, double the number of night trains may be safely passed over the line that can be passed over now. There can be little doubt that it will prevent a great number of accidents from trains running into each other, and placed at mouths of tunnels, will be of great service. The inventor of this ingenious contrivance is Mr. John King, lace manufacturer, Heanor.—*Mechanics' Magazine.*

DISTRIBUTION OF RAILWAYS.

A curious paper has been submitted to the French Academy of Sciences, by M. Lalanne, showing that the apparently fortuitous distribution of Railways over the surface of a large country is in reality subject to certain laws, which may be stated as follows: 1. The meshes of a network of railways, as their number increases, tend to assume a triangular form. 2. These triangles have a tendency to form groups of six each round a certain point, which, therefore, is the nucleus of a hexagon. 3. When a pentagon happens to replace the hexagon, there generally is a heptagon somewhere, which makes up the deficiency, so that the number six really represents the average number of lines starting from each point. 4. There are certain exceptional points, such as the capital of the country, towards which more than six lines converge; in this case the number of lines does not exceed twelve. 5. In those districts where the network is still incomplete, there are centres from which only three lines diverge, instead of six; in that case they make equal angles with each other, thus leaving space for the three remaining lines. This strange regularity, now observable in the networks of France, England, and North America, depends upon a primordial law which Buffon calls the reason of reciprocal obstacles. Rivers, mountains, forests, or even the mere inequality in the productive force of different soils, have contributed towards the formation of these regular meshes. Among the consequences which M. Lalanne deduces from this theory of his, there is this, that the distance between two agglomerations of population of the same order and near each other, must be an exact multiple of the distance between two agglomerations of an inferior order. Thus, the average distance between two capitals of departments in France is eighty-seven kilometres; that between two contiguous *chefs-lieux d'arrondissements*, is forty-three and a half kilometres; and between two contiguous cantons, fourteen and a half kilometres; so that the difference between two prefectures is equal to twice the distance between two sub-prefectures, six times that between two cantons, and twenty-four times the average distance between two communes.—*Galignani's Messenger.*

RAILWAY ROLLING STOCK.

THE number of locomotives possessed by English Railway companies at the close of 1862 was 5140; of passenger carriages 12,584; of other vehicles attached to passenger trains, 4891; of waggons or trucks used for the conveyance of minerals, live stock, and general merchandize, 153,589; and of other carriages or waggons, 4270—making a total of 180,474. At the same date the number of locomotives at work on Scottish railways was 885; of passenger carriages, 1854; of other vehicles attached to passenger trains, 623; of waggons or trucks used for the conveyance of minerals, live stock, and general merchandize, 27,952; and of other waggons, 188—making a total of 31,503. The railways of Ireland, again, possessed at the same date 373 locomotives, 927 passenger carriages, 423 other vehicles attached to passenger trains, 5513 waggons or trucks used for the conveyance of minerals, live stock, and general merchandize, and 309 other waggons—making a total of 7545. We thus arrive at a total for the United Kingdom of 6393 locomotives (which, at £2600 each, would represent a capital of £16,634,800), 14,565 passenger carriages, and 197,758 vans, trucks, &c.—making a combined general total of 218,716. The value of this immense plant must be estimated at £40,000,000. It may be added that each mile of railway in England possessed last year twenty-two vehicles of various kinds (including locomotives), while each mile in Scotland had only eighteen, and in Ireland barely five. A comparison of this kind affords a valuable means of forming an estimate as to the relative productibility of English, Scotch, and Irish railways.

RAILWAY STATISTICS.

THE traffic receipts of railways in the United Kingdom amounted, for the week ending the 5th of December, 1863, on 11,028 miles, to £563,720, and for the corresponding week of the previous year, on 10,578 miles, to £517,950, showing an increase of 450 miles, and of £45,770 in the receipts. The cost of repairing and renewing the rolling stock of our different railways, is £1,243,714 per annum, or about eight and three-fourths per cent. of the total expenditure of the companies. This sum does not, in all cases, include the cost of repairing the locomotives. If we value the entire rolling stock at £27,000,000, and deduct (say) £10,000,000 as the cost of the locomotive engines, the value of the wooden rolling stock will remain at £17,000,000; and upon this amount the annual depreciation is (say) £1,250,000. It is not to our credit as machinists that foreigners have paid much more attention to these things than we have. On various parts of the Continent carriages are to be seen far more elegant in form and finish, and of very much less weight, than our heavy passenger vehicles. In America, passenger-carriages, mails, and goods-vans, are now very generally built of plates of corrugated and ridged iron, and such carriages (" metallic cars," as they call them) are said to be stronger, considerably lighter, cleaner, more comfortable at all seasons, more durable, and less affected by noise than wooden vehicles. The cost of iron in this country is so much below that in America, that anything that could be produced at a selling price on that side of the Atlantic might certainly be produced here at even a less rate. Iron-framed passenger-carriages have already been constructed in this country; it might be well if the principle were more largely tried.—*Builder.*

SUBSTANCES FOR PREVENTING AND REMOVING BOILER INCRUSTATIONS.

The following list of substances which have been used, with more or less success, in preventing and removing the incrustations which are formed by using hard water in boilers is given in the *Mechanics' Magazine*:—

Potatoes.—By using about one-fiftieth of potatoes to the weight of water in a boiler, scale will be prevented, but not removed. Their action is mechanical; they coat the calcareous particles in the water, and prevent them from adhering to the metal.

Extract of Tannin.—A mixture has been used of 12 parts chloride of sodium, 2½ parts caustic soda, ⅛ extract of oak bark, ½ of potashes, for the boilers of stationary and locomotive engines. The principal agent in this appears to be the tannin of the extract of the oak bark.

Pieces of Oak Wood, suspended in the boiler and renewed monthly, prevent all deposit, even from water containing a large quantity of lime. The action depends principally upon the tannic acid.

Ammonia.—The muriate of ammonia softens old incrustations. Its action is chemical; it decomposes the scale. In Holland it has been used with satisfaction in the boilers of locomotives. About 2 ounces placed in a boiler twice per week have kept it clean, without attacking the metal.

Fatty Oils.—It is stated that oils and tallow in a boiler prevent incrustations. A mixture composed of 3 parts of blacklead and 18 parts tallow, applied hot, in coating the interior of a boiler, has given great satisfaction in preventing scale. It should be applied every few weeks.

Molasses.—About 13 lbs. of molasses, fed occasionally into a boiler of 8-horse power, have served to prevent incrustations for six months.

Sawdust.—Mahogany and oak sawdust have been used to prevent and remove scale; but care must be exercised not to allow it to choke up pipes leading to and from the boiler. Catechu contains tannic acid, and has also been used satisfactorily for boilers.

A very small amount of free tannic acid will attack the iron; therefore, a very limited quantity of these substances should be employed.

Slippery Elm Bark.—This substance has also been used with some success in preventing and removing incrustations.

Soda.—The carbonate of soda has been recommended by Professors Kuhlman and Fresenius of Germany, and Crace Calvert of England. It is now employed with satisfaction in the boilers of engines in Manchester.

Tin Salt.—The chloride of tin is equal to the muriate of ammonia, and is similar in its action in preventing scale.

The *Extract of Tobacco* and *Spent Tanners' Bark* have been employed with some degree of satisfaction. The sulphate (not the carbonate) of lime is the chief agent in forming incrustations. By frequent blowing off, incrustations from carbonate of lime in water will be in a great measure prevented.

Mr. Alexander Delrue, of Dunkirk, France, has patented compositions to prevent and remove incrustations. The compositions are composed entirely of vegetable matters, and are prepared by dissolving or infusing in hot water the bark of the oak and pine, as well as the leaves of the sumach-tree ground and reduced to the state of a coarse powder; this infusion is concentrated to a density of about 10 deg. Beaumé, and to it is added a quantity (say from 15 to 30 per cent.) of cream of tartar (bitartrate of potassa) and spirit of turpentine. In employing this liquid to prevent incrustation in steam boilers, a quantity of it is introduced from time to time into the steam boilers; the quantity of the liquid required varies according to the capacity of the boiler, three pints of the liquid being generally sufficient for every thousand pints of water in the boiler, to prevent incrustation forming for about ten days.

COAL SUPPLY IN ENGLAND.

Mr. Robert Hunt, the Keeper of the Mining Records in the Museum of Practical Geology, London, has published a valuable series of Mining statistics, showing the extent and probable duration of the mineral resources of this country. Coals stand at the top of the table, as three-fourths by value of our mineral produce annually consists of this article, so indispensable to our manufacturing and maritime supremacy We therefore learn, with something deeper than regret, that "the rate of exhaustion which is going on over our coal-fields still increases. From 3052 collieries, there were used and sold in 1861, 83,635,214 tons. Two millions and a half tons were wasted in the process of working and burned at surface on the collieries of Durham and Northumberland alone. The total waste must therefore have been very large, although information thereof could not be correctly obtained." There is also a large waste in the actual consumption of coal in this country for domestic purposes, not alluded to by Mr. Hunt, that is not likely to diminish so long as coals are cheap. At present, we probably burn much more fuel in warming our chimneys than our rooms; but if coals were to be permanently double the price they are now, ingenuity would soon find out the way to utilize that which we now squander. The year's produce from the principal coal-fields is shown by the following figures:—Tons in 1861—19,145,000 from Durham and Northumberland; 12,196,000 from Lancashire; 9,375,-000 from Yorkshire; 7,254,000 from Stafford and Worcester; 6,691,000 from South Wales; 5,116,000 from Derby and Notts; 11,081,000 from all Scotland.—*Mechanics' Magazine.*

WELCH'S DOUBLE-ACTION PATENT REGISTER STOVE.

This invention is intended to warm one or two rooms, supplying them with fresh but heated air, by one and the same fire, while also promoting ventilation, and preventing draughts—purposes long striven for in various ways. The draught from the open fire, instead of flowing upwards and into the chimney, flows downwards (towards the feet), and into an iron box behind the fire; and from thence through sheet-iron pipes into the chimney. By this means, not only is a better open fire obtained, but a stream of fresh air is passed over the pipes in the air chamber, and led into the room or into the bedroom above: thus obtaining more than double the warmth, it is estimated, of an ordinary fire, but capable of regulation at pleasure. If the ash-pan is drawn a little outwards the downward draught ceases, and the stove then acts like those in ordinary use. As regards ventilation, by supplying a room liberally with fresh warm air, the foul air from the combustion of gas, etc., and from exhalations from the lungs, is brought below the breathing level and swept into the fire. A hollow fender, connected with the warming apparatus, is also a part of this invention, which may at will be filled with heat from the fire, and this warmth brought to the feet, corresponding with that of hot water. This hollow feet-warming fender is not necessarily a part of the stove.—*Builder.*

UTILIZATION OF WASTE IN THE IRON MANUFACTURES.

Chemical analysis has demonstrated that the thousands of tons of cinders drawn from the puddling and re-heating furnaces, which at most rolling-mills are thrown away as useless, contain invariably from 25 to 50 per cent. of metallic iron, combined and mixed with sulphur, silica, lime, and alumina, forming a very peculiar brittle compound, defying the most ingenious devices of our ironmasters to separate. Professor Fleury, of Philadelphia, states that, near

Troy and the Albany Iron Works, at Troy, New York, many thousand tons of this puddling-cinder are spread over the streets, every 100 lb. of which contain from 30 lb. to 55 lb. of good iron. After many unsuccessful attempts, he has finally succeeded in extracting good cast as well as wrought-iron, and has even been so fortunate as to produce from this refuse material a good quantity of cast steel. Two great difficulties had to be overcome. 1st. The oxides and metallic iron in these cinders are combined with silica and other substances in such a peculiar way that, by re-melting the same in the puddling, cupola, or other furnace, very little of the metallic iron can be extracted; the combination withstands even the high heat in a steel crucible. 2nd. By re-working the cinder with lime alone, or with lime mixed with charcoal and clay, the product is red short, and often red and cold short. The sulphur, silicon, and phosphorus remain still combined with the iron; all attempts to extract good neutral iron from the puddling-cinder by dry admixture of lime are unsuccessful; no other means remain but to destroy or loosen the tenacious chemical combination of these substances before they were placed in the furnace. Unslacked burnt lime possesses the peculiar property of decomposing silicates during hydration, or slacking, as it is commonly called. Taking advantage of this fact, Professor Fleury mixed a proper percentage of powdered burnt lime with the fine-ground cinder, and, after wetting the whole with water, exposed the mixture to the drying influence of the atmosphere. The dry compound was then heated in a common puddling-furnace, and treated like pig iron. He obtained 50 per cent. of wrought iron, which, however, retained still some traces of sulphur. To extract these last traces of sulphur, he dissolved in the water which he used for slacking the lime a small percentage of a chlorine salt, and his expectations were thoroughly realized. The Professor states that the process is also applicable to the working of siliceous ores, and can be performed in the puddling, cupola, or blast furnace. The preparation of the cinder, cost of lime, salt, &c., does not exceed 2 dols. per ton; and, if properly worked, the result is invariably a good quality of iron.—*Illustrated London News.*

ENGLISH AND SWEDISH IRON.

Experiments of an important nature have been made at the fortress of Carlberg, in Sweden, upon the respective merits of armour-plates made in England, France, and Sweden. Messrs. John Brown and Co., of Sheffield, sent two plates, one 12 ft. by 2 ft. 6 in., and one 6 ft. by 3 ft. 8 in. Messrs. Petin, Gaudet and Co., of Lyons, sent two plates, each of 7 ft. 6 in. by 3 ft. 3 in. The Montala Ironworks Company of Sweden, sent two plates of 12 ft. by 2 ft. 6 in., and one 6 ft. by 3 ft. 8 in. All the plates were of 4½ inches thickness, and then bolted to a teak target backed with iron plating, and supported by a massive stone pier. The two upper plates in the target were the French, and each was secured by 11 bolts. The next plate below was the longest, Swedish, and this was secured by 29 bolts. Below this was a tier of two short plates, one Swedish and one English, each secured by 24 bolts, and the lowest plate was a long English, secured, like the Swedish, by 29 bolts. Each plate received six shots from the ordinary 68-pounder naval gun. The French and Swedish plates broke to pieces, and the English plates remained uninjured and free from cracks. The shot used were of Swedish iron, and exhibited great toughness as compared with the shot used in the English service—the core or centre of the shot, after striking, being of double the weight of the core of the English shot.—*Army and Navy Gazette.*

PRESERVATION OF IRON AND STEEL.

Cavalier Novi, formerly Lieut.-Colonel of the Ordnance, has read at the Royal Institution of Naples a paper entitled "Substances for the Preservation of Iron, Cast-Iron, and Steel." It was approved and inserted in the Reports of the Academy. After having enumerated the principal means for preserving iron adopted by the ancients, and still more recently down to modern times, he confines his attention to the three following compositions for coating iron works:—1. Varnish composed of resinous matter, such as essence of turpentine, galipot, resin, colophony, etc. 2. Varnish in the composition of which there is quick essence of coal, tar, and dry pitch of the same tar. 3. Varnish, the composition of which is derived from asphalte and its quick essences, mixed with oxides and various coloring substances. He concludes by saying that the future preservation of iron depends on the positive use of asphalte and its results. The French Government have directed that experiments should be made on these compositions.

MANUFACTURE OF IRON AND STEEL.

Messrs. Williamson, of Parliament-street, and Picard of Lyons, have provisionally specified an invention, the object of which is to run molten iron or steel directly from a converting vessel capable of rotating motion, into moulds or receivers. For a large casting they pour into one mould, or into a receiver placed over it, the iron or steel produced in several converting vessels by means of conveying gutters, which gutters are in communication with the converting vessels. Sometimes they make the converting vessel portable and remove several to the mould.—An invention which relates to ball, mill, and puddling furnaces employed in the manufacture of Iron and Steel, has been provisionally specified for Mr. Thos. Wright, of Coldbrook Ironworks, New Brunswick. The improvements consist in building such furnaces in pairs, with a stove formed in the neck, to receive the metal preparatory to its being passed forward into the body of the furnace, and in applying a blast of atmospheric air to such furnaces, either hot or cold, as required, whereby he obtains a more uniform heat, producing a better quality of the manufactured metal, with a larger yield also, effecting a saving in fuel, and a diminution of manual labor.—*Builder.*

CAST IRON GIRDERS.

Dr. Percy, the eminent metallurgist, on visiting the remains of the German Bazaar, in Langham-place, after a destructive fire, remarked that several of the cast iron girders of the building were much bent, and the cast iron columns distorted by the operation of the fire—a circumstance of considerable importance with reference to the use of cast iron for building purposes. The girders were 13 ft. long, and 13 in. deep in the middle, tapering off slightly towards each end, and flanged, as usual, at the bottom. Several had fallen to the ground, of which only a few were broken; and of those which remained entire two were bent laterally in a striking and nearly equal degree. The flexure was gradual from end to end; the deviation from a straight line at the ends was 32 in. No cracks could be anywhere detected. Many of the cast iron columns, which were still upright, had been singularly twisted at the upper part, as though the metal there had been softened by heat, and yielded, without cracking, to the effect of pressure from above. As far as Dr. Percy and his friend, Mr. James Fergusson, could judge, there was no very decided evidence of fracture in either girders or columns, from the injection of water upon them; and yet, from the fused glass and other objects which lay scattered about, it is certain that they must have been exposed to a pretty high temperature. Dr. Percy considers these results to deserve attention from engineers and architects, and that it would be desirable that specimens of these bent girders and twisted columns should be preserved in some public museum, where they might at all times be accessible for reference. A collection of objects in illustration of accidents, such as the bursting of boilers, breakage of railway axles and tires, railway collisions, etc., would be as interesting as it assuredly would be important in a practical point of view.

RAILROAD LAW.

Recent Decisions in the States of New York, Massachusetts, Pennsylvania, and Ohio.

I.—NEW YORK.

1. The articles of association of a railroad company, formed under the general railroad act, stated that the subscribers associated themselves together to form a company "for the purpose of constructing a railway in the counties of Kings and Queens." The third article stated the object of the company to be "to construct a railroad, to commence in the city of Brooklyn, at some convenient point, and to terminate at Newtown, Queens county; the railroad to be located in Kings and Queens counties, and its length to be about twenty-five miles. There was a village and also a township of Newtown; the village being about twenty-five miles from Brooklyn, and the boundary of the town being also the boundary of the city of Brooklyn; *held* that without construing the word "Newtown," in the articles, to mean the village, and supposing it to be used to signify the township, there was nothing in the articles themselves to sanction a construction which would terminate the road at the boundary between Newtown and Brooklyn, and restrict the road wholly to the city. *Mason* v. *Brooklyn City and Newtown Railroad Company.* 35 *Barbour's Rep.*, p. 373.

2. That the natural interpretation of the language was to be built into Newtown, and that it was to pass through the two counties named, in reaching from the one terminus in Brooklyn to that in Newtown. *Ibid.* 35 *Barbour's Sup. Ct. Reports*, 698.

3. When a corporation, chartered for the purpose of constructing a railroad, has located its line, it cannot change the location and adopt a new route, unless the power to do so is expressly granted in its charter, and then only in the manner indicated. When the power thus conferred upon a company has once been exercised, it is exhausted. Per EMOTT, J. *Ibid.* 35 *Barbour's Sup. Ct. Reports*, p. 698.

4. When authority is given to locate and construct a road, upon a route to be indicated, in a certain manner, that route, when thus indicated, is in effect incorporated in the charter as if the authority thus conferred were expressly and distinctly confined to the precise route laid down in the subsequent proceedings; and the powers of the company are as finally and effectually limited to that precise line of road, as if such were the express provisions of the charter. Per EMOTT, J. *Ibid.* 35 *Barbour's Sup. Ct. Reports*, p. 698.

5. But a map of a portion of the route intended to be adopted by the company, filed in the County Clerk's office as described by the statute, cannot control or modify the charter of the company; and where the charter of the articles of association and the map

are in conflict, the map must yield. It cannot work a change of the terminus, or an abandonment of the road. *Ibid.* 35 *Barbour's Sup. Ct. Reports*, p. 698.

6. Such a map will be considered a description of a portion only of the route—as in fact but a part of the map required by the statute; so that when a similar of the residue is filed, both may be considered as one map. *Ibid.* 35 *Barbour's Sup. Ct. Reports*, p. 698.

7. And such a map, professing to be a map of only that portion of a railroad, lying between certain streets in a city, will not justify the conclusion that the railroad begins and ends within the limits of the city, when the articles of association show that the company was organized for the purpose of constructing a railroad from the city to a point beyond its limits. *Ibid.* 35 *Barbour's Sup. Ct. Reports*, p. 698.

8. The plaintiff having paid his fare from New York to Albany, in a passenger train on the defendants' road; after travelling a part of the distance, stopped at H. over Sunday, giving up his ticket and receiving a check in exchange. On the ensuing Monday he got upon a freight train and continued his journey in a caboose-car, used for transporting persons who accompany or are in charge of the train or its freight, and for the occasional transportation of passengers paying the ordinary fare. His fare was, at first, demanded and paid, but subsequently the conductor returned him the money, and allowed him to ride in the train, by virtue of his ticket. While so riding, the plaintiff was injured by means of a collision. *Held* that after receiving the plaintiff on a train upon which other persons were carried for hire, demanding fare from him, then returning it, and recognizing his ticket as evidence of a contract authorizing him to be carried, without further charge, it was too late for the defendants to say that he was wrongfully there, or was guilty of any fault in leaving the ordinary passenger train and travelling upon a freight train. *Edgerton* v. *New York and Harlem Railroad Company.*

9. Held, also, that it did not lie in the mouths of the defendants to say that the caboose-car was so manifestly dangerous that the plaintiff was guilty of negligence in getting into it to ride. And that there was nothing in the conduct of the plaintiff to prevent his recovering for his injuries, if they were sustained in consequence of any fault or misconduct of the defendants. *Ibid.* 35 *Barbour's Sup. Ct. Reports*, p. 698.

10. Carriers of passengers are bound to carry safely those whom they undertake to carry, as far as human care and foresight will go. Where an injury is sustained by a passenger in consequence of anything in the construction or management of the vehicle or the machinery of transportation, the carrier is responsible if any exercise of care or foresight would have prevented it. Per EMOTT, J. *Ibid.*

11. When it is proved that a car, running at a very moderate speed, upon a railroad, went off the track, and, coming in contact

with a stationary object, was dashed in pieces and destroyed, it is for the railroad company, in an action by a passenger to recover damages for personal injuries, to show that they had used every means which skill and prudence could dictate to have their road in perfect order, and their cars constructed of the best materials, and in the most approved manner. Per Emott J. *Ibid.*

12. Where no cause is directly or positively assigned by the evidence for such an occurrence, the inference is that it was occasioned by some defect in the vehicle or track; and, whether it could have been discovered and remedied, is a question for the jury. *Ibid.*

13. In an action against carriers of passengers, to recover damages for a personal injury, an allegation in the complaint that the occurrence happened, and the injuries of the plaintiff were received by the plaintiff, through the negligence and want of care of the defendants, and not through any want of care, or neglect, or default on his part, is sufficient to include any negligence; and the adding of other allegations which are mere surplusage, will not have the effect of excluding the facts from the consideration of the court or the jury. *Edgerton* v. *New York and Harlem Railroad Co.*, 193.

14. A railroad company cannot escape liability for an injury sustained by a passenger in consequence of its negligence, because the passenger was transported in a freight train, and in a car not specially constructed to carry passengers, where it appears that he was so carried with the knowledge and consent of the company —notwithstanding the 40th section of the general railroad law— when there is no proof that there were any printed regulations of the company posted up in the train, and there were no passenger cars attached. *Ibid.* 35 *Barbour's Sup. Ct. Reports*, 699.

15. A passenger upon a railroad has a right to leave the train on which he is travelling, at any point between the place of starting and that to which he has paid his fare, and to resume his journey in whatever car or vehicle the company provides. If the company receives him into a car as a passenger, he is there rightfully. *Ibid.* 35 *Barbour's Sup. Ct. Reports*, 699.

16. Where a railroad car in which passengers are riding is, while moving along—whether at high or low speed—under the control of the company's servants, and without the agency, apparently, of any causes but those within their control, thrown upon the track and dashed to pieces, the presumption is that the accident was occasioned by the neglect of the company. *Ibid.*

17. Property was delivered to a railroad company at Sing Sing by B., claiming to be the owner, and placed in a car for transportation to New York. Before it had been removed from Sing Sing, a complaint was made by C. to a magistrate, that the property had been stolen from the true owner by B. The magistrate issued a search warrant, under which a constable took the property from the carrier, forcibly, and brought it before the magistrate; who ordered it to be delivered to C., the agent of the owners. Held, that the subject matter being within the jurisdiction of the Justice,

and his proceedings regular in form, the railroad company was protected from liability in an action by B. *Blevin* v. *Hudson River Railroad Co.* 35 *Barbour's Sup. Ct. Reports*, 674.

COMMON CARRIERS.

18. The defendant being a common carrier of goods by canal, between Ithaca and New York, the plaintiff shipped four firkins and one tub of butter upon the defendant's boat, at Ithaca, for New York. The plaintiff directed the captain of the boat to "sell the butter" when he arrived in New York. On reaching the dock at New York, he gave up the charge of the boat to the defendant, and the butter was taken out of the hold and put upon the deck of the boat. During the day the captain sold two firkins and one tub of the butter, and the residue (two firkins) were stolen from the deck that afternoon or evening, while the boat was in charge of a person placed there by the defendant. *Held*, that the defendant's responsibility as a common carrier had ceased when the butter was stolen. That when the consignee left the two firkins on the deck of the boat, without directing what should be done with them, the defendant ceased to be answerable, except as a warehouseman. *Labar* v. *Tabor.* 35 *Barbour's Sup. Ct. Reports*, 674.

19. It is not unlawful, nor against public policy, for a railroad company to convey passengers by stage to and from one of its stations and an adjacent village, in connection with and as a part of its business of transporting passengers upon its road; nor is a contract made by it, thus to carry a passenger, *ultra vires. Buffit* v. *Troy and Boston Railroad Co.*, 420. 36 *Barbour's Sup. Ct. Reports*, p. 698.

20. Such a contract is lawful, and the railroad corporation is stopped from denying its validity. *Ibid.* 36 *Barbour's Sup. Ct. Reports*, p. 698.

21. Where a railroad company employs an individual to convey passengers to and fro between a village and a station on the railroad, in stage sleighs furnished, together with the horses and drivers, by him, such company is liable in damages for any injuries sustained by a passenger in consequence of the overturning of a stage-sleigh through the negligence of the owner or his servant. *Ibid.*

22. When a contract was made in the city of New York, between R. and H., a person professing to act as agent for three lines of public conveyances (including the New York Central Railroad Co.) running in connection with each other, to transport R. and her baggage from New York to Coburg in Canada, and she received from him three tickets, one of which was for a passage over the Central Railroad, and such ticket was accepted by the conductors upon the railroad, as evidence of R.'s right to ride upon the cars as passenger; they marking it, and taking it up at or near the end of the route, in the usual manner, without demanding any fare of her;

held, that there was sufficient proof of an undertaking on the part of the Central Railroad Company to transport R. and her goods over its road; and that the company's conductors, whose business it was to look to such matters, having accepted and treated R.'s ticket as sufficient, the law would presume the undertaking made by H. on behalf of the company was valid and binding upon such company, until the contrary appeared. *Glasco* v. *N. Y. Central R. R. Co.* 36 *Barbour's Sup. Ct. Reports*, p. 698.

23. The obligation of a railroad company is to take what is delivered and received as baggage from a passenger in the baggage car of a passenger train in which the passenger takes his passage, and take it along with, and deliver it to the passenger, at the place of destination, in the usual manner of transporting and delivering baggage. *Ibid.* 36 *Barbour's Sup. Ct. Reports, p.* 698.

24. The obligation is the same, whether the baggage is within the quantity allowed to a passenger, to be carried without any charge, other than the ordinary fare of the passenger; or whether it is an extra quantity, for which an additional charge is made. *Ibid.* 36 *Barbour's Sup. Ct. Reports, p.* 698.

25. If it be taken as the baggage of the passenger, whether ordinary or extra, it is to be carried with the passenger; unless there is some agreement to the contrary. *Ibid.* 36 *Barbour's Sup. Ct. Reports*, p. 698.

26. Where proceedings were taken by the Auburn and Rochester Railroad Company, before a county judge, under the acts of 1836 and 1838, incorporating said company, for the appointment of a jury of appraisers to assess the value of the land required for the construction of its road through a particular county, and one of the owners of land taken was an infant; it was held that it was indispensable that some proper person should be appointed to appear for such infant before the jury of appraisers, to represent her and attend to her interests on the appraisement. *Hotchkiss* v. *Auburn and Rochester Railroad Co.* 36 *Barbour's Sup. Ct. Reports*, p. 600.

27. Held also, that although an attorney was appointed to appear before the jury and protect the interests of the infant, on the appraisement, yet if he failed to attend before the jury, or to represent her interests there, his appointment was nugatory. *Ibid.*

28. That the statute was complied with simply by the making an appointment of attorney for the infant owner, by the county judge, sufficient in form; but that it was the duty of the railroad company to see that some reliable person was appointed, residing in the vicinity, who should in fact personally appear before the jury and protect the interests of the infant; and that until such appointment and appearance, the jury had no jurisdiction of her person, to entitle them to proceed to appraise the land, or the damages for taking the same. *Ibid.*

29. The statute was designed to secure the actual attention of some fit person, before the jury, as guardian or attorney, to attend personally to the interests of the infant upon the appraisement, and

without such appearance, all the doings of the jury, in the proceeding, are entirely unauthorised and void. *Ibid.*

II. MASSACHUSETTS.

1. In assessing damages occasioned to a railroad corporation by the location of a highway across its track, supposed benefit by an increase of travel on the railroad cannot be set off. 14 *Gray's Mass. Reports*, 654.

2. A railroad corporation is entitled to damages for the construction of another railroad across its track, although such track is laid upon piles over tide-water. *Grand Junction Railroad and Depôt Co.* v. *County Commissioners.* 14 *Gray's Mass. Reports*, 654.

3. In a petition and warrant for the assessment of damages occasioned by the crossing of one railroad by another, the place injured is sufficiently described as a "part of the land and bridge heretofore held and occupied by them for railroad purposes, measuring about five rods in length and forty feet in width, and lying a little west of the draw in their bridge from Charlestown to Somerville, and nearly contiguous thereto," with a reference added to the filed location, and actual construction of their road. *Id.* 14 *Gray's Mass. Reports*, 654.

4. Two railroad corporations authorized by statute jointly or severally to locate, construct, and maintain a railroad, if they file a joint location are jointly liable for damages. *Id.* 14 *Gray's Mass. Reports*, 654.

5. A location filed by a railroad corporation with the County Commissioners, by which alone the true location upon the ground cannot be fixed and ascertained, is nevertheless sufficient if by a plan which is made part thereof and filed therewith the location can be determined. *Id.* 14 *Gray's Mass. Reports*, 654.

6. An award under Statutes 1845, c. 191, and 1857, c. 291, of commissioners appointed to determine the terms upon which connecting railroad corporations shall transport each other's passengers and freight and perform the business of each other, must be returned into court. *Boston and Worcester Railroad* v. *Western Railroad.* 14 *Gray's Mass. Reports*, 654.

7. It is no objection to an award of commissioners under statutes 1845, c. 191, and 1857, c. 291, establishing the compensation to be paid by each of two railroad corporations to the other, for drawing passengers and freight over its railroad, that the award gives to either corporation different amounts for carrying passengers and freight to the point of connection from the same station upon its road, where they are to be carried to different stations upon the other road. *Id.* 14 *Gray's Mass. Reports*, 654.

8. Commissioners appointed to determine the terms upon which connecting railroad corporations shall transport the passengers and freight and perform the business of each other, cannot, under statutes 1845, c. 191, and 1857, c. 291, include in their award any

time before the filing of the petition for their appointment. *Id.* 14 *Gray's Mass. Reports*, 654.

9. Commissioners appointed under statute 1845, c. 191, "to determine the rate of compensation to be paid" by one railroad corporation entering upon the road of another, for drawing its cars, passengers, and merchandise, may fix the times at which such trains shall be drawn if not agreed upon by the parties; and may award to the first corporation the right to run a certain number of independent special trains over the other's road, and to fix the times at which they shall be run, provided such times are not within fifteen minutes of the time of any regular passenger train thereon, and the stations at which they shall stop; and also to choose whether all its cars so drawn shall be drawn independently of or in connection with the trains of the other road. *Lexington and West Cambridge Railroad* v. *Fitchburg Railroad*, 266. 14 *Gray's Mass. Reports*, 654–5.

10. It is no objection to an award of commissioners appointed under St. 1845, c. 191, to determine the rate of compensation to be paid by one railroad corporation for the drawing of its cars, passengers, and merchandize over the road of another, that it assumes the number of passengers each month holding different kinds of tickets to be in proportion to the number of the ordinary independent and connected trains; or that it makes the compensation to depend upon the number of passengers and amount of merchandise, and upon the classes of tickets held by the passengers. *Id.* 14 *Gray's Mass. Reports*, 655.

11. A reservation in the charter of a railroad corporation of a right to authorize other railroad corporations to enter upon and use this railroad, extends to a branch railroad purchased from another corporation, whose charter contained no such reservation, although the legislature, since the purchase, have enacted that the corporation purchasing "shall have all the powers and privileges, and be subject to all the duties, restrictions, and liabilities set forth in that charter." *Id.* 14 *Gray's Mass. Reports*, 655.

12. Commissioners appointed under St. 1845, c. 191, to determine the rate of compensation to be paid for drawing the cars, passengers, and merchandise of one railroad corporation over the road of another, may include in their award a period before their appointment, if subsequent to the filing of the petition in court, and not covered by agreement of the parties; and their award, when accepted by the court, will relate back to that time. *Id.* 14 *Gray's Mass. Reports*, 655.

13. It is no objection to an award of commissioners under St. 1845, c. 191, that it declares that each railroad corporation shall indemnify the other against all losses happening through its own or its servants' fraud and gross negligence or want of skill. *Id.* 14 *Gray's Mass. Reports*, 655.

14. An award of commissioners under St. 1845, c. 191, is not invalidated by declaring that one railroad corporation, in case of the cars of another not arriving within ten minutes after time at

the junction of the two roads, shall provide and "be allowed for an independent train to be taken as soon as it conveniently can be;" and that frequent unreasonable want of punctuality in the arrival of such cars at the junction shall be compensated for in damages. *Id.* 14 *Gray's Mass. Reports*, 655.

15. A railroad company which is bound to erect and maintain a sufficient fence, is liable in damages if a horse feeding in an adjacent pasture escapes, through a defect in the fence, and is run over and killed by the cars, without proof of any care on the part of the owner to prevent such an escape. *Rogers* v. *Newburyport Railroad Co.* 1 *Allen's Mass. Reports*, p. 16.

16. Evidence of notices to the owner that the horse had escaped two or three times before, and been upon the track, is immaterial. *Ibid. Allen's Mass. Reports*, vol. 1, p. 643.

17. A railroad company which is not bound to erect and maintain a fence is not liable in damages if a cow, feeding in an adjacent pasture, escapes through a defect in the fence, and is run over and killed by the cars, without proof of due care on the part of the owners to prevent such an escape. *Stearns* v. *Old Colony and Fall River Railroad Corporation.*

18. The Statute of 1846, requiring railroad corporations to erect and maintain fences upon both sides of any railroad which they might thereafter construct, does not apply to a railroad which was located and partially constructed at the time of its passage. *Ibid.* 1 *Allen's Mass. Reports*, p. 644.

19. When in a suit against a railroad company for an injury received while passing along a highway, an issue is upon the unreasonable or negligent conduct of the company in the use of the highway at the time complained of, its usage at other times has no legitimate bearing upon this issue, and evidence respecting such usage is incompetent. *Gahagan* v. *Boston and Lowell Railroad Company. Allen's Reports*, 187.

20. The plaintiff having attempted to prove that a flagman, employed by the company, was a careless and intemperate person, the defendants have a right to show that he was careful, attentive, and temperate; and these facts may be proved by persons who have seen his conduct, and need not be proved by experts. *Ibid.* 1 *Allen's Mass. Reports*, p. 644.

21. A railroad company has no right to use a highway as a part of its freight yard; but it has a right to pass and repass over a highway in making up its trains and shifting its cars, provided this is done only to a reasonable extent and in reasonable manner, without encroaching upon the rights of others who have an equal right to use it. *Ibid.* 1 *Allen's Mass. Reports*, p. 644.

22. If the whole evidence upon which a plaintiff's case rests shows that he did not use due care, but was careless, the court may rightfully instruct the jury as matter of law that the action cannot be maintained; and an attempt to pass between cars in motion, propelled by an engine, if no reason appears to justify the

attempt, shows such want of care as to fall within this rule. *Ibid.* 1 *Allen's Mass. Reports*, p. 644.

23. A railroad company is responsible for an injury occasioned by want of proper care and prudence on the part of its servants in the management of a train which is under their exclusive care, direction, and control, although the train belongs to another company. *Fletcher* v. *Boston and Maine Railroad.*

24. But if such injury is occasioned by the negligence of another railroad company, whose car, for the purpose of being loaded by the plaintiff, has been placed upon a side track of the defendants which is in constant use by other roads, such other company is bound to use reasonable care to prevent a collision; and if it fails to do so, and the plaintiff receives an injury from a collision while engaged in loading the car, he cannot recover against the company whose car caused the collision. *Ibid.* 1 *Allen's Mass. Reports*, p. 644.

25. If such injury results from the negligence of another railroad company which has a joint right with the defendants to use the defendants' track, under a lease from the defendants, and which is accordingly running trains over the defendants' road on its own account, the defendants are not responsible. *Ibid.* 1 *Allen's Mass. Reports*, p. 644.

26. "Ordinary care" has relation to the situation of the parties and the business in which they are engaged, and varies according to the exigencies which require vigilance and attention, conforming in amount and degree to the particular circumstances under which it is to be exerted. *Ibid.* 1 *Allen's Mass. Reports*, p. 644.

27. A railroad passenger ticket which is dated, and bears upon its face a printed statement, "Good only two days after date," ceases to be valid after the expiration of the two days. *Boston and Lowell Railroad Co.* v. *Proctor*, p. 267.

28. The charter of a railroad company required the road from Northborough to Southborough to be located as far north as a certain point, and in the location a curve was made in order to reach that point, and the road was thence continued towards Southborough by an acute angle. *Held*, that the subsequent continuation of the railroad for about a mile and one-half northerly from the point of the angle to the village of Marlborough, was unauthorized. *Brigham* v. *Agricultural Branch Railroad Company*, p. 316.

29. In estimating the damages sustained by a railroad company by the laying out of a highway across their railroad, the jury have no right to take into consideration any supposed future benefit to them from a probable increase of business in consequence of the establishment of the new highway; and evidence of payments of money by them for accidents at their several crossings, and of the comparative profit of the local and other travel over their railroad, is inadmissible. *Boston and Maine Railroad* v. *County of Middlesex*, p. 324.

30. A railroad corporation which has duly located its road across

a public highway, and acquired a right to construct it there, at a certain grade, without any restriction as to the number of tracks, or the place where they should be laid, is authorized to lay and maintain as many tracks as are essential to the convenient transaction of its business; and for that purpose may make any necessary alteration in the surface of the highway. *Commonwealth* v. *Hartford and New Haven R. R.* 14 *Gray's Mass. Reports*, 653.

31. A railroad corporation is entitled to damages for land taken by the laying out of a public highway across its railroad, subject to its use for said road; and for the expense of erecting and maintaining railroad signs and cattle guards at the crossing, and of flooring the same, and keeping it in repair, but not for any increased liability from accidents for the increased expense of ringing the bell, or for its liability to be ordered by the county commissioners to build a bridge for the highway over its track. *Old Colony and Fall River R. R.* v. *County of Plymouth.* 14 *Gray's Mass. Reports*, 653.

III.—PENNSYLVANIA.

1. In an issue under the act of 19th February, 1849, to assess the damages done to the plaintiff's water-power by the destruction of the defendant's railroad, it is error to reject evidence that the cause of mischief complained of could be removed for $140. *Barclay Railroad and Coal Company* v. *Ingham.* 36 *Penn. State Reports*, 570.

2. A water power situated on one of the smaller streams of the State is such a property as a railroad company is liable to make compensation for, if damaged by the construction of their road; although the stream may have been declared a public highway by act of Assembly. *Id.* 36 *Penn. State Reports*, 570.

3. In a proceeding to obtain the use of a landing or wharf for a lateral railroad, under the act of April 24th, 1843, an appeal lies from the action of the reviewers to the court to which their report is to be made, there to be tried by a jury. *Homer & Roberts' Lateral Railroad.* 37 *Penn. State Reports*, 564.

4. On the appeal in such cases the only question to be tried is the amount of compensation to be awarded for the use of such wharf or landing. The jury have no right to pass upon the question of necessity, location, etc. *Id.* 37 *Penn. State Reports*, 564.

5. When an appeal is allowed by law, no writ of error will lie until the appeal has been tried, and the final judgment of the court has been entered thereon. *Id.* 37 *Penn. State Reports*, 564.

6. A person subscribed for twenty shares of the stock of a railroad company, June 16th, 1847, "provided that the construction of said road is prosecuted," but retained his subscription in his own hands until 1854, when the book containing it, with other subscriptions obtained by him as agent, was delivered to the company. In an action to recover the subscription, it was *held* that the contract did not take effect, nor did the statute of limitations begin to run, until the delivery of the book containing it; and that the court

erred in refusing to charge the jury that the subscription was to be treated as a contract from the time when it was delivered to the company. *Pittsburg and Connellsville R. R. Co.* v. *Plummer.* 37 *Penn. State Reports*, 564.

7. Where the defendant sent to the company a letter in 1853, more than six years from the date of his subscription, submitting the names of stockholders received by him, including his own, stating the number of shares held by each, and promising to hand over "the notes taken for the first instalment of five per cent. when the road should be put under contract from West Newton to Connellsville," followed by the delivery to the company of the book containing the subscriptions a few months later, it was held that the defendant had thereby recognised the obligation assumed by his subscription as continuing; that, if conditional, it became absolute on the performance of the condition by the railroad company; and that there was error in the charge of the court that the letter was not a new obligation, or an acknowledgment of the original subscription. *Id.* 37 *Penn. State Reports*, 564.

8. Where a railroad company provides a platform or other safe means of exit from their cars at a station, it is the duty of passengers to leave it by the way provided, unless it be unsafe, or a justifying necessity exist to escape from peril or injury to life or limb. And it is error to admit evidence to be given to the jury that persons were in the habit of getting out of the cars on the side opposite the platform. *Pennsylvania R. R. Co.* v. *Zebe & Wife.* 37 *Penn. State Reports*, 564.

9. Under a charter which makes no provision for consequential damages, a railroad company is responsible for all injuries which are the direct and immediate consequence of the construction of the railroad to the whole tract of land through which it may pass. *Watson* v. *Pittsburgh and Connellsville Railroad Co.* 37 *Penn. State Reports*, 564.

10. The exclusive appropriation of a part, the inconvenience arising from a division of the property, or from increased difficulty of access, and the cost of additional necessary fencing, are alike the direct and immediate result of such construction. *Id.* 37 *Penn. State Reports*, 564.

11. The measure of damages is the difference between what the whole property would have sold for unaffected by the railroad and what it would have sold for affected by it. *Id.* 37 *Penn. State Reports*, 564.

12. When the damages are assessed before the completion of the road, the opinion of the witness as to what will be the value of the land after the road is completed, is inadmissible. *Id.* 37 *Penn. State Reports*, 564.

13. When the damages are assessed after the completion of the road, the difference in the value of the land before the location and after the completion of the road may be shown by the opinion of witnesses, confining to the consideration of the direct and necessary consequences of the construction of the road. *Watson* v. *Pitts-*

burgh and Connellsville Railroad Company. 38 *Penn. State Reports*, 564–5.

14. It is not error to admit in evidence a contract of subscription varying from that declared upon, where it worked no injury to defendants, who were proved liable otherwise by acts of participation in the company's affairs, such as voting, acting as directors, judges, etc., and active exertions to obtain a municipal subscription on the faith of a subscription certified to have been made by the parties so acting. *Hays and Black* v. *The Pittsburgh and Steubenville Railroad Co.* 38 *Penn. State Reports*, 81.

15. Such acts are not merely evidential of an original subscription, but are conclusive, amounting to an estoppel upon the parties against denying it. It is primary and not secondary evidence. *Id.* 38 *Penn. State Reports.*

16. Calls made by the treasurer under general authority given by the board are valid, although the resolutions did not specify the amount of each call. *Id.* 38 *Penn. State Reports.*

17. An omission to record a call for a particular instalment is supplied by the record of a call for all other unpaid instalments. *Id.* 38 *Penn. State Reports.*

18. Entries of credit on the books for stock assigned are worthless if founded on a transfer which did not discharge the assignor's liability. *Id.* 38 *Penn. State Reports.*

19. Terms of present grant used in an act of incorporation will be interpreted as only a promise to grant if the given right be with reference to what does not at the time exist. They are but a legislative promise, which the judiciary will not enforce. *North Branch Passenger Railway Co.* v. *City Passenger Railway Co.* 38 *Penn. State Reports*, 361.

20. A right is a relation of a person or persons to some person or thing, and cannot from its very nature arise or exist in advance of the persons and things related, and of which it expresses the relation. *Id.* 38 *Penn. State Reports.*

21. A passenger railroad company to whom by their act of incorporation was granted the right "to connect with any passenger railway now constructed *or hereafter to be constructed*, so as to give them a complete route from Fairmount to the Exchange," cannot, under that right, connect with another passenger railway which was not made, nor the right of making granted at the time the claimants' act of incorporation was passed. The alleged right at the time of its creation had nothing to which it could attach, or on which it could rest, and was therefore no right at all. *Id.* 38 *Penn. State Reports.*

22. Lands purchased by a railroad company beyond what are actually dedicated to corporate purposes, are bound by the lien of judgments against the corporation, and are liable to be levied in execution and sold by the sheriff as are the lands of any other debtor; but the purchaser at such sale takes only that which is not necessary for the full enjoyment and exercise of the corporate franchise, no matter how acquired by the corporation. *The Ply-*

mouth Railroad Company v. *Colwell and Jacoby.* 39 *Penn. State Reports*, 337.

23. A canal basin is not a legitimate incident to a railroad having no authorized canal connection, and is not protected from levy and sale on execution against the company. *Id.* 39 *Penn. State Reports.*

Where, under their charter, a railroad company could appropriate only four rods of ground in width, except at deep cuts and fillings or at points selected for depôts, or engine or water stations, and no locomotive road, as contemplated in the charter, was constructed within the five years limited therein for the completion, but a horse road only, ground cannot be thereafter appropriated for engine or water stations. That should have been done within the five years required by the act of incorporation. *Id.* 39 *Penn. State Reports.*

24. On the trial of an appeal from the award of damages by appraisers for land taken by a railroad company in the construction of their road, evidence of the price paid or amount received for land in the neighborhood in particular instances is inadmissible; the only proper test is the opinion of witnesses as to the value of the land taken in view of its location and productiveness, its market value, or the general selling price of land in the neighborhood. *East Pennsylvania Railroad Co.* v. *Heister.* 40 *Penn. State Reports*, 560.

25. The jury may allow the actual damages incident to taking the road arising from inconvenience in crossing the railroad and interfering with crossings already established, which the plaintiff has sustained, as also from the failure or neglect of the company to construct the crossings as required by law, but not for making the crossings themselves; they were to be made by the company. *Id.* 40 *Penn. State Reports*, 560.

26. It was not error to reject evidence offered on the part of the company to prove that the plaintiff had offered to claim no damages, if the company would locate the road where he wished it, and that when called on he declined to designate the location he desired; for it was only a proposition accepted by the company at the time, and not binding on the plaintiff afterwards. *Id.* 40 *Penn. State Reports*, 560.

27. One subscribed in 1853 for twenty shares of the stock of the Pittsburgh and Connellsville Railroad Company, on the express condition that the company "should locate and construct their railroad along the route contemplated by the Meyer's Mill Plank Road Company for their road;" paid one instalment, part of the second, but delayed the payment of the balance as the calls were made, until the company, before the road was *constructed* along the route mentioned, suspended operations, after which payment was refused on the ground that, though the road had been *located* by the company, they had not *constructed* it according to the condition in the subscription. In an action brought therefor by the company, it was *held*

That the promise of subscription being precedent to that of construction upon the part of the company, the defendant could not insist upon performance by the railroad company, while he refused performance on his part; and that the road having been located as stipulated, and completed so far as the means of the company would allow, it was a compliance with the condition, and the plaintiffs were entitled to recover. *Miller* v. *Pittsburgh and Connellsville Railroad Co.* 40 *Penn. State Reports*, 560–1.

28. That the condition in the contract of subscription was not a condition precedent and did not require the completion of the road before payment could be required, but only that when located and constructed it should occupy the route designated, the undertaking being on the part of the subscriber to pay as calls should be made by the directors, and on the part of the company to locate as stipulated and construct as fast as their means would allow. *Id.* 40 *Penn. State Reports*, 561.

29. That the suspension of operations made by the directors long after the payments upon defendant's stock had been due, was not a defence in an action brought against him for the unpaid balance thereon. *Id.* 40 *Penn. State Reports*, 561.

30. Where the company had received subscriptions on a guarantee that they would pay interest on stock "as soon as paid" until the road was finished, interest would not accrue until the stock was fully paid; and where but a small part of the stock had been paid for by the defendant, he could not in a suit against him for the balance set up the non-payment of interest on his stock by the company as a breach of condition. *Id.* 40 *Penn. State Reports*, 561.

31. Under the Lateral Railroad Act of 1832, and its supplement of April 20, 1858, the determination of the necessity of the proposed road after an appeal from a favorable report of viewers, is exclusively for the court, and is not to be submitted to the appellate jury for re-trial; the only question for them is the amount of damages. *Brown* v. *Peterson & Corey.* 40 *Penn. State Reports*, 561.

32. In proceedings under the Lateral Railroad acts it is not essential, though proper, that all the owners of land over which the proposed railroad is to pass should be named in the petition; and if a mistake be made as to the real owner, the court may direct the damages assessed by the viewers to be paid to the proper party on proof of the facts. *Boyd et al.* v. *Negley.* 40 *Penn. State Reports*, 561.

33. Where one was named as a reputed joint owner of a tract over which the railroad was located, in connection with the real owners, when she was not a joint owner but only had an annuity issuing out of the land; and her name was stricken from the record by leave of the court after the report of viewers and before the final assessment of damages, it is not a fatal defect in the petition or proceedings. The owners of the land were named, and they could show that the proposed road was unnecessary, or failing in that, could have their damages assessed, which was all they were entitled

to under the law; nor were they compelled to appeal in order to prevent her participation in the damages, for the assessment was not an adjudication between them, and if it had been it is no ground for reversing the action of the court below, where the damages had been assessed for the rightful owners: nor can *they* complain that their tenant was not named in the petition, for such omission was not a defect therein. *Boyd et al.* v. *Negley.* 40 *Penn. State Reports*, 561.

34. It is not a valid objection to the petition that it represented the desire of the petitioner to make, construct, and use his proposed railroad with double or single track, as may be found most suitable for carrying his coal, or coal of other parties thereon; for the law not only authorizes such a petition, but the owner of a lateral railroad may be required to carry the coal of other parties upon it. *Id.* 40 *Penn. State Reports*, 562.

It is not necessary that the grades of the road should appear in the petition or on the plot. *Id.* 40 *Penn. State Reports*, 562.

35. If the petitioner already has the right of way sought by another route, that fact is proper evidence to submit to the viewers or to the court below on the question of the necessity of the road; but it has nothing to do with the question of damages, and is not evidence for the appellate jury. *Id.* 40 *Penn. State Reports*, 562.

36. It is not error in the court to permit the petitioner, pending an appeal as to damages, to amend his petition so as to include other coal lands purchased since the commencement of proceedings, as the amendments could not change or affect the matter in controversy between the parties. *Id.* 40 *Penn. State Reports*, 562.

37. Under the supplementary Lateral Railroad Act of April 20, 1858, the question of the necessity of the road is wholly with the viewers and the court; the appellate jury can only pass upon the question of damages. *Id.* 40 *Penn. State Reports*, 562.

38. Before an appeal from the report of viewers of a proposed lateral railroad is sent to an appellate jury for trial, the court should approve or disapprove the finding of the viewers respecting its necessity; for if the court does not concur in opinion with the viewers, there is nothing to be tried. *Id.* 40 *Penn. State Reports*, 562.

39. Where a subscriber to the capital stock of a railroad company, who has been released from the obligation of his subscription, subsequently votes at an annual election of directors, was himself elected a director, acts as director and as stockholder, and pays money to the company, his acts are evidence of a subscription of some kind, and, in the absence of proof of a special contract, warrant the inference that he had reässumed his original obligation. But they are shorn of their importance when a special contract accounting for them is shown. *Pittsburgh and Connellsville Railroad Co.* v. *Stewart.* 41 *Penn. State Reports*, 567.

40. Even if the original subscription had not been realized, a new contract between the company and the subscriber, authorizing him to pay in materials at a future time instead of cash on call, would

supersede the original contract. *Id.* 41 *Penn. State Reports*, 567.

41. Subscriptions made before a company is organized, must be unconditional. But after the organization the company may stipulate with subscribers that they may pay in any manner mutually agreed on, and it can enforce a subscription only according to its conditions. *Id.* 41 *Penn. State Reports*, 567.

42. The act of the president of an incorporated company, in accepting conditional subscriptions, is binding on the company. *Id.* 41 *Penn. State Reports*, 568.

43. A payment by the subscriber in cash without call after a special contract that he might pay in materials, will not estop him from setting up that contract as a defence against a claim to the payment of the whole subscription in cash. *Id.* 41 *Penn. State Reports*, 567.

44. The Pennsylvania Railroad Company being about to purchase the rolling stock and bonds of the Sunbury and Erie Railroad Company, and to lease it for the term of nine hundred and ninety-nine years, the lessee agreeing by the contract to keep the road in repair, maintain its equipment, and pay thirty per cent. of the gross earnings for taxes, interest on bonds, etc., and the balance, if any, to the lessors, on bill in equity filed by a stockholder in both companies for a preliminary injunction against the proposed purchase and lease, it was *held* that the intended contracts were valid because within the corporate powers of the two companies under the acts of Assembly of April 13th, 1860, and April 23d, 1861, and that they were not assignments in trust for the benefit of creditors with preferences. *Gratz* v. *The Pennsylvania Railroad Co.* 41 *Penn. State Reports*, 568.

45. The act of March 7th, 1861, authorizing the State Treasurer to cancel $3,500,000 of the bonds of the Sunbury and Erie Railroad Company, and directing the satisfaction of the mortgage for $7,000,000, is not a violation of Sec. 4, Art. II. of the Constitution of the State relating to the Sinking Fund, and is therefore Constitutional; and the mortgage for $5,000,000, executed March 30th, 1861, under the provisions of that act, is the first lien on that part of the Philadelphia and Erie Railroad leading from Williamsport to Erie, and second only to the $1,000,000 mortgage on the part of the road between Williamsport and Sunbury. *Id.* 41 *Penn. State Reports*, 568.

46. A bond filed by a railroad company when locating their road is a security for all damages that may occur from the construction also; both are but one injury, and a bond filed for one is therefore a security for all. *Wadhams* v. *The Lackawanna and Bloomsburg Railroad Co.* 42 *Penn. State Reports*, 566.

47. The offer of a bond by a railroad company is an assertion by one of the parties that they cannot agree upon the damages caused to the property of the landowner; and the action of the court approving the sureties and directing the bond to be filed, involves an adjudication that everything had been done to entitle

the company to have the bond filed. *Id.* 42 *Penn. State Reports*, 566.

48. A railroad company is liable for injuries resulting from the negligence, violence, or carelessness of its conductors in removing from the cars a passenger who refused to pay his fare or produce his ticket, in consequence of which he died. *The Pennsylvania Railroad Co.* v. *Vandwĕr.* 42 *Penn. State Reports*, 566.

49. The proviso of the first section of the act of April 14th, 1834, relative to the removal of suits brought by and against railroad companies to the Common Pleas of any adjacent county through which the road of the company is not located, etc., does not apply to the case of an appeal from the report of the viewers appointed to assess the damages occasioned by the location and construction of the road, when it assumes the form of a suit or action against the railroad company. *Pinneo* v. *Lackawanna and Bloomsburg Railroad Co.* 43 *Penn. State Reports*, 566.

50. Where the jury had viewed the ground occupied by the railroad, it was held not error to refuse to permit the plaintiff to ask a witness on the trial whether the roads crossing and recrossing the railroad rendered it more or less dangerous for horses, cattle, teams, etc. The question was immaterial. *Id.* 43 *Penn. State Reports*, 567.

51. In an action by a widow against a railroad company to recover damages for the loss of her husband's life, the court instructed the jury that if the deceased knew that the "fast line" was approaching, and knew his danger in time to escape, and did not, then the fault was his own, and there could be no recovery.

IV.—OHIO.

1. Where a township through which a railroad might be located was by a statute "authorized to subscribe to the stock of said railroad," *held*, that while under such authority the contract of subscription might contain terms and conditions affecting its subject matter and the consideration to be paid and received, the making a subscription and paying money for stock could not be made a consideration to sustain a contract giving the township a claim to control the general conduct and discretion of the directors of the railroad company in matters involving the pecuniary interests of the company and its stockholders to an amount far exceeding the subscription of the township. It was not the intention of the legislature to authorize the township to obtain by its contract such a claim, or the directors of the company for the time being, as to limit the power and discretion of future Boards of Directors. *Id.* *Port Clinton R. R. Co.* v. *Cleveland and Toledo R. R. Co.* 13 *Critchfield's Ohio State Reports*, 545.

2. Where two railroad companies in their agreement for consolidation inserted an article to provide for the completion and running of the route of one of the companies, and the directors of the consolidated company failed to comply with such provisions;

held, that if the duty thus created was owing to all the stockholders, one of the stockholders could not sustain an action against the directors to enforce a compliance therewith; and that if the duty was owing to a class of stockholders, having in respect to the matter an interest or right distinct from another class, any proceeding to obtain relief for a refusal or neglect on the part of the directors to discharge the duty, must bring before the court not only the directors of the company, but the two classes of stockholders. *Id.* 545.

3. The defendant, by a verbal arrangement made with the D., X. and B. Railroad Company, gave to the latter company the right to construct a track on the side of defendant's road-bed for the purpose of connecting the road of the said D., X. and B. Company with defendant's road. Said connecting track passed over a bridge previously constructed by defendant for its track, and which foot passengers had been permitted to use for the purpose of transit. The plaintiff, in passing on foot over said bridge at night, fell through the same, between the rails of the connecting track, by reason of its imperfect covering, and was injured. *Held*, that if the nuisance complained of was created solely by the D., X. and B. Company in the construction of said connecting track, and said company had the sole ownership, possession, and use of said track, the contract between the two companies giving the defendant no power of control in the construction or use thereof, the defendant cannot be held liable for the plaintiff's injury, although the defendant may have had a reversionary interest in the premises, subject to the easement of the D., X. and B. Company. *Gwathney* v. *L. M. R. R. Co.* 12 *Critchfield's Ohio State Reports*, 92.

4. In an action to recover of a railroad company for injuries received by a brakeman while in the service of the company, by reason of the breaking of the chain and giving way of the brake while working it, owing to a defect therein, whereby he was thrown from the train and injured; *held:* 1. That it was the duty of the company to use all reasonable and ordinary care in providing safe and well equipped brakes for the brakemen; and that if the company, in neglect of such duty, have procured a defective and improper brake, and placed the brakeman to work the same without an opportunity to know such defect, and he was thereby injured, a right of action would thereupon arise against the company; 2. That if the existence of such defect at the time of the accident was owing to the neglect of other operatives of the road, supposed to be competent, whose duty it was to have inspected said brake, but who neglected so to do, and negligently suffered the same to continue in use when not road-worthy, unknown to the company, it is not liable therefor, inasmuch as such delinquent inspector is to be regarded a fellow servant of the brakeman in a common service. *C. and X. and L. M. R. R. Co.* v. *Webb.* 12 *Critchfield's Ohio State Reports*, 475.

5. The use on land, the property of a railroad company, of en-

gines and cars running at a high rate of speed, though dangerous, is a reasonable use of land, because it is for a proper object and a highly beneficial purpose, and the danger may be avoided by proper care. If the owners of cattle permit them to run at large in the vicinity of an unenclosed railroad track, and do not choose to avoid danger to their cattle by keeping them within their own enclosures, they can ask no more than that the agents of the railroad company in the legitimate conduct of its business, running its trains with a speed regulated by the grade of its road, the capacity of its locomotive power and the safety of persons and property carried, shall, with due regard to the safety of persons and property in their charge, being the paramount consideration, exercise what "in that particular business would be an ordinary and reasonable care to avoid unnecessary injury to animals casually coming upon their unenclosed road." A railroad company, in determining the rate of speed at which its train shall run, such rate being otherwise reasonable and proper in view of the object to be accomplished, is not bound to consider the increased risk to cattle running at large in the vicinity of its track, and lessen the speed on that account. *C. O. R. R. Co.* v. *Lawrence.* 13 *Critchfield*, 678.

6. When there is nothing in the running of a train or in its rate of speed, at a particular time and place, inconsistent with the general and legitimate conduct of the business of a railroad company, the occasion and necessity therefor do not properly concern the owner of cattle running at large; and he cannot properly inquire whether the rate of speed was greater than usual for a particular train at a particular place, and what was the object of such increased rate of speed. The inquiry should be, "whether, under all the circumstances of the case, the defendants exercised reasonable and proper care in running their engine to avoid injury to the cattle of the plaintiff." And the facts and circumstances which may be relied upon to show a want of *proper* care, are for the exclusive consideration of the jury. *Id.* 13 *Critchfield's Ohio State Reports*, 678.

7. In a proceeding by a railroad company under the railroad act of 1848, authorizing an appropriation of lands, on which to construct a railroad, the company described the land to be appropriated as "fifty feet wide on each side of said railroad, as last surveyed through sub-division lots Nos. 1, 2, 3, and 4, fractional section No. 1 of township 10, south of range 7 east, commencing on the north bounds thereof, thence westerly and southerly on and near the boundaries thereof to a point in the west line of said No. 4, near the north-west corner; also, lots Nos. 11, 12, 13, 14, and 15 of the sub-division of river tract No. 87, in said county." The application was filed February 28, 1851; and notice given March 4, View made and report filed April 21st, and possession taken by the company, April 22, 1851. In an action by a subsequent purchaser of the lands of the former owner, with notice to recover the same from the company, on proof that said road was

surveyed and staked out previous to the first of April, and found staked out by the viewers: *Held*, that said description was sufficiently certain in the appropriation proceedings. *C. and T. R. R. Co.* v. *Prentice et al.* 13 *Critchfield's Ohio State Reports*, p. 373.

8. If, in any case, it would be competent for a court to decree the specific performance of a contract to operate a railroad, requiring as it would personal acts involving the continuous exercise of skill and judgment, under varying circumstances and emergencies, it could only be in a case where the demand for the exercise of such a power was stringent, and the circumstances such as to authorize the court in making an order to limit its duration as to time, and to define, to some proper and reasonable extent, the mode and manner in which it should be obeyed. *Port Clinton R. R. Co.* v. *Cleve. and Toledo R. R. Co.* 13 *Critchfield's*, 544.

9. The P. C. Railroad Company leased its franchises and the road for the term of ninety-nine years, renewable for ever, to the C. and T. Railroad Company, which was a company created by the consolidation of the T. N. and C. Railroad Company and the Junction Railroad Company. The consideration was in the form of covenants—to pay taxes, to assume debts, to finish the road, and to operate and manage the road in such a manner as would not forfeit or endanger the franchises and corporate rights of the lessor. It appears that only a small sum of money had ever been paid in by the stockholders of the P. C. Company, which had never been expended; that the cost of any work on the road previous to the lease had been defrayed by the Junction Company, and that this work had been done and the organization of the P. C. Company made under the general law of the State, to enable the Junction Company to extend its line in a manner its charter did not permit. *Held*, that the P. C. Company was not entitled to a specific performance of the covenant in the lease to operate the road. *Id.*

INVENTIONS OF THE YEAR.

Railroad Cars—Freight Cars—Dumping Cars—Locomotives—Steam Engines—Car Trucks—Car Springs—Car Couplings, etc.

The Nos. affixed are the official Nos. of the Patents at Washington. This Summary is taken from "THE SCIENTIFIC AMERICAN," published at New York.

Freight Car.—CHARLES R. FOOTE and JAMES ORTON, Williamstown, Mass.: I claim, *First.* A car body of cylindrical or an approximate form, with wheels fitted on its periphery and arranged to rotate with its contents or load on the rails, substantially as herein set forth. *Second.* The frame, D, in combination with the car body, A, the journals of the latter being fitted in bearings in the former substantially as described. *Third.* The oblong bearings, c, c, in the frame, D, in combination with the shoes, E, placed on said frame and all arranged to operate as and for the purpose set forth.—No. 41,212.

[This invention relates to a new and improved freight car designed more especially for transporting or carrying coal-oil and other liquids, grain in bulk, etc. The invention consists in constructing the body of the car of cylindrical or an approximate form, and encompassing the same with bands provided with flanges to serve as wheels. The body of the car is provided with an axle, the journals of which are fitted in oblong bearings in a frame and arranged in connection with self-acting brakes, all being combined in such a manner that the body of the car will rotate as it is drawn along, and it is believed several advantages are obtained over the ordinary freight cars in use.]

Railway Carriage.—N. F. BRYANT, East Boston, Mass. Patented Aug. 18, 1863: I claim constructing a car truck with divided axles, or an axle to each wheel, such axle being supported or journaled at each end thereof; that the opposite axles are movable towards or from the longitudinal centre of the car, the construction being for the purpose of adapting the car to tracks of different gauges, as set forth. I also claim the automatic combination, consisting not only of the chocks, or their equivalents, applied to the truck frame and wheels, and the chock rails, or their equivalents, applied to the track, but the two tracks of different gauges and their wheel-changing track, or the same, and its flange-guide rails, the whole being arranged and so as to operate substantially as specified. And in combination therewith I claim the projections or guides, n, n, for the purpose specified.—No. 1,611.

Street Car.—J. A. MILLER, New York City: I claim, *First.* The combined arrangement of a momentum-saving friction brake, substantially such as herein described, with the hand-wheel and shaft, which serves to operate the ordinary brake, and with the treadle, d, sliding-clutch, c, and drum, b, or their equivalents, all constructed and operating in the manner and for the purpose substantially as set forth. *Second.* The arrangement of the ring, H, with springs, I, in combination with the sliding disk, G, and axle, C', of a street car, constructed and operating in the manner and for the purpose substantially as herein shown and described.—No. 41,386.

[This invention consists in the arrangement of a momentum-saving friction brake in combination with the hand-wheel and shaft, which serves to operate the ordinary brake, and with a treadle and sliding-clutch, in such a manner that by the act of turning the hand-wheel, whereby the ordinary brake is applied, the momentum-saving brake is also brought in operation, and by stepping on the treadle the ordinary brake is taken off and the momentum-saving brake assists in starting the car. Mr. Miller's address is 200 Broadway, New York.]

Railroad Car.—JAMES WITHYCOMBE and CHARLES REIBLEIN, Cleveland, Ohio: I claim supporting the bolsters, F F', of railroad cars, by the beams, C C C' C', and E E', arranged and operating as and for the purpose set forth.—No. 41,409.

Car Brake.—W. S. MORROW (assignor to WARWICK MARTIN, ROSALINE N. AMBLER, and ELIZABETH JOHNSON), of Chicago, Ill. Ante-dated June 22, 1863: I claim, *First.* The arrangement of the two drums, A A' and B, with the chains, a c and c′, in combination with the tumbling-rod, R, constructed and operating substantially as and for the purposes herein delineated and set forth. *Second.* I claim the arrangement of the drum, A A′, constructed in two parts, with the vertical shaft, and the chains, c and c′, when constructed, arranged, and operating, substantially as and for the purposes herein shown and described.—No 41,042.

Car Brake for Railroads.—WM. S. MARTIN, Waukegan, Ill. Ante-dated Sept. 20, 1863: I claim, *First.* The combination of the shaft, A, the friction wheels, B B′, the clutches, C C′, springs, S S′, and slides, D D, with the chain, b, arranged and operating as and for the purposes herein delineated and described. *Second.* I claim the peculiarly-constructed lever for moving the shaft, A, marked, H, whereby said shaft is moved forward in the desired direction, whether the lever, H, is moved forward or backward, arranged and operating substantially as shown and set forth. *Third.* I claim communicating motion to the friction wheels, B B′, by the impact thereof upon the wheels of the cars, when said friction wheels are used in combination with the shaft, A, the clutches, C C′, the springs, S S′, the slides, D D′, the lever, H, and the chain, b, operating as and for the purposes specified and shown. —No. 41,013.

Railroad Car Truck.—A. F. SMITH, Norwich, Conn.:—I claim, *First.* Suspending the car to the truck by freely swinging links of so short radius that the gravity of the parts alone will effectively sustain the lateral motion at high velocities, substantially as herein set forth. *Second.* The employment of the within-described fixed straps, M, swinging suspending links, N, joint, m, and bars, a b, or their respective equivalents arranged substantially as shown, whereby the vertical strain is borne by the top of the bearing beam, A, and base of the swing beam, B, as usual, and a shorter radius of lateral motion secured with the advantage specified. —No. 40,957.

Railroad Dumping Cars.—THOMAS A. M'FARLAND, Meadville, Pa.: I claim the movable dirt box, A A, the revolving drums, M and N, the levers, G and F, the ropes P and Q, and pulleys, 1 2, when the same are constructed as described, and in the aforesaid combination for the purposes set forth.—No. 42,862.

Stock Car.—WM. STARK, Bronson, Mich. Ante-dated July 21, 1864: I claim, *First.* The arrangement of the X-shaped hinges, p, in combination with the shutters, o, and hooks, r, as and for the purpose set forth. *Second.* The arrangement of the vertically movable eye-bolts, m, in combination with the hinged caps, l, apertures, k, and hooks, m′, as and for the purpose described.—No. 43,720.

[The object of this invention is to facilitate the feeding and watering of the stock, to provide for a thorough ventilation of the car, to increase the capacity of the same by introducing a movable deck, and to provide the means for sprinkling the stock in the car in an easy and ready manner.]

Dumping Car.—W. R. MAFFIT, Wilkesbarre, Pa.: I claim the rockers, B, and cross rails or bearers, D, applied in combination with the car body, A, and truck frame, E, in the manner and for the purpose substantially as herein shown and described.—No 44,539.

[The main object of this invention is to make a dumping car as low as possible, to reduce or avoid the expense of shovelling the material. The invention consists in the application to a car of transverse rockers, supported by cross rails or screws which are secured to the under side of the truck frame in such a manner that the rockers are brought down to the ground as near as possible, and the car can be tilted sideways to an angle of 45 degrees or more, while the platform or bottom of the same is comparatively low and close to the surface of the truck frame.]

Machine for Loading Hay.—HENRY MAYCOCK.—No. 44,540.

Dumping Cart.—THEODORE BLODGETT, Belchertown, Mass.: I claim the combination and arrangement of the eccentrics, F F, with the shaft, G, the scoop, D, its lifting chains, E E, and the operative mechanism of such shaft. I also claim the arrangement of the scoop, D, on the axle of the supporting wheels in combination with the arrangement of the scoop-elevating machinery on the thills, as specified. I also claim the combination of the hinged door, e, and its holding mechanism, f g, with the scoop, D, elevating mechanism and the wheels and thills, or their equivalents, for connecting one or more draft animals to the cart.—No. 44,068.

Railway Truck adapted to the different Gauges of Tracks.—CHARLES D. TISDALE, East Boston, Mass., assignor to himself and Barna W. Tisdale, Boston, Mass.: I claim the application of the wheels to the axle by means of sleeves or tubular shafts, as described, and combining with the latter and the axle a means or mechanism for fixing the sleeves at different distances apart on the axle in order to adapt the wheels to tracks of different gauges, in manner as specified. I also claim the combination of the clutch-box, D, the flanges, G H, and the semi-circular clutch, E, the same being made and applied together and to the axle, B, and the tubular shaft or wheel-sleeve, C, and so as to operate substantially as specified. I also claim the combination of the stopper, F, and the bolt, N, the two clutch-boxes, D D, and their clutches, E E, the whole being constructed and applied to and so as to operate with the axle and the wheel-sleeves or hollow shafts, substantially as hereinbefore explained. And with the wheels applied to the axle by means of sleeves or tubular shafts as described, and these latter and the axle provided with a means or mechanism for fixing the sleeves at different distances apart on the axle, and for the purpose of adapting the wheels to tracks of different gauges, I claim the application of a "feather connection" (viz., the rib, a, and groove, b), or its mechanical equivalent, to one of the sleeves only of the axle, the other sleeve being free to revolve as well as to slide on the axle.—No. 43,163.

Car Truck.—CHARLES T. TISDALE, East Boston, Mass., assignor to himself and JOSEPH H. CLAPP, Boston, Mass.: I claim the new or improved wheel-locking mechanism, or combination consisting of the double catch, D, the elastic band, E, and either one or two grooves, c, d, and applied to the wheel-sleeve and axle, and so as to operate therewith substantially as herein specified.—No. 44,694.

Track-Clearer for Railroads.—MR. J. ADAMS, Bedford, Pa.: I claim the application of this combined snow-plow and excavator to snow obstructions on railroads for their removal, using for that purpose the aforesaid combined snow-plow and excavator, or any other substantially the same, and which will produce the same effect.—No. 41,468.

Car Brake.—WM. D. GOODNOW, Albany, N. Y.: I claim extending the brake bars, F F, over and beyond the jaw braces, f f, and connecting them thereto by means of the yoke, i i, or their equivalents, substantially as and for the purposes set forth. I also claim in combination with the plank or hang-frame, E, of the car body, and the brake bars, F F, the guide and safety rods, k k, arranged and operating substantially as and for the purposes set forth. I also claim the combination and arrangement of the brake bars, F F, lever, G G′, connecting-bar, N, car-bearing, E, and truck wheels, B B, constructed and operating substantially in the manner and for the purposes shown and described.—No. 44,718.

Car Brake.—A. J. AMBLER, Chicago, Ill., assignor to himself and GUSTAVUS SHEPARD, New York City: I claim the employment or use, in connection with a tensonial chain, F, and a brake chain, G, of fixed and sliding sheaves arranged substantially as herein shown, or in any equivalent way, so that by operating the tensonial chain, F, a movement will be imparted to the brake chain, G, to set or apply the brakes, and the slack of the tensonial chain be taken up by the falling of the sliding sheaves when the power is taken off from said tensonial chain. I further claim limiting or controlling the maximum power of the brakes by limiting the rising and falling movement of the sheaves, E E′, by having the axles, b, of said sheaves fitted in slots, a, in the bars, D″ D″, or other fixtures, substantially as set forth.—No. 44,036.

Mode of operating Brakes of Railroad Cars.—ALFRED BERNEY, of Jersey City, N. J., assignee by mesne-assignment of CHARLES B. TURNER, of Buffalo, N. Y. Patented Nov. 14, 1848, and extended: I claim, *First*, the combination of a sliding-bumper with a rod and a brake system and an interposed spring, the combination being substantially as specified and operating substantially as described. *Second.* The combination of a sliding-rod, a bumper, a guide or cheeks, and a locking-plate, all substantially as set forth, whereby the spring forms a connection either between the bumper and the car-body or the bumper and a system of brakes, substantially in the manner and for the purpose set forth; and *Third.* A locking-plate, in combination with a sliding-rod, capable of operating a brake system and a bumper, whereby the bumper may either be permitted to or prevented from communicating motion to a brake system under a mode of operation substantially as herein before set forth.—No. 1,783.

Operating Brakes of Railroad Cars.—ALFRED BERNEY, of Jersey City, assignee by mesne-assignment of CHARLES B. TURNER, of Buffalo, N. Y. Patented Nov. 14, 1848, and extended: I claim, *First.* The combination of these three elements, viz.: A lever having the characteristics specified; two connections between said lever and two systems of brakes, and a connection between said lever and a windlass, the whole being combined and working together to produce results substantially such as are specified under a mode of operation substantially as set forth. *Second.* A combination of four levers and their connecting rods, arranged with reference to each other, and operating substantially as specified, whereby pressure may be exerted on four rubbing surfaces on the same side of a car, substantially in the manner and under the conditions hereinbefore described.—No. 1,784.

Dumping Apparatus.—FRANK FICHT, Isle Royal Mine, Michigan: I claim the combination of the recesses, b b, with the rails, A A′ A2, or their equivalents, substantially as herein shown and described. I also claim the employment of the wheels, G, in combination with the above named parts, substantially as herein shown and described. I also claim the employment of the skip or car, B, in combination with the above-named parts, substantially as herein shown and described.—No. 44 412.

[This invention pertains to the class of devices that are employed for elevating ores, minerals, earthy matters, and other substances from mines, wells, excavations, and subterranean places of all kinds.]

Watchman's Clock.—WILLIAM WINTER, Plainfield, N. J.: I claim the application to the face of a clock of the tell-tale dial, D, made of slate or other similar material, and marked with figures from 1 to 12, in combination with a hole, f, in the lid, B, and with suitable gear-wheels, causing said tell-tale dial to revolve with the same speed as the hour-hand, substantially as and for the purpose set forth —No.43,616.

[This invention consists in the application to the face of a clock or watch of a movable dial-plate, which is made of slate or other suitable material capable to receive and show the mark of a pencil, or other instrument, and marked with the figures from 1 to 12, the same as the main dial of the clock, and which revolves with the hour-hand under a hole cut into the edge of the lid, which is closed by means of lock and key in such a manner that said disk or tell-tale dial can only be reached through the hole in the lid, and that when a night watchman, or other person having a similar charge, is instructed to pass the clock at certain stated hours, and to make a mark with the pencil on the tell tale dial whenever he passes, his employer or superintendent is enabled to read off on said dial at what hour the watchman has passed the clock and made his mark, and by opening the lid of the clock the tell-tale dial can be readily cleaned and rendered fit for future use.]

Railroad Pumps.—JOHN B. ATWATER, of Chicago, Ill.: *First.* I claim the cylinders, A and B, connected with the pipe, C, in combination with the piston, D, and box, E, or its equivalent, when constructed and operating substantially as and for the purpose set forth. *Second.* In combination with the foregoing, I claim the application of a weight, attached to the upper end of the stem, a, of the piston, D, substantially as and for the purpose herein set forth. *Third.* In combination with a piston, weighted as above described, I claim the application of a body of air, between the piston and the water to be elevated, substantially in the manner herein described.—No. 44,501.

Locomotive.—GEORGE THOMAS, Frankfort-on-the-Main, Germany, assignor to Bernhard Schaffer and Christian Budenberg, New York City: I claim the application to a locomotive of horse pipes, d e* g, with or without an additional air chamber, F, and with suitable stop valves, a a* g′, in the manner and for the purpose substantially as herein shown and described.—No. 44,055.

[This invention consists in the use of an ordinary locomotive as a steam fire-engine, either by connecting the force pump or pumps of said locomotive with an air chamber or by applying the power or a portion of the power of a locomotive to any other pump or device for forcing a current of water through a suitable pipe or pipes, in such a manner that with very little extra expense an ordinary locomotive can be transformed to a fire-engine or pumping-engine, and used as such in cases where it may be desirable.]

Truck for Locomotives.—LEVI BISSELL (assignor to the Locomotive Safety Truck Company), New York City. Patented Aug. 4, 1857: I claim, *First.* Connecting the truck with the frame of the locomotive so that it shall be free to move laterally under the frame in combination with the means herein described or their equivalents thereof, by which the weight of the locomotive resting on the trucks acts automatically to resist the lateral motion of the truck and retain it in a central position while running on the straight parts of the track, and to aid in restoring it to such position when passing from curved to straight parts of the track, substantially as set forth. *Second.* Connecting the truck and body of the locomotive at a point between the axles of the truck and driving wheels, so that the truck may move laterally under the locomotive substantially as described, to compel the axles of the truck and driving wheels to assume positions parallel or nearly so with the radii of the curves of the track, or at right angles with the rails on the straight parts of the track, as specified.—No. 1,794.

Feed-water Heater for Locomotives.—DAVID POLLOCK, Lancaster, Pa. Ante-dated Jan. 17, 1864: I claim, *First.* One or more circulating chambers in combination with the tank and heaters, substantially as and for the purpose set forth. *Second.* I claim the tubular bars or grates, G G, in the furnace or fire-box in combination with one or more circulating chambers for heating the feed water, substantially as set forth. *Third.* I claim one or more pipes, K K, attached to the fire-grate heater and extending above the grate, as herein described for the purpose set forth. *Fourth.* The valve, M, with the float, Q, attached, in combination with the circulating chamber, tank, and heaters, substantially as and for the purpose herein described. *Fifth.* The pipe, V, with the stop, W, arranged as shown for the purpose specified. *Sixth.* I claim combining with the heater, G G, in the fire-box, the safety valve, U, for the purpose herein set forth. *Seventh.* The heater, H H, in the smoke-box, constructed with the circular pipes, substantially as shown and described. *Eighth.* I claim the reheating pipe, N N, constructed as and for the purpose specified. *Ninth.* I claim the hose or pipes, F and L, in combination with the tank, heaters, and circulating chamber as and for the purpose described.—No. 41,319.

Locomotive Wheel.—MARY JANE MONTGOMERY, New York City: I claim, *First.* The application of a corrugated beam of metal, constructed substantially as described, to wheels of locomotive engines, cars, vehicles, and carriages of all kinds. *Second.* The combination of the aforesaid corrugated metal beam, C, with the metallic tire, D, in the construction of wheels of locomotive engines, cars, vehicles, and carriages of all kinds, substantially as described.—No. 42,958.

Pump Gear.—HENRY and FREDERICK J. L. BLANDY, Zanesville, Ohio: We claim the employment in combination with a counter-shaft, B, for driving the feed-pump of an engine, of a friction wheel, E, on the main-shaft of the engine, a friction wheel, F, on the said countershaft, and an intermediate idle friction wheel, G, suspended from a lever or its equivalent, substantially as herein specified.—No. 43,387.

[This invention consists in transmitting the motion from the crank shaft of a steam engine to a counter-shaft for working the feed pump by means of a system of friction wheels, one of which is arranged as an idle wheel to be thrown in and out of gear as required to connect the pump with and disconnect it from the engine, the object being to effect such connection and disconnection in a more easy manner than can be done by the means heretofore used, and to relieve the engine of all avoidable friction, and the driving gear of the pump of all avoidable wear when the pump is not in operation.]

Locomotive Engine.—ISAAC H. CONGDON, Springfield, Ill.: I claim the jet pipes, DD, communicating with the exhaust pipes, C C, and employed in conjunction with the hopper shaped box, E, and discharge pipe, E, to cause the sparks, etc. to pass out and be deposited at the under side of the engine and at the same time deaden or extinguish the same, substantially in the manner and for the purpose specified.—No. 43,898.

Composition for Coating Steam Pipes, Boilers, etc.—JOHN CHILCOTT, of Brooklyn, N. Y. Ante-dated Sept. 19, 1864: I claim the non-conducting composition, composed of silica, gypsum, and coal-tar pitch, with or without hair, substantially as herein described.—No. 44,517.

Method of Operating Cut-off Valves.—GREEN B. MCDONALD, of Louisville, Ky. Ante-dated Jan. 2, 1864: I claim, *First.* The piston H, fitted with a valve or valves, b b, and the cylinder, I, furnished with a side passage, c, and valve or cock, d, and containing oil or other liquid, applied in combination with each other and with the induction or cut-off valve, A, to operate substantially as and for the purpose herein specified. *Second.* The passages, f f, in the said cylinder, I, arranged and operating in combination with the said piston, H, substantially as and for the purposes herein described.—No. 41,083.

[This invention relates to what are known as the drop cut-offs, in which the closing of the induction valve or other valve employed for cutting off the steam is effected by the weight of the valve itself, or by a weight or spring connected therewith, after such valve has been liberated from its opening mechanism. It consists in certain novel means of regulating the closing of the said valve, after its liberation, either by means of a manual adjustment or under the control of a governor.]

Self-regulating Pressure Valve.—AUGUSTINE CAMPBELL, Brooklyn, N. Y. Ante-dated Sept. 22, 1862: I claim, *First.* A pressure regulator composed of a flexible diaphragm, and of the following elements combined and arranged on the opposite sides thereof as follows, to wit, on one side of said diaphragm a balanced valve connected thereto without packing, through a free communication between the proper surfaces of the valve and that side of the diaphragm, and on the other side of said diaphragm a loaded lever performing the double functions, 1st, of resisting the pressure upon the diaphragm with the force desired; and 2d, of indicating to the attendant when the pressure has reached, and approximately how much it exceeds that required. *Second.* I claim so arranging the parts of the above described apparatus that water will accumulate, or may be introduced to protect the diaphragm from injury by the contact of the steam or other fluid, substantially in the manner herein set forth.—No. 43,833.

Valve Gear for Steam Engines.—T. W. BOWERS, Cincinnati, Ohio. Ante-dated January 27, 1864: I claim, *First.* Operating the valve, H, by the lifters or their equivalents, when they are arranged within the valve-chamber, as shown, and for the purpose described. *Second.* The combination of the valves, H, rock-shaft, m, and cranks, m, with the weights, m‴, substantially as described, and for the purpose set forth. *Third.* The several devices in combination, by which the port or steam-valves and the exhaust or outlet valves are operated, when combined substantially as described and for the purpose set forth. *Fourth.* The combination of the forked sliding-bar, L, with the vibrating bar, K, and cam-rod, D, when constructed and arranged, substantially as described. *Fifth.* The construction and arrangement of the connecting-bar, g, and palls, r r, with the cranks, m′ m′, when constructed substantially as described and for the purpose set forth.—No. 43,757.

Safety Valve Arrangement.—WM. S. HUNTINGTON, Andrusville, N. Y., assignor to himself and JAMES ROBERTSON, Alexandria, Va.: I claim, *First.* The combination of the levers, C I′, rods, E L M, spring pawl, K, and cam, N, operating in the described connection with the circular guide, H. *Second.* I claim the combination with the spring-balance, D, of the lever, I′, spring pawl, K, and notches, h, for the purpose explained.—No. 41,580.

Governor Cut-off Valve.—K. H. LOOMIS, Baltimore, Md. I claim the employment in combination of the block, A, secured to stem, d, arm, e, wrist-pin, h, face-plate, f, stud, g, in the manner substantially and for the purpose of regulating the flow of steam to the cylinder of steam engines, as set forth.—No. 43,920.

Balanced Slide Valve.—ALEXANDER BUCHANAN, New York City: I claim, *First.* The attachment of the valve-cover to the back or cover of the steam chest by means of hooks, l l, and eye-bolts, m m, or their equivalents, substantially as and for the purpose herein specified. *Second.* The attachment of the valve-cover to one end of the steam-chest by braces having flexible connections which permit the cover to rise from the valve, substantially as and for the purpose herein specified. —No. 44,849.

[This invention relates to the protection of the back of the valve from the pressure of the steam by means of a valve-cover attached to the back or cover of the valve-chest, and it consists in a novel mode of supporting and sustaining such valve-cover, whereby it is enabled to adapt itself to the back of the valve in such manner that the valve will work against it perfectly steam-tight, but without binding or unnecessary friction; and that in case of the engine being suddenly reversed the valve may be permitted to be lifted off the seat, and thereby prevent the compression of any steam that may have been shut in the cylinder.]

Cylindrical Steam Valve.—WM. H. AKINS, Dryden, N. Y.: I claim the solid plug or plugs, E E′, provided with cavities, e e′, and fitted in cases, F F′, with ports f f* f** f′ f′* f′**, to operate in combination with the annular steam-chambers, g g′, each divided off in three compartments, to communicate with the interior of the cylinder, with the steam pipe, and with the exhaust pipe, in the manner and for the purpose substantially as herein shown and described.—No. 43,824.

Valve-Gear of Steam Hammers.—JOHN T. TURNER, Bridgewater, Mass.: I claim combining the oscillating valve with the hammer by means of a lever, I, one end of which is connected by a rod, h, with an arm on the centre spindle of the valve, and the other end of which is arranged between two tappets, j and k, all substantially as herein specified.—No. 43,612.

Valve for Steam Engines.—JOHN JACOB MILLER (assignor to himself and ERNST PRUSSING), Chicago, Ill. Ante-dated Feb. 15, 1863: I claim, *First.* The combination of the fixed cylindrical seat, A, and cylindrical valve, D, with an adjusting wheel, G, or other substantially equivalent device to regulate the effective stroke of the said valve, as explained. *Second.* The spring, J, and pin, K, used in the described combination with the aperture, g, in the wheel, G, and the slot, f, in the valve-rod, F, to lock the said wheel to the said rod or permit it to be turned up or down thereon, as and for the purpose explained.—No. 43,949.

Valve-Gear for Steam Engines.—ROBERT HEYS, Philadelphia, Pa.: I claim, *First.* The valve-spindle, D, of a steam engine, the link, E, eccentric rod, G, and arm, F, in combination with the weighted lever, k, and link, h, or their equivalents, whereby the motion of the governor-rod may be imparted to the link, as set forth for the purpose specified. *Second.* The wheels, N and N′, lever, P, and pawls, e and e′, with the shield, t, when the position of the latter is regulated by the governor, and when the whole is applied to the raising and lowering of the link, E, substantially as and for the purpose herein set forth.—No. 43,114.

Slide-Valve for Steam Engines.—WILLIAM HUSTON, of Wilmington, Del.: I claim a valve, D, with channel, d, and apertures, e e, f, arranged in combination with the seat, A, and ports, a a′ b b′ c, substantially as and for the purpose set forth. Also the exhaust, c, applied in combination with condenser exhausts, b b′, and valve, D, or its equivalent, in the manner and for the purpose substantially as described.—No. 44,632.

[This invention consists in a valve with a double exhaust—one into the chimney or open atmosphere and the other into a condenser, in such a manner that through the first or ordinary exhaust the pressure of the steam in the exhaust-end of the cylinder is reduced to that of the ordinary atmosphere, or nearly so, and the condensation of the remaining steam can be effected in the same manner and by the same means as by a common low-pressure condensing engine.]

Valve for Steam Engines.—D. B. TRAVIS, La Crosse, Wis.: I claim the combination with two slide valves, A A, of two movable three-portet valve-seats, F F, and a system of six ports in the permanent seat, the whole constructed, arranged, and operating substantially as and for the purpose herein set forth.—No. 40,142.

[This invention consists in a novel system of movable valve-seats and stationary, and movable ports, in combination with slide valves in a steam engine, whereby the engine is enabled to be reversed and stopped very quickly and easily.]

Steam Engine Governor.—H. D. SNOW, Rochester, N. Y.: I claim the employment of steam pressure in marine governors, as a means for counter-balancing the centrifugal force of the revolver.—No. 44,466.

Valve-Gear for Steam Engines.—TISDALE CARPENTER, Providence, R. I.: I claim the employment in a steam or other engine of one or more right and left-hand screws, f f′, pinions, h h, and racks, i i, combined with each other with the regulator and with the induction valve-operating mechanism, and coöperating substantially as described to produce the necessary variations in the operation of the valves for the regulation of the engine.—No. 40,905.

Improvement in Air Valves for Steam Radiators.—GEORGE W. BLAKE, New York, N. Y.: I claim the combination of the brass or composition rod to which the valve is attached, or on which it is formed directly, with one of the iron tubes of a tubular radiator, or to any part of the interior of the shell of any other kind of radiator, substantially as and for the purpose herein specified.—No. 44,155.

[This invention consists in the employment within one of the iron tubes of the tubular radiator, or within the shell of any other radiator, of a brass or composition metal rod, secured at one end to the tube or shell, and having at the other end a valve fitted to a stationary seat, whereby the difference of expansion under changes of temperature between the brass or composition of which the bar is composed, and the iron of which the tube or shell is composed, is caused to leave the valve open until the radiator is full of steam, and then to close it.]

Rotary Steam Valve.—HERMAN HAUPT, Cambridge, Mass.: I claim an equilibrium valve constructed as described, with reference to the steam, gas, air, or water induction and eduction openings or passages and partitions, for operation substantially as set forth. The herein described arrangement of balance-valves for operation in the manner and for the purposes described, whereby the usual outside contrivances for actuating the valve may be dispensed with as set forth.—No. 43,910.

Railroad Rails.—GEORGE D. TELLER, Buffalo, N. Y.: I claim, *First.* A secondary rail, E, made of steel or the best quality of iron, and inserted into a groove made in the top of the main rail, for the purposes and substantially as described. *Second.* The part, e′, whether made of iron or other elastic material, in combination with the main rail, A B, and secondary rail, E, for the purposes and substantially as set forth. *Third.* Making the rails, A and B, with a tongue in one and a groove in the other as represented at c′ (or the equivalent thereof), in combination with the bolts, D, for the more securely locking or fastening the said parts together, as described.—No. 44,562.

Railroad Rail.—WM D. O'BRIEN, Brooklyn, N. Y.: I claim the crescent-shaped rail forming a roof or cap to the sills, as and for the purposes specified. And I claim forming the under side of the joint-plate, e, of city railroads, concave to set on to the convex surface of the wood prepared to receive said plate, for the purpose of preventing the lodging of water beneath the said joint-plate and the rotting consequent thereon, as set forth.—No. 43,599.

Railroad Rail.—SIDNEY A. BEERS, Brooklyn, N. Y.: I claim the manufacture and use of compressible railroad rails; such compressibility resulting from the irregular form of the web, or shank of the rail, which thus becomes a spring of more or less elasticity, in proportion to the extent of departure from a direct or vertical line; as set forth, or by the use of any other form which will secure or promote elasticity between the base and face of the rail.—No. 42,636.

Journal Box for Railroad Cars.—JOHN O. SCOTT, New York City: I claim the employment of a series of loose conical-ended rollers, E F, between grooved journals, B, and boxes, C, in the manner and for the purpose before stated and described.—No. 42,881.

Packing for Journal Boxes.—JONATHAN CONK, Red Bank, N. J.: I claim a packing, for the purpose specified, composed of the zostera marina (grass wrack, sea-eel grass), or other sea-grass, dried or cured, and saturated with any suitable lubricating substance.—No. 41,197.

[This invention is designed as a substitute for cotton waste and other similar fibrous materials which have hitherto been used as a packing for the journal boxes of railroad car-axles, the shafting of machinery, and for other purposes where packing is applied in machinery.]

Journal Box.—E. S. DICKINSON and WM. D. NELSON, New York City. Ante-dated Sept. 18, 1864: I claim, *First.* The employment or use in a journal box for car axles, of an oil chamber provided with a valve, I, so constructed and arranged that said valve will, under the motion of the car, oscillate or roll so as to intermittingly open and close the oil passage, and gradually supply the journal with oil and keep it in a properly lubricated state. *Second.* The combination of the two parts, A B, projecting ears or flanges, a f, screws, C′, and shoulders, c and e, when the said parts are constructed and arranged as herein described, and operated in the manner and for the purposes specified *Third.* The packing plate, C, fitted in the rear of the journal box and provided with the collar or bushing, D, substantially as and for the purpose herein set forth.—No. 44,407.

Journal Box.—G. G. HUNT, Bridgeport, Mass.: I claim the employment of a box, A, having hollow sides and hollow bottom, in combination with the axle, C, and wick, G, all in the manner herein shown and described, for the purpose set forth.—No. 41,221.

[This invention consists in the employment or use of a journal box with hollow sides and bottom, whereby an oil fountain is produced, from where the oil is carried up to the axle by means of one or more wicks, said wick or wicks being acted upon by weights or springs in such a manner that they are always held in close contact with the axle, and that they carry up the requisite supply of oil without allowing any waste.]

Oil Box for Railroad Cars.—EDWIN F. HURLBUT & RANSOM S. POTTER (assignors to themselves and Nathan S. Bouton), Chicago, Ill.: We claim, *First.* Casting or fastening a door or lid into a frame, substantially as shown and for the purposes described. *Second.* The combination of the loose lugs or ears, letter D, with the oil box, substantially as shown and for the purposes described.—No. 42,732.

Railroad Car Seat.—A. S. BABBIT, Keeseville, N. Y.: I claim the application to car-seats or other fixed articles of furniture to be used in a movable conveyance, of flanged blocks, c, provided with shanks, b, that pass up through plates, a, which are suspended from springs secured to the top ends of the shanks, b, and made to support the car-seat, or other article, substantially as described, so that said blocks can be readily secured to some fixed portion of the movable conveyance and their shanks with the springs will form yielding guides to keep the seat or other article in place and render it comfortable for the person using the same.—No.44,379.

[The object of this invention is to support by springs car-seats or other fixed articles of furniture to be used in a movable conveyance, such as berths or benches in vessels, said springs being connected to the legs of the seat or to the frame of the fixed article of furniture, so that they stretch when the seat or other article of furniture is occupied, and that the stems or cores round which the springs are wound form guides for the legs or frame and prevent the seat or other article of furniture changing its place spontaneously.]

Railroad Car-Seat.—CONRAD B. LASHAR, New York City: I claim a movable seat combined with the stationary seats, substantially as specified, when the movable seat is forward of and higher than the stationary seat, as set forth.—No. 44,536.

Railroad Chair.—WELLS HENDERSHOTT, Batavia, N. Y.: I claim, *First.* Making a rail-chair and coupling for railroads, connected by a hinge or hinges at the bottom, with the inclined planes, b b and f f, so that the pressure and weight of the cars will firmly hold the rails, and when the weight is removed the hold will be relaxed and allow the rails to expand and contract for the purposes described, and in the manner as substantially set forth. *Second.* I claim the inclined planes in combination with the hinge, for the purposes described and as set forth. *Third.* I claim the hinge connecting the two parts of the chair and coupling for the purposes described, and substantially as set forth. *Fourth.* I claim the inclined planes for the purposes described and as set forth. *Fifth.* I claim in combination with said rail-chair and coupling a rail that may be turned over, with both the top and bottom sides alike. *Sixth.* I claim in combination with said rail-chair and coupling the supporter for the middle of the rail, constructed in the manner and for the purposes described. *Seventh.* I claim the projections, d d, extending below the chair into the opening, c, in the bottom of the box upon which the chair rests, for the purposes described and substantially as set forth. *Eighth.* I claim the box, a a, in which the chair or coupling is placed, for the purposes described and substantially as set forth. —No. 42,480.

Railroad Chair.—GREEN B. MCDONALD, Louisville, Ky.: I claim the base plate, A, provided with the pendant flange, B, and the lip, D, in combination with two or more hooks, C C, all arranged substantially as and for the purpose set forth.—No. 42,098.

[This invention consists in constructing the chair with a base plate, a bottom flange, and a lip, and using in connection therewith two or more hooks; whereby the chair may be adapted to suit rails of any size or pattern, or to connect two rails of different sizes.]

Railroad Chair.—E. ST. JOHN, Elmira, N. Y.: I claim the combination with the sustaining bar, B, and bed piece, C, of the clamp, E, all applied to each other and to the rails, A A′, and cross-ties, D, substantially as and for the purposes herein shown and described.—No 42,885.

Railroad Chair.—AMOS RANK, Salem, Ohio: I claim, *First.* A two-part railroad rail chair, which is constructed with double supporting cheeks, d d, interlocking base portions, g g′ g′, and a laterally holding bolt, b, passing through the neck of the rail, substantially as described. *Second.* The combination of the tongues, g g′ g′, cheeks, d d, flat bolt, b, and key-pin, h, with the slotted end rails, A A, substantially as described.—No. 44,455.

Portable Railroad Switch.—PHYLANDER DANIELS, Leroy, N. Y. I claim the two bars, A A′, constructed as shown and provided with the clamps B B′, in combination with the bars, C C′, G G′, either or both pairs connected to the bars, A A′, by joints and secured in position, substantially as and for the purposes set forth. I further claim the plate F, when used in combination with the bars, A A′, C C′, for the purpose set forth.—No. 43,103.

[This invention consists in the employment or use of jointed bars, provided with clamps and fitted to the rails in such a manner that the device may be used as a temporary switch without disturbing the rails, and applied at any point, no frogs nor any other parts, except those pertaining to or forming a part of my invention, being required. The invention is also applicable to the adjusting of cars on the track, and may be applied to the rails with the greatest facility, to answer that end.]

Railroad Switch.—REUBEN LEZOTT, Plattsburgh, N. Y.: I claim the movable heads as attached to the horizontal rod, as herein described and for the purposes set forth.—44,537.

Car Brake.—GEORGE S. MILLER, Thompsonville, Conn., E. B. PECK, Bridgeport, Conn., and WILLIAM OLMSTED, Thompsonville, Conn., assignors to said G. S. Miller and E. B. Peck: We claim the employment of the flanges, G H, upon the axle, B, in combination with a double-acting lever, J, and connecting-rod, I, substantially as and for the purpose described.—No. 41,744.

Shoe for Car Brakes.—JOSEPH WOOD, of Red Bank, N. J.: I claim the shoe, A, and sole, B, when one is dovetailed to the other, and when they are so held together by a retaining pin or bolt, m, or its equivalent, that on withdrawing the same the sole can be readily detached from the shoe as specified.—No. 41,114.

Car-Wheel for Railroads.—THOMAS CURTIS, New Hudson, Mich.: I claim the application to the wheels of railroad cars of the movable spurs, B B, operating substantially as and for the purposes set forth and described. I also claim, in combination with, or for use in connection with wheels armed with such movable spurs, the use and application of the additional rail, E, for such spurs to act against, substantially as and for the purposes set forth.—No. 44,078.

Method of applying Steam-power to Car Brakes.—WM. LONGRIDGE, Neverton, Md.: I claim the steam cylinder, O, and steam chest, I, provided respectively with the piston, Y′, and valve, J, and communicating with each other and the boiler, A, substantially as described, when said parts are applied to or connected with a car-brake, to operate in the manner substantially as and for the purpose set forth. I also claim the connecting of the stem, K, of the valve, J, with the bar, E, provided with a spring, D, the latter being connected with the brake-cam, Z, and piston-rod, Y, to operate as described. I also claim the particular manner of connecting the valve-stem, K, with the bar, E, by means of the wheel, F, and rack, L, in connection with the lever, G, for raising the valve, J, and the notched bar, H, for holding said lever, for the purpose herein specified. I also claim the escape-valve, V, applied to the cylinder, O, substantially as shown when used in connection with the foot-rod, X, and for the purpose herein set forth. I further claim the arrangement of the lever, U, pulley, m, at the end of the piston-rod, Y, rod T, attached to one end of lever, U, and the brake-chain, Z, attached to the opposite end and passing around the pulley, m, substantially as and for the purpose set forth.—No. 42,385.

Mode of Operating Railroad Cars.—CHARLES E. WILLIS, New York City: I claim, *First.* The brake-levers, H H', arranged in combination with each other and with the hinged shoes, J J', and screws, I I', in the manner and for the purpose substantially as described. *Second.* The combination of the brake-levers and guide-wheel levers with each other and with the screws, I I', or their equivalents, constructed and operating substantially as and for the purpose specified. No. 44,574.

Automatic Railroad Switch.—J. A. LANZIROTTI, Paris, France: I claim combining with locomotives, tenders, or carriages in front of the train, a series of adjustable rods to operate at the sides of the rails, levers, or other appliances, arranged in diverging lines of rails at different elevations, or more or less projecting laterally, so that by the adjustment of the said rods the switches at the points of contemplated change of rail may be worked automatically, substantially as herein shown and described.—No. 41,074.

Signal Switch for Railroads.—HORACE H. BARNES, Mexico, N. Y.: I claim the arrangement of the segment rack, F, pinion, I, shaft, G, lantern, J, and box, K, with the switch-lever, C, and frame, D, in the manner herein shown and described.—No. 40,898.

[This invention consists in a novel application of a lantern or lamp to the lever of a switch, as hereinafter shown and described, whereby the lantern or lamp will be turned automatically as the switch is moved or adjusted, and different colored lights exposed to show the position of the switch during the night.]

Joint for Railroad Rails.—R. H. LAMBORN, Altoona, Pa.: I claim the use of the channel-bar, C, in combination with the yokes or clevises, B B, fastened under the said channel-bar in any suitable manner (for the purpose of securing the ends of the track-rails as described), the same being constructed and arranged together substantially as described and set forth. I also claim in combination with the track-rails, channel-bar, and yokes or clevises, arranged together as described, the employment of the wedge-keys, D D, for the purpose of fastening the said parts together as described and set forth.—No. 41,437.

Car Spring.—G. ADOLPH RIEDEL, Philadelphia, Pa.: I claim, *First.* Constructing a spring in one or more sections which have one or more sheets, plates, or layers, in which each sheet has a plurality of resilient parts, centrally arranged or otherwise, substantially in the manner and for the purpose above set forth. *Second.* The washers, C C C, when interposed between the spring-plates, B B B, substantially in the manner described. *Third.* Combining one or more central washers, F, with the resilient parts of the spring, substantially as described and for the purpose above set forth.—No. 43,708.

Railroad Car-Window Fixtures.—JOHN D. HALL (assignor to himself and Osborn Conrad), Philadelphia, Pa.: I claim, *First.* The combination of the rod, A, the finger-piece, C, the thumb-piece, B, the box and support, D, the spring, H, the ratchet, E, and the ratch or strip, F, substantially in the manner and for the purposes set forth. *Second.* The angular faced rollers, G I J, and the spring, L, with roller, in combination with the angular groove, constructed and operating as and for the purpose described.—No. 44,770.

Window for Railroad Cars.—GEORGE MANN, Jr., Ottawa, Ill.: I claim the supplemental window attached to the side of the car at the exterior of the ordinary or usual window, in the manner substantially as herein described, to admit of the adjustment of the supplemental window in an oblique position relatively with the side of the car, as and for the purpose specified.—No. 41,079.

Railroad Signal.—F. J. B. HUBERT and F. C. A. DEROCQUIGNY, New York City: I claim, *First.* The pulley, D, provided with the ratchet, F, and chain, C, in combination with the signal-disk, B, suspended on a horizontal axis or shaft, substantially as herein shown and described, and all used in connection with the pawl, i, and arm, i, attached to the hub or collar, f, the arm, M, attached to shaft, J, and the lever, P, connected to arm, M, and provided with the upright plate, R, all being arranged to operate substantially as set forth. *Second.* The arm, K, attached to shaft, J, in combination with the drop catch, N, arranged to operate as and for the purpose specified. *Third.* The colored glass, S, in the signal disk, B, in combination with the lamp or lantern in an aperture, b*, in the upright, A, when operated by the mechanism, as above set forth and for the purpose specified.—No. 41,341.

[This invention relates to a new and improved signal for railroads for the purpose of preventing trains from coming into collision, and also to prevent them from passing on wrongly adjusted switches, and on drawbridges when the draws are open.]

Railroad Signal.—LEWIS FITZPATRICK and WM. GARDNER, Nicholsville, Ohio: We claim the arrangement of the treadle or trigger, F, connected by devices, C H I I′ J K L M, or their equivalents, to a bell, N, suspended near a railway crossing, by which the said trigger is depressed, and the bell rung by all trains approaching the crossing, and only deflected by trains leaving the crossing, substantially as set forth.—No. 43,841.

Railroad Turn-out.—ISAAC N. PILLSBURY and N. E. WARREN, Cleveland, Ohio: We claim the herein-described mode of adjusting the tracks and turnouts of street and other railroads, so that the cars from either end of the tracks can enter upon the turn-out in straight lines from either end, and pass the two points of intersection at either end before making or entering upon the curve, in the manner and form as herein set forth.—No. 41,018.

Car Spring.—FRANCIS E. OLIVER, New York City: I claim an improved spring composed of two or more metallic C-shaped plates, united at their upper and lower edges by suitable bearing caps, and combined with a central compensating spring of india-rubber, gutta-percha, or other equivalent elastic material, substantially in the manner and for the purpose herein set forth.—No. 42,682.

Car Spring.—ULYSSES B. VIDAL, Philadelphia, Pa.: I claim the arrangement of the pyramidal springs, B B′, to stand in alternate inverted positions, in the manner and for the purpose herein shown and described. I also claim having one side of the box divided into as many separate movable parts, A′ A″, as there are tiers of springs, as and for the purpose herein shown and described.—No. 42,519.

Car Spring.—WILLIAM MARSHALL, New York City: I claim the combination of the springs, C D, and levers, B, arranged substantially as shown, and either with or without the box, A, to operate in the manner as and for the purpose set forth.—No. 43,121.

[This invention consists in the employment or use of spiral springs arranged and combined with levers in such a manner that a strong and durable spring will be obtained, and one which may be constructed at a very moderate cost. The object of the invention is to obtain a spring which will possess as much elasticity as the ordinary elliptic or semi-elliptic springs, and be equally as durable, and still be capable of being cheaply constructed and readily repaired when necessary; the elliptic or semi-elliptic springs, although far preferable to any hitherto constructed, being too expensive for general use and applied only to the more expensive style of cars.]

Spark-Arrester.—JAMES RADLEY and MARGARET HUNTER (administratrix of John W. Hunter, deceased), New York City. Patented Jan. 22, 1850. Reissued Jan. 16, 1855: We claim, *First.* The arranging of a series of chambers and channels between conically-shaped plates, the channels being so formed as to cause the products of combustion to impinge against that side of each of the dirt chambers, which has the springs and caps, and thereby force the sparks, dirt, etc., into them, in the manner described herein. *Second.* We claim the piece, p, suspended in the central aperture at the top of the spark-arrester, arranged and operating in the manner and for the purpose substantially as hereinbefore described. *Third.* We claim the double cover or top for the formation of a second series of dirt passages, arranged and operating in the manner and for the purpose substantially as hereinbefore described.

Locomotive Car-Truck.—ROBERT H. LONG (assignor to himself, JOSEPH GRICE, of New York, and SAMUEL B. GRICE), Philadelphia, Pa.: I claim the combination at one end of the car or locomotive of a four-wheel truck, C′, and a vibrating truck, E′, pivoted together and to the car body in the manner and for the purpose herein set forth.—No. 43,739.

[The object of this invention is to enable railroad cars to turn or curve more freely, more especially on curves of short radius such as are used in city railroad tracks; and to this end it consists in the combination at one end of the car of a four-wheel truck or frame, and a vibrating truck or frame, the four-wheel truck having the axles arranged within it in the usual manner, and being pivoted between the axles to the vibrating truck or frame, and the latter being pivoted to the main frame or body of the car at a point not over or between the axles.

Car-Coupling.—HENRY A. BUCK, Meadville, Pa.: I claim the drop, B, curved and fitted in grooves or recesses in the draw-head, A, as shown in connection with the coupling pin, C′, and the link or shackle, C, all arranged to operate substantially as and for the purpose specified.—No. 42,343.

[This invention relates to a new and improved car-coupling of that class which are commonly termed self-coupling, and it consists in the employment or use of a suspended drop placed within the draw-head and arranged in such a manner as to support the coupling-pin when the latter is set or adjusted for coupling, and at the same time so arranged as to be out of the way of the link or shackle, when the latter enters the draw-head, and prevented from being acted upon by the link or shackle until the latter reaches the proper point to receive the coupling-pin, thereby avoiding a casual dropping of the coupling-pin before the link or shackle can receive it.]

Car-Coupling.—ELIAS M. WRIGHT, Wyandot, Kansas: I claim the coupling, D, constructed, arranged, and operating in combination with the nearly hemispherical cavities, b, b, in the bumper-heads, substantially as and for the purpose herein set forth.—No. 42,897.

Car-Coupling.—J. T. LOWREY, of La Fayette, Ind.: I claim, *First.* The combination of the pin, D, and the pivot-rod, E, in their said arrangement in a railroad car-bumper, and for the purposes set forth in the foregoing specification, viz., the production of a self-adjusting coupling. *Second.* Also the cuts, F and H, in the bumper and in combination with said pin and pivot-rod, whereby said pin obtains room to swing. *Third.* Also, the groove, G, in the interior of the bumper and in its combination with said pin and rod; which groove, by being narrower than the link-chamber beneath it, keeps the link from rising unduly, and thus keeps it in its horizontal position. *Fourth.* Also the rubber in said groove, G, assisting the pin in recovering its perpendicular.—No. 41,308.

Railroad Car-Coupling.—RALPH CARKHUFF, Lewisburg, Pa.: I claim in a car-coupling, the use and combination of the rack, G, pinion, H, and key, F, for the purpose set forth.—No. 42,835.

Car-Coupling.—EBENEZER CAREY (assignor to himself and HORACE H. HAWLEY), Burlington, Iowa: I claim the suspended or swinging-plate or pin-support, B, fitted within the draw-head, A, and provided with a projection, f, at its upper end, in combination with the pin, C, and link or shackle, D, all arranged to operate substantially as herein described.—No. 43,734.

[This invention relates to a new and improved car-coupling which is self-acting or self-coupling, and it consists in the employment or use of a suspended pin support, a pin of peculiar construction and the ordinary link or shackle, all arranged and combined with a draw-head in such a manner as to form a simple and efficient coupling of the kind specified.]

Pneumatic Railway.—THOMAS WEBSTER, Rammell, London, England. Patented in England, on Feb. 10, 1860: I claim, *First.* A pneumatic railway or tube in which the carriages are placed inside the tunnel or tube, but are independent of the tunnel or tube and are wholly supported and in their motion are guided and directed by two or more rails, grooves, or trams, and in which the pneumatic pressure is applied over the whole or transverse area of the carriage. *Second.* The contrivance for filling up with soft material the space between the interior of the tunnel or tube, and the outside of the carriage, as applied to pneumatic railways and tubes, as above described. *Third.* The use of several smaller or branch air passages leading into the tube at different points, either with or without self-acting valves, so as gradually to reduce the velocity of the carriage as applied to pneumatic railways and tubes, as above described.—No. 42,509.

Atmospheric Railway.—ALEXANDER ALLISON and JAMES HALLIWELL, London, Great Britain: We claim, *First.* The valve, a, whether employed for railway or other purposes, and when used in combination with the chamber, w, or without said chamber, constructed substantially as described. *Second.* The curbed bar, e, for removing the valve, a, from the aperture, d, and returning the same after the passage of the piston-rod, f, substantially as described. *Third.* The elastic packing bands, j, when used on a piston-head, for the purpose and substantially in the manner specified. *Fourth.* The cone-valve, H, whether used in a solid piston-head or in combination with the elastic band, j, constructed and arranged for the purpose and substantially in the manner specified. *Fifth.* The device for operating the cone-valve, H, constructed and arranged substantially in the manner specified, *Sixth.* The frame, f, with guide-rollers, s, so arranged with reference to the bottom of the carriage, P, as to allow the piston, D, to follow the dip of the tube at the crossings, and to prevent any vertical motion of the carriage affecting the said piston. *Seventh.* The frame, I, with guide-rollers, r, so arranged with reference to the frame, f′, as to prevent the oscillation of the carriage, P, being communicated to the piston, D. *Eighth.* The branching of the tube, A, at N, Fig. 5, and the branching of the aperture, d, at y, in connection with the dip of said tube for the purpose of conveniently shunting the train or passing from one line of rails to another.—No. 44,376.

Marine Railway. — C. H. EDWARDS, Quincy, Mass.: I claim the construction of the ways of a marine railway, so that the upper surface upon which the rolls traverse shall form a vertical curve substantially as described, and for the purpose as set forth.—No. 41,426.

Car-Coupling.—N. S. WHITE (assignor to himself and RICHARD VAUGHN), Port Chester, N. Y.: I claim the sliding-stop, F, arranged with springs, d, and a cam, I, in connection with the arms, C, D, E, attached to a hub, a, placed loosely on the shaft, B, said parts being applied to a draw-head, A, and all arranged to operate in the manner substantially as and for the purpose herein set forth.—No. 44,571.

[This invention relates to a new and improved car-coupling of that class which is commonly termed self-coupling, and it consists in the employment or use of a vertical sliding-stop arranged with springs and a cam, in connection with a pin fitted on a shaft or axis provided with two arms, all being arranged within or applied to a draw-head in such a manner that a very simple and efficient car-coupling of the kind specified is obtained.]

Car-Coupling.—JAMES WIDNEY, Allegheny City, Pa.: I claim the combination and arrangement of the projections, g and h, trigger, B, and pin, C, with the ordinary coupling-link, the whole being constructed, combined, arranged and operating substantially as herein described and for the purpose set forth.—No. 43,447.

Car-Coupling.—JAS. M. GOW, Rock Island, Ill.: I claim the coupling-pin, B, provided with an arm or projection, h, having a pin, i, passing transversely through for the pin to swing upon and describe a short arc under the action of the entering link or shackle, substantially as set forth. I also claim in combination with the pin, B, thus suspended, the projections, f f, at the lower parts of the sides of the pin, in connection with the curved ledges, g, at each side of the recess, d, to serve as a support for the pin, as set forth. I also claim the grooves, k k, at each side of the opening, b, and slot, c, in combination with the pins or screws, l l, the projections, f f, of the pin, B, and the recesses, m, in the sides of the slot, c, all arranged substantially as and for the purpose specified. I further claim the shoulder, n, on the back part of the pin, B, when arranged in relation with the back part of the slot, c, for the purpose herein set forth.—No. 43,399.

[This invention relates to an improvement on a car-coupling, for which Letters Patent were granted to this inventor, bearing date Feb. 9th, 1864.]

Mode of connecting Cars to Trucks.—ALFRED BRIDGES, Newton, Mass.: I claim, *First.* In railroad cars the spring, H, on the truck-frame, so combined and arranged with the suspension-rod, G, or its equivalent, that it controls both vertical and side motions, substantially as herein set forth. *Second.* I claim the combination of the two springs, H and N, with the truck-frame, D d, substantially in the manner and for the purposes herein specified. *Third.* I claim the thimble, h, when used with the spring, H, truck-frame, D d, suspension-rod, G, and pedestal, F, substantially in the manner and for the purpose herein specified.—No. 44,278.

Car-Coupling.—WILLIAM H. FORKER, Meadville, Pa., assignor by mesne-assignments to HENRY BALDWIN, JR., Philadelphia, Pa. Ante-dated Sept. 18, 1864: I claim the combination of the arm, C, and spring, D, hinged drop-pin, D', and projection, e, constructed and arranged as described, and operating in connection with the draw-head, A, and link or shackle, B, in the manner and for the purposes specified.—No. 44,484.

[This invention relates to an improved car-coupling, of that class which are commonly termed self-coupling, and it consists in the employment or use of a drop-pin connected by a joint to an arm pivoted at the upper part of the draw-head, and having a spring bearing against the under side of its back part; all being arranged in such a manner that an ordinary link or shackle in the draw-head of one car may, on entering the draw-head of an adjoining car, engage itself with the drop-pin, and form a connection between the two cars, while the parts being few and combined and arranged in a simple way, insure durability, and prevent the liability of the coupling getting out of perfect working order.]

Car-Coupling.—HENRY FAKE, Chicago, Ill.: I claim the two bars, D D', provided with hooks, d d, at their outer ends and fitted within the draw-head, A, on the pin, C, between the projections, B B, in combination with the springs, G G J J, and the sliding-bars, E E H H, all arranged substantially as and for the purpose herein set forth.—No. 44,085.

[The object of this invention is to obtain a car-coupling by which the danger of coupling by hand will be avoided, and one which will accommodate itself to all variations in the track, that is to say, admit of working or playing both horizontally and vertically under the movement of the cars, as the latter pass over the track or rails.]

Car-Coupling.—JAMES M. GOW, Rock Island, Ill.: I claim the combination of the draw-pin, B, when slotted and otherwise constructed, as herein shown and described, with the slotted draw-head, A, all the parts operating together, as set forth.—No. 41,502.

[This invention consists in a slotted draw-pin supported by a pivot in the upper part of the draw-head and projecting through a slot in the under side of the same, in combination with the ordinary coupling-link, in such a manner that the link, on entering the draw-head will push back the draw-pin and allow it to catch between said link and shoulder in the under side of said draw-head, and in uncoupling two cars nothing is required but to raise the draw-pin in its slot high enough to release the link.]

Car-Coupling. — HENRY BLACKMORE (assignor to himself and ADAM APPLE), Pittsburgh, Pa.: I claim the use, in combination with a coupling-box, of a hinged pin, so constructed substantially as described, that the draught-bar will push the hinge-piece of the pin back when it enters the coupling-box, and that so soon as the draught-bar has entered the cavity of the coupling-box, the movable part of the coupling-pin will drop down into the draught-bar or link, thus securely locking it in place.—No. 42,041.

Axle Box for Car Trucks.—WM. LOUGHRIDGE, Weverton, Md.: I claim, *First.* The stuffing box composed of the leather, B, or its equivalent, annular socket, a, metallic packing, b, and pressure plate, E, substantially as described. *Second.* The arrangement of the springs, d d', and rods, F F, with the socket, a, and pressure plate, E, all arranged to operate substantially as and for the purpose set forth.—No. 45,058.

Railroad Car Journal.—W. G. SMITH (assignor to himself, JOHN F. BARNEY, and JACOB A. WILDER), Chicaco, Ill: I claim, *First*, The journal, I, when disconnected from the shaft of the wheel, substantially as and for the purposes set forth. *Second.* Constructing a journal disconnected from the shaft varying in size, that is, having two or more different diameters, substantially as herein described. *Third.* The combination and arrangement of the journal, I, the friction wheels, R and L, and the hollow hub, C, when constructed and operating substantially as specified. *Fourth.* The combination and arrangement of the journal, I, the journal box, D, provided with the face plate, E, and the hub, C, when constructed and operating substantially as herein delineated and set forth. *Fifth.* The combination and arrangement of the journal, I, the washer, P, and the hollow hub, C, when arranged substantially as herein described.—No. 45,124.

Sleeping Car.—JOSEPH SUTTER, New York City. Ante-dated Nov. 3, 1864: I claim, *First.* Sustaining the backs in a horizontal position by means of the swinging link, f, applied in the manner and for the purposes specified. *Second.* I claim the folding extension piece, g, applied to the back and employed between one back and the other when in a horizontal position, as set forth. *Third.* I claim the spring head rest, l or l', constructed and applied in the manner and for the purposes set forth. *Fourth.* I claim the protecting bars, h, connected by the slotted bars, i, and slide bars, k, at the ends of the backs, forming the sides of the lounge or berth, for the purposes and as specified. *Fifth.* I claim the folding extension leaves, g', turning up under the seats or reaching from one seat to the next, for the purposes and as specified.—No. 45,092.

Locking Door for Railroad Cars.—E. W. MORSE, Chicago, Ill.: I claim, *First.* A locking device in a car or other structure with sliding doors, constructed and operated substantially as above described. *Second.* I also claim protecting the bolt of the lock by means of the guides which hold the door to the rail on which it slides, substantially as and for the purpose set forth.—No. 45,165.

[This invention consists of a device for locking the sliding doors of freight cars, by which the bolt is concealed within the guides which hold the door to the rail on which it moves.]

Locomotive Smoke Stacks.—SETH HAM, of Philadelphia, Pa., assignor to himself and WM. H. MCCAFFERTY, of Alexandria, Va.: I claim, *First.* The curved deflecting plate, E, and inner journal-shaped casing, D, arranged in respect to the inside pipe, A, and outer casing, B, substantially as and for the purpose specified. *Second.* The plate, E, inner casing, D, and plate, C, with its flange, a, arranged in respect to each other and the inner pipe and outer casing substantially as set forth for the purposes described.—No. 45,204.

Shoe for Car Brakes.—JOSEPH WOOD, Red Bank, N. J.: I claim, *First.* The sole, B, its lugs, c and c', and lug, d, in combination with the shoe, A, the latter and the sole being constructed and adapted to each other so as to be secured by a simple pin, i, substantially as specified. *Seeond.* A groove or grooves, x, formed in the face of the sole, substantially in the manner and for the purpose set forth.—No. 45,106.

Low-Water Detector for Steam Boilers.—BERNARD SCHAFFER, of Buckau, Magdeburg, Prussia, assignor to himself and CHRISTIAN BUDENBERG, of New York City: I claim, *First.* The employment or use of the ball shaped valve, C, in combination with the adjustable float, D, and whistle, A, as described, leaving the valve free to accommodate itself to the motions of the float, and preventing the valve from sticking by the motions of the float. *Second.* The arrangement of the tube, r, and set screws, s s, in combination with the float, D, and valve stem, C', as specified, whereby the float can be adjusted to the desired position, and a free communication between the interior of the float and the steam space of the boiler is effected.—No. 45,207.

THE IRON HORSE.

From "The Knickerbocker."

THERE were noble steeds in the days of old,
They were fierce in battle, in danger bold;
They clanked in armor, and shone in gold,
  And they bore their riders with lordly pride;
But the IRON HORSE, there were none like him!
He whirls you along till your eye is dim,
Till your brain is crazed, and your senses swim,
  With the dizzy landscape on either side!

He springs away with a sudden bound,
His hoof unshodden, spurns the ground,
His nostril dashes its foam around,
  Like the first faint clouds of a thunder shower:
And a stated moment he ever hath,
When he rushes forth on his iron path,
And woe to him who shall rouse his wrath,
  By curbing him in, beyond the hour!

While other steeds must be champing hay,
Must repose by night, and be fed by day,
Let the Iron Horse have his level way,
  And he asks for no more than his fire and water.
He wears no bridle, nor curbing-chain,
He brooks no spur, and he needs no rein;
Only set him forth on the open plain,
  And he'll be the last horse to weary or loiter!

All seasons and times he will fearless brave,
Whether hot shines the sun, or th' north winds rave;
He flies o'er the earth, and he rides the waves,
  Like a shadowy cloud o'er the harvest fields:
He neighs aloud, as he dashes by,
And the fire-sparks flash from his gleaming eye,
And vales resound, and the hills reply,
  To the rapid rush of the flashing wheels.

His breath is hot as the siroc's blast,
As it hisses forth through his iron teeth,
And it rolls up slow, when he hurries past,
  Like the morning mist, in a snowy wreath.
And you'd better stand in the van of war,
Where the vollied death-shots fly free and far,
  And thousands fall, ere the fight is done,
  Than to cross the path that he flies upon,
Whenever the hurled and loud-rattling car,
  Like a thunder-gust, comes roaring on!

But not alone for his matchless speed,
Do we sing the praise of this noble steed.
"Such a fellow for business," the Yankees say,
  Can nowhere be found, in the old world or new;
He will toil all night, he will toil all day,
  And it's hard to tell what he *cannot* do.
With the old-fashioned method of working with tools,
  Our mechanics and artists have nearly all done;
For they find it much easier to sit on their stools,
  While the work of twenty is done by one.

Not only the SPEED of this Iron Horse
Is such, that he leaves far behind in the course
  All the fleetest racers that ever were shod;
He's the fastest WORKMAN that ever you saw;
He'll set more card-teeth, and braid more straw,
  Than all the fair maids from New York to Cape Cod.
To be sure he won't work alone, but then
Not a fig would he give for his choice in men;
  Only let him have one, howe'er loose his wits,
And he'll spin you a yarn, or knit you a stocking,
With all the grave matrons that ever came flocking
  To a gossiping party in old Massachusetts.

They say, besides, to raise cabbage and beets
In an hour, is but one of his many feats;
He will warm your room, and cook your dinner,
  And when it is ready, he will tell you so;
And to this, you must add, he's a mere beginner,
  Who learned his trade scarce a year ago:
The western men have taught him to mow,
  To plough the field, and grind their wheat,
And he's all the same, in rain or snow,
  In the winter's cold, or the summer's heat.

In the land of stern habits, he turns off clocks,
With such a fearful rapidity, it shocks
  All the sober bounds of a man's belief;
Give him but rags, and lo! once or twice round,
He'll hand out a BOOK, all printed and bound,
  And paged off, in order, from leaf to leaf!
    If he learns for the future as fast
    As he has for a few years past,
And acquires, by the way, the habit of meddling,
The Yankees will certainly send him out peddling!

Had the animal lived in old Homer's day,
  When Jupiter used such a store of thunder,
The forges of Vulcan, where deep they lay,
  Half rending the crater of Ætna asunder
With their ceaseless roar, and thundering shocks,
  Would have proved to be built for a useless trade;
And Vulcan, ruined by th' fall of stocks,
  Would have turned the Cyclops off unpaid;
For a thunderbolt, forged by the Iron Horse,
And hurled by him on its flaming course,
Would have proved to mortals a hotter curse,
Would have bellowed louder, and blasted worse,
Than all that the king of the gods ever hurled
From his starry throne o'er a frighten'd world.

It is human nature to make or mar;
So in modern times they have taught him war;
And he throws a ball, they say, moreover,
With perfect ease, from Calais to Dover.
A common cannon, when once exploded,
Will fire not another shot, till loaded;
He stops not to murder by such a dull scheme,
For he pours his balls in a ceaseless stream.
Had he stood in the straits of Thermopylæ,
  With only one of the three hundred men,
  Who fought their last in the narrow glen,
To turn his front on that tossing sea
Of Persian plumes, as they onward came,
He had stolen the fame of the Spartan name,
And Xerxes' ranks had been widely strown,
In a sea of gore, that was all their own.

Would you know still more of this noble steed?
  The voice of the tempest is roaring loud,
And the howling blasts, in their viewless speed,
  O'er the ocean are hurrying the darkening cloud.
The Storm-Spirit rides on the foam-crested wave,
  And the Deep is roused to his fiercest wrath;
Oh! whose is the arm that hath power to save
  The vessel that flies on his stormy path?
The wrecks are whelmed in old ocean's caves,
And the sailors sink to their unknown graves,
While their dirge is sung by the sounding waves.

But see! there's a ship! yet it hath no sail;
Perchance it is strown on the rushing gale,
But it hath no mast! still onward it comes,
  All bright and beautiful, alone,
When the tempest howls, and the roused deep foams.
She sends up a cloud, that is wreathed in fire!
  Ah! her hapless fate must full soon be known!
The lightnings of heaven have smote her in ire:
But no! those wreaths are too bright for smoke:
  'Tis the rolling breath of the Iron Horse!
In vain the winds from their caves have broke,
  He drags the ship on her foaming course;
With convulsive heaving, he paws the wave,
  And the ship hath no need of mast or sail,
For his alone is the power to save
  From the gathered rage of the sea and gale!

But not alone on the stormy sea,
  Not alone through the vales of the northern clime,
Where he travels now so gloriously,
Shall his destined path in the future be;
He shall cross the Alp and the Apennine,
His voice shall be heard by the winding Rhine;
  By the fallen fanes of the olden time;
He shall send the roar of his rolling car,
Through the wide domains of the northern Czar;
Through Sarmatia's wilds, and the Switzer's snows,
And along the vales where the Danube flows;

Where the Moslem hears the Muezzin's cry,
"To prayer! to prayer!" he shall hurtle by;
Where the deep blue heaven of Asia smiles,
O'er her storied plains and countless isles,
And the flowers that breathe in the balmy air,
Are bright as the pearls that are shining there;
Where the Afric sun pours his scorching beams
On the thirsty sands and the wasted streams;
Where the Pharaohs, in their kingly pride,
Were rolled by night in the Red Sea's tide,
'Neath the palm-trees' boughs, the banyan's shade,
His iron path-way shall yet be laid.

On our mountain ridges his chariots gleam,
He follows the track of the winding stream;
He will carry us forth from our early homes,
  To the fairy scenes of the glowing West,
Where the Father of Waters in grandeur roams,
  Through broad savannahs in verdure drest.
Away! away! with his ceaseless roar,
The valley and stream he will hasten o'er:
Away! away! where the prairie lies,
Like an emerald sea, 'neath the fair blue skies,
With naught in view save the waving grass,
The flowers that bend as his chariots pass,
And in black and fearful host afar,
  The countless herd of the buffalo,
That start at the gleam of his shining car,
  And away, loud bellowing and thundering go,
With a speed that no foot of the deer can surpass.

The prairie-horses shall toss the mane,
  Tear the ground with their hoofs, and neigh aloud,
When this stranger-steed o'er their free domain,
  Comes rushing on, like a flying cloud;
Bnt he heeds them not, as he onward speeds,
With a tread as loud as a thousand steeds.
A sound shall be heard through the mountain caves,
  A sound, through the gloom of the pathless glen,
Like the hollow murmur of breaking waves,
  Or the measured tramping of mail-clad men;
'Tis the Iron Horse; he hath passed the bound
Of the wild sierras that fenced him round;
He hath no more on the land to gain,
His path is free to the western main!

RAILROAD CHRONOLOGY.

"*Bid harbors open, public ways extend;*
Bid temples, worthier of God, ascend;
Bid the broad arch the dang'rous flood contain,
The mole projected, break the roaring main;
Back to his bounds their subject sea command
And roll obedient rivers through the land."

POPE.

THERE were short roads, called tram-ways, in and about Newcastle, England, so early as the middle of the 17th century; but they were made of wood, and were used for transporting coals a moderate distance from the pits to the place of shipping. They are thus mentioned in 1676: "The manner of the carriage is, by laying rails of timber from the colliery to the river, exactly straight and parallel; and bulky carts are made with four rollers fitting those rails, whereby the carriage is so easy that one horse will draw down four or five chaldron of coals, and is an immense benefit to the coal merchants."—(*Life of Lord-Keeper North.*) They were made of iron, at Whitehaven, in 1738. The first considerable iron railroad was laid down at Colebrook Dale in 1786. The first iron railroad sanctioned by Parliament (with the exception of a few undertaken by canal companies, as small branches to mines) was the Surrey Iron Railway (by horses), from the Thames at Wandsworth to Croydon, for which the Act was obtained in 1801. The first great and extensive enterprise of this kind, where steam was used in England, was the Liverpool and Manchester Railway, commenced in October, 1826, and opened September 15, 1830.*

The following were among the earliest roads constructed in Great Britain:—

Railways.	*Opened.*	*Railways.*	*Opened.*
Surrey (by horses)	1805	Dundee and Arbroath	April, 1840
Stockton (by horses)	Sept. 1825	London and Brighton (part)	May, 1840
Canterbury and Whitstable	May, 1830	London and Southampton	May 11, 1840
Liverpool and Manchester	Sept. 15, 1830	Lancaster and Preston	June, 1840
Edinburgh and Dalkeith	1831	Manchester and Birmingham	June, 1840
Bolton and Leigh	June, 1831	York	June, 1840
Dundee and Newtyle	Dec. 1831	West Durham (part)	June, 1840
Warrington	1833	Preston and Wyre	July, 1840
Bodmin and Wadebridge	1834	North Midland	July, 1840
Leeds and Selby	Sept. 1834	Maryport	July, 1840
Dublin and Kingstown	Dec. 17, 1834	London and Blackwall	July 4, 1840
Whitby	May, 1836	Great Western	Aug. 1840
Newtyle and Cupar Angus	Feb. 1837	Glasgow and Ayr	Aug. 1840
Paisley	April, 1837	Northern and Eastern (part)	Sept. 1840
Grand Junction	July 4, 1837	Chester and Birkenhead	Sept. 1840
Manchester and Bolton	May, 1838	Birmingham and Gloucester	Sept. 1840
London and Birmingham	Sept. 17, 1838	Chester and Creide	Oct. 1840
Sheffield	Oct. 1838	Taff Vale (part)	Oct. 1840
Preston	Oct. 1838	Manchester and Leeds	Oct. 1840

Up to the year 1836 there had been passed 164 Acts, viz.:—

Year	Acts	Year	Acts	Year	Acts
1801	1	1815	1	1827	6
1802	2	1816	1	1828	11
1803	1	1817	1	1829	9
1804	1	1818	1	1830	8
1808	1	1819	1	1831	9
1809	2	1821	1	1832	8
1810	1	1823	1	1833	11
1811	3	1824	2	1834	14
1812	2	1825	5	1835	18
1814	1	1826	6	1836	35

The Surrey Iron Railway Company was formed in 1801, for making and maintaining a railway from the town of Wandsworth to Croydon—nine miles. Cost, £60,000; a double line of rails.

* Haydn's Dictionary of Dates.

1802.—The Carmarthenshire Railway or Tramroad Company—sixteen miles—cost £35,000.

YEAR 1827.—The Granite Railroad, chartered in 1825, was opened for business, three miles, from Quincy to the Neponset River, Massachusetts—the first railroad in the United States. It was constructed with a flat rail, laid on longitudinal wooden sills, for which stone sills were afterwards substituted.

Mauch Chunk and Summit Hill Railroad, Pennsylvania, commenced operations in the coal regions of Pennsylvania. This was the second railroad in the United States. The loaded cars descend by their own gravity.

Baltimore and Ohio Railroad Company chartered by States of Maryland and Virginia.

1828.—The Liverpool and Manchester Railroad projected—the trade between the two cities then being 1,200 tons daily. In the British Almanac for 1829 may be found George Stephenson's estimate of materials and cost.

The Baltimore and Ohio Railroad was commenced (July 4th) with formal ceremonies.

1829.—The subscribers to the Thames Tunnel enterprise met in London—June.

October.—A prize of £500 awarded to George Stephenson, for the best locomotive—speed attained, thirty miles an hour.

December 30.—The Welland Canal, connecting Lakes Ontario and Erie, opened for travel and commerce.

The Carbondale and Honesdale Railroad (from the Delaware and Hudson Canal to the Northern or Lackawanna coal fields) opened for business. The second railroad in the State of Pennsylvania.

The Mill Creek and Mine Hill Railroad, Pennsylvania, also opened to business.

Chesapeake and Delaware Canal, thirteen and a half miles, finished (from Delaware City, on the Delaware River, forty-two miles from Philadelphia, to Back Creek, a branch of Elk River, Chesapeake Bay). This canal was used for four years for travel between Philadelphia and Baltimore.

Among those who labored to introduce the era of steam in the iron manufacture, and all those branches which it subserves, several citizens of New York and its vicinity were early engaged. Its direct agency in the several departments of the iron business has been as a new creation; and its numerous applications to machinery of all kinds has constantly augmented the demand for iron, and extended the field for labor, capital, and skill, to a degree impossible without it. In this connection, Christopher Colles, John Stevens, Chancellor Livingston, and Robert Fulton appear among the earliest laborers. The name of Stevens is associated with that of Fitch in the first application of steam to navigation; and his patented improvements in the engine of Savery, the boiler, bellows, etc., were among the earliest granted by the new Government. In the year following, the splendid success of Fulton on the Hudson, the steamboat Phœnix, built by John C. Stevens, and navigated by his son, Robert L. Stevens, from New York to Philadelphia, was probably the first that traversed the Atlantic. When the grand idea of a canal through the State, suggested by Colles, was advocated in New York, Stevens proposed a railroad instead, which would, if followed, have given the Empire State the precedence in that unequalled system of internal communication. To her vast system of canals, secured by the efforts of DeWitt Clinton and others, and to her magnificent railways, in connection with steam, New York owes the development of her great iron resources, no less than of the great agricultural capabilities of the State. Her immense foreign commerce is equally the result of steam-power applied to ocean travel.*

1830.—*March* 29.—James Rennel, a noted engineer, died in London, aged 88.

September 15.—The Liverpool and Manchester Railroad opened for business—(commenced in 1826). Mr. Huskisson accidentally killed.

The Boston and Lowell Co. Railroad incorporated—25 miles.

Baltimore and Ohio Railroad opened for travel—14 miles—to Ellicott's Mills.

1831.—Charters granted to the Boston and Providence Railroad Company, and the Boston and Taunton Railroad Company.

* History of Manufactures in the United States, by Bishop. Philadelphia, 1861.

Baltimore and Susquehanna Railroad opened for travel, as far as seven miles—(now the Northern Central Railroad, Baltimore to Harrisburg).

The Mohawk and Hudson Railroad, afterwards (in 1847) known as the Albany and Schenectady Railroad, and in 1853 made a part of the New York Central, was chartered in 1826, commenced in 1830, and finished in 1831. It was one of the first roads in the United States on which locomotives were used. It was constructed with inclined planes and stationary engines.

Two new railroads commenced in England: I. Newcastle and Carlisle Railway. II. Leicester and Swannington Railway.

1832.—*August.*—Work commenced on the Boston and Worcester Railroad.

Newcastle and Frenchtown Railroad, Delaware (from the Delaware Bay to Chesapeake Bay), ten miles, opened to travel, mainly for passengers.

The Dundee and Newtyle Railroad—eleven miles—opened for travel; speed, one hour and a quarter for the whole distance.

December 22.—Camden and Amboy Railroad opened for travel.

1833.—Act of Parliament for the construction of the London and Birmingham Railway; also the London and Greenwich Railway. Confident expectations and promises that the speed on this railway might reach twenty miles an hour.

The Philadelphia and Trenton Railroad—28 miles—opened to travel.

1834.—The Camden and Amboy Railroad was the first constructed in the State of New Jersey, sixty-one and a half miles. Chartered in 1830; partially opened for business—14 miles—in December, 1832, and finished in 1834.

Philadelphia and Columbia Railroad (82 miles) opened for travel. (Now a part of the Pennsylvania Central Railroad.)

May, 1834.—The Railroad between Charleston and Hamburg (S. C.), 136 miles, opened for business.

Dec. 1.—The Baltimore and Ohio Railroad opened.

Baltimore and Port Deposit Railroad Company chartered (for a road from Baltimore City to Port Deposit, on the Susquehanna River, 36 miles).

1835, *July* 6.—Boston and Lowell Railroad (incorporated 1830), 26 miles, opened for business June 27; Boston and Providence Railroad, 41 miles, June 2d, in part; Boston and Worcester Railroad opened for business, July 6.

August 25.—Baltimore and Washington Railroad completed for passengers.

Dec. 7.—The railroad from Nuremberg to Firth opened—the first in Germany.

May 5.—The first railroad in Belgium finished—Brussels to Malines—12¾ miles.

July 16.—First severe accident on the London and Birmingham Railway.

1836.—*June* 23.—The steamboat Novelty made an experimental trip from New York to Albany with Anthracite coal as fuel.

August 1.—The Utica and Schenectady Railroad commenced business.

The Bangor and Piscataquis Railroad, chartered in 1833, was opened for travel this year, being the first road built in the State of Maine.

The New Jersey Transportation and Railroad Company opened its road for bnsiness in 1836, between Jersey City and New Brunswick, being the second road constructed in the State. (Eight miles, Newark to Jersey City, opened in 1834.)

1837.—*June* 19.—Railroad from Baltimore to Wilmington, Del., partly opened for travel.

Aug. 11.—Accident on the Portsmouth and Roanoke Railroad; three passengers killed.

The railroad from Harrisburg to Lancaster (36 miles) opened for travel in 1837.

Nov. 10.—Providence and Stonington Railroad, 41 miles, opened for public travel.

Aug. 26.—A railroad from Paris to St. Germain opened.

Dec. 29.—American steamer Caroline burnt by the Canadians at Schlosser.

The Boston and Providence Railroad opened for travel—the first in Rhode Island.

1838.—*Sept.* 16.—The railway from London to Birmingham opened for business the entire length—time, 4 hours, 48 min.

Miles of railroad completed in New York, 218; cost, $5,065,000; miles commenced, 938; capital, $16,000,000; additional miles authorized, 1704.

Steamers Great Western and Sirius, at New York from Bristol and Cork, April 23.

The Philadelphia, Wilmington and Baltimore Railroad partly opened for travel.

London and Southampton (now Great Western) Railroad in part opened, 23 miles.

Sept. 2.—Railroad from Ghent to Ostend opened for travel.

Dec. 23.—The Nashua and Lowell Railroad, in New Hampshire, was opened for business; commenced in 1837; the first in the State.

The Hartford and New Haven Railroad was partly opened for travel this year, being the first in the State. Commenced in 1836, and finally completed in 1839.

1839.—The Western Railroad, Mass., opened for business October 1st.

The Philadelphia and Reading Railroad (58 miles) opened for travel and the coal trade; and the Williamsport and Elmira (Pa.), 25 miles.

Railroad from Wilmington, Del., to the Susquehanna River, 35 miles, opened for travel (now a part of the P. W. and Balt. Railroad).

April 7.—Opening of the railroad from Leipsic to Dresden.

Aug. 2.—Opening of the railroad from Paris to Versailles.

The railroads of the State of Illinois at this time were eight in number, with a mileage of 1341 miles; cost $11,470,000.

The Trenton branch of the Camden and Amboy Railroad, and that portion between Trenton and New Brunswick, N. J., were finished in 1839. It has paid annual dividends averaging twelve per cent. for twenty-seven years. The State gave the exclusive right to this road for carrying passengers between New York and Philadelphia for the sum of $200,000 in its stock, with a transit duty on passengers. The State now derives an annual income of $200,000 from dividends and transit duties.

1840.—The Norwich and Worcester Railroad was opened for travel, being the second in the State of Connecticut.

The number of miles of railroad in Massachusetts completed was 337 miles; annual revenue, $11,741,000.

The Eastern Railroad of Mass. (from Boston to Portland) in course of construction.

July 1.—The New Bedford and Taunton Railroad (Mass.) opened for business.

July 18.—The steamer Britannia, the first regular packet of the Cunard Line, arrived at Boston from Liverpool, after a passage of fourteen days and eight hours.

Railroad from Annapolis, Md., to the Baltimore and Ohio Railroad finished (22½ miles).

The following railroads in Great Britain were finished this year:

Lancaster and Preston, 20½ miles; North Midland, 72¼; Hull and Selby, 30¾; Preston and Wyre, 19½; Slamannan, 12½; Chester and Birkenhead, 14½; Chester and Creide 20½; Stockton and Hartlepoole, 8¼, &c. Total miles, 207¾.

The following lines are partially opened:

London and Brighton (total), 61; Manchester and Birmingham, 72¼; Birmingham and Gloucester, 23; Maryport and Carlisle, 28; Glasgow and Greenock, 22⅛; Northern and Eastern, 30; Taff Vale, 41½; London and Blackwall—total, 94¼.

1841.—*March* 30.—The Glasgow and Greenock Railway opened for travel (22¼ miles).

June 30.—The Great Western Railway opened throughout (Paddington to Bristol, England).

August 12.—The first passage made through the Thames Tunnel, by Sir I. Brunel.

Sept. 1.—Railway opened for travel from Cologne to Aix La Chapelle.

Dec. 24.—Accident on the Great Western Railway train, England. Eight persons killed and sixteen wounded.

1842.—*Feb.* 9.—Judgment against Boston and Worcester Railroad Company—$13,000—in favor of Ostinelli for personal damage.

Aug. 10.—The Manchester and Birmingham Railway opened for travel.

May 26.—London and Dover Railway opened for travel to Tunbridge.

May 8.—Accident on the railroad from Paris to Versailles; 70 persons killed.

Aug. 24.—Death of Benjamin Wright, aged 72 years, at New York city; a director and one of the chief constructors of the Erie Canal; one of the earliest engineers of the State of New York.

1843.—The Central Railroad of Georgia (Savannah to Macon), 190 miles, opened.

April 1.—Destruction of the Railroad dépôt at Schenectady, N. Y., by fire.

July 2.—Cunard Steamer Columbia, from Boston for Liverpool, lost off Seal Island.

Up to 1843, inclusive, 1583 miles of railway had been completed in Belgium, viz.:

	MILES.		MILES.
1835	12¾	1840	200
1836	27¼	1841	225
1837	87	1842	261¼
1838	156	1843	326¼
1839	188		
		Total,	1483½

March 25.—The Thames Tunnel opened to the public for foot passengers.

Aug. 26.—Destruction of the U. S. Steamer Mississippi in the bay of Gibraltar.

Nov. 20.—Death of Professor Hassler of the U. S. Coast Survey, aged 74.

1844.—The year 1844 witnessed important railway movements in England. The great Southern and Western Railway of Ireland was chartered—from Dublin to Cashel, 98½ miles. About 797 miles were authorized by Parliament this year. The total number of miles of railway constructed in Great Britain in 1844, was 241 miles.

Feb. 27.—Death of Nicholas Biddle at Philadelphia, aged 58 years.

1845.—The cost of railways completed in the United Kingdom, to the end of this year, was £70,680,000; expended on roads in course of construction, £67,-359,000; and required for their completion, £563,203,000—a total of £701,242,000; in addition to which there were 643 new companies proposed.

1846.—The railroads in operation in England and Scotland this year were 1862 miles in length, at a cost of £67,740,000. In Ireland only 89 miles, at a cost of £1,296,000; and in the United States, 4864 miles.

At this time there were only 61 miles of railroad in operation in the State of Maine, and 35 miles in New Hampshire.

The Legislature of Massachusetts this year chartered eighteen railroad companies, with a proposed capital of $5,800,000.

September 21.—Death of Captain W. G. Williams, U.S.A. Railroad Engineer.

During the year ending November 1, 1846, the number of miles of railway completed in the United Kingdom was 438 miles. The railway interest had assumed such magnitude, and so many "bogus" lines had been proposed, that a Board was appointed in England, as "Her Majesty's Commissioners of Railways," consisting of Sir Edward Ryan, Captain Henry R. Brandeth, R. E., and Edward Strutt, M.P.

1847.—Providence and Worcester Railroad opened for travel; the second road in the State of Rhode Island.

Railroad property in England, Ireland, and Scotland became exceedingly depressed in the year 1847; and the extraordinary calls for subscriptions led to a panic in the money market, and the suspension of the Bank Act in England.

1848.—The Vermont Central Railroad, the first in the State, was opened this year as far as Northfield, 53 miles—one of the most disastrous railroad enterprises ever undertaken in the United States.

The Suspension Bridge near Niagara Falls was finished this year, by Mr. Ellet, engineer, who first crossed it July 29th.

The Legislature of Massachusetts chartered this year nineteen new railroad companies, with a capital of $7,105,000.

Death of George Stephenson, the celebrated engineer, August 12th, aged sixty-seven years; born January 9, 1781.

Parliamentary returns show that the miles of railway authorized in Great Britain to the end of 1847, were 13,300 miles, viz.:—

	Acts.	*Miles.*	*Capital Invested.*
1801 to 1840	299	3,000	£69,000,000
1841	19	15	18,000,000 (1841–1844)
1842	22	67	
1843	24	91	
1844	48	797	
1845	120	2,883	59,000,000
1846	272	4,790	121,000,000
1847	184	1,663	35,000,000
1848	83	—	18,000,000
Totals,	1,071	13,300	£320,000,000

1849.—*October* 14.—A railroad convention at St. Louis; 465 delegates recommend the construction of the Pacific Railroad.

About 870 miles of railway were opened in the year 1849, in the United Kingdom, viz.: 630 miles in England, 108 in Scotland, and 132 miles in Ireland.

A Railway Insurance Company (indemnity for damage or loss of life) was this year established in London.

December 11.—The Boulogne and Amiens Railway opened for travel.

December 12.—Death of Sir Marc Isambert Brunel, the engineer, aged 81 years.

From the fall of dividends on all the lines, and continued pressure of calls, the distrust of all railway property became such, that towards the autumn of 1849, large masses of it were practically unsaleable. The retrospect of the third quarter of 1849 is the most dismal picture it has ever been our duty to lay before our readers. Gloom, panic, and confusion appeared to have taken full possession of the railway market, and a commensurate depression in the value of all lines, good, bad, and indifferent, has been the result. A glance at the market will suffice to convey a knowledge of the overwhelming depreciation which now exists—a depreciation including even the principal lines, the main arteries of the internal traffic of the country. Within the last few weeks the stock of the London and North-Western Railway has fallen 20 per cent. In some of the journals the loss in September, 1849, sustained by the then holders of railway shares, has been estimated at so large an amount as 180 millions sterling. (Alison's Europe.)

The following table exhibits the variations in the price of the stock of the leading railways, from January, 1846, to January, 1852, when the gold discoveries set in:

	January 1st,						
	1846	1847	1848	1849	1850	1851	1852
London & North-Western	215	196	150	121	101	123	118
Great Western	195	150	105	93	58	77	86
South-Western	150	170	120	94	61	66	87
Midland	150	130	107	100	45	47	57
Brighton	135	118	82	62	80	87	95
South-Western	190	120	90	70	57	66	64
York & North Midland	210	190	144	140	34	44	44

—Tooke and Newmarch, v. 360, 361.

Thus, even after the lapse of seven years, the prices of railway stock, till the gold discoveries came into play, which they did in 1852, were, even in the most favorable cases, little more than half, in many only a third or a fourth of what they had been at the beginning of the period.

1850.—*September* 9.—An accident occurred on the Western Railroad, at Washington Summit, between Albany and Springfield: three passengers were killed.

June 25.—Railroad jubilee at Burlington, Vermont.

Pennsylvania Coal Company Railroad, 47 miles, opened for the coal trade.

July 31.—Railroad Convention at Portland, Maine, in favor of a railroad from Portland to British provinces. Forty-four miles of the Atlantic and St. Lawrence Railroad (Portland to Montreal) in operation this year. Railroad from Portland to Augusta, Portland to Somersworth, in course of construction. Also Troy and Rutland Railroad; Whitehall and Rutland Railroad; Fitchburg and Worcester Railroad; Connecticut Valley Railroad; Connecticut and Passumpsic Railroad; Cocheco Railroad; Portsmouth and Concord Railroad.

July.—The European and North American Railway suggested by the British Association for the Advancement of Science, at Edinburgh.

The British Railway Acts reduced from 83 (in 1848) to 35 in 1849, and to 30 in 1850.

The increase of railway receipts in the United Kingdom from 1842 to 1850, was as follows:—

1842	£4,341,000	1845	£6,669,000	1848	£10,059,000
1843	4,842,000	1846	7,639,000	1849	11,013,000
1844	5,610,000	1847	8,975,000	1850	12,755,000

Decrease of average weekly receipts, per mile, from £60 in 1848, to £43 in 1850.

December 4.—Death of Mr. Milne, author of Treatise on Annuities and Insurance.

1851.—*September.*—Telegraphic communication established between Dover and Calais.

1852.—*June* 1.—Telegraphic communication first established between England and Ireland (between Holyhead and Kingston), 70 miles.

November 1.—Direct telegraphic communication between London and Paris.

1853.—The total length of railroads in the United States in 1853 was 14,494 miles.

Sixty-two persons were killed by railroad accidents this year in Massachusetts.

July 18.—The Atlantic and St. Lawrence Railroad, from Portland to Montreal, was opened through the whole length, 292 miles.

January 6.—Accident on the Boston and Maine Railroad, whereby the only son of President Pierce was killed.

August 12.—A collision occurred on the Providence and Worcester Railroad, whereby twelve persons were killed, and twenty-five were wounded.

January 12.—Baltimore and Ohio Railroad, 379 miles, from Baltimore, Maryland, to Wheeling, on the Ohio River, opened for travel.

January 3.—Accident on the North-Western RR., England. Ten persons killed.

October 26.—Capt. J. W. Gunnison, U.S.A., engineer, killed by Indians, in Utah.

December 9.—Railroad riots at Erie, Pennsylvania.

Opening of the South Wales Railway, from Carmarthen to Haverfordwest.

1854.—*May* 22.—The railway between Susa and Turin, Sardinia, inaugurated.

Oct. 25.—Railway from Flensburg to Gonning, Schleswig, opened.

Providence, Hartford, and Fishkill Railroad opened to Hartford.

Providence, Warren and Bristol Railroad (R. I.) opened for travel.

Charter granted by Congress to the Metropolitan Railroad Company (for a road from Washington to a junction with the Baltimore and Ohio Railroad, near the Point of Rocks, on the Potomac, 41 miles; not yet completed—a road much needed for Government transportation in the years 1861–1864.

Jan. 17.—Repetition of railroad riots at Erie, Pa.

April 30.—The first railroad in Brazil opened for travel.

1855.—*Jan.* 28.—The first train passed over the Panama Railroad.

Nov. 1.—Accident to first excursion train on the Pacific Railroad bridge, on the Gasconade River—twenty-five persons killed.

1856.—*Nov.* 12.—Great railroad jubilee at Montreal, two days.

May 1.—Destructive fire at the Harlem Railroad Dépôt, New York; loss $100,000.

June 16.—Grand Trunk Railroad, Canada, to Guelph, 87 miles from Toronto.

July 16.—Collision on the North Pennsylvania Railroad with a Sunday-school excursion train. Forty persons killed.

Oct. 6.—Death of W. Francis Whishaw, aged 52, in London, an eminent English civil engineer.

Sept. 18.—A railroad Convention at Cincinnati; sixty delegates present from the leading Eastern and Western railroads.

1857.—The Legislature of Massachusetts chartered this year sixteen new railroad companies; capital $4,822,000.

April 24.—Death of Capt. A. I. Swift, U.S.A., of the engineer corps.

June 30.—The Trent Valley R.R. opened with great *éclat*; Sir Robert Peel present.

Sept. 22.—A deputation from the Liverpool Stock Exchange arrived in London to confer with railway companies, to check the undue absorption of capital for new routes. The calls for this month only were £2,726,000, and for October, £3,493,000.

Sept. 30.—A public meeting of bankers and merchants at Manchester; resolutions passed exhorting railway companies to defer their fresh calls for dues in September—many millions sterling in amount.

Oct. 4.—A meeting of bankers, merchants, and manufacturers at Birmingham, to ask for relief from the pressure in the money market.

Oct. 25.—The restrictive clause in the Bank of England charter removed, and great relief instantly felt.

March 21.—Death of William Scoresby, at Torquay, an early Arctic explorer.

Jan. 16.—Leopold Redpath found guilty of forging fictitious shares of stock of the Great Northern Railway; sentenced to transportation for life.

March 12.—Accident on the Grand Trunk Railroad near Hamilton, Canada—seventy persons killed.

May.—Opening of the Memphis and Charleston Railroad celebrated at Memphis.

July 1.—Accident on the Cincinnati and Marietta Railroad; four persons killed and twenty wounded.

1858.—*Oct.* 9.—The first overland mail from San Francisco reached St. Louis—24 days, 13½ hours.

Nov. 11.—Formal opening of the Detroit and Milwaukee Railroad.

1859.—*Sept.* 16.—Riot on the Erie Railroad near the Bergen Tunnel—two days.

Nov 1.—Accident to an excursion train of thirteen cars on the Chicago and North-Western Railroad at Johnson's Creek; ten persons killed.

Nov. 24.—First train of cars passed over the Victoria Bridge, Montreal.

Nov. 29.—Governor Wise takes possession of the Winchester and Potomac Railroad, prior to the execution of John Brown.

Feb. 22.—Formal opening of the Hannibal and St. Joseph Railroad.

March 16.—Railroad Convention at Buffalo; 46 railroad companies represented.

April 17.—Railroad riot at Panama.

June 27.—Accident on the Michigan Southern Railroad; 33 persons killed.

Oct. 12.—Death of Robert Stephenson, aged 56 years (born October 16, 1803).

1860.—Ten miles of horse railroad in use in the city of Baltimore.

THE PACIFIC RAILROAD.—The Secretary of the Interior in his Annual Report for December 1864, says:

"There can be no doubt that the public resources will be much increased by the immediate working of the mines to the extent of their capacity, and by the settlement of those regions by an enterprising and industrious population, though no direct income should be derived from the sale of the lands. It is therefore worthy of consideration, whether it would not be expedient to grant all, or such portions of the lands as are requisite to insure the construction of the necessary railroads, and the conversion of the sterile lands to a condition of fertility. The benefits resulting from such roads would not be confined to the product of the mines. A new highway, at all times except from obstruction by snow, would be open to the Pacific. Passing by the valley of the Rio Grande to El Paso, it would receive a large portion of the rich commerce of Central and Western Mexico. These benefits are so obvious and of such surpassing importance, that I do not hesitate in expressing my earnest conviction that the government should embrace any suitable opportunity which may be offered to secure the completion of a railroad upon the terms suggested.

"It appears from a communication of Gen. Dix, the President of the Union Pacific Railroad Company, that it has, since the adjournment of Congress, expended more than half a million of dollars upon the main line of the road leading westward from Omaha, of which one hundred miles have been permanently located, and forty miles are in process of construction.

"The company has surveyed lines to Salt Lake City, through the South Pass, Laramie plains, Bridger's Pass by way of Timpanagos and Weber rivers, to determine the most feasible route. Parties have also been engaged in explorations in Colorado Territory through Berthold's Pass and up the Caché la Pendre River, and also in examining the topography of the country in the vicinity of the 100th meridian of longitude, and in locating the line from Omaha to Fort Kearney. Considering the limited time which has elapsed since the action of Congress enabled this company to prosecute the work with energy, satisfactory progress has been made, and the country has no reason to apprehend any tardiness in the prosecution of this great enterprise.

"Under the Acts of Congress of July 1, 1862, and July 2, 1864, making grants of land to aid the construction of railroad and telegraph lines to the Pacific coast, the initial point of the main line of railroad from the Missouri River westward has been fixed at Omaha, Nebraska, and the definite location of the road for one hundred miles west from that point has been approved by the President. The route of the Pacific Railroad of California has been selected, and a map of the preliminary location thereof, from Sacramento eastward to the great bend of the Truckee River in Nevada, has been filed in this department. The lands along these routes for twenty-five miles, on both sides, have been withdrawn from market, pursuant to the requirements of the act of 1862."

THE MUTUAL LIFE INSURANCE COMPANY

OF NEW YORK.

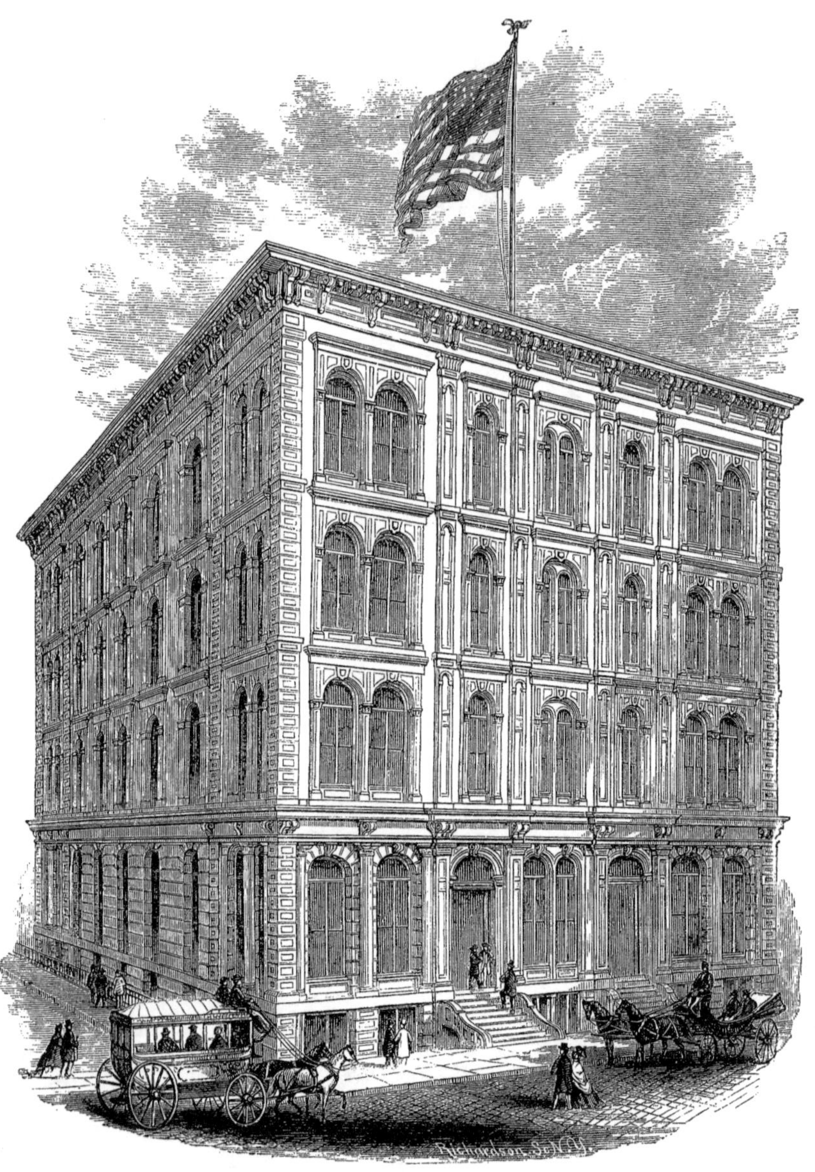

Offices of

THE MUTUAL LIFE INSURANCE COMPANY OF NEW YORK,

President, F. S. WINSTON: *Secretary,* ISAAC ABBATT; *Actuary,* SHEPPARD HOMANS.

NOS. 140, 142, 144, AND 146 BROADWAY, N. Y.

Erected 1864.

THE ATLANTIC BANK, NO. 142; THE SAFE DEPOSIT COMPANY OF NEW YORK, NO. 146.

Engraved for the Railroad and Insurance Almanac for 1865.

EXTRACTS FROM THE NINTH ANNUAL REPORT OF THE INSURANCE COMPANIES OF MASSACHUSETTS.

January 1, 1864.

How Life Insurance fares in the midst of this our civil revolutionary war, is a question on which, we are happy to say, this report will throw a cheerful light. Among the blessings which our rebellious masters threw away, because more than their equal share of liberty was not good enough for them, was a pretty large interest in our northern mutual life insurance companies, they having none of their own. Our companies were no losers by this, as we have explained in former reports. On the other hand, not a few of them profited by the forfeiture of Southern policies to an amount far greater than sufficient to cover the subsequent war risks of their members. Still there were two questions which caused some solicitude to the guardians of these institutions. First, whether the continuance of the war would not diminish their business; and second, whether it would not increase the mortality so as to impair their funds. So far as the twenty-five companies now doing business in Massachusetts are concerned, the year ending November 1, 1863, answered the first question, that their business had experienced an increase of thirty-seven per cent. in its cash receipts, and thirty-two and a half per cent. in the amount insured; that is, the amount of insurance has increased from one hundred and ninety-six millions of dollars to about two hundred and sixty millions, and the annual revenue from seven and a half millions to ten and a quarter millions. It answered the second question by showing the ratio of the number of deaths to the lives insured scarcely a shade higher than in any of the former years in which we have noted it. In some particular companies the losses by deaths on war risks may have slightly exceeded the extra war premiums received, but in the aggregate the military exposure thus far has not impaired the funds of the companies, nor has it produced such an effect on the aggregate mortality as would have attracted particular notice in time of peace. The light mortality which has always characterized our American life insurance companies, has still prevailed. The policies terminated by death have been 873, while by the combined experience of the English companies, they should have been 1165. This evidence of safe and successful operation in the midst of a struggle which might be expected to paralyze every institution looking beyond the safety of the present, shows what an amount of reserved force there is in the loyal part of the republic, and ought to teach traitors a lesson of despair in their work of destruction.

LIFE INSURANCE COMPANIES.

Whole-Life Policies of Twenty-five Life Insurance Companies doing business in Massachusetts, outstanding November 1, 1863, *arranged according to the years in which they were issued, each year ending November* 1.

[From the Ninth Annual Report of the Insurance Companies of Massachusetts.]

MASSACHUSETTS HOSPITAL LIFE INSURANCE COMPANY.

YEAR.	Number of Policies.	Amount Insured.	Net Value.	Ratio of Value to Amount.
1830	1	$2,000 00	$1,115 84	55.78
1834	2	5,000 00	2,793 93	55.90
1835	1	5,000 00	1,955 70	39.11
1837	1	1,500 00	680 73	45.36
1838	1	3,000 00	1,093 47	36.42
1839	1	1,000 00	503 63	50.36
1840	1	2,000 00	1,150 82	57.56
1850	1	3,000 00	640 69	21.35
1852	1	500 00	77 36	15.47
1855	1	3,000 00	257 26	8.57
1856	1	1,500 00	137 83	9.18
1857	1	3,000 00	266 76	8.89
1859	2	5,000 00	435 74	8.71
Totals	15	$35,500 00	$11,109 77	31.30

NEW ENGLAND MUTUAL LIFE INSURANCE COMPANY.

YEAR.	Number of Policies.	Amount Insured.	Net Value.	Ratio of Value to Amount.
1844	62	$194,941 00	$69,679 55	35.74
1845	92	259,700 00	88,353 59	34.03
1846	112	283,900 00	80,902 15	28.48
1847	114	270,145 00	75,503 59	27.94
1848	78	214,650 00	52,736 84	24.57
1849	111	281,200 00	70,583 80	25.10
1850	76	206,000 00	49,212 92	23.88
1851	89	237,400 00	48,377 15	20.37
1852	105	329,650 00	64,270 06	19.50
1853	105	314,938 00	49,510 29	15.72
1854	140	482,950 00	70,517 39	14.60
1855	196	701,000 00	95,291 24	13.59
1856	248	828,600 00	94,565 53	11.41
1857	183	646,600 00	63,985 56	9.89
1858	311	1,218,650 00	107,929 17	8.85
1859	463	1,578,000 00	120,509 86	7.63
1860	688	2,056,000 00	132,855 44	6.46
1861	548	1,666,900 00	80,534 53	4.83
1862	1,056	2,878,621 00	103,576 22	3.60
1863	1,317	3,971,036 00	78,536 09	1.98
Totals	6,094	$18,620,881 00	$1,597,430 97	8.57

STATE MUTUAL LIFE INSURANCE COMPANY OF MASSACHUSETTS.

YEAR.	No. of Policies.	Amount Insured.	Net Value.	Ratio of Value to Amount.
1845	28	$62,256 61	$20,300 51	32.60
1846	85	154,070 99	46,277 02	30.03
1847	103	195,555 14	59,489 81	30.43
1848	125	224,620 99	59,301 56	26.39
1849	87	151,546 38	37,276 39	24.60
1850	51	100,934 09	24,627 42	24.41
1851	65	85,458 50	17,843 96	20.78
1852	75	108,583 76	22,392 71	20.62
1853	113	154,900 35	28,462 38	18.37
1854	49	82,425 01	13,627 92	16.54
1855	26	51,877 46	7,533 73	14.52
1856	52	89,225 11	11,548 84	12.94
1857	130	207,595 20	21,672 41	10.44
1858	73	115,215 26	11,506 76	9.99
1859	99	162,385 34	14,577 23	8.98
1860	107	173,749 05	12,148 83	6.99
1861	133	186,960 35	8,121 43	4.34
1862	87	114,500 00	3,773 74	3.29
1863	112	152,800 00	2,809 86	1.84
Totals	1,600	$2,574,659 59	$423,292 51	16.44

BERKSHIRE LIFE INSURANCE COMPANY OF MASS.

YEAR.	No. of Policies.	Amount Insured.	Net Value.	Ratio of Value to Amount.
1851	3	$7,600 00	$1,371 08	18.03
1852	15	26,050 00	4,463 06	17.14
1853	33	67,400 00	11,050 12	16.39
1854	84	178,000 00	26,955 92	15.14
1855	52	101,200 00	12,417 94	12.27
1856	116	270,550 00	32,288 01	11.93
1857	93	219,900 00	23,506 89	10.69
1858	64	130,000 00	12,429 95	9.56
1859	107	201,200 00	15,384 13	7.64
1860	150	287,750 00	18,325 67	6.37
1861	106	191,100 00	8,344 24	4.36
1862	54	96,200 00	2,833 76	2.95
1863	123	245,200 00	5,418 14	2.21
Totals	1,000	$2,022,150 00	$174,788 91	8.64

NORTH AMERICA LIFE INSURANCE COMPANY, N. Y. CITY.

YEAR.	No. of Policies.	Amount Insured.	Net Value.	Ratio of Value to Amount.
1862	10	$30,500 00	$912 95	2.99
1863	501	1,157,750 00	21,844 64	1.88
Totals	511	$1,188,250 00	$22,757 59	1.91

MASSACHUSETTS MUTUAL LIFE INSURANCE COMPANY.

YEAR.	No. of Policies.	Amount Insured.	Net Value.	Ratio of Value to Amount.
1851..............	15	$17,100 00	$3,556 29	20.80
1852..............	55	93,300 00	16,986 16	18.20
1853..............	31	55,300 00	8,121 87	14.68
1854..............	48	88,380 00	12,896 77	14.59
1855..............	87	176,100 60	23,379 49	13.28
1856..............	125	273,600 00	35,440 08	12.95
1857..............	118	274,700 00	32,663 40	11.89
1858..............	237	532,400 00	49,147 22	9.23
1859..............	398	870,200 00	66,561 06	7.65
1860..............	463	962,400 00	57,964 35	6.02
1861..............	388	819,700 00	38,870 02	4.74
1862..............	454	1,029,100 00	33,400 49	3.25
1863..............	767	1,831,500 00	36,928 69	2.02
Totals...........	3,186	$7,023,780 00	$415,915 89	5.92

MUTUAL LIFE INSURANCE COMPANY OF N. Y.

YEAR.	No. of Policies.	Amount Insured.	Net Value.	Ratio of Value to Amount.
1843..............	103	$556,291 92	$229,684 12	41.30
1844..............	131	614,139 23	247,885 54	40 36
1845..............	243	1,003,275 31	393,604 55	39.24
1846..............	273	939,880 97	351,035 77	37.34
1847..............	337	1,397,380 06	491,157 49	35.14
1848..............	421	1,588,214 39	531,853 84	33.48
1849..............	496	1,776,629 53	553,044 59	31.12
1850..............	420	1,285,519 07	381,766 87	29.70
1851..............	289	863,972 90	238,891 40	27.65
1852..............	325	1,214,830 66	313,151 21	25.76
1853..............	368	1,384,736 61	330,301 89	23.84
1854..............	539	1,930,935 84	411,819 47	21.32
1855..............	678	2,894,205 27	576,586 06	19.92
1856..............	928	3,528,399 62	613,896 41	17.40
1857..............	850	3,129,785 98	471,107 41	15.05
1858..............	914	3,413,630 25	454,140 87	13 30
1859..............	1,060	3,638,204 05	405,492 00	11.14
1860..............	1,146	3,858,104 51	359,198 07	9.31
1861..............	837	2,844,089 69	220,371 73	7.75
1862..............	1,259	3,621,944 14	205,652 24	5.68
1863..............	1,969	5,762,205 72	158,045 15	2.74
Totals...........	13,586	$47,246,375 72	$7,938,686 68	16.80

JOHN HANCOCK MUTUAL LIFE INSURANCE CO. OF MASS.

YEAR.	No. of Policies.	Amount Insured.	Net Value.	Ratio of Value to Amount.
1863..............	140	$258,600 00	$8,185 09	3.16

MUTUAL BENEFIT LIFE INSURANCE COMPANY OF N. J.

YEAR.	No. of Policies.	Amount Insured.	Net Value.	Ratio of Value to Amount.
1845	122	$455,500 00	$141,493 47	31.06
1846	547	1,663,800 00	488,383 88	29.34
1847	474	1,401,100 00	372,402 95	26.58
1848	377	1,090,530 00	279,690 75	25.67
1849	366	1,013,650 00	235,094 31	23.18
1850	186	610,800 00	128,393 74	21.01
1851	171	509,200 00	101,874 03	20.01
1852	152	508,800 00	92,016 28	18.08
1853	164	521,200 00	86,944 75	16.69
1854	174	620,570 00	91,351 30	14.72
1855	169	543,700 00	70,179 49	12.91
1856	206	726,850 00	85,846 75	11.81
1857	207	778,700 00	77,237 14	9.92
1858	379	1,316,350 00	114,719 10	8.71
1859	731	2,568,900 00	181,592 40	7.07
1860	913	3,141,065 00	182,250 07	5.80
1861	658	2,381,000 00	106,207 67	4.46
1862	1,213	4,254,150 00	142,462 49	3.35
1863	2,687	9,137,157 00	200,866 13	2.20
Totals	9,896	$33,243,022 00	$3,179,006 70	9.56

NEW YORK LIFE INSURANCE COMPANY.

YEAR.	No. of Policies.	Amount Insured.	Net Value.	Ratio of Value to Amount.
1845	13	$43,000 00	$12,399 86	28.83
1846	56	154,850 00	44,498 73	28.75
1847	86	239,866 00	66,013 44	27.51
1848	86	258,850 00	64,723 47	25.01
1849	141	426,300 00	99,618 14	23.36
1850	216	680,597 00	150,103 54	22.06
1851	241	748,700 00	153,300 21	20.47
1852	185	485,200 00	87,944 91	18.12
1853	110	344,250 00	64,962 00	18.87
1854	106	329,400 00	50,072 49	15.20
1855	122	324,150 00	43,565 42	13.44
1856	188	541,700 00	62,464 46	11.53
1857	154	468,050 00	45,588 89	9.74
1858	167	616,900 00	54,256 17	8.79
1859	297	975,075 00	70,078 54	7.18
1860	435	1,317,250 00	80,858 56	6.14
1861	508	1,424,775 00	72,671 04	5.10
1862	2,103	5,137,755 00	213,542 44	4.17
1863	4,077	9,851,276 00	265,435 20	2.69
Totals	9,291	$24,367,944 00	$1,702,097 51	6.98

CONNECTICUT MUTUAL LIFE INSURANCE COMPANY, HARTFORD.

YEAR.	No. of Policies.	Amount Insured.	Net Value.	Ratio of Value to Amount.
1847	209	$442,150 00	$120,431 33	27.22
1848	457	974,710 00	236,711 12	24.28
1849	1,204	2,822,389 50	644,626 50	22.82
1850	1,279	2,877,270 00	634,669 18	22.05
1851	954	1,165,100 00	434,931 37	20.09
1852	329	740,600 00	127,677 17	17.23
1853	296	778,400 00	129,291 19	16.59
1854	405	1,099,920 00	154,789 64	14.06
1855	314	821,300 00	100,347 94	12.22
1856	309	862,400 00	98,774 55	11.45
1857	300	835,600 00	82,807 06	9.92
1858	494	1,502,495 50	133,050 03	8.85
1859	604	1,711,464 00	128,752 32	7.52
1860	1,155	3,426,751 00	206,436 24	6.02
1861	920	2,680,955 00	124,312 34	4.64
1862	1,463	3,910,842 00	123,829 41	3.17
1863	4,134	10,990,600 00	237,812 05	2.16
Totals	14,826	$38,642,957 00	$3,719,249 44	9.62

UNION MUTUAL LIFE INSURANCE COMPANY OF MAINE.

YEAR.	No. of Policies.	Amount Insured.	Net Value.	Ratio of Value to Amount.
1849	15	$45,900 00	$9,992 84	21.77
1850	332	758,917 00	177,572 62	23.40
1851	215	484,490 00	99,191 01	20.46
1852	91	195,350 00	38,229 91	19.57
1853	58	111,800 00	19,093 18	17.08
1854	35	84,350 00	13,013 24	15.42
1855	25	60,800 00	6,399 48	10.52
1856	45	129,150 00	13,409 05	10.39
1857	31	81,250 00	8,724 25	10.74
1858	139	384,550 00	32,847 07	8.54
1859	197	501,900 00	34,243 90	6.82
1860	207	489,750 00	26,473 21	5.40
1861	131	295,100 00	11,199 34	3.79
1862	271	596,800 00	17,903 70	3.00
1863	869	2,045,750 00	41,255 03	2.02
Totals	2,661	$6,265,857 00	$549,547 83	8.77

SECURITY LIFE INSURANCE COMPANY, N. Y.

YEAR.	No. of Policies.	Amount Insured.	Net Value.	Ratio of Value to Amount.
1862	96	$194,000 00	$6,144 87	3.17
1863	579	1,197,500 00	22,262 60	1.86
Totals	675	$1,391,500 00	$28,407 47	2.04

UNITED STATES LIFE INSURANCE COMPANY, N. Y. CITY.

YEAR.	No. of Policies.	Amount Insured.	Net Value.	Ratio of Value to Amount.
1850	67	$149,550 00	$31,599 89	21.14
1851	63	145,800 00	31,398 32	21.53
1852	61	138,625 00	26,794 79	19.33
1853	60	141,800 00	22,564 91	15.91
1854	90	232,500 00	34,458 97	14.81
1855	112	297,800 00	35,877 36	12.05
1856	309	692,000 00	81,529 69	11.78
1857	263	637,000 00	61,079 34	9.59
1858	251	607,880 00	55,168 34	9.07
1859	265	616,850 00	43,586 05	7.06
1860	372	777,700 00	44,963 17	5.78
1861	282	541,350 00	24,314 73	4.49
1862	325	652,312 00	20,927 82	3.21
1863	740	1,718,360 00	32,555 68	1.89
Totals	3,260	$7,349,527 00	$546,819 06	7.44

MANHATTAN MUTUAL LIFE INSURANCE COMPANY, N. Y.

YEAR.	No. of Policies.	Amount Insured.	Net Value.	Ratio of Value to Amount.
1850	13	$35,728 00	$8,931 51	24.99
1851	138	415,739 00	88,613 56	21.32
1852	95	349,537 00	65,937 17	18.86
1853	120	401,979 00	72,560 07	18.05
1854	162	581,407 00	88,820 60	15.27
1855	112	378,307 00	52.243 78	13.81
1856	196	616,779 00	75,651 35	12.26
1857	235	725,141 00	81,306 75	11.21
1858	333	1,010,299 00	96,629 58	9.56
1859	434	1,352,419 00	95,082 21	7.03
1860	438	1,364,989 00	77,226 42	5.66
1861	472	1,626,980 00	77,329 20	4.75
1862	752	2,650,004 00	85,310 89	3.22
1863	1,289	4,435,751 00	86,845 34	1.96
Additions	—	58,898 00	24,127 60	40.96
Totals	4,789	$16,003,957 00	$1,076,616 03	6.73

GUARDIAN LIFE INSURANCE COMPANY, N. Y. CITY.

YEAR.	No. of Policies.	Amount Insured.	Net Value.	Ratio of Value to Amount.
1859	11	$31,500 00	$2,116 73	6.72
1860	103	219,600 00	11,157 47	5.08
1861	98	182,750 00	7,812 36	4.27
1862	309	561,872 00	17,623 29	3.14
1863	604	1,144,070 00	22,078 92	1.93
Totals	1,125	$2,139,792 00	$60,788 77	2.84

NATIONAL LIFE INSURANCE COMPANY, MONTPELIER, VT.

YEAR.	No. of Policies.	Amount Insured.	Net Value.	Ratio of Value to Amount.
1850	75	$115,958 95	$29,858 14	25.75
1851	70	126,148 14	30,598 84	24.35
1852	29	57,375 33	12,544 63	21.85
1853	54	89,542 70	17,118 83	19.11
1854	34	61,356 65	9,573 63	15.60
1855	39	75,046 86	11,767 22	15.68
1856	132	220,709 75	29,028 91	13.15
1857	107	198,957 52	22,714 63	11.42
1858	58	135,011 10	13,092 63	9.69
1859	119	183,604 31	15,612 93	8.50
1860	142	240,165 51	13,270 38	5.52
1861	78	107,500 00	4,393 55	4.08
1862	95	158,000 00	4,830 66	3.06
1863	161	234,450 00	5,348 35	2.28
Totals	1,193	$2,003,826 82	$219,753 33	10.99

CHARTER OAK LIFE INSURANCE COMPANY, HARTFORD, CT.

YEAR.	No. of Policies.	Amount Insured.	Net Value.	Ratio of Value to Amount.
1850	32	$44,500 00	$9,920 20	22.27
1851	164	299,600 00	57,317 69	19.12
1852	84	133,100 00	23,317 75	17.52
1853	185	315,483 33	48,683 37	15.43
1854	195	393,350 00	54,082 38	13.75
1855	165	330,800 00	40,232 76	12.16
1856	113	173,650 00	20,881 48	12.03
1857	297	529,400 00	54,539 36	10.30
1858	380	655,300 00	51,519 26	7.86
1859	295	621,500 00	41,656 02	6.70
1860	219	361,923 00	19,5[illegible]0 61	5.40
1861	156	261,500 00	11,455 77	4.38
1862	124	243,678 00	7,757 85	3.18
1863	517	1,177,100 00	29,775 29	2.53
Totals	2,926	$5,540,884 33	$470,689 79	8.49

EQUITABLE LIFE INSURANCE COMPANY, N. Y. CITY.

YEAR.	No. of Policies.	Amount Insured.	Net Value.	Ratio of Value to Amount.
1859	105	$491,500 00	$36,525 15	7.43
1860	279	950,050 00	54,882 77	5.77
1861	305	793,900 00	38,074 23	4.80
1862	714	1,711,350 00	50,635 12	2.96
1863	1,002	2,693,200 00	53,772 06	2.00
Totals	2,405	$6,640,000 00	$233,889 33	3.52

PHŒNIX LIFE INSURANCE COMPANY, HARTFORD, CONN

YEAR.	Number of Policies.	Amount Insured.	Net Value.	Ratio of Value to Amount.
1851	11	$11,500 00	$2,135 63	18.57
1852	60	67,900 00	11,642 94	17.15
1853	91	109,500 00	17,095 09	15.61
1854	138	163,300 00	22,883 38	14.02
1855	96	120,600 00	15,187 97	12.59
1856	102	128,100 00	14,258 79	11.13
1857	102	151,700 00	14,585 26	9.61
1858	110	125,000 00	10,051 45	8.03
1859	150	170,100 00	11,757 96	6.91
1860	202	239,500 00	13,779 67	5.75
1861	175	211,000 00	9,844 58	4.66
1862	450	817,034 00	31,600 75	3.87
1863	715	1,228,600 00	25,476 06	2.07
Totals	2,402	$3,543,834 00	$200,299 53	5.65

WASHINGTON LIFE INSURANCE COMPANY, N. Y.

YEAR.	Number of Policies.	Amount Insured.	Net Value.	Ratio of Value to Amount.
1860	145	$456,500 00	$27,917 71	6.11
1861	110	319,500 00	16,406 16	5.13
1862	211	481,550 00	15,637 83	3.25
1863	288	725,250 00	14,584 00	2.01
Totals	754	$1,982,800 00	$74,545 70	3.76

HOME LIFE INSURANCE COMPANY, N. Y. CITY.

YEAR.	Number of Policies.	Amount Insured.	Net Value.	Ratio of Value to Amount.
1860	180	$471,700 00	$28,603 18	6.09
1861	523	1,256,800 00	62,402 23	4.96
1862	553	1,271,900 00	39,655 44	3.12
1863	1,676	3,221,350 00	63,071 67	1.96
Totals	2,932	$6,221,750 00	$193,892 52	3.12

GERMANIA LIFE INSURANCE COMPANY, N. Y. CITY.

YEAR.	Number of Policies.	Amount Insured.	Net Value.	Ratio of Value to Amount.
1860	75	$226,000 00	$13,785 82	6.09
1861	184	500,800 00	24,527 16	4.90
1862	438	843,000 00	26,219 87	3.11
1863	1,933	2,826,350 00	51,553 21	1.82
Totals	2,630	$4,396,150 00	$116,086 06	2.64

KNICKERBOCKER LIFE INSURANCE COMPANY, N. Y.

YEAR.	No. of Policies.	Amount Insured.	Net Value.	Ratio of Value to Amount.
1853	53	$100,447 00	$20,240 15	20.16
1854	40	103,628 00	21,690 54	20.94
1855	12	35,420 00	6,025 24	17.01
1856	22	67,420 00	10,745 80	15.93
1857	25	70,500 00	7,657 33	10.86
1858	46	141,400 00	11,159 69	7.89
1859	61	182,250 00	13,560 46	7.44
1860	56	183,000 00	10,625 30	5.80
1861	107	314,300 00	14,380 08	4.57
1862	236	567,050 00	17,893 45	3.16
1863	595	1,344,575 00	27,317 53	2.03
Totals	1,253	$3,109,990 00	$161,295 57	5.19

WISCONSIN MUTUAL LIFE INSURANCE COMPANY, WIS.

YEAR.	No. of Policies.	Amount Insured.	Net Value.	Ratio of Value to Amount.
1859	105	$291,500 00	$20,906 02	7.17
1860	216	444,850 00	25,903 27	5.82
1861	355	483,400 00	20,979 97	4.34
1862	791	896,900 00	29,073 05	3.24
1863	1,466	1,594,950 00	32,986 69	2.07
Totals	2,933	$3,711,600 00	$129,849 00	3.49

ALL THE LIFE INSURANCE COMPANIES COMBINED.

YEAR.	No. of Policies.	Amount Insured.	Net Value.	Ratio of Value to Amount.
1830	1	$2,000 00	$1,115 84	55.78
1834	2	5,000 00	2,793 93	55.90
1835	1	5,000 00	1,955 70	39.11
1837	1	1,500 00	680 73	45.36
1838	1	3,000 00	1,093 47	36.42
1839	1	1,000 00	503 63	50.36
1840	1	2,000 00	1,150 82	57.56
1843	103	556,291 92	229,684 12	41.30
1844	193	809,080 23	317,565 09	39.24
1845	498	1,823,731 92	656,151 98	35.96
1846	1,073	3,196,501 96	1,011,097 55	31.64
1847	1,323	3,946,196 20	1,184,998 61	30.04
1848	1,544	4,351,575 38	1,225,017 58	28.14
1849	2,420	6,517,615 41	1,650,236 57	25.31
1850	2,748	6,868,774 11	1,627,296 72	23.68
1851	2,488	6,117,808 54	1,309,400 54	21.39
1852	1,662	4,449,401 75	907,446 11	20.39
1853	1,841	4,891,676 99	926,000 09	18.93
1854	2,239	6,432,472 50	1,076,553 64	16.73

ALL THE LIFE INSURANCE COMPANIES COMBINED—*Continued.*

YEAR.	No. of Policies.	Amount Insured.	Net Value.	Ratio of Value to Amount.
1855..............	2,206	6,915,306 59	1,097,292 38	15.86
1856..............	3,092	9,150,633 48	1,280,467 53	13.98
1857..............	3,096	8,957,879 70	1,069,442 44	11.93
1858..............	3,956	11,905,081 11	1,207,647 29	10.15
1859..............	5,503	16,153,551 70	1,318,430 71	8.16
1860..............	7,691	21,648,807 07	1,418,336 21	6.55
1861..............	7,074	19,090,360 04	982,552 36	5.15
1862..............	13,064	32,719,062 14	1,201,198 33	3.67
1863..............	28,261	68,945,380 72	1,524,763 48	2.21
Additions...........	—	58,898 00	24,127 60	40.96
Totals...........	92,083	$245,525,587 46	$23,255,001 05	9.47

RAILROAD LITERATURE.

Those who wish to examine the early and the progressive history of the Railroad system, may find much information on the subject in "*Bishop's History of American Manufactures*," in the "*British Almanac and Companion*" for 1830 to 1860; and in the periodical works mentioned below. For the latter list we are indebted to "*Poole's Index to Periodical Literature.*"

Rail, Champions of the. Blackwood's Magazine. 70: 739.

Railroad Accidents, how far Preventible. Edinburgh Review, 94: 49. Same art. Living Age, 31: 49. Same article, Eclectic Magazine, 24: 1.

Railroad across Florida Peninsula. (G. R. Fairbanks) De Bow's Review, 7: 44.
——— and Locomotive Engines. Quarterly Review, 42: 377.
——— and Steamboat Statistics. Hunt's Magazine, 10: 381, 474. 12: 290.
——— Atlantic and Pacific. (Prof Forshey and J. D. B. De Bow) De Bow's Review, 3: 474.
——— Baltimore and Ohio. (P. Cruise) North American Review, 28: 166.—Niles's Register, 47: 123.
——— between Cairo and Suez. Westminster Review, 42: 428. Same article, Living Age, 4: 205.
——— between Charleston, Savannah, and Nashville. South. Quar. Rev. 8: 298.
——— Convention, Southern and Western. (Mr. Sykes) De Bow's Rev. 11: 621.
——— Convention, South-Western. De Bow's Review, 12: 543.
——— Enterprise. New Englander, 9: 321.
——— Enterprise and New York. (J. B. Jervis) Hunt's Magazine, 15: 456.
——— Enterprises at the South. (J. D. B. De Bow) De Bow's Review, 3: 559.
——— Fall River. Hunt's Magazine, 17: 303.
——— from New York to New Orleans. (C. M. Emerson) De Bow's Rev. 7: 338.
——— History and Economy. Southern Quarterly Review, 13: 372.
——— Hudson and Mohawk. (S. D. W. Bloodgood) Journal of Science, 21: 141.
——— Hudson River. (J. B. Jervis) Hunt's Magazine, 22: 278.
——— Influence on Landed Property. De Bow's Review, 11: 585.
——— Iron and the Tariff. (J. E. Bloomfield) Hunt's Magazine, 12: 66.
——— Legislation in New York. (F. Whittlesey) Hunt's Magazine, 15: 546.—(V. B. Varnum) Hunt's Magazine, 21: 163.
——— Literature. Living Age, 5: 333.
——— Liverpool and Manchester. Monthly Review, 123: 253.—Niles's Register, 37: 77. 40: 174.
——— Locomotion, Andraud's. (W. S. Chace) Hunt's Magazine, 17: 40.
——— Michigan Central. Hunt's Magazine, 18: 94.
——— Mississippi and Atlantic. Hunt's Magazine, 17: 67.
——— Mobile and Ohio. With map, (F. B. Clark) Hunt's Magazine, 19: 579.—(L. Froost) De Bow's Review, 3: 328.
——— Movement in Virginia. (P. Clark) Hunt's Magazine, 13: 459.
——— Movement, Western. (J. W. Scott) Hunt's Magazine, 12: 323.
——— New York and Erie. (F. Hunt) Hunt's Magazine, 14: 35.—(V. M. Drake) Hunt's Magazine, 15: 359.—(E. Dwight) Hunt's Magazine, 22: 371.
——— Pennsylvania Central. (J. A. Wright) Hunt's Magazine, 16: 263.
——— Philadelphia and Reading. (C. G. Childs) Hunt's Magazine, 16: 210.
——— Prospects and Progress. (J. D. B. De Bow) De Bow's Review, 12: 492.
——— Prospects, South-Western. (R. Beebe) De Bow's Review, 12: 420.
——— Reading. Hunt's Magazine, 16: 415.

Railroad to the Pacific. (W. Darby) Am. Whig Rev. 1: 424. 10: 311. 12: 539.—Dem. Rev. 23: 405. 25: 243. 27: 536.—Hunt's Mag. 15: 477. 16: 278.—(C. H. Davis) Hunt's Mag. 18: 467.—(M. F. Maury) Hunt's Mag. 18: 592.—(A. Whitney) Hunt's Mag. 19: 527.—(J. M. Niles) Hunt's Mag. 21: 72.—(W. Darby) Hunt's Mag. 21: 194.—Hunt's Mag. 21: 616.—(M. F. Maury) Southern Literary Messenger, 14: 344.

——— Red River and Mississippi. (W. H. Sidell) De Bow's Review, 12: 409.

——— Southern Atlantic and Mississippi. De Bow's Review, 1: 22.

——— Statistics. Hunt's Magazine, 2: 347. 4: 48, 567. 8: 185, 292. 9: 95, 184. 10: 381, 274. 11: 371. 12: 290. 13: 385. 15: 209, 609. 16: 115, 324. 17: 101, 211. 18: 94, 220. 19: 115, 214.

——— Western. (J. Sparks) North American Review, 24: 475.—(N. Hale) North American Review, 28: 522.—Hunt's Magazine, 10: 474.

Railroads. Ed. Rev. 60: 46.—Dem. Rev. 21: 338.—Blackw. Mag. 58: 633.—Mus. 6: 282.—(W. R. Casey) Hunt's Mag. 9: 144.—(J. W. Scott) Hunt's Mag. 13: 250.—Niles's Reg. 28: 54. 29: 184. 32: 282, 300. 33: 74. 40: 132.—Living Age, 2: 247. 11: 497.

——— American. (N. Hale) North American Review, 44: 435.

——— American and Belgian. American Almanac, 1840: 124.

——— and Canals. Quarterly Review, 31: 349.—United States Lit. Gaz. 4: 11.

——— and Manufactories, Reciprocal Influences of. (H. Smith) De Bow's Review, 11: 468.

——— and Metropolitan Improvements. Westminster Review, 45: 462.

——— and Transports at Home and Abroad. De Bow's Review, 9: 513.

——— Comparative Fares on, in United States. Hunt's Magazine, 18: 97.

——— English. (J. E. Bloomfield) Hunt's Magazine, 13: 353.

——— English, Accidents on. Hunt's Magazine, 15: 97.

——— First Application of Steam on. (J. E. Bloomfield) Hunt's Mag. 14: 245.

——— History and Progress of. Monthly Review, 124: 592.

——— How should they be Managed? (D. M. Balfour) Hunt's Magazine, 23: 188.

——— Importance of. Hunt's Magazine, 12: 152.

——— in England and Abroad. Edinburgh Review, 85: 271.

——— Influence of. (J. M. Niles) De Bow's Review, 5: 454—Banker's Magazine, 5: 303.

——— in Ireland.—See "Ireland."

——— in Italy. (C. E. Lester) Hunt's Magazine, 17: 250.

——— in Massachusetts. Hunt's Mag. 6: 94.—(E. H. Derby) Hunt's Mag. 14: 29.—(E. H. Derby) Hunt's Mag. 15: 234.—(D. M. Balfour) Hunt's Magazine, 18: 381.—(N. Hale) Hunt's Magazine, 18: 662.—(E. H. Derby) Hunt's Magazine, 23: 304.—(N. Hale) North American Review, 28: 522.

——— in Missouri. De Bow's Review, 8: 571.

——— in New York. Hunt's Magazine, 10: 476. 18: 544.—(A. C. Flagg) Hunt's Magazine, 25: 281, 415, 505, 694.

——— in the South and West. Southern Literary Journal, 1: 161.

——— in the United States. American Almanac, 1847: 160. 1848: 198.—De Bow's Review, 12: 667.

——— Moral Influence of. New England Magazine, 2: 288.

——— Past History of. Fraser's Magazine, 17: 421.

——— Present Condition and Prospects of. Fraser's Magazine, 18: 43.

——— State Tolls on. Hunt's Magazine, 18: 63.

——— to New Orleans. (J. G. Barnard) De Bow's Review, 8: 444.

——— Wood's Treatise on. American Monthly Review, 3: 126.

Railway Administration and Improvement. Westminster Review, 42: 1.

——— Atmospheric. Westminster Review, 40: 470.—Eclectic Magazine, 1: 100, 513.—Living Age, 1: 302. 4: 43. 6: 114.

——— Companies and Railway Law. Fraser's Magazine, 43: 114.

——— Consolidation and Government. Eclectic Review, 4th s. 21: 292.

——— Gauge Dispute. Fraser's Magazine, 33: 743.

Railway How we got up the Glenmutchkin. Blackwood's Magazine, 58 : 453.
——— Improvement. Westminster Review, 44 : 225.
——— in India. Eclectic Review, 4th s. 31 : 135.
——— Investment. Westminster Review, 44 : 497.
——— Legislation. Quarterly Review, 74 : 120.
——— Literature. Dublin University Magazine, 34 : 280.
——— London and North-Western. Quarterly Review, 84 : 1. Same article, Living Age, 20 : 579.
——— Management. Westminster Review, 53 : 410.
——— Potentates. Fraser's Magazine, 36 : 213. Same article, Eclectic Magazine, 12 : 106. Same article, Living Age, 14 : 586.
——— Progress. Westminster Review, 52 : 435.
——— Prospects in India. Fraser's Magazine, 37 : 414.
——— Rhapsody. Blackwood's Magazine, 58 : 614.
——— System of Europe. American Whig Review, 4 : 485.
——— System of Great Britain. North British Review, 11 : 305. Same article, Eclectic Magazine, 18 : 470.—De Bow's Review, 7 : 523.
——— System, Origin of. Living Age, 16 : 208.
——— Systems of Europe and America. De Bow's Review, 3 : 138.
——— Traction, Economy of. Westminster Review, 48 : 416.
——— Travelling and Toll Question. Westminster Review, 39 : 359. Same article, Eclectic Museum, 2 : 522.
——— Trip, A. Fraser's Magazine, 22 : 238, 577.
——— Witness in London, Letter from a. Blackwood's Magazine, 62 : 68.
Railways. Fraser's Magazine, 29 : 503. 32 : 719. 33 : 97. 39 : 607. 40 : 106.—Blackwood's Magazine, 58 : 1, 633.
——— English. With map, Bank. Mag. 2 : 325.—Eclec. Rev. 4th s. 31 : 521.
——— in Great Britain. Banker's Magazine, 1 : 490.
——— in Ireland. Dublin University Magazine, 13 : 376.
——— Plea for Ancient Towns against. Blackwood's Magazine, 54 : 398.
——— Reports on. Eclectic Review, 4th s. 8 : 326.

WORKS ON RAILROADS.

History of the Railroads and Canals of the United States: exhibiting their progress, cost, revenue, expenditures, and present condition. By Henry V. Poor, late editor of the "Railroad Journal." Vol. First, 8vo. pp. 612. Price $6.

Locomotive Engineering and the Mechanism of Railways: A treatise on the principles and construction of the locomotive engine, railway carriages, and railway plant. Illustrated with sixty large engravings and numerous woodcuts. By Zerah Colburn, Esq., Civil Engineer. Published by John Wiley, New York.

England's Policy. Among the recent pamphlets are, I. "A few words of advice to the Maltese," etc. II. "English Governors and Foreign Grumblers." III. "A Letter to his Grace the Duke of Newcastle: by Four of the Elected Members of the Council of Government of Malta." In one of these the following paragraph occurs:

England is growing old and cold, with her best life-blood drained out of her by the lancet of Emigration, and would fain lie down and be at rest. What she says now on all occasions is, "Let me doze quietly to the hum of Manchester spindles and the drone of Peace-party speeches; but, for Heaven's sake, do not expect me to do anything which you young folks call high or noble, chivalrous or self-sacrificing! I did all that long ago, when I was young and foolish; but it cost a mint of money and a world of trouble; and now I only want to be permitted to make a little more money and doze quietly on my bags."

NEW ENGLAND RAILROAD SHARES.

Market Values at Boston.

Railroad Companies.	1862. Lowest and Highest.		1863. Lowest and Highest.		Dividends. When payable.		Dividends. 1862.	1863.		Jan. '64	Par.
Boston and Lowell........	92	108½	103	108½	Jan.	July	2¾	4	3	3	500
Boston and Maine.........	105	129	121	135½	Jan.	July	6	4	4	4	100
Boston and Providence....	105½	130	121	142½	Jan.	July	8	4	4	4	100
Boston and Worcester....	107	132½	127	150¼	Jan.	July	8	4	4	5	100
Cambridge (horse).........	95	112½	109¼	135½	Apl.	Oct.	9	4½	4½	..	100
Chelsea (horse) Pref......	36	47	47	53	Apl.	Oct.	8	4	4	..	50
Cheshire (Pref.)..........	12	22¼	20	52	Jan.	July	0	0	0	2	100
Concord................	52¼	62	60	67	May	Nov.	7	4	4	..	50
Connecticut River.........	77	107⅛	103½*	114⅝	Feb.	Aug.	6	3	3	3	100
Connt. and Passumpsic....	5	30	30	51	Jan.	July	0	0	0	0	100
Eastern..................	54½	96	93	115	Jan.	July	0	3	3	3	100
Fitchburg	95½	112¾	109	124½	Jan.	July	6	3	3	4	100
Malden and Melrose (horse)	5	40	5	35	Mar.	Sept.	0	0	0	..	100
Manchester and Lawrence.	99	115	111	122½	May	Nov.	7	4	4	..	100
Metropolitan (horse)......	48¾	70½	55	82½	Jan.	July	8	5	5	3	50
Michigan Central........	47	97	92	127	Jan.	July	6	5	6	6	100
Middlesex (horse)........	59	101	97	112½	Jan.	July	4	4	4	3	100
Nashua and Lowell......	109	125	117½	135	May	Nov.	8	4	4	..	100
New York Central.......	79⅝	107¾	107	140	Feb.	Aug	6	3½	3½	5	100
Northern (N. H.).........	48	65½	63	74	June	Dec.	4	2	2	..	100
Old Colony and Newport..	102	126½	119	151	Jan.	July	6	3	3	†3	100
Portland and Saco........	99	113½	106*	115	June	Dec.	6	3	3	..	100
Providence and Worcester.	103	125	120	134	Jan.	July	8	4	4	4	100
Somerville (horse)	19¾	29	29	37	May	Nov.	5	2½	2½	..	50
South Shore............	4¾	6¼	6*	19½	Jan.	July	0	3	0	0	25
Vermont and Canada.....	97	136	132	169½	June	Dec.	8	4	4	..	100
Vermont and Massachusetts	9⅝	22¾	22½	43¼	None.		0	0	0	..	100
Western................	111	147	140	171	Jan.	July	8	4	4	5	100
Wilmington.............	42	61½	59¾	74½	Apl.	Oct	9	5‡	5	..	50
Worcester and Nashua....	52	67	65	83	Jan.	July	$4	$2	$2	2½	75

† Old Colony 40 per cent. extra in Stock, Jan. 1864. ‡ Wilm.

JOURNAL OF INSURANCE LAW.

Cases Decided in the Courts of Pennsylvania, Maryland, New York, Massachusetts, and Ohio, in the Years 1862 *and* 1863.

I.—PENNSYLVANIA.

1. THOUGH the term enemies, when rigidly construed, means public enemies, so that the policy in strictness would hardly cover the loss; yet as indemnity is the object of insurance, and as it is a rule in marine policies that, where the loss is of a *like nature* with the specified peril, or substantially within its meaning, the underwriters are liable, the loss would be covered by the peril of "enemies" insured against in the policy. 43 *Penn. State Reports*, 555.

2. The United States Government has so conducted and treated the contest between it and the Confederate States, so called, as to make it a war in substance as essentially as it could be between foreign powers. 43 *Penn. State Reports*, 555.

3. The judgment of an inferior court will be maintained if sustainable on any ground, though the reasons given in the court below be insufficient; so that where in the court below it was *held* that the loss was covered by the term "enemies," and in the Supreme Court that it was in any event covered by the words "all such losses," the judgment would be affirmed. 43 *Penn. State Reports*, 555.

4. Under a clause in a policy of insurance which provides that it shall become void on assignment unless notice thereof be given at the office of the company, and the same approved and endorsed on the policy by the secretary or other authorized officer, an approval of and consent to an assignment, written and signed by the president on a separate piece of paper, and attached to the policy by a wafer, is a sufficient endorsement within the meaning of the policy. *The Penn. Ins. Co.* v. *Bowman.* 44 *Penn. State Reports*, 560.

5. Insurance money for loss by fire occurring after contract for sale of property insured, belongs to the vendee. *Reed* v. *Lukens.* 44 *Penn. State Reports*, 560.

6. A condition in a policy of insurance that it should cease from the time that the property insured should be "levied on or taken into possession or custody, under an execution or other proceeding at law or equity," does not apply to a wrongful levy made upon the property as that of another person. *Phila. Fire Ins. Co.* v. *Mills.* 44 *Penn. State Reports*, 560.

7. If an insurance company on notice of loss refer the insured to their resident agent for settlement, and instruct the agent to procure a statement of the loss, he is thereby invested with full authority to receive and extend the time for furnishing it; and if given within the time required by the agent, though after thirty days from the fire, the condition in the policy requiring it to be

made within that time is not broken. *Lycoming Ins. Co.* v. *Schollenberger.* 44 *Penn. State Reports*, 560.

8. Where there was any evidence as to the authority given to the agent by the company to act in the premises, and of an actual waiver of condition on the part of the agent, it was for the jury; and though a waiver must be intentional and clearly proven, the sufficiency of the evidence relating thereto is for the jury, whose error in judgment thereon can be corrected only by motion for new trial. *Id.* 44 *Penn. State Reports*, 561.

9. In an insurance of a single property (a coal breaker), under a valued property where the insured, immediately after its destruction by fire, wrote to the company, stating that his "coal breaker" burnt down this morning, giving the number of his policy and the amount of his insurance, such a statement of loss, though in the preliminary notice, was substantially a particular statement, and a compliance with the condition requiring it. *Id.* 44 *Penn. State Reports*, 561.

10. Where, under a condition requiring payment of assessments within thirty days from demand and avoiding the policy until paid, a balance remained unpaid beyond that time and on the day of the fire, but was paid the same day to the agent, and by him reported to the company without objection on the part of either of them, such receipt is a waiver of the forfeiture, and that breach of condition cannot be set up against recovery on the policy. *Id.* 44 *Penn. State Reports*, 561.

11. It is not a bar to a recovery on the ground of waiver, that the declaration averred a performance of all the conditions precedent, and the proof was of a dispensation with and waiver of performance, for the defect was amenable as matter of right; and after verdict, especially where the case was tried as if there had been no omission, the *narr.* will be treated as if amended. *Id.* 44 *Penn. State Reports*, 561.

12. Whether an action on a policy of insurance may be maintained by an assignee of a policy, in his own name, where it has been assigned with consent of the company, and premium note of assignee has been paid, received, and substituted in place of that of assignor: *quere.* *Lycoming Ins. Co.* v. *Shreffler.* 44 *Penn. State Reports*, 561.

13. But where the same action had before been brought up on error, the parties standing the same upon the record, the objection to the maintenance of the action in the name of the assignee alone should then have been made; but as it was not, it must be treated as waived. *Id.* 44 *Penn. State Reports*, 561.

14. The report of loss made out by the agent of the company is not evidence to go to the jury as to the amount of loss in an action upon the policy, though accompanied by the affidavit of the party insured. *Id.* 44 *Penn. State Reports*, 561.

15. The particular statement of the plaintiff, though not evidence of the extent or amount of the loss, may be used to refresh the memory of the witness. *Id.* 44 *Penn. State Reports*, 561.

An unadjusted and unliquidated claim for a loss upon a policy of insurance against fire is subject to attachment in the hands of the insurance company. *Girard Fire Ins. Co.* v. *Field.* 45 *Penn. State Reports*, 559.

II.—MARYLAND.

1. An insurance policy under seal was issued to "J. McGowan & Sons" for one year, with a covenant that it should continue so long as the "assured or their assigns" shall pay the premium, and the company shall accept and receive the same from them. At the time the policy was issued the firm of "J. McGowan & Sons" was composed of the plaintiffs *and another party* who retired from the firm during the *first year*, and the business was conducted by the plaintiffs under the same name; the day preceding the expiration of the policy, the premium for the *second year* was paid and a renewal receipt endorsed upon the policy, stating that the company had received the premium from "J. McGowan & Sons," under the policy "*which is hereby continued in force*" for another year. A loss occurred during the *second year*, and upon an action by the plaintiffs to recover therefor; *held:*

1st. That the renewal receipt is not a *parol* and *new* contract with *other parties*, on which an action of assumpsit may be brought, but is simply an extension for another year of the original *sealed* contract; and the plaintiffs, not being the covenantees nor their assignees, cannot maintain an action of *covenant* upon the policy.

2d. But whether specialty or parol, no action can be maintained on the contract except by the *parties insured;* it is a joint contract, and whatever sum could be recovered would be *in solido*, and no one of the parties insured can sue alone for his proportion; these plaintiffs therefore cannot maintain the action. *Baltimore Fire Insurance Company* v. *McGowan.* 16 *Maryland Reports*, 617.

2. If advances be made by the charterer on freight simply on the personal credit of the owner, who is bound to repay the same as a debt, independent of the issue of the voyage, the charterer has no insurable interest in the amount so advanced as freight. *Lee* v. *Barreda.* 16 *Maryland Reports*, 618.

3. But where, by the terms of the charter party, the charterer has a lien upon the freight for his advances, he has an insurable interest, on account of such lien, to the extent of his advances, which he may insure in general terms as freight. *Id.* 16 *Maryland Reports*, 618.

4. Where a charter party stipulates that the charterer, if required, shall advance a sum "not exceeding one-third of the freight, which is to be in part payment of the freight, together with the cost of insurance on such advances," it gives the charterer a lien upon the freight for his advances. *Id.* 16 *Maryland Reports*, 618.

5. The terms of a charter party, by which the charterer has the right to retain the amount advanced out of the freight, gives him a lien on the freight which he may insure, notwithstanding he had

the right to reclaim the amount upon failure of the voyage. *Id.* 16 *Maryland Reports*, 618.

6. An insurance policy insuring A, and making "*the loss, if any, payable to*" B, is to be regarded as having been, at its inception, assigned to B with the assent of the company, and he is entitled to its benefit without procuring a transfer of the policy from A assented to by the company as in ordinary cases. *National Fire Insurance Co.* v. *Crane.* 16 *Maryland Reports*, 618.

7. The president and secretary of an insurance company, not being stockholders therein, are competent witnesses for the company in an action upon a policy executed by the company. *Id.* 16 *Maryland Reports*, 618.

8. Where the fact of a prior insurance was notified to the company at the time the policy was issued, the want of the endorsement of such prior insurance on the policy cannot be urged in a court of equity in a cause otherwise free from objection, whatever effect it may have at law. *Id.* 16 *Maryland Reports*, 618.

9. The endorsement of a prior insurance on the policy could only have been made by the company, and if omitted the assured is not at fault if he has notified the company of the existence of such prior insurance. *Id.* 16 *Maryland Reports*, 618.

10. There is a distinction in cases where the preparation of an instrument belongs to the party to become liable under it; he ought to be dealt with more strictly, and insurance contracts are within this principle. *Id.* 16 *Maryland Reports*, 618.

11. Equity will interpose not only in cases of fraud but also of mistake, where a policy is drawn up in a form different from the application, or anything is omitted which it was the duty of the company to insert or endorse on the instrument. *Id.* 16 *Maryland Reports*, 618.

12. It may be true as a general rule that when a loss has happened from the perils covered by a fire policy, and the insurer claims exemption under the clause of the policy against unauthorized alterations increasing the risk, and providing that any loss *happening by reason of such alterations* shall not be paid, the *onus* is on him to prove the facts which entitle him to exemption. *Howell's Executors* v. *Baltimore Equitable Society.* 16 *Maryland Reports*, 619.

13. But where there is a total destruction of the building by fire, and the claim is for the whole loss, and it is shown to have resulted either altogether or to an unknown extent from an unauthorized alterations which increased the risk, the loss must fall on the assured unless he furnishes proof of some loss occasioned by other causes than such alteration. *Id.* 16 *Maryland Reports*, 619.

14. Under the clause of a fire policy making it void if any unauthorized hazardous trade increasing the risk is carried on in the building, the fact that such trade was carried on avoids the policy, no matter what was the cause or origin of the fire, or that such trade was carried on by the tenant of the assured without his knowledge or consent. *Id.* 16 *Maryland Reports*, 619.

15. A deed of real estate to a married woman under the Act of 1842, Ch. 293, Sec. 1, vests her with the legal estate in fee, but not to her sole and separate use; in such property the husband still retains his marital rights, and such interest of the husband is an insurable interest. *Mutual Insurance Co. in Baltimore County* v. *Deale.* 18 *Maryland Reports*, 592.

16. In an ordinary contract of insurance the interest of a husband in property conveyed to his wife would be covered by an insurance of the property as his, and his omission to state the nature and extent of his interest, where no inquiry is made, will not avoid the policy. *Id.* 18 *Maryland Reports*, 592.

17. But in the case of a mutual insurance company whose charter, to which the insured was bound by the contract of insurance, makes all premium notes liens on the real estate of the assured to meet losses, the title of the assured is a most important consideration of the contract, and a material misrepresentation or concealment in regard to it will render the contract void. *Id.* 18 *Maryland Reports*, 592.

18. A mutual insurance company whose charter gave it "full power and authority to make insurance on any kind of property," may insure the interest which a husband has in property conveyed to his wife. *Id.* 18 *Maryland Reports*, 592.

19. Where a party in his application for insurance in a mutual insurance company called the property "his property," and the policy refers to such application, this does not constitute a *warranty* on his part that he held the fee-simple thereto unincumbered, a breach of which, by the existence of the legal title in his wife, would render the policy void. *Id.* 18 *Maryland Reports*, 592.

20. Whether a misrepresentation or concealment by the assured in a mutual insurance policy of the true nature and extent of his interest in the property insured will avoid the policy, depends upon its materiality to the risk, and the question of materiality is a question of fact to be submitted to the jury. *Id.* 18 *Maryland Reports*, 592.

21. In the case of a mutual insurance company where there is a lien created on the property insured, a representation or concealment as to title may be material to the risk, which would not be so in an ordinary case, but its materiality is a question for the jury, and the court cannot assume it as a matter of law. *Id.* 18 *Maryland Reports*, 593.

22. The defendant (the company) has a right to ask for a specific instruction directing the attention of the jury to the particular fact in which the alleged misrepresentation or concealment existed. *Id.* 18 *Maryland Reports*, 593.

23. An insurance company is not chargeable with notice at the time of insurance of the state of the title to the premises insured as disclosed by the land records, so as to prevent its relying, in order to defeat the action on the policy, on any objection to the title of the assured, which might have been ascertained by inspection of such records. *Id.* 18 *Maryland Reports*, 593.

24. Where a stockholder and agent of an insurance company filled up, at the request of the assured, an application for insurance, and presented it to the company, he is a competent witness for the company to testify as to such matters, for he was therein the agent of the assured. *Id.* 18 *Maryland Reports*, 593.

25. Assumpsit is the proper remedy upon a contract not under seal for additional insurance, endorsed on a policy, there being nothing in the original covenant continuing it in force as a specialty, and binding the company by subsequent endorsements of additional insurance. *Id.* 18 *Maryland Reports*, 593.

III.—NEW YORK.

1. *Held*, that by force of the 20th section of the act of 1853, the prohibition in regard to the amounts of the premium notes contained in the 13th section, applies to, and is to be observed by, companies formed under the act of April 10th, 1849, and which were in existence at the time the act of 1853 took effect. *Barbour's Sup. Ct. Reports*, *Volume* 36, *p.* 685.

2. *Held*, further, that the giving of such notes was an act not merely *ultra vires*, but was an act expressly prohibited by law. *Ibid.*

3. Policies of insurance are not deemed, in their nature, incidents to the property insured; and do not cover any interest which a person other than the insured may have in the property, as heir, grantee, mortgagee, or creditor, unless there be a valid assignment of the policy. *Wyman* v. *Prosser*. *Ibid. p.* 685.

4. The contract of insurance, being a mere personal contract, in no way attached to or running with the real property insured, it does not pass with it either to a grantee or an heir. The executor or administrator is the only one who can take the contract and enforce it. *Ibid. p.* 685.

5. A stipulation in a policy of insurance, that the insurance shall be void, in case the assured, or any other person with his knowledge, shall have existing, during the continuation of the policy, any other insurance on the property, not notified to the insurers, and mentioned in or indorsed upon the policy, is a material part of the contract between the parties. *Gilbert* v. *Phœnix Ins. Co.* *Ibid.* 372.

6. The parties to a contract of insurance have a right to stipulate between themselves as to the nature and kind of evidence by which the assent of the insurers to other insurances shall be manifested. And when they have thus stipulated, the court has no power to substitute any other kind of evidence differing in kind or degree. *Ibid.* 685.

7. Accordingly, a condition (made a part of the contract) that notices of all previous insurances on the property shall be given to the insurers and indorsed upon the policy, or otherwise acknowledged in writing, at or before the time of making the insurance,

otherwise the policy shall be void; and a similar condition in reference to subsequent insurances, together with a stipulation in the body of the policy that the insurance shall be void in case the insured shall have any other insurance upon the property during the continuance of the policy, not notified to the insurers and mentioned in or indorsed upon the policy, constitutes a valid agreement; and the failure of the insured to have other insurances effected by him mentioned in or indorsed upon the policy, or acknowledged in writing, will render the policy void. *Ibid.* 685.

8. Where a policy of insurance declares expressly, in the body thereof, that the same is made and accepted in reference to the terms and conditions thereunto annexed, one of which conditions is, that in case of any loss on or damage to the property insured, it shall be optional with the insurers to rebuild or repair the buildings within a reasonable time, on giving notice of their intention to do so, within thirty days after receiving the preliminary proofs of loss; and if, within the specified time after proof of loss, the insurers serve upon the insured written notice of their intention to rebuild the building destroyed, no action will lie upon the policy to recover the amount of the loss, until the neglect of the insurers to comply with their offer to rebuild within a reasonable time. *Beals* v. *Home Ins. Co.* *Ibid.* 614.

9. The insurers having elected to pay the loss by restoring the building burned, they cannot be required to pay in any other way *Ibid.* 686.

10. No action will lie upon the policy after the insured has refused to enter upon the premises to rebuild, and has himself proceeded to rebuild, without waiting for the expiration of the thirty days within which the insurers were entitled to make the election to rebuild. *Ibid. p.* 686.

11. A clause in a condition, giving the insurers thirty days within which they shall have the option to rebuild, is not repugnant to another part of such condition in which it is stipulated that the company will pay the loss "within sixty days." *Ibid.* 686.

12. Where a promissory note, on its face, is payable at such time or times as the directors of a mutual insurance company may, agreeably to their charter and by-laws, require, the presumption is, that it was given and taken as and for a premium or deposit note; and no recovery can be made on such a note, unless it has been duly assessed. *Sands* v. *St. John.* *Ibid.* 628.

13. But the plaintiff may allege and prove that the note, notwithstanding its form, was given and taken as and for a capital stock note, and used as such in organizing the insurance company, and recover the whole amount thereof, without showing that it has been assessed; such notes being paid absolutely at maturity. *Ibid.* 686.

14. Actions on capital stock notes must be brought within six years next after the causes of action accrue thereon. *Ibid.* 686.

15. An action may be commenced on such a note without any

actual request or demand of payment, at the expiration of twelve months, or twelve months and three days, from its date; and the statute of limitations will then commence running on the same. *Ibid.* 686.

LIFE INSURANCE.

16. One having an interest in the continuation of the life of another, as his creditor, may insure the life of the debtor, and the contract for that purpose will be valid. *Rawls* v. *American Life Ins. Co.* 36 *Barbour's Rep.* 357.

17. The fact that the debt is due to the creditor as a member of a partnership, and from another firm, of which the person whose life is insured is a member, does not alter the rule. *Ibid.* 689.

18. If such a policy of insurance is valid in its inception, the circumstances that the statute of limitations had run against the debt, before the occurrence of the death, will not affect it. *Ibid.* 686.

19. The interest of the creditor, in the continuance of the life of the debtor, cannot be held to have ceased entirely because the statute of limitations has operated against the debt. *Ibid.* 686.

20. It is not necessary that the party holding a policy on the life of another should have an insurable interest in such life at the time of the death, to make the policy valid, if it was valid in its inception. *Ibid.* 687.

21. A life policy is not regarded as a mere contract of indemnity. *Ibid.* 687.

22. A clause in a life insurance policy provided, in case "of a bodily injury to the insured of so serious a nature as wholly to disable him from following his usual business, occupation, or pursuits," for the payment of £5 per week during the continuance of such disability. The insured, a solicitor and registrar of a county court, was confined to his bedroom for several weeks by a sprained ancle, and was consequently unable to attend to his business: *Held*, that he was "wholly disabled," within the meaning of the policy, and was therefore entitled to recover. *Hooper* v. *Accidental Death Ins. Co.* 5 *Hurl. and Nor.* 546.

FIRE INSURANCE IN LONDON.

For many years previous to 1832, the principal fire insurance offices of London kept fire brigades at their individual expense. But the large expenses they separately incurred led to the formation in that year of one consolidated brigade, for the purpose of promoting economy as well as greater efficiency. The London Fire Brigade thus commenced its operations under the united sanction of, and from funds contributed by, most of the leading insurance offices in London. The expense was at first £8,000, the men employed eighty, and the number of stations nineteen. In 1834, immediately after the destruction by fire of the Houses of Parliament, the offices seized the occasion to direct the attention of the Government to the insufficient protection against fire in the great public buildings in London, and suggested that the parochial engines should be placed under the inspection of the commissioners of police—a recommendation not adopted by the Government. Since that time the annual cost of the brigade has reached the sum of £25,000 in the last year, the stations are twenty, and the number of men employed, 127. The insurance offices, alarmed at the growing expense and responsibility, again in February last addressed the Secretary of State for the Home Department, stating their wish and intention to give up the brigade at as early a date as might be consistent with the formation of new and efficient arrangements for the protection generally of the metropolis against fire. A moderate expense they did not object to incur, but the expense has now assumed a magnitude which they cannot continue to bear, and they consider that the public of London have no claim whatever on their respective offices for protection against fire.

To these representations great force is added by the evidence of Mr. Newmarch, who states before the committee that he believes the total value of property insurable against fire within six miles of Charing Cross (the area of the Metropolitan Board of Works) is not less than £900,000,000. Of this not more than about £300,000,000 is insured, and this property insured now bears, therefore, through the medium of the fire offices, the expense of the present fire brigade establishment. In addition to this, it must be observed that the London Fire Brigade, a body of incalculable importance and acknowledged merits, has no legal standing or authority whatever. It exists, so to speak, upon sufferance. A man might set fire to his own house, endangering his neighbors, and unless overborne by force, positively refuse to allow the insurance office engines to put the fire out. Nor is this all; notwithstanding the ability and zeal of this fire brigade, it is admitted on all hands that on its present scale it is totally inadequate for the general protection required. All the way from Charing Cross to Richmond there is only one large and one small station. There is no station north of Holborn. The existing stations have been very naturally planted by the insurance offices where most property was insured, and not with reference to public safety. If any large district of London were to be materially increased by buildings of a smaller description, it might not be the interest of the offices to protect them by incurring the additional expense of a new station. In thirty years they have only increased the number of their stations once, whence it appears conclusively that the mere increase of houses is not taken into consideration.

A Parliamentary return has just been published of all sums paid for duty on insurance against fire during the past year, by each of the fire insurance companies of the United Kingdom. From this document it appears that the sums paid by the London offices, which amount in the aggregate to £986,210, stand as follows when arranged in the order of their respective totals, including the duty paid in Ireland :

DUTY PAID BY THE LONDON FIRE INSURANCE OFFICES DURING THE YEAR 1861.

Sun	£219,244	General	£17,893
Phœnix	137,565	Unity	17,076
Royal Exchange	87,589	Royal Farmers'	12,551
County	72,157	Hand-in-Hand	10 334
Imperial	66,734	Law Union	8 056
Alliance	51,538	Church of England	5,599
Globe	47,884	Mercantile (one quarter)	5,174
Atlas	45,380	Commercial Union (one quarter),	3,457
Law	38,225	State	3,103
London	34,829	United Kingdom Provident	1,545
Guardian	34.487	Emperor	742
Union	33,191	Preserver	45
Westminster	31,809		

The following is a similar table with regard to country offices, the aggregate amount of which is £489,630 :

DUTY PAID BY THE COUNTRY FIRE INSURANCE OFFICES IN ENGLAND AND WALES DURING THE YEAR 1861.

Norwich Union	£84,138	Queen	£8,563
Royal	67,470	Provincial	7,890
Liverpool and London	65,977	Essex and Suffolk	7,229
West of England	61,492	Midland Counties	5,590
Manchester	42,178	Nottingham and Derby	5,145
Leeds and Yorkshire	29,053	Salop	4,147
Lancashire	25,212	Sheffield	3,732
Yorkshire	23,307	Norwich Equitable	3,166
Birmingham	16,086	Hants, Sussex, and Dorset	2,308
Kent	15,794	Shropshire and North Wales	2,086
Birmingham District	9,058		

With respect to Scotch and Irish offices the following is the return of duty paid, in the order of their respective totals:

North British	£34,975	Scottish Provincial	£10,871
Scottish Union	33,586	National	7,089
Northern	21,942	National (Irish)	7,134
Caledonian	13,636	Patriotic (Irish)	6,596

The total amount of duty received in the United Kingdom for the year 1861 was £1,611,677, being £53,060 in excess of the previous year:

London offices paid	£986,210	Scotch offices paid	£122,105
Country offices paid	489,630	Irish offices paid	13,732

The following is an abstract from the Parliamentary return showing the sums insured at each office on farming stock, exempt from duty. Under this head the totals insured by the London offices are as follows, the aggregate amount of property protected being £39,064,898:

Value of Farming Stock (exempt from duty) insured by London Offices during the Year 1861.

Sun	£8,664,947	Union	£329,496
County	8,027,913	Westminster	246,593
Phœnix	4,589,915	Law Union	176.385
Royal Farmers'	4,421,483	General	154,603
Royal Exchange	4,362,478	Law	148,709
Alliance	2,896,169	State	61,802
Atlas	1,315,392	Mercantile	49,381
Globe	1,120,356	Hand-in-Hand	42,760
Imperial	954,785	Church of England	24,502
Unity	682,263	United Kingdom Provident	12,416
London	398,399	Emperor	5,770
Guardian	372,981	Commercial Union	5,400

Of the Value of the Farming Stock insured at each of the Country Offices, including Scotch and Irish, the following are the totals, amounting to £34,530,709.

Norwich Union	£10,062,302	Leeds and Yorkshire	£682,257
Yorkshire	3,267,284	Salop	561,898
Provincial	1,770,361	Nottingham and Derby	482,745
West of England	1,546,138	Shropshire and North Wales	346,630
Essex and Suffolk	1,477,873	Lancashire	328,322
Midland Counties	1,234.471	Birmingham District	291,421
Kent	1,107,066	Norwich Equitable	255,129
Manchester	1,031,884	Hants, Sussex	161,363
Royal	1,015,742	Sheffield	66,740
Liverpool and London	962,076	Queen	29,463
Birmingham	779,323		

SCOTCH.

North British	£1,715,185	Scottish Provincial	£779,426
Scottish Union	1,680,347	National	543,465
Northern	1,319,920	Stewarton, Dunlop, and Fenwick Mutual Society	22,706
Caledonian	825,906		

IRISH.

Patriotic	£112,165	National	£70,100

MARINE DISASTERS OF THE YEAR 1863.

COMPILED BY ISAAC H. UPTON, SECRETARY, NEW YORK.

TOTAL LOSSES.

Month.	Ste'mers	Ships.	Barks.	Brigs.	Sch'ners	Total.	Tonnage.
January	3	13	10	13	13	52	23,429
February	2	 6	 8	 8	31	55	16,244
March	1	 7	 6	 9	13	...36	14,808
April	4	 6	 9	 7	25	52	16,326
May	1	12	 7	 3	 6	...29	13,874
June	4	 8	11	 7	19	...49	21,323
July	2	 8	 8	 5	10	...33	13,965
August	3	10	 5	 5	 9	32	13,598
September	......	 5	 2	 5	14	26	6,714
October	1	 9	 5	10	10	35	13,838
November	4	 8	11	 4	15	42	10,844
December	3	 5	10	 6	26	50	17,072
Total for 1863	28	97	92	83	...191	...491	
Total Tonnage	21,652	81,242	36,220	18,721	24,200	......	182,035

PARTIAL LOSSES, YEAR 1863.

Month.	Ste'mers	Ships.	Barks.	Brigs.	Sch'ners	Total.	
January	7	32	16	 8	25	...88	....
February	7	16	26	13	33	95	....
March	3	17	...12	10	28	70	....
April	2	22	 7	15	34	80	....
May	......	12	 4	 8	11	35	....
June	2	10	 3	 3	17	35	....
July	2	19	 3	 4	19	47	....
August	3	18	 3	13	17	58	....
September	4	27	 5	 8	28	72	....
October	3	15	15	12	19	64	....
November	5	34	14	10	29	82	....
December	5	21	13	19	33	91	....
Partial Losses	43	...243	...125	...123	...283	...817	....
Total Losses	28	97	92	83	...191	...491	....
Total and part, 1863	71	...340	...217	...206	...474	..1,308	....
Total Vessels, 1862	44	...233	...219	...189	...325	..1,010	....
Total Vessels, 1861	49	...232	...182	...168	...322	.. 953	....
Total for three years	...164	...805	...618	...563	..1,121	..3,271	....

MARINE DISASTERS FOR 1864.

TOTAL LOSSES.

Month.	Ste'mers	Ships.	Barks.	Brigs.	Sch'ners	Total.	Tonnage.
January	2	9	7	5	16	39	13,866
February	3	13	7	5	18	46	20,224
March	2	13	4	7	27	53	21,185
April	4	6	6	12	21	49	16,638
May		5	3	5	[Sloop 1... 5	19	6,973
June	1	8	4	4	11	28	11,277
July	5	3	11	3	12	34	11,469
August	1	7	6	4	28	46	12,341
September	2	5	3	9	10	29	8,428
October	5	5	7	6	23	46	15,337
November	1	12	10	7	23	53	21,200
December							

PARTIAL LOSSES, YEAR 1864.

Month.	Ste'mers	Ships.	Barks.	Brigs.	Sch'ners	Total.	
January	7	25	14	14	39	99	
February	2	23	16	13	25	79	
March	4	18	12	17	37	88	
April	7	22	35	29	71	164	
May	1	12	9	11	23	56	
June	5	9	4	8	18	46	
July	1	7	4	6	17	35	
August	2	17	4	6	14	43	
September	6	16	8	8	18	56	
October	8	9	8	5	18	48	
November	6	29	21	17	42	115	
December							

ESTIMATED LOSS OF THE YEARS 1861, 1862, 1863, 1864, IN THE U. S.

	January.	February.	March.	April.
1864	$1,245,500	$1,560,300	$1,220,100	$1,750,500
1863	1,430,200	1,175,000	1,340 000	1,950,000
1862	1,825,600	1,529,200	2,340,800	1,416,300
1861	2,930,600	2,403,700	2,648,500	1,617,550
Total................	$7,431,900	$6,668,200	$7,549,400	$6,734,350

	May.	June.	July.	August.
1864	$950,000	$635,300	$1,650,400	$1,475,800
1863	2,100,000	2,230,000	1,800,000	1,250,000
1862	1,735,700	960,000	647,000	428,000
1861	2,825,600	923,500	932,500	576,900
Total................	$7,611,300	$4,748,800	$5,029,900	$3,730,700

	September.	October.	November.	December.
1864	$1,150,600	$1,275,400	$1,516,500	....
1863	1,560,000	1,075,000	950,000	$1,750,000
1862	616,000	1,412,000	1,716,000	1,964,000
1861	956,450	700,850	1,314,500	1,100,000
Total................	$4,283,050	$4,463,250	....	....

Total, 1864....................................	
" 1863..........................	17,535,200
" 1862..........................	16,590,600
" 1861..........................	18,930,650
Grand Total, United States.......................	

THE BRITISH WRECK REGISTER AND CHART FOR 1863.

WE find from the return of the Registrar-General of Seamen, recently published, that during the past year 413,972 vessels, representing a tonnage of nearly 62,000,000, entered inwards and cleared outwards from British ports. The estimated value of the goods carried on board these ships was upwards of £400,000,000 sterling.

But our object at present in dealing with the dry but instructive statistics detailed in the annual return of the Board of Trade is not to follow out the train of thought naturally suggested by these figures. We will at once, therefore, proceed to deal with the important facts which are brought by this accurate Register under our notice.

We accordingly find that the number of wrecks and casualties, including collisions, reported as having occurred on the coasts of the United Kingdom during 1863, is 2001. This number, which is in excess by 174 of the wrecks reported in 1862, is above the annual average of the ten years ending 1863. The numbers for the last five years are as follows, viz.:—1859, 1416; 1860, 1379; 1861, 1494; 1862, 1827; and 1863, 2001; total, 8117. The fearful increase in 1863 was owing to the great number of casualties in the gales of October, November, and December of that year, and the marked increase in 1862 is owing mainly to the 542 wrecks and casualties which happened in the gales of January, October, and December.

One word as to the character of those three fearful gales in 1863. It will be remembered by many that the first of these gales occurred on the 30th of October, and was in part indicated by the steady fall of the barometer from 29·84 in. on the 27th to 29·10 in. on the 29th; and although it rose slightly to 29·32 in. on the morning of the 30th, it was but to fall with greater rapidity to 28·80 in. by 3 30 P.M., when the unprecedented pressure of 29½ lb. to the square foot took place in the force of the wind.

The second storm which we have to notice occurred on the 21st of November, and was foretold by a rapid decline of the barometer from 29·91 in. on the night of the 20th to 29.70in. by the morning of the 21st, and then to 29·44 in. by 5 P.M., accompanied as before by an extreme gust of wind of 17½ lb. to the square foot, the great pressures continuing only between 4 and 5 P.M.

The third, and by far the most remarkable storm occurred on the 2d of December, and was amply presaged by the rapid fall of the barometer from 29·46 in. on the night of the 1st, to 28·84 in. on the morning of the 2d; the wind, however, did not begin to blow violently till 2 30 P.M., where a sudden gust of 9 lb. was recorded; from 2 30 to 2 50 P.M. the pressure varied from 5 lb. to 9 lb.; it then increased greatly in force; at 2 50 P.M. there was a pressure of 16 lb., and at 2 55 P.M. one of 22½ lb.

We may surely learn from these examples—firstly, that the chief severity of a gale may be expected at or near the time of *minimum* barometer reading; and, secondly, that after the *minimum* has passed the worst of the gale has passed, and that the storm will moderate as the barometer readings increase.

It is an interesting fact that our fishermen are rapidly educating themselves in the use of the barometer, and many without doubt have been the instances where the watching of the barometer indications has saved valuable lives and much property. The National Lifeboat Institution has about 100 of these instruments at its lifeboat stations, and the Board of Trade about the same number at other places. Aided by a diagram or chart showing the daily variations of the barometer, a glance at it by the fisherman clearly tells what he is to expect from coming weather, and we confidently believe that if similar precautions were taken by our seamen—in addition to exercising due vigilance in the use of the lead—the prevention of a large number of shipwrecks every year would inevitably follow.

Out of 2001 wrecks and casualties in 1863, 882 are reported to have occurred by stress of weather, and 214 from various and unknown causes. Again, 61 were lost from defects in the ships or in their gear or equipment, and 176 from inattention and negligence. The loss of 1096 vessels by stress of weather, and various other causes unknown, we must charitably suppose, was inevitable; yet we cannot help thinking that if the storm warning signals on the coast had been diligently attended to a considerable proportion of those 1096 shipwrecks might have been avoided; but the loss of 237 ships from negligence and defects in their equipments is inexcusable, and calls loudly for investigation, if not on account of the valuable property thus lost for ever to the country, surely on that of the precious lives sacrificed on these disastrous occasions, in order that every effort might be made to prevent such an annual waste of life and property.

During the same period 5096 lives were saved by lifeboats and the rocket apparatus, fishing boats, and other means. In the absence of these appliances the sacrifice of human life would no doubt have been terrible to contemplate.

The number of collisions reported in 1863 is 331, against 338 in 1862, and 323 in 1861, 317 being the annual average of the seven years ending 1863. Of these 331 collisions 216 happened at night, and 115 in the day-time, 133 were caused by "bad look-out," "neglecting to show lights," and "neglect or misapplication of the road at sea." The remainder were more or less the result of "accident," "unsound gear," or "negligence."

Here, again, there can be no doubt that with proper precautions and a good look-out, a very large proportion of these dreadful accidents might have been prevented.

During the past six years 399 lives have been lost from collisions in our seas—a truly distressing fact; and if fishing smacks and boats were not often at hand to render prompt and efficient services to the poor people, this large number would undoubtedly be enormously increased.

"The life and property lost by collisions at sea—ever increasing with extending trade—are so appalling," says Sir David Brewster, "that no expense should be spared in indicating the approach of vessels during ocean fogs or heavy falls of snow. A small dioptric apparatus, with a Bude or a Drummond light, ought to be a part of every ship's equipment, whether of war or of commerce. A floating reef is a more dangerous enemy than one fixed on a shore, and there is no source of protection against its shock but the light which indicates its approach."

The wreck chart, published with the register, has a melancholy interest, and many a widow and orphan can point on it to the site whereon perished all that was dear to them in this world. The site of each of the 2001 shipwrecks and casualties during the past year can be distinctly traced out on that chart.

The total number of wrecks and casualties from all causes reported during the year 1863 is 2001, against 1827 reported in 1862. It is above the number reported during any one of the eight years preceding, and is 661 above the annual average of the eight years ending 1862. The tonnage of these wrecks is thus given:—

	VESSELS.
Vessels under 50 tons	404
51 and under 100 tons	494
101 " " 300 "	867
301 " " 600 "	158
601 " " 900 "	46
901 " " 1200 "	18
1201 " upwards	14
Total	2001

Of the total number of ships to which casualties have happened in 1863, 1649 were British ships, 272 foreign ships, and the country and employment of 80 were unknown.

This is a lamentable disclosure. The bravery and skill of our seamen are proverbial, but we regret to add that their recklessness is also unrivalled; and hence, after making due allowance for the greater number of British ships, this striking contrast between the loss of British and foreign vessels on the shores of the United Kingdom is accounted for.

The greatest number of casualties happened to ships laden with coals, ores, bricks, etc., or, in other words, to ships of the collier class, as will be seen from the accompanying list, viz.:—

Colliers laden	614
Colliers light	114
Iron and copper ore, etc	146
Stone, etc	115
Timber	101
Fishing smacks and other laden vessels	689
Vessels in ballast (not colliers)	174
Passengers and general cargo	48
Total ships	2001

The winds most fatal during 1863 were from the N.W., W.N.W., S.W., W.S.W., and W. During the former year, 1862, the most fatal winds were S.S.W., S.W., W.S.W., W., and N.W.

Again, it appears that 614 casualties happened with the wind at and under force 7, or from a calm to a moderate gale, and that 1050 happened with the wind above force 7, or from a fresh gale to a hurricane.

The number of persons who perished in 1863 from wrecks was 620, while in 1862 it was 690.

It is satisfactory to know that, notwithstanding the larger number of casualties in 1863, there is a great falling off in the number of lives lost, and that it is 161 below the annual average of the last twelve years.

The total number of lives lost from 1854 to 1863 is really frightful to contemplate. It was 7786, and this, let it be remembered, is not a casual loss. It is a continual, if not an ever increasing one. The drain on our sailors and fishermen goes on year after year, notwithstanding all the benevolent and strenuous efforts made at the present day to stay the ravage. The sea is dreadfully exacting in its demands, and season after season, when the equinoctial gales blow, when the winter sets in, our shores are converted into altars, on which the ocean, as during last winter, offers his victims by hundreds. It is unlikely that we shall ever effectually obtain the mastery over the waves; but even at this moment we are able to contend successfully with them in their blind efforts to swallow up life against our endeavors to save. During the fearful gales of October, November, and December last, nearly 500 lives were rescued by lifeboats alone; and undoubtedly a very large proportion must have perished in the absence of these noble services.

The lifeboat men at Ramsgate, Holyhead, and many other places on the coast during that fearful December hurricane experienced it, and they saved altogether 246 lives that would otherwise probably have perished.

The number of lives saved during the past year was 5096, and the total number of lives rescued by lifeboats, the rocket and mortar apparatus, smacks, and other means during the past eight years, is 25,254—a number sufficient to man a considerable fleet.

The Board of Trade, the Coastguard, and our boatmen and fishermen, continue to work cordially with the National Lifeboat Institution in the great and important work of saving the lives of shipwrecked persons on our coasts, and by means of its lifeboats and of fishing boats, to the crews of which it has given liberal rewards for their laudable exertions, it has contributed to the saving of nearly 14,000 persons.

There are at present 182 lifeboats on the coasts of the United Kingdom belonging to the Royal National Lifeboat Institution and other bodies. The mortar and rocket apparatus stations now number 239, and are under the management of the Coastguard and the Board of Trade.

During the past year 417 lives (besides 17 vessels) were saved by the lifeboats of the National Institution alone, and upwards of 300 by shore boats and other means, for which it granted rewards. A sum of £1297 was expended by the institution in rewards, and £13,819 on its various establishments round the coasts of the British Isles.—*London Insurance Record, Oct.* 1864.

MARINE INSURANCE IN HAMBURGH.

From the year 1837 *to* 1863, *both inclusive.*

The following tables show the progress of the various companies, including some private insurances:

I. The table represents the annual losses paid, each year, 1837–1861, *—II. Expense and Interest.—III. Totals, losses, and expenses.—IV. Average each year.—V. Profits annually.—VI. Net loss annually.*

Receipts.

Year.	Number of Companies.	Number of Transactions.	Charges on the same in Banco Marks.*	Sums Insured in Banco Marks.*	Premiums received in Banco Marks.*	Average per cent.
1837	18	3,335	2,126,000	195,667,000	3,048,839	1.56
1838	19	3,535	2,298,500	219,163,600	3,222,625	1.47
1839	19	3,545	2,207,000	246,281,400	3,570,953	1,45
1840	20	3,705	2,303,000	260,696,300	3,776,635	1.45
1841	20	3,705	2,303,000	266,375,200	3,746,648	1.41
1842	21	3,865	4,599,000	233,181,400	3,270,711	1.40
1843	22	4,015	2,849,000	248,977,800	3,444,451	1.38
1844	23	4,215	2,969,000	270,894,700	3,726,411	1.38
1845	23	4,215	3,134,000	304,143,400	4,461,454	1.47
1846	24	4,475	3,485,000	278,040,600	4,174,543	1.50
1847	23	4,275	3,005,000	333,812,500	4,939,245	1.48
1848	23	4,275	3,005,000	236,793,500	4,778,420	2.02
1849	22	4,095	2,897,000	258,247,200	4,025,956	1.56
1850	22	4,095	2,897,000	278,156,600	4,175,606	1.50
1851	22	4,095	2,897,000	278,916,500	4,171,531	1.50
1852	22	4,095	2,897,000	288,311,500	4,286,628	1.49
1853	23	4,275	3,125,000	357,431,200	5,528,724	1.55
1854	23	5,975	3,825,000	443,457,590	6,958,775	1.57
1855	23	5,975	3,825,000	459,301,660	7,214,065	1.57
1856	25	6,285	4,011,000	564,528,250	8,186,365	1.45
1857	25	7,435	4,893,000	614,027,660	8,526,590	1.39
1858	24	7,235	4,713,000	424,762,160	6,163,670	1.45
1859	20	5,745	3,979,000	459,943,190	6,534,545	1.42
1860	21	5,905	4,075,000	484,863.210	6,538,450	1.35
1861	22	6,055	4,120,000	472,915,660	6,511,950	1.37
1862	20	5,445	3,765,000	464,215,900	6,366,300	1.37
1863	22	5,515	3,759,000	494,821,900	6,543,770	1.32

* Marc banco, forty cents per dollar.

Disbursements.

Year.	Losses paid.	Expenses and Interest.	Total Banco Marks.*	Average per cent.	Profit Banco Marks.*	Loss Banco Marks.*
1837	2,508,557	289,367	2,797,924	1.43	250,915	—
1838	2,561,757	311,242	2,872,999	1.32	349,626	—
1839	2,230,608	295,786	2,526,394	1.03	1,044,559	—
1840	3,062,503	330,138	3,399,641	1.30	376,994	—
1841	3,053,917	336,010	3,383,927	1.27	362,721	—
1842	2,704,385	334,871	3,039,256	1.30	231,345	—
1843	3,355,419	388,732	3,744,151	1.50	—	299,700
1844	3,515,090	397,242	3,912,332	1.44	—	185,921
1845	5,252,431	389,033	5,641,464	1.85	—	1,180,010
1846	3,553,899	380,321	3,934,220	1.41	240,323	—
1847	3,517,408	403,534	3,920,942	1.17	1,018,303	—
1848	4,355,370	443,581	4,798,951	2.03	—	20,531
1849	3,210,888	413,700	3,624,588	1.40	401,368	—
1850	4,054,017	403,854	4,457,871	1.60	—	282,265
1851	3,455,827	401,522	3,857,349	1.38	314,182	—
1852	4,593,380	400,139	4,993,519	1.73	—	706,891
1853	4,559,308	662,416	5,221,724	1.46	307,000	—
1854	5,791,000	867,775	6,658,775	1.50	300,000	—
1855	5,341,745	861,820	6,203,565	1.35	1,010,500	—
1856	7,236,810	747,055	7,983,865	1.41	202,500	—
1857	6,780,525	915,565	7,696,090	1.25	830,500	—
1858	6,503,815	989,855	7,493,670	1.76	—	1,330,000
1859	5,411,560	869,585	6,281,145	1.37	253,400	—
1860	5,750,965	869,985	6,620,950	1.37	—	82,500
1861	5,662,045	849,905	6,511,950	1.37	—	—
1862	Not yet ascertained.				—	212,000
1863					—	—

* Marc banco, forty cents per dollar.

BOSTON LOSSES AND INSURANCE.

List of Boston Fire Losses and Insurance for 33 years.

Year	Losses.	Insurance.	Year	Losses.	Insurance.
1829	$118,540	$52,750	1847	222,273	162,085
1830	23,620	4,320	1848	300,525	216,992
1831	68,195	40,975	1849	123,660	76,167
1832	74,613	25,713	1850	386,107	192,937
1833	69,405	37,925	1851	492,849	215,315
1834	107,440	45,970	1852	515,167	295,056
1836	130,295	55,125	1853	150,772	106,880
1837	32,118	20,238	1854	537,604	361,047
1838	140,004	61,191	1855	409,353	287,832
1839	77,973	58,632	1856	258,231	533,787
1840	102,975	36,920	1857	390,657	316,207
1841	102,611	44,533	1858	761,370	646,210
1842	127,666	90,086	1859	521,383	471,853
1843	164,083	95,252	1860	617,213	405,923
1844	234,591	169,450	1861	1,107,569	806,433
1845	226,338	155,205	1862	367,429	120,909
1846	172,993	87,159			

Population of Boston.

Year	Population	Year	Population
Year 1829	61,892	Year 1849	138,000
" 1839	85,000	" 1854	160,000
" 1844	114,000	" 1859	177,000

NEW AND PROJECTED RAILROADS.

MAINE.—It is proposed to connect Portland with Halifax by rail, *viâ* Bangor and St. John, N. B. 300 of the 582 miles are now completed. The computed distances to St. John are as follows:

From Bangor to Mattawamkeag................	55	miles.
" Mattawamkeag to New Brunswick frontier..	50	"
" New Brunswick frontier to St. Andrew's line	5	"
" St. Andrew's line to St. John..............	75	"
	185	miles.

A branch to Fredericton, from Hartt's Mills, will be 20 miles. By the new routes the distances will be:

From St. John to Woodstock and Houlton,	125	miles.
" Bangor to Woodstock and Houlton,	165	"
" St. John to Fredericton	62	"

VERMONT.—The Montreal and Vermont Junction Railway has been under contract from the Canada line to the Junction with the Stanstead, Shefford, and Chambly Railway.

CONNECTICUT.—A union has been effected (subject, of course, to legislative sanction), between the Boston and New York, and the Boston, Hartford and Erie Railroad Companies. This was apparently the only measure likely to remove difficulties, hitherto insurmountable, in the way of completing an important line, not only of local travel, but a great link in the chain of western railroad communication, *viâ* the Erie and Great Western broad gauge route.

NEW HAMPSHIRE.—An extension of the Boston, Concord and Montreal Railroad is contemplated, from Littleton, N. H., to the Grand Trunk Railroad at Northumberland.

MASSACHUSETTS.—The Agricultural Branch Railroad was proposed early in 1864, from Northboro' to Pratt's Corner, in Sterling.

By an Act of the New York Legislature of April last, the three corporations which held divided sway over the Hartford and Erie line were merged into one, and this last consolidation scheme puts the entire route, including branches to Providence, etc., entirely under the control of a single company.

RHODE ISLAND.—The Fall River and Newport Railroad was opened for travel in the year 1864; giving direct communication by rail between Boston and Newport. From the latter point the steamers for New York will leave hereafter, instead of Fall River. This road passes to Fall River, thence to Tiverton, Bristol, Portsmouth, Grover, and Newport.

NEW YORK.—The Albany and Susquehanna Railroad is partly in operation.

Buffalo.—The Atlantic and Great Western Railroad Company propose a branch road from Salamanca (the present eastern terminus of their road), to Buffalo.

Goshen.—A new Railroad has been proposed from Goshen (on the Erie Railroad) to the village of Montgomery, ten miles—to be known as the Montgomery and Erie Railway, with a capital of $105,000.

Oswego.—The Oswego and Rome Railroad was placed under contract in 1864. The road is leased to the Rome and Watertown Railroad Company.

Otsego County.—A Railroad is in contemplation from a point on the Albany and Susquehanna Railroad into Otsego County, through Cherry Valley, Springfield, Bridgwater, and Sangerfield; and through Oneida, Madison, and Onondaga counties to Auburn.

THE Atlantic and Great Western Railroad was opened for travel as far as Akron, O., in 1864, passing through Jamestown, N. Y., Meadville, Pa., Warren and Ravenna, O., to Akron and Mansfield—a distance of 269 miles from Salamanca, where the road joins the New York and Erie. The western terminus will be at Dayton. From the latter city the Cincinnati, Hamilton and Dayton Railroad is laying another rail, to connect with the Ohio and Mississippi Railroad at Cincinnati, thus giving a broad gauge road from New York to St. Louis, a distance of 1200 miles. When complete, the main road will have a line:

In New York of	48½ miles.
In Ohio	246 "
In Pennsylvania	92½ "
	387 miles.
Eastern Coalfields branch and extension,	33 "
Western	11 "
Cleveland	50 "
Mahoning road (and branch)	78 "
	559 miles.

PENNSYLVANIA.—An extension of the Alleghany Valley Railroad is proposed to the mouth of the Mahoning River, in Armstrong County. The branch line will be from Franklin to Mahoning, *viâ* Brady's Bend.

Connellsville.—The portion of the Pittsburgh and Connellsville Railroad between Connellsville and Cumberland (Md.), 87 miles, has been in course of construction this year.

Penn Haven.—The Penn Haven and White Haven Railroad has been in course of construction during the year 1864. The route begins at Penn Haven, on the Lehigh, nine miles above Mauch Chunk, and skirts that stream 16 miles to White Haven, where it connects with the plane of the Lehigh Navigation Company to Wilkesbarre.

Erie.—The Philadelphia and Erie Railroad was completed in the year 1864. This road runs from the City of Philadelphia. An excursion train passed on the route on the 4th of October. At Sunbury the track is 423 feet above tide-water, at Erie 573 feet. From Sunbury, westward, the track rises gently for 150 miles. The road has been in course of construction for the long period of fourteen years; having been commenced in 1852. From Sunbury to West Creek Summit, 157 miles, the road skirts the Susquehanna River.

Kittanning.—The portion of the Allegheny Valley Railroad between Kittanning and the mouth of the Mahoning, is being rapidly built. It is proposed to extend the road to Brady's Bend, and thence to Franklin.

The Bald Eagle Valley Railroad, from Tyrone to Lock Haven, connecting the Pennsylvania Central and Philadelphia and Erie Railroads, was opened through, from Bellefonte to Lock Haven, in December, 1864, and trains are now about to be run regularly over the route. This road is about seventy miles in length, and forms an important connection between different portions of the State, and between the East and the West.

MARYLAND.—The Western Maryland Railroad was projected some years ago; only forty miles are thus far laid towards its construction. The proposed extension will terminate at Hagerstown, in Washington county. The Baltimore and Ohio Railroad Company also propose a branch road, from or near Harper's Ferry to Hagerstown.

NEW JERSEY.—The Burlington County Railroad, branch to Princeton, was opened for travel May 10, 1864.

Perth Amboy.—The Perth Amboy and Woodbridge Railroad was put in operation in October, 1864. It is a branch of the New Jersey Railroad; commencing at Rahway, and passing through the village of Woodbridge, and terminating at Perth Amboy, a distance of eight miles. Dummy-engines convey the trains in about thirty minutes.

The Raritan and Delaware Bay Railroad.—The steamboat Sea Shore leaves Robinson street wharf (north side) daily, Sundays excepted, at 6 00 a.m. and 4 00 p.m., connecting at Port Monmouth with trains for Long Branch, Middletown, Red Bank, Shrewsbury, Farmingdale, Bergen, etc., and furnishes an indirect route from New York to Philadelphia.

ILLINOIS.—The Air-Line Railroad from Chicago, *viâ* the Chicago and North-Western Railroad and the Iowa and Nebraska Railroad, has been in the year 1864 in course of construction as far as Boonesboro, on the Des Moines River, 345 miles west of Chicago.

IOWA.—The McGregor Western Railway is in active operation between North McGregor and Monona.

IN the year 1864 Congress passed laws granting public lands to the States of Iowa, Minnesota, and Wisconsin, to aid the construction of railroads in those States, viz.:—

Iowa.—Act of May 12, 1864. 1. For a railroad from Sioux City to the south line of the State of Minnesota, at a point between the Big Sioux River and the west fork of the Des Moines River, to be selected by the State. 2. To the McGregor Western Railroad Company, from a point in South McGregor, westerly until it intersects the first-named road in the county of O'Brien. The alternate sections within ten miles of these roads are granted; the intervening lands not to be sold under double price.

MINNESOTA.—A railroad bridge was put under contract in June, 1864, to cross the Mississippi about two miles above St. Paul.

New Grants.—By Act of May 12, 1864, four additional alternate sections of land are granted to aid the construction of a railroad from St. Paul and St. Anthony, *viâ* Minneapolis, to the southern line of the State, near the Big Sioux. (This road will probably connect with the first-named road under "IOWA.") 2. By Act of May 5, 1864, alternate sections of land are granted to Minnesota, to aid the construction of a railroad from St. Paul to the head of Lake Superior. (The terms for the carrying of the mails over this road to be regulated by Congress.)

KENTUCKY.—The Legislature of Kentucky has passed an Act to amend the charters of the Louisville and Frankfort Railroad Company, and of the Lexington and Frankfort Railroad Company, authorizing them to build a branch road to Covington or Newport.

MICHIGAN.—Routes have been surveyed in 1864 for roads from Eagle Harbor, from Copper Harbor, and from Lac Belle.

LAKE SUPERIOR.—Hitherto the route to market for the ores of Lake Superior has been over the Iron Mountain Railroad to Marquette, thence through Lake Superior, the Sault St. Marie Canal, and St. Mary's River, to the lower lake ports. A new route has been this year in course of construction, through the Peninsula Railroad, from the mines to Bay de Noquette of Lake Michigan.

KANSAS.—Forty miles of the Eastern Division of the Union Pacific Railroad had been graded early this year. A second section of forty miles was located in the spring.

OHIO.—Surveys were made a year ago for the railroad bridge over the Ohio, from Belpre to Parkersburg, so as to give a railroad connection with the Parkersburg branch of the Baltimore and Ohio Railroad.

Marietta.—The work on the Marietta and Cincinnati Railroad, from Loveland, was put under contract early in 1864. The route will run from Loveland five miles down the Little Miami to Milford; thence, *viâ* Duck Creek Bottom, Madisonville, Sharpsburg, Ross' Run, and Mill Creek, to Cincinnati.

Junction Road.—This road was chartered in 1849 by the States of Ohio and Indiana. The route contemplated is, from Hamilton, (where it will connect with the Cincinnati, Hamilton and Dayton Railroad, and with the Atlantic and Great Western Railroad), passing through Butler county, Ohio; Union, Fayette, Rush, Shelby, Hancock, and Marion counties, in Indiana; passing through the towns or villages of Hamilton, Oxford, College Corners, Liberty, Connersville, Rushville, Morristown, and Indianapolis. The portion from Hamilton to Connersville is completed. From Connersville to Indianapolis, fifty miles, the work is in course of construction.

The Connersville and Newcastle Junction Railroad, about twenty-five miles, connects the main line at Connersville with the Indiana Central, at Cambridge City.

WISCONSIN.—The Milwaukee and St. Paul Railroad commenced, about a year ago, the work on the Watertown Division of the road, between Mississippi Junction and Milwaukee.

Janesville.—Surveys were made early in 1864 for a railroad from Janesville, Wisconsin, to Winona, Minnesota.

Railroad Grants.—By Act of Congress, May 5th, 1864, alternate sections of land are granted to the State to aid the construction of a railroad from St. Croix River or Lake to the west end of Lake Superior; and from a point of said road to Bayfield.

2. To aid the construction of a railroad from the town Tomah, Monroe county, to the St. Croix River or Lake.

3. For a Railroad from Portage City, Berlin, Doty's Island, or Fond-du-lac, north-westerly to Bayfield; thence to Superior, on Lake Superior. (These roads are declared to be public highways for the use of the Government of the United States, free from toll or charge for the transportation of troops or property of the United States.)

PACIFIC RAILROAD.—The first forty miles of the Union Pacific Railroad [Eastern division], from the State line between Kansas and Missouri, and from the City of Wyandot to the City of Lawrence, were opened for travel and freight on the 19th November, 1864. This great work may be considered as fully inaugurated, with the best prospects of National benefits.

CANADA.—The Canadians are urging the construction of a road from Canada to the Pacific; giving a continuous route from Halifax to New Westminster. The distance from the head of Lake Superior by proposed route or routes to Cariboo is about 1800 miles; and from the head of navigation to the Pacific much less.

NICARAGUA.—A railroad is contemplated from Monkey Point, on the Atlantic, to Corinto on the Gulf of Monsieu, *viâ* Lake Nicaragua and Lake Managua.

THE RAILWAY THROUGH THE ALPS.—We are glad to learn that this scheme is progressing, and that it is likely to be attended with a success commensurate with the magnitude of the undertaking. There are at present in Switzerland three gentlemen representing the Board of Directors of the Central European Railway Company, namely, Mr. Cave, sheriff of London and Middlesex, Mr. Walford, a director of the Financial Corporation, and Mr. J. W.

Maclure, of Manchester. They went out to inaugurate the commencement of the works. The object of the line, as is known, is to connect the lines running from Ostend and Rotterdam to Basle, with the Lombardian and Italian systems, thereby shortening the overland route to India by about 400 miles, or 60 hours, and making England independent of France, by affording a rail route through Belgium and Switzerland, neutral countries, in the event of a European war. The line to be made will leave the Lombardo-Venetian Railway at Como, and run by Chiasso, Lugano, and Bellinzona to Biasca. Thence it will take either the pass of the St. Gothard or the Luckmanier Pass, according to the decision of the Swiss Federal Government. A letter from a member of the deputation states that the deputation, with the local representatives of the Company, Signor Cattaneo, and others, visited the works at Lugano, where they were received with salvoes of artillery. The united bands of the canton of Ticino played in front of the hotel where the deputation stayed, and the Mayor, with the leading inhabitants, paid them complimentary visits, prior to their interview with the Government of the canton. It was hoped that very shortly about ten miles of the line would be open for traffic. The deputation were to meet the Federal Government at Berne, where they expected to learn what the Government subvention would be. The line from Como to Biasca is estimated to cost about a million and a half, of which about £750,000 is already issued and held by British capitalists.

It is well known that the whole length of the tunnel, when completed, will be 12,220 metres. The machine used for the purpose is M. Sommelier's perforator, set in motion by compressed air. It consists of a piston working horizontally in a cylinder, and carrying a chisel fixed upon it like a bayonet, which at each stroke dashes with violence against the rock to be pierced. Each time the chisel recoils, it turns round in the hole, and as the latter is sunk deeper and deeper, the frame, or shield, which carries, not one, but nine perforators, advances in proportion. While the chisel is doing its work with extraordinary rapidity, a copper tube of small diameter keeps squirting water into the hole, by which means all the rubbish is washed out. Behind the shield there is a tender, which, by the aid of a pump set in motion by the compressed air, feeds all these tubes with water. The noise caused by the simultaneous striking of all the chisels against the rock is absolutely deafening, enhanced as it is by the echo of the tunnel. All at once the noise ceases, the shield recedes behind it, and the surface of the rock is perceived riddled with eighty holes, varying in depth between eighty and ninety centimetres. These holes are now charged with cartridges, slow matches, burning at the rate of sixty centimetres per minute are inserted, and the workmen retire in haste. The explosion seems to shake the mountain to its base; when all is over, the ground is found covered with fragments of rock, and an advance equal to the depth of the holes has been obtained.

HORSE RAILROADS IN THE UNITED STATES.

Estimates of City Horse Railroads in Operation.

Year 1864.

Owing to the want of official data, of a late date, the following summary is only an approximation of the facts:

	Length of Route. Miles.	Length of Track. Miles.	Cost of Roads and Equipment.
Portland, Me.	7.0	8.5	$160,000
Boston, Mass.	138.0	169.0	4,250,000
Worcester, Mass.	5.2	5.7	90,000
Springfield, Mass.	4.0	4.0	50,000
Hartford, Conn.	7.0	8.7	150,000
New Haven, Conn.	8.0	11.5	15,000
New York City, N. Y.	104.0	179.0	8,976,000
Albany, N. Y.	13.0	21.0	500,000
Brooklyn, N. Y.	91.4	143.2	3,610,000
Buffalo, N. Y.	13.0	19.0	450,000
Rochester, N. Y.	10.0	19.5	200,000
Syracuse, N. Y.	5.2	5.6	130,000
Troy, N. Y.	10.3	12.0	182,000
Utica, N. Y.	2.0	2.0	50,000
Jersey City, N. J.	10.0	15.0	300,000
Hoboken, N. J.	9.6	10.9	300,000
Newark, N. J.	15.2	17.7	750,000
Trenton, N. J.	4.0	4.0	50,000
Philadelphia, Pa.	167.0	192.0	4,500,000
Pittsburgh, Pa.	21.7	32.5	410,000
Baltimore, Md.	7.0	9.0	220,000
Cleveland, Ohio	5.0	5.0	120,000
Cincinnati, Ohio	17.5	29.0	620,000
Chicago, Ill.	8.0	13.0	250,000
St. Louis, Mo.	26.5	36.0	720,000
New Orleans, La.	10.0	10.0	200,000
Totals	719.6	982.8	$27,353,000

TAXATION OF RAILROADS.

The Assessment and Collection of the Tax on the Gross Receipts of Railroads, Canals, Steamboats, &c.

TREASURY DEPARTMENT, OFFICE OF INTERNAL REVENUE, WASHINGTON, *August* 16, 1864.

SECTION 103 of the Act of June 30, 1864, imposes upon every person, firm, company, or corporation owning or possessing or having the care and management of any railroad, canal, steamboat, ship, barge, canal-boat, or other vessel, or any stage-coach or other vehicle, engaged or employed in the business of transporting passengers or property for hire, or transporting the mails, or any canal, the water of which is used for mining purposes, a duty of two and one-half per centum upon the gross receipts, and three per centum upon the gross receipts of any toll-road, ferry, or bridge. And section 109 provides for the mode and time of the returns, and the assessment and collection of the duties imposed, except in the cases of the owners or proprietors of stage-coaches and other vehicles, which are specially provided for by the regulation of the Secretary of the Treasury, hereto appended.

The owner, possessor, or party having the care and management of any railroad, canal, &c., is made subject to the tax, and must, of course, make the returns and pay the tax as prescribed.

There are but few cases where there will be any difficulty in determining who is the owner, possessor, or party having the care and management, and liable to the duty. Where the owner is known, and the railroad, canal, &c., is under his control, he is the party liable. Where another party than the owner has the possession, care, and management, doing the business and receiving the freight or fare, such other party is the one liable. Where the owners or proprietors of a canal own the boats and themselves manage the business, they are liable. If, however, they do not own the boats, but permit others who do to use their canal for an agreed or fixed rate of toll or compensation, they having no other interest in the business of transporting passengers or goods, then such owners or proprietors are not liable; but the owners of the boats are. If one railroad or other transportation line is leased to another, the lessee managing the business, the lessee and not the lessor is the proper party to make the returns.

The duty is imposed upon the gross receipts, hence the expenses paid for tolls, canal or otherwise, towing, pilotage, wharfage, State or other taxes, and the like, cannot be deducted any more than the expense of motive power or labor employed.

Where property or passengers are transported over several lines, each must return the amount received by them; and the fact that the price for the whole is collected by one, does not render that one liable to return and pay the duty on the whole, but only on the portion belonging to their own line.

The term "other vehicle" will include all coaches, wagons, hacks, drays, carts, omnibuses, and the like, engaged in the transportation of property or passengers *for hire.*

Where a party uses his own vessel or vehicle for the transportation of his own property, he is not liable to the duty.

An occasional transportation of property or passengers does not render a party liable, but the assessor or assistant assessor must judge whether or not, under all the circumstances, the party is engaged in the business.

A livery-stable keeper may let his carriages to any persons applying therefor, who may take them and transport themselves or others, or transport property of their own or others, and such livery stable keeper will not be liable; but if the livery-stable keeper engages in the business of transporting passengers or property for hire he would be liable. In the one case he for the time parts with the control and possession of his carriage; in the other case he retains it. Other cases may arise where the circumstances and conditions are varied, and the test may be different. No definite rule can be laid down which will apply to all cases. The questions which will arise are questions of fact to be decided by the assessor or assistant assessor, subject, of course, to an appeal in proper form to this office.

The transportation of property, passengers, or mails between ports of the United States and foreign ports is exempted from the duty. When, therefore, property, persons, or mails are transported from a port of the United States to a port in the British provinces, and are again transported from some port in the provinces to another port in the United States, the party so transporting from port to port is exempt from tax; but the receipts for transportation to or from such port within the limits of the United States must be returned.

Any person or persons, firms, companies, or corporations, owning or possessing, or having the care or management of any steam vessel for the transportation of passengers, must include in the returns of the gross amount of receipts, as required by section 109, all sums received for lodging, including receipts for the use of berths and staterooms; and railroad companies will include the amounts received for the use of sleeping-cars.

When, according to the custom of any steam vessel, the expenses of board are included in the charges made for transportation, the assessor will make the proper allowance therefor.

This tax, as well as that imposed upon express companies by section 104, is upon the *gross receipts,* and therefore no deduction can be allowed from the receipts of a railroad or steamboat company on account of sums received from any express company, nor can any express company be allowed to deduct the amounts paid to railroad or steamboat companies.

The towing of boats and rafts by tug-boats is not considered transportation, and no tax is to be assessed upon the receipts therefor.

The law authorizes all such persons, companies, and corporations to add the tax to their rates of fare, notwithstanding any limitation which may exist by law or by agreement; but no such authority is given for an addition of the tax to a bill for freight.

When the owner or agent of any toll-road or bridge shall accompany his monthly return with an affidavit to the effect that the gross annual receipts of such road or bridge do not exceed the amount necessarily expended in keeping such road or bridge in repair, and the assessor is satisfied that such is the fact, no tax will be assessed.

Where goods had been transported by any such person or company and delivered at the place of destination before the first of July, no tax will be assessed, although the bills for freight may have been collected subsequently; and the tax for any subsequent month will be upon the receipts for freight delivered in such month, without reference to the time when the goods were shipped, or when the bills are collected.

The returns of receipts for transportation, and the other returns required by section 109, except as to the receipts of circuses and travelling exhibitions, must be made in the district where such persons or company have their principal place of business. If they have no place of business, then the returns must be made in the district where they reside. In cases where no residence is known, but a transportation line extends through several districts, a special regulation will be made, upon a statement of the circumstances and course of business to this office, which will protect the party from the annoyance of being required by the assessors to make returns in more than one district.

Under the authority conferred upon the Commissioner by section 115, it is prescribed that the returns of circuses and other travelling exhibitions, representations, and shows shall be made in the district where they exhibit: *Provided*, that the proprietor or proprietors thereof may, before they leave any district in which they so exhibit, make a statement under oath to the assessor of the gross amount of their receipts in such district, giving their residence, or their principal place of business, if any they have, with a request that the said assessor shall transmit the same to the assessor of the district in which they so reside or have their place of business, and the assessor shall thereupon transmit a copy of said statement to the assessor of the district of their residence or principal place of business, and at the end of each and every month such proprietor or proprietors may make their returns as provided by law in such district, and pay the duties therein as provided by law.

TREASURY DEPARTMENT, WASHINGTON, *August* 15, 1864.

By section 103 of the act of June 30, 1864, every person, firm, company, or corporation, owning or possessing, or having the care and management of any stage-coach or other vehicle, engaged or employed in the business of transporting passengers or property for hire, or in transporting the mails of the United States, is subject to a duty of two and one-half per centum upon the gross receipts of such stage-coach or other vehicle; but the mode and time of assessment and collection of such duty are not provided.

In accordance with the provisions of section 176 of the said act, it is therefore prescribed that any person, firm, company, or corporation, owning, possessing, or having the care and management of any stage-coach or other vehicle engaged as aforesaid, shall, within ten days after the first day of each and every month, make return to the assistant assessor of the district, stating the gross amount of their receipts for the month next preceding, which return shall be verified by the oath or affirmation of such owner, possessor, manager, agent, or other proper officer, in the same manner and form as prescribed in the case of the returns of railroads, steamboats, and other vessels; and shall also, on or before the last day of the month, pay to the collector of internal revenue the full amount of duties which have accrued on such receipts for the month aforesaid.

GEORGE HARRINGTON,
Acting Secretary of the Treasury.

ACT OF JUNE 30, 1864.

RAILROADS, STEAMBOATS, FERRY-BOATS, AND BRIDGES.

SEC. 103. *And be it further enacted,* That every person, firm, company, or corporation, owning or possessing, or having the care or management of any railroad, canal, steamboat, ship, barge, canal-boat, or other vessel, or any stage-coach or other vehicle engaged or employed in the business of transporting passengers or property for hire, or in transporting the mails of the United States, or any canal the water of which is used for mining purposes, shall be subject to and pay a duty of two and one-half per centum upon the gross receipts of such railroad, canal, steamboat, ship, barge, canal-boat, or other vessel, or such stage-coach or other vehicle: *Provided,* That the duty hereby imposed shall not be charged upon receipts for the transportation of persons or property, or mails, between the United States and any foreign port; and any person or persons, firms, companies, or corporations, owning, possessing, or having the care or management of any toll-road, ferry, or bridge, authorized by law to receive toll for the transit of passengers, beasts, carriages, teams, and freight, of any description, over such toll-road, ferry, or bridge, shall be subject to and pay a duty of three per centum on the gross amount of all their receipts of every description. But when the gross receipts of any such bridge or toll-road shall not exceed the amount necessarily expended to keep such bridge or road in repair, no tax shall be imposed on such receipts: *Provided,* That all such persons, companies, and corporations shall have the right to add the duty or tax imposed hereby to their rates of fare whenever their liability thereto may commence, any limitations which may exist by law or by agreement with any person or company which may have paid or be liable to pay such fare to the contrary notwithstanding.

INTERNAL GENERAL AVERAGE.

The uncertainty which exists in laws relating to General Average, is a serious evil—and it is to be hoped that the merchants and underwriters of all maritime countries will continue to exert themselves in favor of coming to some understanding. An Act of Congress would settle the question in the United States, and an Act of Parliament in England; but such Acts will never be passed unless the parties immediately interested move in the matter with determination. A letter from Mr. J. Russell Bradford, delegate from Boston to the Social Science Congress at York, England, gives the rules adopted by the Congress.

There were present, delegates from the Chambers of Commerce of Bremen, Hamburg, and Lubeck, from the Belgian Government, the Chambers of Commerce at Antwerp, the Board of Underwriters at Antwerp, the Comité des Assurances Générales at Paris, the Russian Government, the Corporation of Sunderland, the Board of Underwriters at Amsterdam, the Netherlands Trading Company, the Shipowners' Society of Amsterdam, the Chamber of Commerce of Hull, the Shipowners' Society of London, the Belgian Government, Lloyd's Salvage Association, the Committee of Lloyd's, the Chamber of Commerce of Liverpool, the Liverpool Underwriters' Association, the Sunderland Shipowners' Society, the Board of Trade of Boston, U. S., the Board of Underwriters of Boston, U. S., the Chamber of Commerce of New York, the New York Board of Underwriters, the New Orleans Board of Underwriters, and the Shipowners' Association of Liverpool, besides several Adjusters from London, Liverpool, Glasgow, and elsewhere.

AVERAGE RULES, FRAMED AT YORK IN 1864.

At a Congress of Delegates, appointed by various Governments and Commercial Associations of Europe and America, held at York in September, 1864, under the Presidency of Sir James Wilde and Sir Fitzroy Kelly, the following rules were adopted:

Sec. 1. A jettison of timber or deals, or any other description of wood cargo, carried on the deck of a ship in pursuance of a general custom of the trade in which the ship is then engaged, shall be made good as General Average, in like manner as if such cargo had been jettisoned from below deck.

No jettison of deck cargo, other than timber or deals, or other wood cargo, so carried as aforesaid, shall be good as General Average.

Every structure not built in with the frame of the vessel shall be considered to be a part of the deck of the vessel.

Sec. 2. Damage done to goods or merchandise by water which unavoidably goes down a ship's hatches opened, or other opening made, for the purpose of making a jettison, shall be made good as General Average, in case the loss by jettison is so made good.

Damage done by breakage and chafing, or otherwise from derangement of stowage consequent upon a jettison, shall be made good as General Average.

SEC. 3. Damage done to a ship and cargo, or either of them, by water or otherwise in extinguishing a fire on board the ship, shall be General Average.

SEC. 4. Loss or damage caused by cutting away the wreck or remains of spars, or of other things which have previously been carried away by sea peril, shall not be made good as General Average.

SEC. 5. When a ship is intentionally run on shore because she is sinking or driving on shore or rocks, no damage caused to the ship, the cargo, and the freight, or any or either of them, by such intentional running on shore, shall be made good as General Average.

SEC. 6. Damage occasioned to a ship or cargo by carrying a press of sail shall not be made good as General Average.

SEC. 7. When a ship shall have entered a port of refuge under such circumstances that the expenses of entering the port are admissible as General Average, and when she shall have sailed thence with her original cargo, or a part of it, the corresponding expense of leaving such port shall likewise be so admitted as General Average; and whenever the cost of discharging cargo at such port is admissible as General Average, the cost of reloading and stowing such cargo on board the said ship, together with all storage charges on such cargo, shall likewise be so admitted. Except that any portion of the cargo left at such port of refuge, on account of its being unfit to be carried forward, or on account of the unfitness or inability of the ship to carry it, shall not be called upon to contribute to such General Average.

SEC. 8. When a ship shall have entered a port of refuge under the circumstances defined in Section 7, the wages and cost of maintenance of the master and mariners, from the time of entering such port until the ship shall have been made ready to proceed upon her voyage, shall be made good as General Average. Except that any portion of the cargo left at such port of refuge on account of its being unfit to be carried forward, or on account of the unfitness or inability of the ship to carry it, shall not be called on to contribute to such General Average.

SEC. 9. Damage done to cargo by discharging it at a port of refuge shall not be admissible as General Average, in case such cargo shall have been discharged at the place and in the manner customary at that port with ships not in distress.

SEC. 10. The contribution to a General Average shall be made upon the actual values of the property at the termination of the adventure, to which shall be added the amount made good as General Average for property sacrificed; deduction being made from the shipowners' freight and passage money at risk, of two-fifths of such freight, in lieu of crew's wages, port charges, and all other deductions; deduction being also made from the value of the property of all charges incurred in respect thereof subsequently to the arising of the claim to General Average.

SEC. 11. In every case in which a sacrifice of cargo is made good as General Average, the loss of freight, if any, which is caused by such loss of cargo, shall likewise be so made good.

INSURANCE COMPANIES IN BOSTON.

1864.

	Incorp.	President.	Secretary.
Alliance Insurance Co.	1850	R. S. S. Andros	W. H. C. Copeland.
American Insurance Co	1818	J. Ingers. Bowditch	Andrew C. Dorr.
Arkwright Mutual Fire Ins. Co		Waldo Higginson	E. H. Sprague.
Boston Insurance Co.	1823	Peter W. Freeman	Henry Washburn.
Boston Manuf. Mutual Fire Ins. Co.	1850	William Amory	Edward E. Manton.
Boylston Fire and Marine Ins. Co	1825	Joseph W. Balch	Noah S Jenney.
China Mutual Insurance Co	1853	Francis Bacon	George L. Deblois.
City Fire Insurance Co	1850	Samuel P. Heywood	Austin W Benton.
Conway Fire Insurance Co. Agency		James S. Whitney	David C. Rogers.
Eliot Fire Insurance Co	1849	G. A. Curtis	William H. Lathrop.
Equitable Safety and Mar. F. I. Co.	1839	John Clark	J. Theodore Clark.
Fireman's Insurance Co	1831	Thomas C. Amory	Shubael G. Rogers.
Franklin Insurance Co.	1823	William M. Byrnes	Edmund B. Whitney.
Howard Fire Insurance Co		J. W. Daniels	E. Brown.
Manufacturers' Insurance Co	1822	Samuel Gould	James J. Goodrich.
Massachusetts Mutual Fire Ins. Co.	1798	Charles Wells	Charles B. Cuming.
Mechanics' Mutual Fire Ins. Co.	1836	Solomon Hovey	Osborn B. Hall.
Mercantile Marine Ins. Co	1823	Stephen H. Bullard	William B. Coffin.
Merchants' Insurance Co	1816	Thomas C. Smith	James C. Braman.
National Insurance Co	1832	Huon H. Bean	George W. Kuhn.
Neptune Insurance Co	1831	Caleb Curtis	George F. Osborn.
New Engl. Mutual Marine Ins. Co.	1839	George C. Lord	Benjamin Lyon.
North American Fire Ins. Co.	1851	Albert Bowker	Charles L. Pitts.
Prescott Fire and Marine Ins. Co.	1855	Franklin Green, Jr.	P. E. Eddy.
Shoe & Leather Deal. F. & M. I. Co.	1855	John C. Abbott	Cyrus M. Stimson.
State Mutual Fire Ins. Co	1843	Pelham Bonney	Leonard B. Adams.
Suffolk Fire Insurance Co	1859	John H. Lunt	Edward Foster.
Tri-Mountain Mutual Fire Ins. Co.		Timothy H. Smith	P. Divine.
Union Mutual Fire Insurance Co.	1843	Enoch Hobart	George G. Field.
United States Insurance Co	1825	Robert B. Williams	Closing business.
Washington Insurance Co	1824	Isaac Sweetser	Benjamin Sweetser.
John Hancock Mutual Life Ins. Co		George P. Sanger	George B. Ager.
Massachusetts Hospital Life Ins. Co.	1823	George W. Lyman	Moses L. Hale.
Union Mutual Life Insurance Co.	1848	Henry Crocker	Whiting H. Hollister.

MARINE INSURANCE COMPANIES IN THE CITY OF NEW YORK.

Location.	Name.	President.	Secretary.	Capital.
Wall, 51	Atlantic Mutual	John D. Jones	W. T. Jones	....
Nassau, 1	Columbian	Benj. C. Morris	W. M. Whitney	$1,000,000
William, 57	Commercial Mutual	D. Drake Smith	Henry D. King	....
Pine, 39	Great Western	Richard Lathers	W.T. Lockwood	1,000,000
Wall, 35	Mercantile Mutual	Ellwood Walter	C. J. Despard	....
William, 61	New York Mutual	John H. Earle	W. P. Hansford	....
Wall, 43	Orient Mutual	Leop. Bierwirth	Charles Irving	....
Br'dway, 111	Pacific Mutual	Alfred Edwards	Thomas Hale	....
Wall, 49	Sun Mutual	M. H. Grinnell	Ed. R. Anthony	....
Pine, 40	Washington	G. H. Koop	A. S. Macarthy	....

FIRE INSURANCE COMPANIES

IN THE CITY OF NEW YORK.

DECEMBER, 1864.

** *The Card or Prospectus of these Companies may be found among the Advertisement-Pages of this Volume.*

LOCATION.	NAME.	PRESIDENT.	SECRETARY.	CAPITAL.	SHARES
B'dway, 139	Adriatic	William A. Seaver	Frank W. Lewis	$300,000	103a106
B'dway, 170	Ætna	Jacob Brouwer	Hun. G. Beach	200,000	96a 98
Wall, 62	Ætna (Agency)	James A. Alexander, *Agt*	......	......	.....
B'dway, 114	Albany (Agency)	Richard W. Bleecker, *Agt*	......	......	.....
B'dway, 139	Albany City (Agency)	T. H. Crosby, *Agent*	......	......	......
Wall, 67	Albany Mutual	George W. Savage, *Agent*	......	......	......
Wall, 48	American	James M. Halstead	Fred. W. Downer.	200,000	135a138
Pine, 46	American (Agency)	Asa Bigelow, Jr., *Agent*	......	......	......
Fulton, 163	American (Agency)	Samuel G. Walker, *Agent*	......	......	......
B'dway, 128	American Exchange	Henry Butler	William Raynor	200.000	85a 90
Wall, 18	****Arctic**	J. Milton Smith	Vincent Tilyou	500,000	100a105
Wall, 16	Astor	William T. Pinckney	Robert D. Hart	250,000	99a101
Wall, 14	Atlantic (Brooklyn)	John D. Cocks	Horatio Dorr	150,000	140a145
Wall, 64	Atlantic (Providence)	Agency	J. S. Parish	......	......
B'dway, 650	Baltic	William S. Corwin	William H. Kipp	200.000	100a103
Wall, 10	Beekman	Benjamin W. Benson	Elisha H. Cheshire	200,000	100a105
Bowery, 124	Bowery	William Hibbard	George G. Taylor.	300,000	162a168
Wall, 70	Brevoort	James C. Harriott	John G. Haviland	150,000	75a 80
Wall, 2	Broadway	Hiram M. Forrester	John Wray	200,000	140a150
Wall, 18	Brooklyn (Brooklyn)	Francis P. Furnald	John W. Cheney	153,000	190a220
B'dway, 168	Central Park	Abraham Michelbacher	Jos. L. Townsend.	150,000	95a100
Broad, 4	Charter Oak (Agency)	Charles M. Peck, *Agent*	......	......	......
Wall, 67	Citizen's	James M. McLean	Edward A. Walton	300.000	230a240
Wall, 58	City	Richard A. Reading	Samuel Townsend	210,000	142a148
Broad, 4	City (Agency)	Charles M. Peck, *Agent*	......	......	......
B'dway, 156	Clinton	Hugh Lanig	Jas. B. Ames, Jr.	250,000	120a130
B'dway, 161	Columbia	Timothy G. Churchill	Edward Kemeys	500,000	104a106
Wall, 27	Commerce	Benjamin Babcock	William E. Hoxie.	200,000	100a106
Wall, 62	Commerce (Agency)	James A. Alexander, *Agt.*	......	......	......
Wall, 49	Commercial	Joseph Petit	Mat. V. B. Fowler	200,000	134a138
B'dway, 151	Commonwealth	Joseph Hoxie	George T. Haws	250,000	95a100
Wall, 74	Connecticut (Agency)	Ezra White, *Agent*	......	......	......
B'dway, 102	Continental	George T. Hope	Hiram H. Lamport	500,000	180a200
William, 13	Corn Exchange	Robert P. Getty	J. Pryor Rorke	400,000	84a 86
B'way, 180	****Croton Fire In. Co.**	Andrew Wesson	John M. Tompkins	200,000	85a 87
Wall, 71	Eagle	Sanford Cobb	Alex. J. Clinton	300.000	175a185
Wall, 69	East River	Samuel Sloan	Wm. F. Underhill.	500,000	......
Pine, 46	Elliot (Agency)	Asa Bigelow, jr., *Agent*	......	......	......
B'way, 102	Empire City	Lindley Murray	Wm. A. Burtis, jr.,	200,000	170a180
Fulton, 163	Enterprise	Samuel G. Walker, *Agent.*	......	......	......
Wall, 58	Equitable	Richard J. Thorne	John Miller	210.000	182a190
B'way, 130	Excelsior	Eugene Plunkett	Samuel M. Craft	200,000	110a112
B'way, 170	Exchange	James Vannorden	Rich'd C. Combes.	150 000	62a 64
B'way, 200	Firemen's Fund	Nathan B. Graham	Henry Beeckman.	150,000	91a 93
Wall, 7	Firemen's Trust (B'kln)	George Hall.	William Burrell	150,000	110a112
Wall, 33	Firemen's	John V. Harriott	Abner Hayward	204,000	120a125
Wall, 27	Franklin (Agency)	James A. Bancker, *Agent.*	......	......	......
B'way, 172	Fulton	William A. Cobb	James M. Rankin.	200,000	145a150
B'way, 96	Gallatin Fire Ins. Co.	David Clarkson	Henry Baldwin	150,000	100a104
Pine, 1,	Gebhard " "	William D. Waddington	John R. Smith	200,000	103a106
Wall, 4	Germania " "	Maurice Hilger	John E. Kahl	500,000	116a118
G'wich	Globe " "	Leonard Kirby	Alfred A. Reeves.	200,000	115a120
Wall, 17	Goodhue " "	Robert Bage	Fred. W. Macy	200,000	100a102
Pine, 8	Greenwich Fire "	Samuel C. Harriot	James Harrison	200,000	160a161
Wall, 76	Grocers' " "	Sampson Moore	James G. Platt	200.000	111a113
Wall, 11	Hamilton	Richard J. Smith	John C. Winans	150,000	90a 94
Wall, 64	Hampden (Springfield)	Seely & Parsons, *Agents.*	......	......	......
Wall, 45	Hanover	Doras L. Stone	Benj. S. Walcott	400,000	130a134

LOCATION.	NAME.	PRESIDENT.	SECRETARY.	CAPITAL.	SHARES
Wall, 50	****Harmony**	Robert O. Glover	Daniel D. Gassner.	300,000	125*a*130
Wall, 74	Hartford (Agency)	Ezra White, *Agent*			
B'way, 193	****Hoffman**	William Dumont	Joseph W. Wildey.	200,000	104*a*110
B'way, 135	Home	Charles J. Martin	John McGee	2,000,000	188*a*195
B'way, 167	Home (Agency)	Fred'k W. Satterlee, *Agt.*			
B'way, 92	Hope Fire Insurance Co.	Jacob Reese	Thomas Greenleaf.	200,000	105*a*115
Wall, 64	Hope, (Providence, R. I)	Seely & Parsons, *Agents.*			
Wall, 66	Howard	Samuel T. Skidmore	Henry A. Oakley.	300,000	185*a*195
B'way 140	Humboldt	William Mulligan	Alex. Wiley, jr.	200,000	100*a*101
B'way, 100	Importers' and Traders'	Joseph Brokaw	Frank W. Ballard.	200,000	112*a*115
B'way, 207	Indemnity	John Hone	Wm. R. Sheldon.	150.000	107*a*110
Pine, 4	Ins. Co. of N. Am. (Phila.)	James S. Hollinshead			
B'way, 113	International	Charles Taylor	Olwin A. Drake.	1,000,000	100*a*102
Wall, 9	Irving	Mason Thomson	Martin L. Crowell.	200,000	123*a*129
Wall, 60	Jefferson	Thomas Morrell	Sam'l E. Belcher.	200,000	195*a*200
Wall, 67	Jersey City	R. McLaughlin	Jesse Paulmier	150,000	120*a*130
Nassau, 1	Kings County (Brooklyn)	Edward T. Backhouse	Henry Pope	150,000	70*a* 75
Wall, 64	Knickerbocker	George Hodgsdon		280.000	129*a*134
Wall, 14	Lafayette (Brooklyn)	James Freeland	J. B. Thompson, jr.	150,000	100*a*101
Wall, 50	Lamar Fire In. Co	Edward Anthony	Isaac R. St. John.	300,000	120*a*130
Wall, 16	Lenox Fire Ins. Co	George A. Jarvis	Walt. M. Franklin.	150,000	106*a*110
B'way, 163	Liverpool and London	Henry Grinnell, *Agent*	47 William		
Wall, 48	Long Island (Brooklyn)	Benj. W. Delamater	Wm. W. Henshaw.	200,000	135*a*140
B'way, 104	Lorillard Fire Ins. Co	Carlisle Norwood	John C. Mills	500,000	145*a*...
Wall, 68	Manhattan	William P. Palmer	Andrew J. Smith.	500,000	
Pine, 46	Manufacturers' (Agency)	Asa Bigelow, Jr., *Agent*			
Wall, 37	Market	Asher Taylor	Henry P. Freeman	200,000	130*a*135
Liberty, 75	Massasoit, (Agency)	Frame & Hare, *Agents*			
Wall, 31	Mechanics' (Brooklyn)	Daniel Chauncey	Walter Nichols	150,000	135*a*160
Wall, 48	Mechanics' and Traders'	Walter Underhill	James R. Lott	200,000	150*a*160
B'way, 166	Mercantile	William A. Thomson	Wm. A. Anderson.	200,000	105*a*110.
B'way, 106	Merchants'	Cornelius V. B. Ostrander.	John L. Douglass.	200,000	200*a*210
Pine, 46	Merchants' (Agency)	Asa Bigelow, Jr., *Agent*			
Broad, 4	Merchants' (Agency)	Charles M. Peck, *Agent*			
B'way, 108	****Metropolitan**	James Lorimer Graham	Jno. C. Goodridge.	300,000	140*a*145
B'way, 168	Montauk (Brooklyn)	William Ellsworth	Abram M. Kirby.	150,000	130*a*...
Nassau, 1	Morris Inland and Fire	Benj. C. Morris	Wm. M. Whitney.	200.000	105*a*110
Wall, 65	Nassau (Brooklyn)	William M. Harris	Ab'm J. Beekman.	150,000	175*a*180
Wall, 52	National	William S. Thorne	Henry T. Drowne.	200,000	
Pine, 46	National (Agency)	Asa Bigelow, Jr., *Agent*			
Wall, 20	New Amsterdam	David S. Manners	W. H. Dusenberry	300,000	105*a*108
B'way, 111	New England (Agency)	Ithamar Conkey, *Agent*			
B'way, 151	New World	Thomas A. Emmet	Sam'l A. Patterson	200,000	70*a* 71
Wall, 72	New York Fire and Marine.	David Underhill	Ed. C. Dederer	200,000	145*a*150
Wall, 12	Niagara	Jonathan D. Steele	Peter Notman	500,000	119*a*125
B'dway. 114	North American	James W. Otis	Rich. W. Bleecker	500,000	115*a*120
Pine, 46	North American	Asa Bigelow, Jr., *Agent*			
Wall, 62	North American	Jas. A. Alexander, *Agent.*			
Greenwich, 202	North River	Peter R. Warner	John Hegeman	350,000	95*a*100
Wall, 60	North Western	W. Lecount, *Agent*			
Wall, 62	Norwich (Agency)	Jas. A. Alexander, *Agent*			
B'dway, 470	Pacific	Amos F. Hatfield	Thos. F. Jeremiah	200,000	145*a*155
B'dway, 237	Park	Josiah W. Baker	William Jaffray	200,000	135*a*145
Canal, 393	People's	Matthias Clark	William S. Martin	150,000	110*a*112
Wall, 74	Peter Cooper	Nathan C. Ely	William H. Riblet	150,000	108*a*110
Wall, 62.	Phœnix (Brooklyn)	Stephen Crowell	Philander Shaw	500,000	150*a*160
Wall, 74	Phenix (Hartford)	H. Kellogg	Ezra White, *Agent*		
Wall, 8	Relief	James H. Pinckney	Wm. E. Crary	200.000	130*a*140
Wall, 16	Republic	Robert S. Hone	Duncan F. Curry.	300,000	104*a*110
Nassau, 3	Resolute	John E. Uhlhorn	Wm. M. Randell	200,000	113*a*116
Wall, 56	Royal, Liverpool & Lon	A. B. McDonald, *Agent*			
Wall, 67	Rutger's	Isaac O. Barker	Edward B. Fellows	200,000	128*a*135
Wall, 67	St. Mark's	John M. Ferrier	Washington Post.	150,000	90*a* 94
B'way, 166	St. Nicholas	William Winslow	John J. Searing	150,000	71*a* 74
Pine, 31	Security	Joseph Walker	Rich'd L. Haydock	1,000,000	125*a*135
Wall, 74	Springfield, Mass	Ezra White, *Agent*			
Wall, 11	Standard	W. Cripps	Wm. M. St. John.	200,000	120*a*125
Wall, 6	Sterling	Archibald Gracie	A. L. Soularde,	200,000	105*a*110
Wall, 69	Stuyvesant	James Kelly	Abm. P. M. Roome	200,000	91*a* 94
Wall, 49	Sun Mutual	R. A. Reading, *Manager.*		100,000	
Greenwich 187	Star Fire Ins. Co.	George W. Savage	Nicholas C. Miller.	200,000	new.
Wall, 14	Tradesmen's	David B. Keeler	Tim'thy Y. Brown	150.000	127*a*130
William, 61	Union Mutual	Francis S. Lathrop	Ferdinand Stagg	1,550,000	
Wall, 69	United States	Abraham S. Underhill	Washington Ritter	250,000	145*a*150
B'way, 172	Washington	George C. Satterlee	Wm. K. Lothrop	400,000	150*a*160
Pine, 46	Washington (Prov.)	Asa Bigelow, Jr., *Agent*			
Wall, 74	Western, (Mass.)	Ezra White, *Agent*			
B'way, 165	Williamsburgh City	Richard Teneyck	Hubert Giroux	150,000	115*a*120
B'way, 161	Yonkers and New York	Richard L. Franklin	John W. Murray	500,000	118*a*120

Progress of Life Insurance Companies doing Business in Massachusetts, from November 1, 1863, to November 1, 1864.

[From the Returns to the Insurance Commissioners of Massachusetts, Nov. 15, 1864]

COMPANIES.	New Policies Issued.		Policies outstandi'g Nov. 1, 1864.		Net Increase.		Policies terminated by Death.		Gross Premiums received during the year.	Premiums received in Cash.	Net Premium reserve, Nov. 1, 1864. (Exclusive of Capital.)	Guarantee Capital.	Investment in U. S. Gov'rnment Securities.
	Number.	Amount Insured.	Number.	Amount Insured.	Number.	Amount Insured.	Number.	Amount Insured.					
Home Companies.													
New England Mutual......	1,902	$5,852,650	8,165	$24,946,056	1,382	$4,448,325	93	$266,450	$759,133	$440,525	$2,782,075	None.	$400,000
State Mutual...........	258	365,400	1,934	3,172,406	90	151,780	26	29,922	72,865	69,859	560,011	$100,000	193,000
Berkshire..............	242	599,800	1,277	2,639,450	146	427,050	15	36,000	102,676	79,857	302,281	64,000	136,705
Massachusetts Mutual.....	1,583	3,918,150	4,557	10,405,280	1,234	3,172,800	50	107,300	343,246	228,149	732,512	100,000	110,719
John Hancock...........	584	1,360,000	730	1,636,600	556	1,304,500	1	1,000	101,613	45,545	106,545	100,000	63,231
Total.................	4,569	$12,096,000	16,663	$42,799,792	3,408	$9,504,455	185	$440.672	$1,879,534	$863,937	$4.483,426	$364,000	$903,655
Companies of other States.													
Mutual Life, N. Y.........	3,831	$12,270,476	17,193	$59,093,593	2,792	$8,970,607	190	$694,496	$1.740,100	$1,740,100	$11,291,421	None.	$4,916,659
Mutual Benefit, N. J.......	6,388	20,174,625	15,720	51.473,057	5.408	17,451,835	149	501,430	1,834,594	1,156,002	5,411,176	None.	1,253,000
New York, N. Y....	4,502	11,858,858	12.472	23,264,318	2.856	8,171,474	104	306,350	1,504,546	1,214,321	3,160,103	None.	1,256,787
Connecticut Mutual, Ct....	7,583	20,785,188	21,900	57,872,483	6,809	18,904,251	191	471,462	2,005,483	1,098,627	6,931,751	None.	2,049,950
Union Mutual, Me.........	1,514	3,567,900	4,006	9.442,215	[illegible],225	2,949.208	38	88,442	300,196	177,821	922,128	$100,000	16,000
United States, N. Y........	1,162	2,483,920	4,376	9,85[illegible],896	843	1,844,895	40	78,930	320,842	320,842	1,051,565	100,000	570,932
Manhattan, N. Y..........	2,017	6,663,872	6,342	20,787,769	1,375	4,228,412	54	161,750	691,151	426,575	1,649,740	100,000	281,935
National, Vt.............	464	684,300	1,692	2.680,445	331	483,167	29	45,074	78,914	76,454	391,873	25,000	115,940
Charter Oak, Ct..........	1,387	3.955,078	4.114	9,101.412	991	3,240,678	22	48,500	378,413	268,883	673,744	200,000	126,831
Phœnix, Ct..............	1.969	3,302,875	4,127	6,470,309	1,653	2,804,975	28	46,200	150,725	97,377	392,555	100,000	107,550
Knickerbocker, N. A.	1,054	2,499.650	2,164	5,411,650	689	1,728,000	9	32,112	186,486	132,305	395.168	100.000	80,470
Ætna, Ct., *.............	3,744	8,793,150	6,358	13.519.020	....	....	...	....	533,478	290,188	606,343	150,000	132,475
Wisconsin Mutual, Wis.....	3,644	4,889,104	5,945	7.888,578	3,003	4,188,328	26	33,000	296,610	210.144	333,150	None.	26,000
Equitable, N. Y...........	2,640	8.022,150	5,193	15.269,550	2,310	7.247,300	24	65,300	540.237	505,660	791,926	100,000	269,310
Guardian, N. Y...........	1,657	3,473,650	2,734	5,455,238	1,273	2,735,884	9	17,500	200,554	123,215	163,863	125,000	108,824
Washington, N. Y.........	896	2.368.050	1,597	4.337,150	649	1,733,600	14	38,200	144,888	144.888	199,784	125,000	168,355
Home, N. Y..............	2,188	4,237,950	4,771	9.709,400	1,748	3,312,650	30	66,500	320,649	203,827	420,751	125,000	184,145
Germania, N. Y...........	2,715	4,130.206	4.913	7,965.687	2,173	3,360.406	23	36,500	273.866	204,363	258,312	200,000	66,000
Security, N. Y............	1,262	2,488,068	1,885	3,857,818	1,053	2,031,018	8	16,500	106,987	62,736	94,328	110,000	110,000
North America, N. Y..... .	1,087	2,971,700	1,611	4,318,350	870	2,486,400	8	23,000	205,443	165,062	122,511	100,000	128,273
Total.................	51,704	$129,620,770	129,113	$337,777,939	38,141	$97,873,090	996	$2,771,247	$11,814,171	$8,619,400	$35,262,202	$1,760,000	$11,969,436
Grand Total..........	56,273	$141,716,770	145,776	$380,577,731	41.549	$107.377,545	1,181	$3,211,919	$13,193,706	$9,483,337	$39,745,628	$2,124,000	$12,873,091

N.B.—These figures are subject to correction, by further examination of the returns. The number of actual deaths is not quite so great as that of policies terminated by death. The new policies embrace all that were issued and in force in any part of the year, as well as those that were outstanding November 1, except when the returns contain only the latter. The claims by death are mostly paid ; but when they are not so, the "net premium reserve" is what remains after fully providing for them, and all other claims, whether admitted to be just by the Company or not. Of course these figures do not show the standing of any Company, which depends on the relation between its net assets and the net value of its policies. The development of this relation, as well as of the ratio of working expenses to receipts, must await the report of the Commissioners. * This Company not having done business in this State in the previous year, the net increase of its business and loss on policies cannot be stated.

ALPHABETICAL INDEX

TO SUBJECTS CONTAINED IN

THE RAILROAD AND INSURANCE ALMANAC For 1865.

ONE VOLUME OCTAVO, PRICE TWO DOLLARS.

G. W. Carleton, Publisher, New York.

AMALGAM BELLS,
AMALGAM BELLS,
AMALGAM BELLS,
AMALGAM BELLS,

At prices within the reach of every Church, School, Cemetery, Factory or Farm in the land. Their use throughout the United States and Canadas for the past six years has proven them to combine most valuable qualities. Among which are TONE, STRENGTH, SONOROUSNESS and DURABILITY OF VIBRATION, unequalled by any other manufacture. Sizes from 15 to 5,000 lbs., costing TWO-THIRDS LESS than any other metal, or 25 cents per pound; at which price I warrant them twelve months. Old bell metal taken in exchange, or bought for cash. Send for a circular to the manufacturer,

JOHN B. ROBINSON, No. 36 DEY STREET, N. Y.

List of Prices, Weights and Sizes of Farm, Hotel, Steamboat, School-house, Shop and Factory Bell.

These Bells are fitted with Yoke, Standard's Crank and Bolt, complete for use.

Weight of Bell and Hangings.	Diameter.	Cost of Bell and Hangings complete.
15 lbs.	7 inches.	$3 75
20 "	8½ "	5 00
35 "	10 "	8 75
50 "	12 "	12 50
75 "	16 "	18 75
100 "	18 "	25 00
150 "	20 "	37 50
200 "	22 "	50 00
250 "	24 "	62 50

List of Academy, Steamboat, Fire Alarm and Church Bells, with Particulars as to Weight, Sizes, Price of Bells, Hangings, etc.

Weight of Bells.	Diameter.	Price of Bells without Hangings.	Price of Patent Hangings.	Price of Bell and Hangings complete.
225 lbs.	26 inches.	$56 00	$15 00	$71 00
275 "	29 "	69 00	18 00	87 00
375 "	32 "	94 00	22 00	116 00
450 "	34 "	112 00	25 00	137 00
600 "	36 "	150 00	30 00	180 00
750 "	40 "	188 00	35 00	225 00
1,000 "	46 "	250 00	42 00	292 00
1,200 "	48 "	300 00	45 00	345 00
1,400 "	50 "	350 00	50 00	400 00
1,600 "	52 "	400 00	54 00	454 00
1,800 "	55 "	450 00	60 00	510 00
2,000 "	58 "	500 00	62 00	562 00
2,500 "	60 "	625 00	72 00	697 00
3,000 "	63 "	750 00	85 00	835 00
3,500 "	66 "	875 00	87 00	962 00
4,000 "	69 "	1,000 00	100 00	1,100 00
4,500 "	72 "	1,125 00	113 00	1,238 00
5,000 "	75 "	1,250 00	125 00	1,375 00

Larger sizes made to order at 25 cents per pound.

GUARANTEE.—All bells sold at the above prices WARRANTED against breakage by fair ringing, for TWELVE MONTHS from time of purchasing. Should one fail, a new Bell will be given by returning the broken one.

Orders may be sent through the AMERICAN ADVERTISING AGENCY, 389 Broadway, New-York.

☞ In case a Bell breaks after the expiration of the Warrantee, I allow HALF PRICE for the old metal.

JOHN B. ROBINSON, 36 Dey Street, N. Y.

THE

MERCHANTS AND BANKER'S ALMANAC,

FOR

1865.

CONTAINING

I.—Calendar Pages and Record of Prominent Events of the year 1864.
II.—Daily Price of Gold each month in the years 1862, 1863, 1864.
III.—A List of the Banks, arranged alphabetically, in every State and City of the Union—Names of President and Cashier, and Capital of each. (Corrected December, 1864.)
IV.—List of six hundred and eighty National Banks, with the names of the President and Cashier, and Capital and limit of Capital of each. (Corrected December, 1864.
V.—A List of Private Bankers in the United States. (Corrected December, 1864.)
VI.—List of Private Bankers and Brokers in New York City.
VII.—A List of the Banks in Canada—their Cashiers, Managers, and Foreign Agents—Capital and Circulation of each.
VIII.—Governor, Directors and Officers of the Bank of England, 1864.
IX.—List of Banks and Bankers in London, December, 1864.
X.—Alphabetical List of Eighteen Hundred Cashiers in the United States.
XI.—Financial and Commercial Forms in the English, French and Spanish Languages.
XII.—Bank Statistics—New York City Banks, Boston Banks, Philadelphia Banks.
XIII.—Schedule of Revenue Tax on Promissory Notes, Bonds, &c.
XIV.—The National Banks—quarterly returns of 1863, 1864.
XV.—List of the Secretaries of the Treasury from 1789 to 1865—date of appointment, resignation or dismissal of each.
XVI.—The lowest and highest prices at New York, annually, for forty years, of the following articles, with the duties levied each year: Breadstuffs, Candles, Coal, Coffee, Copper, Cotton, Fish, Flax, Fruit, Furs, Glass, Gunpowder, Hides, Hops, Indigo, Iron, Pig Lead, Leather, Liquors, Molasses, Nails, Naval Stores, Oils, Paints, Pork, Beef, Smoked Hams, Lard, Butter, Cheese, Rice, Salt, Seeds, Sheetings, Soap, Spices, Spirits, Sugars, Tallow, Teas, Tobacco, Whalebone, Wines.

To be Continued Annually.

PUBLISHED BY

I. SMITH HOMANS, Jr., Office of the BANKERS' MAGAZINE,

46 Pine Street, New York.

Copies mailed to order—Price, postage free, Two dollars.

www.ingramcontent.com/pod-product-compliance
Lightning Source LLC
LaVergne TN
LVHW011213110826
845150LV00006B/1418

* 9 7 8 1 4 2 5 5 1 7 3 3 5 *